THE SOLIDARITY OF KIN

SUNY series in Native American Religions
Kenneth M. Morrison, editor

The Solidarity of Kin

*Ethnohistory, Religious Studies, and the
Algonkian-French Religious Encounter*

Kenneth M. Morrison

STATE UNIVERSITY OF NEW YORK PRESS

Published by
State University of New York Press, Albany

© 2002 State University of New York

All rights reserved

Printed in the United States of America

No part of this book may be used or reproduced
in any manner whatsoever without written permission.
No part of this book may be stored in a retrieval system
or transmitted in any form or by any means including
electronic, electrostatic, magnetic tape, mechanical,
photocopying, recording, or otherwise without the prior
permission in writing of the publisher.

For information, address State University of New York Press,
90 State Street, Suite 700, Albany, NY 12207

Production by Cathleen Collins
Marketing by Patrick Durocher

Library of Congress Cataloging in Publication Data

Morrison, Kenneth M.
   The solidarity of kin : ethnohistory, religious studies, and the Algonkian-French religious encounter / Kenneth M. Morrison
      p. cm. — (SUNY series in Native American religions)
   Includes bibliographical references and index.
   ISBN 0–7914–5405–3 (alk. paper) — ISBN 0–7914–5406–1 (pbk. : alk. paper)
   1. Algonquian Indians—Religion. 2. Algonquian Indians—Missions. 3. Syncretism (Religion). 4. Jesuits—Missions—Canada. 5. Jesuits—Missions—New England. I. Title: Ethnohistory, religious studies, and the Algonkian-French religious encounter. II. Series.

E99.A35 M66 2002
266'.2'089973—dc21

2001049408

Dedicated to
Geoff Glover
Michael Jewell
Andrea Bear Nicholas and Daryl Nicholas
William Philie
—Where they are, community happens

Contents

Acknowledgments ix

Introduction: Making Sense—Religious Studies and Ethnohistory 1

1. The Study of Algonkian Religious Life: The Methodological Impasse 17
2. Beyond the Supernatural and to a Dialogical Cosmology 37
3. Toward a History of Intimate Encounters: Algonkian Folklore, Jesuit Missionaries, and Kiwakwe, the Cannibal Giant 59
4. The Mythological Sources of Wabanaki Catholicism: A Case Study of the Social History of Power 79
5. Discourse and the Accommodation of Values: Toward a Revision of Mission History 103
6. Montagnais Missionization in Early New France: The Syncretic Imperative 115
7. Baptism and Alliance: The Symbolic Mediations of Religious Syncretism 131
8. The Solidarity of Kin: The Intersection of Eastern Algonkian and French-Catholic Cosmologies 147

Notes 173

Selected Bibliography 223

Index 231

Acknowledgments

Since this volume reexamines diverse and well-known interpretations of Eastern Algonkian religious life and history, my debts are many. My training in Canadian-American history at the University of Maine at Orono focused on the northeastern region and the colonial period that localizes this work. My fellowship year at the McNickle Center for the History of the American Indian at the Newberry Library in Chicago affirmed my research interests. I owe the center a debt not only for precious reflective and writing time, but also for the scholars I met at its seminars and conferences: James Axtell, Robert Berkhofer, Vine Deloria, Jr., Raymond Fogelson, Jeannette Henry, D'Arcy McNickle, Alfonso Ortiz, and Wilcomb Washburn.

I am grateful for another institutional affiliation. My work with the American Indian Studies Center at UCLA, its staff and Faculty Advisory Committee, brought me a practical understanding of the intellectual challenges of Native American Studies in a university context. I owe a special thanks to the center's director, Charlotte Heth, for support that made it possible for me to rethink and rewrite Chapter Three of this volume. I also thank the history graduate students at UCLA—particularly Margaret Beemer, Roger Bowerman, Susan Kenney, and Rebecca Kugel—who shared the excitement of our individual and collaborative work.

Most important of all has been my association with the Department of Religious Studies at Arizona State University. My colleagues as a whole share a conviction that Religious Studies offers new ground for the human sciences. Anne Feldhaus, Joel Gereboff, and Mark Woodward have made valuable contributions to my study and they have my gratitude. Patricia Friedman has helped with a myriad of technical details in preparing the manuscript. As at UCLA, many ASU Religious Studies students have been vital conversation partners on a variety of issues which have shaped this work: Mark Ament, Christie Barker, Lynn Brun, Sara Bush, Kimberly Christen, Dan Coons, Michael Coyle, Tracy Davids, Gretchen Fletcher, John Fulbright, Kenja Hassan, Grace Hoff, Maria Kardamaki, John Lindamood, Ken Lokensgard, Randy McCaskill, Lisa Nelson, Mary Schulte-Dwan, Alon Unger, William Van Norman, and Cynthia Carsten Wentz. I am especially grateful to Mark Leary, Orlando Garcia, David Shorter, and Patricia Farmer Smith for their incisive readings of an early draft.

Over the years I have benefited from many conversations with colleagues in the American Academy of Religion, the American Society for Ethnohistory, and the Society for the Study of Native American Religious Traditions: Jennifer S. H. Brown, Vine Deloria, Jr., Raymond DeMallie, Fritz Detwiler, Sam D. Gill, Howard Harrod, Lee Irwin, Thomas Parkhill, Jordan Paper, Jacqueline Peterson, Melissa Pflug, Ivan Strenski, and Ines Talamantez. No work can proceed without the support of family and friends, and I thank Aaron Anderson, Kim and Jay Berneburg, Noreen Dresser, Joanne Glover, Ric and Cathy Glover, Marcia Hageman, Michael Jewell, Kathleen McGrane, Irin Smith, Jody Tarshis, Thandeka, Martha Townsend, and Michael Cochise Young. Similarly, I have enjoyed rich conversations with several Wabanaki people, particularly Deanna Francis (Passamaquoddy), and Wabanaki scholars, Eunice B. Nelson (Penobscot), Andrea Bear Nicholas, and Daryl Nicholas (Maliseet). I am grateful to Geoff Glover and my mom, Lucille Stewart, for helping to edit the scanned versions of my previously published essays.

I acknowledge a real debt to Arizona State University for both financial support and sabbatical leaves. The National Endowment for the Humanities provided a summer stipend that made it possible to drop off the planet for three months, and thus to take stock about what I knew and needed to know about Native American religious ethnography.

I am also grateful to the following journals for permission to reprint essays: Chapter Three was published as "Towards a History of Intimate Encounters: Algonkian Folklore, Jesuit Missionaries, and Kiwakwe, the Cannibal Giant," *American Indian Culture and Research Journal* 3–4 (1979): 51–80; Chapter Four was published as "The Mythological Sources of Abenaki Catholicism: A Case Study of the Social History of Power," *Religion* 11 (1981): 235–263; Chapter Five was published as "Discourse and the Accommodation of Values: Toward a Revision of Mission History," *Journal of the American Academy of Religion* 53/3 (1985): 365–382; Chapter Six was published as "Montagnais Missionization in Early New France: The Syncretic Imperative," *American Indian Culture and Research Journal* 10/3 (1986): 1–23; Chapter Seven was published as "Baptism and Alliance: The Symbolic Mediations of Religious Syncretism," *Ethnohistory* 37/4 (1990): 416–437.

Special thanks are due to Nancy Ellegate and Cathleen Collins at SUNY Press for the care they have given the preparation and production of this book. I have also been particularly fortunate for the constructive criticism the anonymous reviews for SUNY Press provided.

A special acknowledgment must be given to my brother-in-law, Geoff Glover, who generously constructed, electrified, and remodeled the spaces within which I have worked. Thank you, Bro.

I am thus greatly in the debt of many institutions and persons, but I must add that I am solely responsible for the interpretations that follow.

Kenneth M. Morrison

Johnny #1
The Bradshaw Mountains
Arizona

Introduction

Making Sense—Religious Studies and Ethnohistory

These essays attempt to build bridges between ethnohistory–that joint endeavor between history and anthropology–and Religious Studies. As they have developed, these distinctive fields have pursued an understanding of human reality in very different ways. As they often describe their enterprise, historians deal with cultures diachronically, as they change over time. Anthropologists, conversely, are said to study cultures synchronically, as abstract pattern and structure. The interpretive situation is actually much more complex, but in the early years of the American Society for Ethnohistory scholars worked toward combining both approaches—time and pattern, structure and change. In this sense, the interdisciplinary goal was to understand cultures ethnographically and historically.[1]

Religious Studies, at least as I understand and attempt to practice the discipline, concerns itself with the study of meaning. As a hermeneutical field, Religious Studies attempts to interpret the ways in which life is itself an interpretive experience on the part of its participants. Ethnohistorians also deal with "religion," but tend to see it as either some abstract, institutionalized, and functional part of culture, and/or as subjective belief.[2] Religious Studies scholars pursue religion as meaning (theological, cosmological, humanistic, sociological, historical, interspecies),[3] and I explore some of that pursuit in these essays.[4] Meaning can be treated abstractly, as a culture's existential and normative principles,[5] for example. Meaning can also be understood dynamically, if we are able to reconstruct the play of such principles in what people say and do.

In this effort to bridge the disciplines, I am not alone.[6] Indeed, anyone attempting Native American Studies in any of these disciplinary contexts has found the going challenging. None of these fields adequately comprehend Native American life. A dissonance of disciplinary commitments, methodologies, and interpretive strategies makes both ethnohistory and Religious Studies prime examples of postmodern intellectual confusion and lively response.[7] In these essays (particularly Chapters One, Two, and Eight), I explore the general character of that confusion, assessing some of the major efforts in the past twenty-five years to understand Native Americans' religious traditions, social life, and historical experience.

I heartily agree with many critics who observe that current interpretations are ethnocentric.[8] I differ from most because I make distinctive claims about that ethnocentricism. First, I argue that scholars remain ethnocentric because they have failed to understand the distinctive premises of Native American life. Second, I explore the ways in which they have not understood that those premises constitute genuine conceptual alternatives to scholarly ways of representing other peoples in abstract cultural terms. Third, I claim that those existential principles can be reconstructed. Finally, I contend that those premises can guide us in fitting our interpretation to Native Americans' actual experience and history, or at least whatever of that experience can be reconstructed.

Given the challenges involved in understanding Native American life and historical experience, my aims are limited and focused. I present a series of essays written to explore the complex meaning of Native American and European contact. I am concerned particularly with the ways in which both parties negotiated that meaning in French Catholic missions to Eastern Algonkian peoples. Initially, I did not intend to focus on missionization. The first two historical essays on Wabanaki (Abenaki) Catholicism (Chapters Three and Four) aimed rather to explore the ways in which the Wabanaki people's religious tradition shaped their understanding of the European other, English as well as French. But in the seventeenth century, the French Catholic missions were also a major context for a contested encounter of meanings. Since these missions localized those cultural processes from which has emerged what scholars call a world system, understanding the religious and social change they induced has large implications beyond their particular time and place.[9] Native Americans and European colonizers met in many other situations—economic, diplomatic, and military, for instance—but the missions focused the larger conversation on both sides of the encounter: Who are you? What do you want? What do you mean for us?

The historical essays have developed of their own accord, but in an orderly fashion. I have come to understand them as interdisciplinary hybrids, linked conceptually by a long conversation with other scholars in history, anthropology, ethnohistory, and Religious Studies. During my graduate studies in Canadian-American history in the early 1970s, the field of American Indian history was just developing, albeit mostly in the form of the history of Indian-White relations, and anthropological study was just beginning to provoke new interdisciplinary questions about the cultural patterns of American Indian life. From what was then the emerging field of ethnohistory, I took the conviction that cross-cultural studies must recognize that Native American "others," who are the "subjects" of scholarly study, ought to be engaged in their own terms, in the narratives in which they self-constitute, and in the particular worlds of meaning in which they live. I taught American Indian history and ethnohistory for eight years at UCLA, and found myself increasingly dissatisfied with the main concerns of the field: Indian-White relations, and the development of federal Indian policy.

If the goal was to understand Native American experience, then policy studies were necessary for understanding the colonialist context. I also came to realize that colonialism defined only part of American Indian history. Historians had not explained, for one example, what Robert Berkhofer called the startling and paradoxical survival of Native American identity despite centuries of cultural change, and economic, political, and technical colonialism.[10] Nor had scholars made sense of the prominent role that "religion" played in Native American experience. From first contact to the present, Native Americans have understood contact, and have responded to non-Indians, religiously. They understood that contact challenged their own sense of tribal identity, just as non-Indian diseases, ecological transformations of the land, and dispossession and dispersal from traditional territories undercut their social solidarity.[11] Such massive changes also threatened the peoples' relation to cosmic beings with whom their health and well-being, their ability to make a living, and their location in the cosmos depended. The peoples worried about their own responsibility for such cataclysmic changes: they turned to ritual to diagnose the causes of their condition, to rectify health problems, and to reinvigorate their relations with cosmic, plant, and animal beings, as well as with their ancestors.[12] Ritual performance, I came to understand, was the very way in which Native Americans took responsibility for their historical situation. Meanwhile, for American people in general and for scholars in particular, victimization continued as the main explanation of Native American experience.

I slowly came to realize that Religious Studies might offer some precision in understanding that mythological traditions reflect on the proposition that human life derives from, and constrains, cosmic meaning.[13] Religious Studies affirmed what seemed to me a central purpose of Native American Studies: achieving a representation of Native American realities in which Native American peoples might recognize themselves. I also found that Religious Studies has some distance to go before Native American realities can be understood. Accordingly, the historical essays in this volume attempt to make sense of the historical and ethnographic record in interdisciplinary modes of study, and to assess that record in light of the ethical constitution of Native American life.

My concern for understanding the ethical character of American Indian life aims to create new methodological ground. Some critics of professional American Indian history, as we will see, rail against a pervasive tendency for scholars (here acting out implicit assumptions in popular culture, especially the "Lo! The poor Indian" sentiment) to write moral histories of Indian-White relations. The critics have not recognized, unfortunately, that our tendency to impose subjective constructs on Indian experience, our tendency to moralize, fails simply because scholars' values and those of Native Americans differ greatly. Moreover, scholars seem not to understand that in Native American contexts the moral ideal and social life share common ground, and that the ideal cannot be understood apart from everyday life. Although much will be said about the respective disciplines and their actual and potential relations, I am concerned particularly with their limitations and my own struggle to overcome the shortsighted consequences. In my view (as with many others), the disciplines remain inadequate, imperfect, and illogical extensions of an Euramerican ideological stance that has always made every effort to subsume Native American peoples under Christian, progressive, objective, and other universalizing views of history.[14]

The essays of this volume explore some of the ways in which I have come to think about Native American history, and what I have been able to reconstruct as Native American points-of-view. I've wanted to understand early Canadian missions as the ways in which Algonkian people made sense of difficult, even deadly, post-contact realities. I've also wanted to understand the missions as Algonkian ways of responding creatively to those conditions. Contact created an explosion of uncertainty. Violence between Europeans and tribes devastated by alcohol and disease accelerated at an alarming pace. Contact even amplified intra- and intertribal conflict, but eventually drove home the need for native peoples to achieve a united front against all Europeans, even the well-intentioned. As anthropologist Victor Turner has shown so effectively in his African studies, ritual activities and social order intersect.[15] Disasters, such as those that affected seventeenth-century Algonkian peoples, engender a state of consciousness called liminality. In Turner's view, the concept of liminality captures a root social uncertainty. Liminality has both positive and negative aspects; in either case, liminality is defined by an experience of what Turner calls being "betwixt and between." In good times, liminality might be thought of as the achievement of solidarity, a state of sociality in which selfish, individualistic, and anti-social impulses are contained by a people's fresh commitment to core communal values. In bad times, liminality might be thought of as a kind of social psychosis. Psychotic forms of liminal consciousness respond to a world coming or come apart, and they do so by seeking answers to barely glimpsed, but keenly suffered, problems. In the seventeenth-century Northeast, every aspect of social order needed to be recast, not in some abstract formulation of a cultural policy, but in the social relations of everyday life. Algonkians had no choice but to make sense of the medical, economic, political, and ecological changes that led to their experience of social chaos. Not surprisingly, Eastern Algonkian peoples understood the seventeenth century as an eruption of anti-social evil, the extent of which went far beyond anything in their pre-contact experience.

The devastating events of the seventeenth century can hardly be exaggerated, but Algonkian peoples were able to respond effectively. If these essays have any unity at all, they explore the moral principles of Algonkian lifeways as ways of documenting these peoples' astute assessment of the character of their post-contact situation, and also the viability of their very own ways of making sense. If, in Turner's sense, the incomprehensible constitutes liminal uncertainty (as Turner explores in a variety of cultural settings), those disasters also presented Algonkian people with many opportunities to remake their world anew. Accordingly, these essays seek to privilege Algonkian points-of-view, and they work hard to reconstruct such indigenous perspectives. They are based on a reading of historical and ethnographic texts across the grain of European and Christian biases. They seek to reconstruct some of the ways in which Algonkian peoples discerned their post-contact situation.

As anyone even vaguely familiar with the scholarly literature on the seventeenth-century Northeast realizes, we now have a rich overview of how contact proceeded in real defiance of the religious and political expectations of the colonizers.[16] The enduring challenge is to understand the ways in which missionary and Algonkian purposes sometimes clashed and sometimes converged. In this regard, these essays attend to the missionaries' motivations, teachings, and interventions into Algonkian life. The essays are also unlike most studies that comprise the field of mission history, and indeed of American Indian history. They seek primarily to uncover Algonkian ways of assessing missionary truth claims, and not the other way around. Thus, readers seeking an interpretive balance between Algonkian and missionary positions will find some useful insights, but the essays move closer to Algonkian than to missionary concerns. As readers will also see, the essays have taught me the virtue of learning more and more about less and less.

In all these complex ways, scholars recapitulate the interpretive quandary facing seventeenth-century French Jesuit missionaries in Canada: how to make sense of the Native American other when an adequate self-understanding was, and is, not commonly available. After all, even those persons who profess belief assume that there is a fit between religion and the world, but are not necessarily aware of the cosmic assumptions that play themselves out in their lives. In this sense, theologian George Tinker argues that missionaries—all of them, without exception—engaged in acts of genocide against Native American peoples.[17] For much of the historical encounter, the complex problem Tinker reconstructs has not been appreciated. Like the Jesuit missionaries, non-Indians have continued to blunder in, devising theories of missionization and civilization after the fact. We have not had a theological, historical, and anthropological perspective to ease the ongoing and ethnocentric character of our encounters with Native American peoples. Nor have we understood the economic, political, material, and religious factors that have shaped our colonialist relations with indigenous peoples. Our colonialism has thus proceeded in happenstance ways without regard for Native American actors. We have not been able to conceptualize, let alone manage, the intricacies of cultural contact. As one result, we, as well as Native Americans, have been on a learning curve. For our part, we have practiced the art of the possible whose limits have been defined by the myth of Christian Civilization.[18] We will gain no insight into Native American traditions until we understand the ways in which we are fundamentally committed to Judeo-Christian, as well as the related secular, principles of worldview.

Because these terms are so pervasive, and unconscious, the study of Native American religious life is necessarily fraught with controversy. For one example, in seeking some baseline understanding of Algonkian tradition, I run the risk of conveying the very mistaken notion that there is a pure, aboriginal, and unchanging religious system. Nothing could be further from the actuality. Native American religious peoples have, in fact, been in conversation with each other for thousands of years, and their particular tribal traditions thus express negotiated agreements about the pluralistic nature of reality.[19] In such conversations, and the mythological and ritual adaptions they engendered, we discover only one way in which Native American traditions have always had a collective and changing character.[20]

American Indian peoples have always sought kinship solidarity as a collective goal shared by humans and other personal beings.[21] One need think here not only about the pervasiveness of councils in many cosmogonic traditions, but also the extensive and hardworking institutional forms of kin, village, tribal, and intertribal councils, to recognize the hard-won value of solidarity.[22] But such a recognition is not enough. How we make sense of both individual and collective forms of tradition depends fundamentally on two factors. First, if we are willing to understand that tradition is a dynamic consensus about reality, then we can see that all peoples at all times and in all places participate in that lively process of making cultural, religious, and social sense. Second, if we can come to understand the typical, and often ethnocentric, assumptions that we make about "religion," then we can see the actual need to learn how to think about "religion" from other peoples, and in ways that are faithful to their particular understanding of the ways of the world.[23] I can suggest how we face some of these challenges by comparing two textbook treatments of Native American religious traditions and life: Peggy V. Beck and Anna L. Walters' *The Sacred: Ways of Knowledge, Sources of Life* (1977), and Sam D. Gill's *Native American Religions: An Introduction* (1982).[24]

Beck and Walters begin with what has become a familiar and difficult problem: Native American peoples have no abstract term to convey what non-Indians mean by "religion": sacred text, dogma, institution. For Beck and Walters, there is an inherent contradiction between being religious, on the one hand, and thinking about religion on the other. Their statement of concern is worth reflecting upon:

> Like all peoples throughout the world, Native Americans seek their own way to explain origins and destinies—to face the unknown and learn the power and meaning of natural laws and forces. Religions

attempt to bring an individual or group closer to the source of these powers and laws. A study of the world's religions would show that many symbols, ways of teaching, and ways of expressing the sacred, are universally shared by human beings. The point this textbook makes, however, is that in contrast to many organized religions in the world, Native American sacred ways limit the amount of explaining a person can do. In this way they guide a person's behavior toward the world and its natural laws. Many Native American sacred teachings suggest that if people try to explain everything or to seek to leave nothing unexplored in the universe, they will bring disaster upon themselves, for then they are trying to be like gods, not humans.[25]

For Beck and Walters, these discriminations are directly related to what they see as an unsatisfactory separation between ways of knowing that are typical of the social and behavioral sciences, and "the religious life of the scientists who study them and who perform the experiments." In addition to this distance, they decry the scientific attempt "to dominate and control the unknown, to overcome human frailty or weakness." Beck and Walters see such activities in apocalyptic terms: "This has begun to destroy certain balances and relationships that exist in the world and its ecosystems. By destroying balances of this kind people destroy alternatives—they make it more and more difficult to adapt to change, to crisis, and to the unexpected."[26] In effect, Beck and Walters see the study of Native American traditions as a descriptive enterprise that aims "to better understand the profoundness of strength, beauty, and vitality of this dimension of American Indian People."[27]

As I read their argument, Beck and Walters identify a primary tension that the study of Native American traditions and history must resolve: the core relationship in non-Indian settings between abstract knowledge and manipulative power, both of which proceed in disrespectful ways. They relate, rightly, that Native American traditions do not attempt simply to explain and to control the world. Moreover, they note that these traditions are neither sectarian nor evangelical. We must also account for Beck and Walters' claim that Native American traditions are *practical* systems of *knowledge*. The claim that religious life can be a system of pragmatic references to the actual world proposes, in effect, a way of understanding "religion" that is little explored, and which undercuts many scholarly claims that Native American religious systems are not rational. Beck and Walters' proposition is also controversial because the idea that being religious constitutes a way of being mindful is not commonly accepted.

Unfortunately, Beck and Walters explore these issues in contradictory ways. One can see from this extended quotation that Beck and Walters are strongly opposed to dogmatic religions, or to sciences, which attempt to understand the world in ways that belong properly to the gods, the unknown, natural laws and forces. Such a view needs comment because, while they may be rehearsing a familiar gulf between science and religion, they describe Native American traditions in theistic ways, which may not be appropriate for Native American peoples, and in terms natural scientists would recognize: natural laws and forces. No one would disagree, I suspect, that religious persons concern themselves profoundly with the unknown.[28]

Beck and Walters also fail to mediate between the individual's experience of the world and that of the social group as a whole. They chose "the word spiritual to help us define the word religion." In so doing, they wish to differentiate between "ordinary" and "intangible" reality, and by intangible they mean "spiritual."[29] They understand the spiritual in subjective, emotional terms, contending that "organized religions" often fail to recognize "the emotions and sacred moments that are their guiding vision." They also equate religious emotion with "mystical experience."[30] As a result, therefore, Beck and Walters understand *the sacred* (my italics) in similarly subjectivist ways: "*Sacred* [their italics] means something special, something out of the ordinary, and often it concerns a very personal part of each one of us because it describes our dreams, our changing, and our personal way of seeing the world." They also declare that "the sacred is something that is shared," that the sacred is a collective phenomenon, but they do not do justice to this social dimension.[31] Other subjectivist terms dominate Beck and Walter's narrative, and distract from the collective character of religious life that they also wish to highlight. They think that "reverence," "awe," "divinity,""belief," and the "unseen" can be used to describe Native American religious life. Beck and Walters sum up their view: "As we discuss the sacred, we might say there are two sides to it: the personal, *ecstatic* [their italics] side that individuals find hard to describe, and the part of the sacred that is shared and defined year after year through oral histories, ritual, and other ceremonies and customs." In these ways, Beck and Walters desire to mediate between non-Indian divisions of reality into the objective and the subjective, but use language that focuses on religious emotion. In their way of thinking in terms of analogies, religion can be glossed as divinity = intangible = awe = personal belief. This model focuses on individualistic religious sensibilities, rather than on the collective character of Native American insights into, and responsibility for, the nature of the world. Such an equation does not help us to understand their thesis that Native American religious traditions are real, practical, and collective ways of *knowing* the world.

Whatever the overall usefulness of their perspective, Beck and Walters reveal that any understanding of "religion" rests fundamentally on one's insights about it. Sam D. Gill begins in such a place, but ends with an altogether different definition of religion. Wanting to separate himself from the European equation of religion with church and state—what I call the myth of Christian Civilization—leads Gill toward a less ethnocentric proposition. Accepting the principle not only that humankind shares a single nature, but that being can be defined as *homo religiosus*, Gill crafts an open-ended definition:

> We will consider as religious those images, actions, and symbols that both express and define the extent and character of the world, especially those that provide the cosmic framework in which human life finds meaning and the terms of its fulfillment. We will also consider as religious those actions, processes, and symbols through which life is lived in order that it may be meaningful and purposive.[32]

As we shall see, this definition proposes an understanding of "religion" that is quite different from the assumptions that inform ethnohistorical scholarship.

Gill's view of the religious is both provocative and controversial. In the first place, Gill redefines the noun "religion" as the adjective "religious." He suggests, in so doing, that the abstraction "religion" has something vitally to do with human life as it is actually lived; in this way, Gill's definition speaks to some of Beck and Walters' concerns. Gill also takes a humanistic stance (one that other scholars of Native American life might emulate) which declares that the study of Native American "religions" must concern itself with the actual lives of Native American persons. As a consequence, we should consider the ways in which people *act* religiously, rather than focus on what they ostensibly *believe*. Gill's definition insists that the abstraction "religion" means nothing apart from the human ideation, valuation, and personal and collective activity that constitute meaningful life. As Gill has explored the implications, he has come to propose a performative view of Native American religious life, a view that urges an investigation of the oral and non-verbal modes of cognition and expression, especially those that have a ritual and, therefore, collective character.[33] In addition, Gill's definition avoids an ethnocentric definition of religion in terms of gods, the sacred, worship, belief (and thereby the supernatural), dogma, institution (and thereby both nature and culture). Instead, Gill favors an emphasis that stresses the motivated, responsible actions of persons whose lives attempt an alignment with the purposes of cosmic beings.

As with every other investigator of "religion" inside and outside Religious Studies, the English language trips Gill into a non-humanistic emphasis that distracts from his performative argument. His phrase—"images, actions, and symbols"—raises a thorny question about the religious actor. Images and symbols are, as Gill is well aware, reifications of human behaviors, merely abstractions referring to motivated human interaction. Neither images nor symbols are normally understood (in English, at least) as capable of action in their own right. In any case, and even in this slip of the tongue, Gill relocates our attention on religion as a belief system to one that highlights human religious thought and behavior as an irreducibly socio-linguistic phenomenon.

Thus, one learns from Gill both an explicit and a tacit lesson in thinking about religion and religiousness comparatively, and about the ways in which "religion" may particularly be associated with non-Indian ideological and institutional order, and religiousness with all people whatever their cultural condition. As applied to Native American religious traditions, to distinguish between religion and the religious highlights meaning-making activity, rather than church and belief, and so gives us a more precise concern for not only pursuing Native Americans' points-of-view in general, but also their concern for meaning in local and particular times and places. This concern is well put, because if we are learning anything at all about American Indian religious persons, the conclusion must be that they are, as they have always been, masters of their own meanings.[34] Tacitly, Gill's definition reveals the conceptual distortions associated with reification as a mode of abstraction: to mistake motivated religious activity for religion as a cultural pattern tends to reduce meaning to the mechanical and impersonal functions of symbolic systems.[35] Such a reduction of the purposeful—Religious Studies' scholars call that purposive activity "intentionality"—explains much of what Religious Studies has to offer historians, anthropologists, and ethnohistorians as they attempt to make sense of Native American life.

My readers will notice that I also struggle with this intellectual problem of reification in this volume. In the early essays, particularly in Chapters Three and Four, my newfound enthusiasm for ethnohistory expressed itself in my pervasive use of garden-variety anthropological jargon. My readers will also see, I hope, that the newer essays attempt to balance disciplinary modes of discourse with careful attention to Native American religious life as perception, thought, and behavior. Scholars of Native American life, I have come to learn, must serve many competing masters.

Two essays written for this volume explore the ways in which scholars have either ignored Native American religious life, or have misinterpreted those traditions in ethnocentric ways. Chapter One reviews the major interpretations of Eastern Algonkian life and history, and the ways in which self-described rationalist scholars dismiss those interpretations as romantic and idealist—as non-empirical and subjective belief, in other words. The chapter also demonstrates that both idealists and rationalists misinterpret Algonkian religious traditions, and that they do so in precisely the same categorical ways. Chapter Two assesses a closely related issue, namely the claim of Religious Studies scholar, Åke Hultkrantz, that the concept of the supernatural (and all that such a concept entails) is foundational, and empirically demonstrable, for Native American religious systems. This chapter also engages seriously Hultkrantz's claim that scholars have misunderstood the empirical character of Algonkian religious life. To do so, the chapter reassesses A. Irving Hallowell's trailblazing essay "Ojibwa Ontology, Behavior, and World View." Accordingly, Chapters One and Two question the non-Indian objectivist/subjectivist paradigm that misconstrues Native American religions. These essays identify a major problem that emerges from the complex ways in which European languages tend to emphasize theological, cognitive, and social assumptions that distort Native American realities. The chapters argue, alternatively, that Hallowell articulated a relational, intersubjective understanding of Algonkian religious life that has great value for achieving a cross-cultural perspective.

The historical chapters (Chapter Three to Seven) also focus on problems central to understanding Algonkian religious traditions and their history. The first two, Chapters Three and Four, written while I was still a member of a History Department, deal with the Wabanaki peoples. They address some of the ways in which a careful study of Wabanaki mythological traditions can reveal otherwise undocumented, indigenous perspectives about religious life and intercultural contact. Seventeenth-century European documents reveal little about the moral tensions that the Algonkians recognized both in their tribal lives and in their relations with non-human persons. These essays show that traditions about cannibal giants and the compassionate culture hero, Gluskap, opened a way in which I could see that Algonkians assessed and judged European social behavior in unique terms. While they are themselves not historical documents, nineteenth- and twentieth-century Algonkians used these stories to reflect on their moral and multicultural situation. These stories indicate that the Algonkians recognized ethical criteria by which their ancestors had apparently made sense of the claimed superiority of European colonizers, and which guided their responses to post-contact conditions.[36] These stories not only express a precise way of thinking about social life, some of them articulate a troubled moral rejection of European social life. Thus, an Algonkian way of thinking about the religious meaning of sociality came to direct my inquiry: the stories about the cannibal giants and Gluskap reveal a hitherto unrecognized relational logic that suggests the systematic integrity of Algonkian thought and religious life. I learned that these nineteenth- and twentieth-century stories are also congruent with what can be reconstructed of the seventeenth-century Algonkians' historical behavior.[37] They also helped to explain the Algonkians' revulsion toward the impersonal, profit-seeking, individualistic, and overly abstract hierarchial forms of European life. Chapters Three and Four eventually informed the cultural background of my history of Wabanaki-Euramerican relations, *The Embattled Northeast*. Since that work presented a narrative history of trade, diplomacy, and war, the book did not examine the interdisciplinary issues this present volume reassesses. Religious history, I have come to learn, requires an altogether different methodology.

Chapters Five to Seven, written after I joined a Religious Studies Department, explore the ethnographic and historical course of the Algonkians' relational and religious logic that I discovered among the Wabanaki. This logic, I was learning, escaped the rationality of objectivity and subjectivity scholars commonly apply to Native American history. By center-staging intercultural dialogue—not just discourse, but vitally charged communication—these essays move toward balancing missionary and Algonkian perspectives. Specifically, they reconstruct the dialogical processes by which the Montagnais adjacent to the French settlement of Quebec scrutinized the astounding religious claims of French missionaries. The burden of these chapters is twofold. They establish that a variety of factors impeded the missionaries' ability to communicate with the Montagnais. They also reconstruct the Montagnais' responses to the missionaries to document both their experience of cultural confusion and the traditional logic by which they assessed Jesuit truth claims.

Building on both the opening interpretive and the historical chapters, Chapter Eight assesses the common assertion that Algonkians "converted" to Catholicism. The chapter reevaluates suggestive methodological perspectives from mythological and socio-linguistic studies. This chapter argues by way of a conclusion that Algonkians shaped Catholicism in ways that fit their own ways of thinking about the world, ways that gave them religious means to ensure their ongoing community life. I argue that Algonkians took an active role in missionization and that the result was an intersection, rather than a displacement, of worldviews.

With the exception of some minor editing to eliminate duplication of argument and documentation, and to standardize tribal names, the previously published essays (Chapters Three to Seven) are reprinted here as they first appeared. I have chosen not to recast these essays for several reasons. First, the decision is a matter of personal honesty. Since my overall concern in this book is to critique constructively the literature on the Eastern Algonkian peoples (and by extension the scholarship on Native American life in general), it seems important to let the essays stand. I believe that my readers will better appreciate my broad disciplinary criticism if they can see that I recognize my own gradual shift in understanding. Besides, I would be disingenuous to reproach others for failing to resolve issues with which I have also struggled. In being honest about my intellectual difficulties with understanding Algonkian religious life, I hope also that my readers can see that I am not engaging in personal attacks against the scholarly arguments I critically engage in these essays. Second, the essays themselves present evidence of my growing awareness of the problem of intellectual ethnocentrism; especially in Chapters Three and Four, I could see the missionaries' and even the Algonkians' ethnocentrism, but not my own. Chapters Five to Seven reveal that I came to distance myself from non-Indian cosmological assumptions, including widespread views about "religion," "belief," and "conversion." A comparison of these essays will show my readers that I have won my insights through hard work and reflection. Finally, as I discussed my plan-of-action with Andrea Bear Nicholas, chair in Native Studies at St. Thomas University, two issues emerged clearly. We came to agree that my readers (Native and non-Indian alike) should be able to see both my intellectual struggle and the manner of its self-correction. We also think that it is important to admit that interpretive work only slowly moves toward clarity and that its conclusions must always be open-ended, responsive to new voices, new data, and new methodological perspectives.

Andrea Bear Nicholas also reminds me that, since colonialism continues to affect contemporary Wabanaki peoples, it is important to alert my readers to what my study does not engage. I can imagine the long-range history of colonialism Nicholas has in mind, although this study focuses only on the seventeenth century. That history would include a realistic portrayal of the missionaries' cultural and religious arrogance that led over centuries to the dismantling of native societies, to undermining their leadership, kinship relations, and confidence in their way of life. That history would trace the imposition of authoritarian politics, the rule of alien forms of law, the denial of sovereignty, the processes of economic marginalization, territorial displacement and dispossession, the gradual but inexorable imposition and internalization of alien ways of thinking and valuing. Such a history has yet to be written for the Wabanaki, or any other Native American people. Although they are not this book's primary focus, these issues form the background of the seventeenth-century cases I examine.

Because of the conceptual problems that my early essays rehearse, I have become conscious that the study of comparative cosmology is pivotal to understanding Native American cultural life and its history. If a cosmology is a conceptual map of the world, then it becomes easier to recognize that Native American peoples have distinctive philosophies of being, ways of knowing, and rigorously relational ethical systems. My two Wabanaki essays (Chapters Three and Four) demonstrate that I had not yet come to understand adequately the differences in Native and Euramerican cosmologies. For example, while nothing in these essays suggests that I ever thought that "nature" is an appropriate cross-cultural category, the essay on the cannibal giant (Chapter Three) indicates at least that I was unconscious about the issue, probably because I had not yet appreciated the complexity of Hallowell's contribution to Algonkian studies. In this initial foray into Algonkian worldview, I use "natural" as an adjective either to indicate "world" or to point to the ordinary, given, and ethical character of the Algonkian cosmos. As I apply the term "natural" to the cannibal giants, I seem to associate them with wildness as a characteristic of nature. Such usages are inaccurate since the thrust of that essay is to demonstrate that in Algonkian life cannibals are categorically monstrous because they are anti-social and unethical.[38] In retrospect, I can see that I was unaware of my own categorical assumptions, and also that, by beginning to follow the Algonkians' logic about the cannibal giants, I was starting to see something of the religious character of their social life.

Readers who become concerned with the integrity of my overall argument about the religious character of the Algonkians' social life and non-Indian difficulties in thinking about their worldview (explored in greater depth in Chapter Four on the relationship between myth and Wabanaki Catholicism) will come to understand some of the ways in which this terminological problem can be corrected. "World" or "cosmos" can well substitute for nature, and "unethical" could stand for "natural" as I use these terms in the cannibal giant essay. But I also hope that readers come to appreciate that such a terminological shift would be too easy. What is at issue is not simply a range of terms and their misuse. Far more seriously, such inappropriate terminology reveals how poorly comparative culture was understood in the late 1970s.

Although I had read his work, I had clearly not internalized A. Irving Hallowell's 1960 argument that Algonkian people do not recognize "nature" as a cosmological domain separate from their own. Apparently, I did understand Hallowell's insistence that the term "supernatural" did not apply to Algonkians because they did not recognize nature as a domain separate from human beings. The Wabanaki essays are silent on the issue of supernaturalism, which I first address in Chapter Six. After I began to teach and study Native American religious traditions, I learned that Religious Studies scholars (as I explore in Chapter Two) commonly represent Native American religious life in terms of natural, cultural, and supernatural categories. Some scholars seem to recognize that such categories do not fit Native American cosmologies, but even they fail to explore the categorical difference. Among the cases I discuss, for example, both Calvin Martin (Chapter One) and James Axtell (Chapter Eight) reject the supernatural category and discuss Algonkian traditions as though they were and are supernaturalistic.

The larger issue—that Algonkian and Euramerican cosmologies differ in specific ways—I myself did not yet understand in my Wabanaki studies. Like my colleagues in all the disciplines, I operated in terms of an unconscious cosmological system that I did not recognize as an untested, unverified, and nonempirical explanation of other people's realities. In two essays (Chapters Three and Four), for another example, I use the terms "belief," "faith," "sacral," "spiritual" and "spiritual forces," "otherworldly relations," and "two worlds" as though they were all opposed to nature and culture. Sometimes I used these terms to indicate a subjective, religious state of being. In Chapter Four, I refer to the "conversion" of the Kennebec Wabanaki, but the chapter itself argues for syncretism. In other words, I have come to realize that in the Wabanaki essays I was only partially engaging Algonkian ways of being, knowing, and valuing.

Readers may find it useful to know that my historical training did not include the scholarly study of Native American religious traditions. Not only were such issues completely ignored in Native American Studies (in which I was also self-trained), Religious Studies was also in its infancy. As my overall argument in this volume indicates, scholars still misunderstand both Native American religious traditions and their histories. Not surprisingly, even scholars of religion contest the nature of the field, its methods, and its findings. In these circumstances, such interdisciplinary study combining history, anthropology, and Religious Studies is still uncommon and to its absence can be traced much of the interpretive confusion I document in the new essays in this volume. By highlighting intellectual ethnocentrism, I seek to define several issues with which ethnohistory has struggled in making sense of cultural similarities and differences. Whatever their complicated combinations and permutations, the cases I document in Chapter One (which examines the tension between romantic and rationalist modes of explanation), in Chapter Two (which focuses on the problem of comparative cosmology), and in Chapter Eight (which critiques the description of religious adaptation as conversion) reveal that Religious Studies has much to contribute to understanding religious difference, religious dialogue, and religious change.

As my readers will see, A. Irving Hallowell is pivotal to the understanding toward which I am still moving. In focusing on the Ojibwa view of ontology, Hallowell created the compelling argument that they have a worldview characterized by linguistic, perceptual, cognitive, behavioral, and ethical coherence. In Chapters Six and Seven, and in all the new essays in this volume, I apply Hallowell's findings. In various ways, I argue that Hallowell's particular methodological value is in studying what Thomas Blackburn identifies as a culture's existential and moral postulates.[39] I raise this issue of Hallowell's significance because scholarly readers will notice that in Chapters Six and Seven I do not present a systematic argument about the relationship of Hallowell's thought to the overall study of Native American religions. I have explored something of that relationship in one published essay—"The Cosmos as Intersubjective: Native American Other-than-Human Persons"[40]—in which I conclude that Hallowell's theoretical contributions have gone largely untested, but are highly relevant to the interpretation of Native American religious life. Some of my students have done related work on the Mohave, Quechan, Apache, Blackfoot, and Hopi.[41] Other scholars have come to similar conclusions about the category "person" among the Ojibwa,[42] Odawa,[43] Navajo,[44] Hopi and Zuni,[45] Yoeme,[46] Chumash,[47] Kwakiutl and other Northwest Coast peoples,[48] and Yupik.[49] In addition, a collection of essays on indigenous religions explores my triad—person, power, and gift—for its explanatory significance in several traditions.[50] While these concepts broadly inform my hypothetical orientation toward understanding Native American religious traditions, they do not receive primary exploration in the essays of this volume. But I do argue that these terms point to analytical concerns that pervasive ethnocentric terminology obscures. The categories of person, power, and gift suggest a broad need to rethink Native American religious ethnography as a task that is necessarily preliminary to achieving some ethnographically accurate understanding of Native American religious history.

In these ways, I have come to understand that scholars of religious life have a particular responsibility to define analytical terms applied to cultural comparison. Scholars must test the usefulness of such categories in understanding "religion" for its meaning within distinct traditions, and for understanding the religious encounter between Native and Euramerican peoples. Clearly, such an interpretive enterprise must be deconstructive: scholars must consider whether their own social, cultural, and religious assumptions have misrepresented the views of other people. In this regard, I have come to doubt whether monotheistic assumptions about "religion" can be applied to the religious cosmologies of Algonkian-speaking peoples. I also show that intellectual ethnocentrism drives the need for a reconstructive effort: we can come to appreciate something of the social, cultural, and religious terms within which other people operate.

For the moment, however, I also argue that such a goal will continue to be elusive because scholars represent other peoples in modes of rationality that sometimes ignore, and often fail to explain, alternative ways of being social, of reasoning in relational terms, and of acting ethically in ways that are other-directed rather than self-oriented. Social scientific and reified ways of thinking stress the structural characteristics of native "culture" and "society," as well as Native Americans' economic, technical, and diplomatic relations with non-Indian peoples.[51] Of course, such an analysis can be useful, but it is not quite the same thing as engaging Native American views about their own cultural situation or their motives in relating to Euramerican peoples. Such conceptual abstractions certainly help us to understand important variables in contact situations—differences between large- and small-scale societies, consensual versus authoritarian politics, sharing and profit economies, and experientially oriented and dogmatic religious traditions. At the same time, however, their abstract emphasis tends to miss the motivated, concrete, pragmatic, and deliberate actions of both Native and Euramerican actors.

As a collection of essays written over an extended period of time and that document a long-range process of learning, this volume speaks to the development of Native American Religious Studies in general and Algonkian Studies in particular. I invite my readers to join me in an exercise in hindsight about cross-cultural studies. The new essays in this volume explore interdisciplinary reflections about the adequacy of academic ways of understanding Native American realities. The older essays record thinking-in-process. Together, the essays document how I have grappled with intellectual ethnocentrism. They record a personal and professional struggle I hope my readers will come to recognize is required of all interpretive scholarship.

1

The Study of Algonkian Religious Life

The Methodological Impasse

The essays in this volume explore the well-known and still controversial ground of seventeenth-century French missions to several Eastern Algonkian peoples. These missions have drawn more scholarly attention than any other in North America simply because the French left a remarkable record of their contact with Native Americans. As might be expected, anthropologists, historians, ethnohistorians, and church historians have attempted to formulate viable ways of understanding the meaning of the seventeenth-century encounter.[1] Accordingly, this chapter surveys some of these interpretive stances, and seeks to understand their conflicting views of Algonkian religious life and history.

I focus on a controversy that has developed in the past twenty years between so-called romantic or idealist and rationalist interpretations of contact history. Calvin Martin describes the apparent impasse: "Regarding the Indian side of the Indian-white couplet, one finds platitudes still expressed and condolences extended—expressions of concern and benevolence. But then what? From there on the Indian is usually shoehorned into the dominant culture's paradigm of reason and logic, its calculus of viewing the world and manipulating its parts. The traditional historian colonizes the Indian's mind."[2] Martin stresses the intellectual roots of the enduring problem: the complex, dazzling interpretive machine that derives from "Aristotelian, Augustinian, Calvinist, Baconian, Cartesian, Newtonian, Marxist and many other" perspectives.[3] I address a similar concern. I ask whether scholars have achieved views of Native American religious life that might facilitate an understanding of Native American history from Native American points-of-view.[4] I find, in short, that scholars have not engaged the Algonkian-speaking peoples. Scholars have applied uncritically non-Indian religious categories and have not examined the ostensible fit of those categories with those of Algonkian peoples. Such an imposition of non-Indian ways of thinking constitutes what I mean by intellectual ethnocentrism and, as I will show, the bias is linked to false assumptions about the comparative nature of religion.[5]

THE INTERPRETIVE BASELINE

For much of the twentieth century, historians recognized the problem of intellectual ethnocentrism and attempted to circumvent it. Self-consciously seeking a balanced view of contact, Alfred Goldsworthy Bailey pioneered a social-scientific interpretation of French-Algonkian history in his 1934 doctoral thesis.[6] Quoting William Christie MacLeod at the opening of his preface, Bailey reveals that his interpretation (Bailey gives his study the subtitle, "A Study in Canadian Civilization") substituted a secularized, progressive explanation for partisan religious and nationalist interpretations. "Every frontier has two sides," MacLeod declares. "Its movement forward or backward is the consequence of two sets of forces. To understand fully why one side advances, we must know something of why the other side retreats."[7] MacLeod speaks, it should be observed, a language of victimization. For Bailey, the encounter developed in the ways in which Algonkian peoples discovered and grappled with overwhelming difference: "They were gradually to become more aware of a civilization that had little or nothing in common with their own; a more complex material culture; a specialized European conception of property of which they had at first no notion; a society which was in general more various, but in some respects less rigid than theirs; and a religion which, in its metaphysical and especially in its social aspects, was completely alien to their comprehension."[8] For Bailey, as for many since, Native Americans played a passive, victimized role in post-contact North American history. In his farseeing but imperfectly achieved view, religious orientations shaped the French advance and the Algonkian retreat.

Bailey was very aware of the problem of intellectual ethnocentrism. He began his study declaring that he could not go beyond the reality assumptions of his own view of reality:

> It is difficult, if not impossible, to form an idea of what the Indians thought of the European during the first period of encounter. It is difficult because, as we cannot transcend our own traditional processes, we are bound to read into the actual Indian view one that has been especially conditioned by our peculiar cultural background. That is, the subjective standpoint cannot be eliminated.[9]

Given his attention to evidence from Algonkian ethnography, however, Bailey was not quite so pessimistic in practice. He thought that Algonkian perspectives could be reconstructed. Scholars have, in fact, belatedly acknowledged Bailey's foundational theoretical contributions to what would become the interdisciplinary field now called ethnohistory. A good deal of that recognition singles out his concern for comparative religious life.[10] He recognized, for example, that the French themselves created a major impediment to achieving their aim of culturally and religiously transforming the Algonkian peoples. "Scarcely less important as an obstacle to conversion," Bailey wrote, "was the failure of the French to acquaint themselves with the fact that there was a religion of any kind among the Eastern Algonkians."[11] In actuality, Bailey distinguished himself because he appreciated that Algonkian economics, politics, diplomacy, technology, social/sexual life, mythology, and oral tradition cannot be understood "without some consideration of the religious factor, however brief it may be."[12]

Bailey's characterization of the Algonkian world is significant, not only because his interpretation reveals scholars' early-twentieth-century understanding of comparative religious interpretation, but also for what his description discloses about the long-range interpretive challenge. Bailey writes:

> That is, there were in the primitive cosmogony what we would call a set of extra-physical forces which exerted a continuous and comprehensive influence over the furniture of this world, and the relative potencies of these mystical forces were equated with the relative superiority of the materials which they controlled or with which they were interpenetrated.[13]

Bailey's terminology is both innovative and limiting. The notion that a cosmogony constitutes a coherent worldview has had enduring potential for the study of Native American religious life.[14] Similarly, the idea that physical substance (Bailey's "natural"—"the world," and cultural—"furniture") participates in some otherworldly significance identifies enduring interpretive problems.[15] As we will see, the ground of meaning in Algonkian life has a profoundly interpersonal character that Bailey's terms "extra-physical forces," "potencies," "mystical forces," and "interpenetrated" do not capture.

Bailey's characterization of Algonkian religious life works against itself because he never attempts to overcome the limiting notion of the "primitive," while his effort to ground contact history in Native American worldview was simply ahead of his time. He notes, for one example, that Algonkian theories of disease and curing were more advanced than those of either the English or the French. Bailey also recognizes that Algonkian medicine proceeded in different terms, terms that he cannot quite encompass: "The Montagnais and the Abenaki [Wabanaki] measured up favourably with the English and the French in their knowledge of what, to the contemporary scientific mind, may be termed natural causes, but the category of natural causes was one that could not have been recognized by the native mind which perceived supernatural inter-penetration, or perhaps identity, with the physical environment."[16] To his mind, that supernatural character had to do with an Algonkian misunderstanding of objectivity and subjectivity: "no sharp division separated the habit of mind which led to the use of medicinal herbs from that which had recourse to incantation and exorcism, these two being necessarily involved in the same process."[17] In his gloss of Algonkian cosmology, Bailey identified the significant actors as "supernatural beings,"[18] who were addressed by "sympathetic magic."[19] Although Bailey expresses the terminology of choice in the 1930s, his conceptual strategy is both tentative and imprecise. In comparing Algonkian and French religious orientations, for example, Bailey undercuts the very terms he uses to describe the Algonkian worldview:

> The Indians were, of course, unaware of the idea of natural causation which was the product of the nineteenth century sciences. The distinction between natural and supernatural, between flesh and spirit, which was implicit in the doctrines of the medieval church, and of the Jesuits in New France, was not recognized by such primitive peoples as the eastern Algonkians. Indeed, the terms 'natural' and 'supernatural' tend to become meaningless since the natural and the super nature [sic] were so closely inter-related.[20]

In this way, Bailey identified what would become an enduring ethnographic problem in the study of Algonkian religious life. How can scholars grasp a world organized by terms that depart from those—the natural, cultural, and supernatural terms—of their own cosmology? What is the status of a world in which natural and supernatural distinctions are not made? What alternative distinctions do Algonkians make? What kind of reality does such a world have? Bailey does not explore these questions, but he quotes the anthropologist Diamond Jenness, who suggests that Algonkian reality consisted of nothing more, nor less, than a subjective projection of religious imagination upon the world. The Indian

> peopled his world with numerous "powers," some great, mysterious, and awe-inspiring, some small and of little or no account . . . he . . . gave them such anthropomorphic traits as speech and knowledge, even ascribed to them human or partly human forms. So the "power" of the cataract became its "spirit." . . . The "power" of the cataract was only an attribute, but the "spirit" was a separate existence. It carried the same name as the cataract, and the name heightened its individuality, giving it the status of a definite supernatural being. . . . Some spirits were vague and nameless, others as definitive as the deities of ancient Greece and Rome. But *ultimately* they were *no more than personifications of the mysterious forces* which the Indians saw *working* in nature around them."[21]

In effect, Jenness identifies the religious terminology and associated assumptions that non-Indians have utilized uncritically. He contends that Native American religious systems derive from a supernatural ultimacy, and that the beings of the Algonkian cosmos were nothing more than projected personifications upon nature's mysteries. Jenness uses, moreover, contradictory language in reducing personal beings to impersonal "mysterious forces" that work mechanistically. Such terminological confusions have continued to trouble Algonkian religious ethnography.

RELIGIOUS ETHNOGRAPHY

Although many scholars have acknowledged Alfred Goldsworthy Bailey's pioneering effort to engage Native American points-of-view in contact situations, few followed his lead. That lag between Bailey's innovative effort in 1937 and the emergence of other interdisciplinary work helps explain the excitement and controversy that Calvin Martin's study, *Keepers of the Game: Indian-Animal Relationships in the Fur Trade*[22] ignited. One measure of Martin's success emerged when *Keepers of the Game* received the 1979 Albert J. Beveridge Award of the American Historical Association. Another more revealing measure appeared three years later, as prominent members of the anthropological and ethnohistorical communities assessed Martin's book and found it wanting.

Two of these responses are exemplary for understanding the difficulty ethnohistorians have had in making sense of Algonkian religious ethnography. This difficulty won Martin dismissal as an "idealist" or "romantic" scholar who overestimates religious influences on Algonkians' historical behavior. Charles A. Bishop declares that Martin "is one of the few historians who has attempted to deal with the issue of the role of ideology in Indian culture change. Through his focus upon Indian cognition and how this was related to behavior both in prehistoric times and during the fur trade era, he has made a number of us rethink our positions." In addition, Bishop makes two observations that describe the positive and negative assessments of Martin's position. First, he thinks that "much of what Martin says about aboriginal Algonkian religion appears to be correct." Second, Bishop concludes that Martin has neither the historical data to support his thesis, nor an appropriate methodology by which to make sense of the data he does present.[23] Bruce Trigger agrees with Bishop's basic argument: "I do not deny the importance of trying to understand the fur trade in terms of how it was perceived by the Indians. Nor do I deny that in some instances idealist explanations of historical phenomena may be valid." This is an important caveat, and one that many scholars have acknowledged since the publication of *Keepers of the Game*. Arguably, Native Americans have distinctive religious points-of-view. But Trigger also defines an ideological issue that has troubled ethnohistory since 1979. He writes: "It appears, however, that materialist explanations, which view human behavior primarily as a response to the problems of mortal existence, account for such activities more often than do idealist ones."[24] Stated in another way, Calvin Martin is controversial for both Bishop and Trigger because he stresses the study of irrelevant religious motives, rather than the compelling causalities of economic, political, and technological culture. Such remains the impasse between religious and materialistic understandings of Indian history.

Upon close examination, Calvin Martin's religious ethnography turns out to be as problematic as his much maligned reading of Indian history. As his many critics have detailed, Martin imagines, with little evidence for his claims, that the European fur trade, Christianity, and unprecedented epidemics converged to convince Algonkian peoples that wildlife in general, and the beaver in particular, had declared war upon them. He also argues that they, in turn, retaliated against the animals. Thus, Martin argues that both Native Americans and the animals repudiated the cardinal principles of their common cosmos and of their interdependence. Since virtually everyone agrees that Martin's is a farfetched theory about the effects of the fur trade, it is all the more important to review the character of his religious ethnography. Ironically, his interpretation of the religious nature of Algonkian life is understood as his core contribution to American Indian ethnohistory, although that achievement is also the least examined aspect of his study.

Ostensibly grounded in a close reading of the ethnographic record, Martin's claim to have achieved an accurate reconstruction of the religious principles of Algonkian worldview rings false. As I will demonstrate, Martin has read the ethnographic record in ways that reveal the religious ethnocentrism that has colored most interpretations from the seventeenth century to the present. It may or may not be that Martin is the idealist that Trigger claims. Before Trigger's stand can be assessed, it is crucial to deconstruct the manner in which Martin misinterprets post-contact Algonkian religious life because his view is taken as an accurate portrayal of those religious traditions. We should acknowledge, as do many of his critics, the complexity of the ethnographic and historic issues that Martin has forced us to confront.

It is telling that Martin does not present a systematic argument about the nature of Algonkian religious life or the ways in which it ought to be studied. While a primary concern for Algonkian worldview defines his methodology, Martin does not reflect on the task of achieving an accurate religious ethnography per se. In both the Mi'kmaq (Micmac) and Ojibwa (Anishnaabe)[25] sections of his book, Martin contends that Algonkian peoples have been interpreted in ethnocentric ways. Paradoxically, however, while Martin realizes that his readers, scholars and general public alike, will find his ethnographic argument about Algonkian religious thought and practice difficult to accept, he does little to help them to do so.

Martin declares, for example, that many readers will find his reading of Algonkian ways of thinking "a fantasy," not realizing that, by characterizing the Algonkian religious outlook as a system of "spiritual beliefs,"[26] he sustains the very dismissal of Algonkian worldviews as the "fantasy" he wishes to disclaim. For complex reasons that Martin does not recognize, neither the term "spiritual" nor the term "belief" can be characterized as cross-cultural.[27] For non-Indians, these terms encapsulate the most fundamental and unexamined of suppositions about the nature of reality. These terms are, in other words, at the heart of interpretive ethnocentrism. The term "spiritual," for example, can refer variously (and unsystematically, since most people are neither metaphysicians nor theologians) to a variety of reality assumptions. Spiritual often refers, in the first place, to non-physical beings, that is, the spirits,[28] and frequently to the otherworld dimension in which they are supposed to exist, that is, the supernatural.[29] In the second place, spiritual commonly refers to subjective religious "belief," and thus to refined religious piety, sentiment, and/or religious achievement, that is, a deeply/highly spiritual person. In a related way, belief sometimes points to some posited aspect of reality that is construed variously as non-empirical and imaginative objects of fantasy, or of faith. Both spiritual and belief thus tend to encompass broad entailments that lie at the dualistic heart of Western cosmology, meanings that are particularly rehearsed in the pervasive assumption that reality has both objective and subjective, physical and spiritual, characteristics. Spiritual beliefs, secular materialists have always insisted, have merely a subjective, private, and individual relevance. Given his commitment to this terminology, the same remains true for Calvin Martin because he does not account for the distinctive reality assumptions of the Algonkian peoples.

In describing Algonkian religious views as "spiritual beliefs,"and as "fantasy," Martin argues for a worldview approach to the study of Native American life and history, even while he seems to relegate such a methodology to trafficking with the unreal. Martin writes: "To neglect this 'fantasy,' then, would be to risk inappropriately fantastic, because Westernized, interpretations of baffling events in this early period of contact history."[30] Martin thus declares the need to overcome, or at least to contain, Western bias. He insists on the need to understand that Western bias is itself fantastic, that is to say improbable when applied to other times and places. For Martin, and this may be why materialists judge his interpretation of Native American religious motivation romantic, social science assumes that economic, materialistic, and capitalistic factors defined Algonkian participation in the fur trade. Martin argues to the contrary that the Algonkian worldview simply does not proceed in terms of materialist causality. Unfortunately, Martin argues for a "spiritual" explanation as an alternative to a materialist one, not understanding that he himself continues to exercise the very theological and rationalistic principles of the Western worldview he otherwise criticizes.

Take, as one example, Martin's purpose in quoting pioneer ethnohistorian, Alfred Goldsworthy Bailey. Reflecting on the eagerness with which some Mi'kmaq approached trade with Jacques Cartier in 1534, and on their reactions when the French fired two cannons in the air to dampen their enthusiasm, Bailey wrote: "Clearly the strangers who controlled the thunder were heavily endowed with manito [power], but even the displeasure of the gods could not keep the Micmac from the source of iron, for iron saved them from days of drudgery and enabled them to vanquish their enemies who were as yet armed only with stone, bone, and wood implements."[31] Bailey's claim about the Mi'kmaq's motivation is important to Martin for what it reveals about the "conventional wisdom" that has explained Native American responses to European trade. Martin puts his case succinctly: "There, in poetically encapsulated form, is the usual explanation for the Indian's participation in the trade: European hardware and other trade items were immediately perceived by the Stone Age Indian as being far superior in their utility to his primitive technology and general material culture."[32] Martin disagrees with such a depiction because he insists that Algonkians pursued their own religious understanding of contact events.

Martin does not discuss, however, two features of Bailey's ethnocentric characterization of Mi'kmaq religious life, features that he rehearses throughout his own interpretation. First, Bailey propounds the claim (theory would be too large a concept, because such a claim is seldom assessed by reading European sources against the grain of *their* own ethnocentricism) that Native Americans responded to Europeans with naive and religious awe. Second, Bailey characterized the nature of the traditional beings of Native American cosmology as "gods," but does not compare Native American and western European ontological assumptions about "being" in the world. In other places as well, Martin quotes both primary sources and secondary interpretations that exercise similar ethnocentric religious categories, yet he does not recognize that they do so.[33] Martin's ethnocentrism, like that of all Europeans, expresses itself in terms like "Nature," "supernatural," "beast," "sacred," "spiritual," "belief," and the like.

Martin's use of the term "magic" to describe the causal relations (that is to say power) shaping the Algonkians' world continues to exercise an ethnocentricism that belies his claim of reconstructing Native American points-of-view. "The Indian's was a world filled with superhuman and magical powers which controlled man's destiny and Nature's course of events."[34] Martin relies on Murray and Rosalie Wax to document his claim of Algonkians' cosmic subservience,[35] a claim A. Irving Hallowell had long since laid to rest.[36] In another study, Murray Wax notes that people who live in a "magical world" think and react to the world as a society, "not a mechanism, that is, it is composed of 'beings' rather than 'objects.' Plants, animals, rocks, and stars are thus seen not as 'objects' governed by laws of nature, but as 'fellows' with whom the individual or band may have a more or less advantageous relationship."[37] As I explore in the following chapter, Algonkian people focus on a relational causality in which humans interact reciprocally with other-than-human persons. Martin paraphrases the Waxes: "one is struck by the anthropomorphic nature of animals,"[38] again overlooking Hallowell's denial of Algonkian anthropomorphism.[39] More important, Martin does not seem to appreciate that the Waxes call for a descriptive causal language that appreciates the interpersonal character of the Algonkians' world.

Quoting Martin at length reveals the ways in which he departs radically from the relational principles the Waxes identify, and the ways in which he in fact uses the substantive, objective, chemical, and mechanical tropes they criticize:

The essential ingredient in this peculiar relationship between man and animals, and indeed between man and all of Nature, is Power. Power—called *manitou* in Algonkian—is a phenomenon common among pre-industrial people the world over. Roughly defined, it is the spiritual potency associated with an object (such as a knife) or a phenomenon (such as thunder). To the Micmac, as well as to all the rest of these Eastern Canadian hunter-gatherers, manitou was the force which made everything in Nature alive and responsive to man. Only a fool would confront life without it, since it was only through the manipulation and interpretation of manitou that man was able to survive in this world. To cut oneself off from manitou was equivalent to repudiating the vital force in Nature; without manitou Nature would lose its meaning and potency, and man's activities in Nature would become secular and mechanical.

Ethnologists have frequently compared Power to static electricity in its properties, 'in the sense that it may be accumulated by proper ritual and then be employed in service or discharged by contact with improper objects.' Power, continue the Waxes, 'is never regarded as a permanent and unconditional possession, but may be lost by the same kinds of forces and circumstances as it was gained.' One handles Power according to the principles of ritual. Ritual thus becomes the means of harnessing, or conducting, Power.

It is important to understand this concept of Power if we are to appreciate fully the Indian hunter's role in the fur trade, something which will receive considerable attention in part 3. Suffice it to say, here, that the world of the Micmac was filled with super-human forces and beings—dwarves, giants, and magicians; animals that could talk to man and had spirits akin to his own; and the magic of mystical and medicinal herbs—a cosmos where even seemingly inanimate objects possessed spirits. Micmac subsistence pursuits were inextricably bound up within this spiritual matrix, which, I am proposing, acted as a kind of control mechanism on Micmac land use, maintaining the natural environment within an optimum range of conditions.[40]

When Martin's terms are unpacked it is easier to understand his place in the terminological ethnocentrism I am documenting. Under the guise of presenting a new, ethnographically accurate portrayal of Algonkian religious life, Martin simply rehearses non-Indian religious assumptions. Characterizing the relationship between Algonkians and animals as "peculiar," Martin uses a culinary metaphor—"the essential ingredient"—in a way that draws attention away from the interactional character of Mi'kmaq cosmic life, and focuses, instead, on its abstract "essential" components. The primary ingredient is, Martin declares, a "spiritual potency" associated with "an object" and "a phenomenon," not an intentional being. All three of these impersonal terms depart from the relational character of religious life that the Waxes wish to highlight; unlike Martin, the Waxes stress that power is a matter of motivated behavior—the purposeful interaction—of human and other kinds of beings.

Instead of understanding how relationships emerge from a dialogical interaction between various kinds of beings, Martin abstracts discursive power (read "the ability to persuade") into a "vital force in Nature" that humans must manipulate. Although Martin seems to contrast this interpretation of power with one that is both "secular and mechanical," he cites approvingly a common view that power "is like static electricity in its properties," and can be harnessed, stored, discharged, and conducted like electricity. Thus, when Martin describes the Mi'kmaq world as "filled with super-human forces and beings," including "the magic of mystical and medicinal herbs," one can see that he continues to rehearse an objectivist language in representing Mi'kmaq reality. The only exception to this objective representational strategy consists of Martin's use of subjectivist terms—"spiritual," "magic," and "mystical"—which he does not explicate as relevant for understanding Algonkian worldview.

These subjectivist terms do nothing to help the reader to understand Martin's claim that animals in the Mi'kmaq cosmos "could speak to man and had spirits akin to his own."[41] For Martin, the nub of the matter has to do with understanding that power/manitou is directly related to "the principles of ritual," but he fails to identify these principles. Instead of reconstructing actual instances of Mi'kmaq-animal behavior—a behavioral emphasis any proper religious ethnography ought to stress—Martin is content to see ritual as a "spiritual matrix" that provided the Mi'kmaq some "kind of control mechanism" over "Nature."[42] All of these terms, I submit, rehearse precisely the conceptual confusion I identify as intellectual ethnocentrism.

In addition to the pervasive ethnocentric terms that establish themselves in the Mi'kmaq portion of his book, Martin's reading of the Algonkian mythological tradition is highly selective, superficial, and uncritical. Chapter Three, which claims to survey the Ojibwa worldview, begins with an account of Algonkian cosmology based on two late-eighteenth and early-nineteenth-century texts. Martin uses these historical texts uncritically. He does not comment on their character or veracity, nor does he compare them to other extant myth texts. Nor does Martin seem to appreciate that both accounts are problematic.

His initial paragraph, based on Samuel Hearne's late-eighteenth-century trading journal, recounts the experience of the first female human being. Martin's account presents the story in inexplicable ways: the first woman, we are told, dreams that she sleeps with a handsome young man, "who was in reality her pet dog transformed." Neither the reported dream nor the reality of her dog's metamorphosis particularly supports the paragraph's thesis that in the creation myth "beasts were once related to mankind." In fact, Martin presents the two sentences about the female and her transformed dog without explanation as he suddenly shifts to a giant who appears and begins to shape the land into lakes, rivers, and mountains. The giant then grabs the dog, tears it to pieces, transforms its various parts into fish, animals, and birds, and gives "the woman and her offspring full power to kill, eat and never spare, for that he had commanded [the beings he had created] to multiply for her use in abundance." A textual note reveals that Martin is aware that the "'never spare' injunction" is unusual, and he relates it to the shame Hearne's Indian companions felt at "their wasteful slaughter of game."[43] He does not otherwise contextualize this story, assess the motivations of the storyteller, or explain what the account might mean for our understanding of Algonkian worldview. In effect, Martin overlooks the ways in which humans share being with animals, regardless of their differences in physical appearance. Nor does he explain that the giant is a culture hero, a transformer who establishes the ethical character of human-animal relations, a morality based on human-animal reciprocity, rather than, as the Hearne text suggests, human exploitation.

Martin's second paragraph proceeds as oddly as his first. Here Martin's account, based on David Thompson's turn-of-the-nineteenth-century narrative, purports to describe Cree and Ojibwa cosmogony, although the creation itself (unless Martin means the transformations recounted in the first paragraph) is not conveyed. Instead, Martin introduces the culture hero *Wisekejak*, as the subordinate of the Great Spirit, called *kitchi manitou*, who gives the hero "his solemn commission" "to teach man and beast how to live properly together." Martin's account of Algonkian worldview thus stresses both hierarchy and authority, not the consensual ethics of tribal life. Ignoring the Great Spirit's repeated enjoinders, Wisekejak acts like a trickster, creating havoc in human-animal relations. Exasperated, the Great Spirit destroys all of creation with a flood, but a beaver, an otter, and a muskrat survive and take "refuge with the now distraught *Wisekejak*." Then, the water subsides, and "man and all other life-forms were remade" by some unspecified creator. In a final move, another unidentified actor "stripped" Wisekejak of "his great authority." "From then on he was to be a deceiver only: a trickster-transformer."[44] As we have seen, Martin's critics do not quarrel with this description of Algonkian cosmology, but we should do so.

Martin characterizes "those days of heroes and powerful magic" as a "supernaturalistic world view" even though he seems to understand that such a category does not apply. "I use the world 'supernaturalistic'," Martin writes in a textual note, "as a convenience for the reader. To the Indian the spirit world was not distinguished from the natural world; for him there was nothing supernatural."[45] How such a category is convenient for the reader goes unexplained. Martin certainly ignores A. Irving Hallowell's argument that Western categories, including nature as well as supernatural, distort the Algonkian actuality.[46] Martin also seems oblivious to his own ethnocentrism: he insists on supernaturalism regardless of Algonkian categories. Take, for example, his understanding of kitchi manitou, the Great Spirit. This figure, whom Hallowell characterizes as remote, conceptual, and abstract, rather than as a behavioral presence in Ojibwa life,[47] Martin deifies: "*Kitchi Manitou*, the Great Spirit, was the creator and sustainer of all things." Martin overlooks details he himself provides that suggest that kitchi manitou was hardly sovereign. In the first place, "he was too physically distant and omnipotent to influence affairs directly."[48] Here Martin seems not to notice that the Great Spirit's inability to influence worldly affairs amounts to a significant compromise of his posited omnipotence. Similarly, Martin distorts the history of this figure, claiming that the Jesuit missionaries "equated" kitchi manitou "with the sun," when, in fact, the missionaries reported that Algonkians themselves made the analogy between the Sun and the Jesuits' significant other.[49] Martin is confident that a primacy of being constitutes the Algonkian worldview. He contends that kitchi manitou exercises his will through "a descending hierarchy of subordinate manitous." Martin contradicts immediately this claim of cosmic political hierarchy: he quotes Ruth Landes to the effect that "among the manitos the mighty ones, like the great birds and beasts, were solitary Characters (a respectful appellation for them) who met in smoke-filled councils to discuss cosmic affairs."[50] As a political institution, furthermore, the council among the Algonkians (and other Native Americans as well) articulated a principle of political equality, rather than the hierarchy Martin posits.[51]

Simply put, Martin presents a garbled reading of Algonkian religious life. As he knows, the Algonkian cosmos derives its coherence, system, and regularity in the behavioral actions of persons—humans, animals, plants, and others. To this insight, Martin adds a Western cosmology composed of nature, culture, and supernatural, but does not recognize that this scheme holds that different kinds of increasingly superior beings exist at each level. Consider the following quotation, reminiscent of Diamond Jenness, which reveals the ways in which Martin describes the Algonkian cosmos in contradictory terms:

> Just as everything had a purpose, so everything had its manitou, or spirit, whose power and influence depended on its significance to the Indian. Spectacles of Nature—waterfalls, rivers and lakes, large or peculiarly formed rocks, aged trees—had especially strong manitous. So, too, did the elements, which in the Indian mind were personified: northwind, thunder, lightning, cold, and so forth. All things animate and inanimate had spirit, and hence being.[52]

These sentences are particularly confused. If everything is manitou rather than has manitou, that is to say, if everything is a personal being, then such beings are able to exert intentional power and influence; given such personal autonomy, these beings could not, therefore, owe their "significance to the Indian." It is also apparent that Martin reifies this personal and interpersonal world as "Nature" (which he always capitalizes) in a way that obscures the Algonkian view of the world as an intentional, interactional system. Algonkians do not "personify" because their recognition of persons in the world is a behavioral phenomenon.[53] Indeed, meaning in the Algonkian cosmos emerges in the intersection of the purposeful actions of all persons, human and otherwise. Meaning derives from an interspecies sociality that Martin seems to identify, but which he undercuts with his phrase "in the Indian mind." If spirit, animacy, and being are synonymous for the Algonkians, and they would seem to be, then surely inanimate things cannot have being. Further, Martin reduces the behavioral, interactional, and intersubjective character of the Algonkian cosmos to the "spiritual": "Every activity, whether it be hostile, sociable, subsistence, or whatever, had spiritual overtones; all of his relations and functions were above all else spiritual. . . . On the practical level, this meant that the Indian would approach every situation fortified with spiritual power. Life was, by definition, a spiritual enterprise."[54] Rather than understand that the "spiritual" has relational, and thus behavioral, significance for the Algonkian peoples, Martin draws an analogy between "spiritual" causality and "magical power," "magical charms," and "imitative and contagious" magic. I argue, in short, that to describe Algonkian religious life in other than everyday, real, interactional terms, particularly by recourse to the language of spiritual supernaturalism, theism, and magic, is to fail to make sense of Algonkians in the cognitive terms Martin claims to establish.[55]

In fairness, Calvin Martin reproduces uncritically an ethnographic tradition that has failed to recognize its own religious ethnocentrism. A few ethnographic examples from his Chapter Five will suffice to reveal the pervasive problem. Martin begins with Frank G. Speck's argument that for the Montagnais-Naskapi hunting is a "holy occupation," a characterization that Martin finds "stunning" with no explanation why. From Speck, Martin also derives his notion that hunting is a "magico-religious activity," which is otherwise undefined except as a "spiritual activity."[56] Similarly, Martin relies on the early work of A. Irving Hallowell to describe Ojibwa hunting practices, seeming not to recognize that the mature Hallowell backed away from the categories to which he initially gave prominence. Martin quotes Hallowell's doctoral dissertation on bear ceremonialism: "The animal world often represents creatures with magical or superhuman potencies, and the problem of securing them . . . involves the satisfaction of powers or beings of a supernatural order. Consequently, . . . [s]uccess or failure in the hunt is more likely to be interpreted in magico-religious terms than in those of a mechanical order."[57] As we shall see in the following chapter, when Hallowell came to realize that his first representational strategy, which here stresses magic and supernatural terms, misinterpreted Algonkian religious life, he rejected such a description. Martin also cites John Witthoft, who claims that "animals were gifts of the Creator and of lesser supernatuals," and Adrian Tanner, who says that the Cree treat the bodies of slain animals as "sacred substance," and that the Cree recognize "the mystical power of animals."[58]

By and large, Martin's critics do not provide ethnographic arguments that parallel my own about his misconstruction of the Algonkian worldview.[59] The critics intend merely to test whether Martin's core thesis—hostility between humans and animals resulted in war and over-exploitation of game in the fur trade—fits the Algonkian and other Native American cases. But, for all of that, several critics simply argue that Martin seeks an explanation in the wrong places. For these critics, materialist explanations convey adequately Native American motivations in the fur trade; they also explain their response to epidemic illness and Christianity.[60] The critics claim, moreover, that such "ideological" motivations as Martin seeks probably have little importance. Dean Snow reasons—rightly, I think—that historical causality is systematically complex and that, in this sense alone, Martin oversimplifies the Algonkians' situation. Snow is less correct, I also think, to relegate all that he captures by the term "ideology" to some irrelevant edge of human history. "It seems clear to me," Snow writes, "that in most cultural systems most of the time, ideology has been largely a product of other factors and not itself a factor that significantly influenced other factors either positively or negatively."[61] While Martin is not unique in misinterpreting Algonkian history, a significant group of his critics relegate his very attempt to some largely pointless scholarly activity. Such is the current impasse in the scholarship on the study of Algonkian religious life and history.

THE APPARENT PROBLEM: CULTURAL RELATIVISM

A recent study by anthropologist, archaeologist, and ethnohistorian, Bruce Trigger, refocuses attention on scholars' reconstructions of Native American worldviews, and reveals yet again the enduring impasse. Trigger's essay—"Early North American Responses to European Contact: Romantic versus Rationalistic Interpretations"—rejects out of hand Martin's religious explanation of contact events. I would argue that Trigger makes achieving an accurate religious ethnography central to understanding not only northeastern Indian history in the colonial period, but Indian history throughout the continent.[62] Trigger adopts a tolerant attitude to what he calls relativist, idealist, or romantic interpretations of contact events.[63] Since Trigger contends that relativistic explanations of Native American traditions are now unfortunately dominant,[64] and since he espouses an alternative, rationalist explanation, his argument that idealism and rationalism might be complementary approaches to contact history seems disingenuous, or at least confused. Trigger's proposed mediation between romanticism and rationalism is worthy of careful consideration. He writes: "The problem that confronts historians and anthropologists is not simply to agree that relativistic and rational factors both play roles in human behavior but to determine what roles and how those factors fit together in the larger totality of behavior."[65] The problem actually is, I would argue, that scholars have not appreciated that Native American religious life has a relational, pragmatic character all its own and attends to relational modes of causality in ways whose depths have yet to be plumbed.

Trigger desires to dichotomize culture into rational and irrational spheres, a division that no more describes Native American worldviews than Martin's magical supernaturalism. To Trigger's mind, and contradicting his earlier claim for the value of methodological balance, the middle view which attempts to mediate between material and non-material cultural domains is too general: "Many argue that, especially in spheres of human activity relating to ecology, technology, and the economy, rational calculations involving universal considerations of efficiency and practicality play a more important role than do culturally constrained perceptions of reality, while cultural traditions may play a more important role in determining the content of religious beliefs."[66] In effect, Trigger holds that "religious beliefs" have little to do with the efficiency and practicality of everyday life. Although this middle position is his own formulation, Trigger dismisses it and does not comment on his rejection. Trigger does not notice that as stated this position does not mediate between a subjective idealism and objective rationalism because it constrains religious life to the unreality of posited beliefs, the inefficient, and the impractical. Trigger does not appreciate the ecological, the technical, and the economic as the very contexts that call for motivated religious action.

Trigger himself prefers what he calls a rationalist approach rather than a religious understanding of contact events. With this emphasis, his essay works at cross-purposes. Trigger champions materialist over idealist interpretations. Trigger admits, for example, that, thin as the evidence is for the sixteenth and perhaps the early seventeenth centuries, the data still suggest that Native Americans responded to Europeans in the terms of their traditional worldviews.[67] Trigger even accepts that the evidence suggests that Native Americans' behavior in the early fur trade was, to an important degree, motivated by religious concerns: northeastern peoples were attracted to trade goods that resembled traditional objects of religious value, and they used such objects with traditional religious purposes in mind.[68] While Trigger recognizes that worldview shaped contact events in the sixteenth century, he also argues that a rational pragmatism provoked a cognitive reorientation of Native American worldviews almost from first encounter.[69]

Trigger's argument suggests that utilitarian materialism soon replaced Native Americans' initial religious understanding of European technical culture. He also overlooks that religious understanding in the course of his argument. In contending that Native Americans embraced quickly a rational pragmatism, Trigger would seem to agree with Calvin Martin's view that contact produced a "despiritualization" of Algonkian peoples' worldview.[70] Trigger's conclusion warrants direct quotation: "While the importance of native beliefs should never be underestimated, in the long run a rationalist and materialist analysis of cultural interaction seems to explain far more about what happened to native people following European contact than does an analysis that assigns primary explanatory power to their traditional beliefs."[71] The terms of this conclusion, I would argue, are conceptually ethnocentric: it is problematic to gloss Native American religious orientations to the world as "beliefs," and thereby to dismiss the obvious worldly success of their long-established, and religiously informed, economies. In addition, Trigger seems to argue that the interaction was one-sided, rather than the interpersonal engagement that his term "interaction" would seem to require. Trigger conceives the encounter as shaped by "what happened to" Native American peoples, rather than as mediated by their ability to discern contact events in terms meaningful to themselves.

Certainly, Trigger's argument stresses that Native Americans turned away—reoriented—from tradition in order to participate "efficiently" in the post-contact, utilitarian world. Trigger does not assess with any compelling detail, however, those studies which he claims examine Native American religious systems. In brief, Trigger seems to have set up "romantic," "idealist," and "relativist" scholars as straw men easily knocked down by an effective European pragmatism that Native Americans, in his view, lacked until they reoriented to European social norms.[72] Trigger thus dismisses the old and common claim that Native Americans do not distinguish between "religion," and the social, economic, political, and technical domains of culture.[73] Although he does not identify explicitly the argument as "romantic," he summarizes idealist interpretations of Native American responses to the fur trade: "In modern times historians and economists have concluded that in traditional Indian cultures economic behavior was so embedded in social and political activities that it precluded 'economic rationality' after contact with Europeans."[74] He certainly assumes, to the extent that he can recognize that Native Americans' worldviews did shape their discernment of contact, that a religious view of reality is non-utilitarian and non-rationalistic.

For Trigger, "human behavior is shaped mainly by calculations of individual self-interest, that are uniform from one culture to another."[75] At this level of his argument, Trigger makes an undocumented claim that flies in the face of the ethnographic evidence. As A. Irving Hallowell has long since established on the basis of a careful reading of the *Jesuit Relations*, the "modal personality" of the Algonkian peoples did not conform to the individualism typical of Europeans. Instead, as members of small-scale kin groups, Algonkian peoples were other-oriented and pragmatically concerned for the ill-effects that attend to those individuals who did not take the well-being of others into consideration.[76] I would be inclined to meet Trigger halfway: sixteenth- and seventeenth-century Native Americans were capable of pragmatic self-interest, although I would argue that they tended to orient practically to the well-being of the primary group. I would also argue that they operated within worldviews that combined ethical and practical objectives. While I would argue that Native Americans stressed ethical practice in the early contact period, Trigger emphasizes asocial self-interest.[77]

Trigger's argument rehearses a deep-seated European confusion about the relationship between "religion" and the world, a tension Trigger defines as an eighteenth- and nineteenth-century conflict between rationalism and romanticism. From the materialist end of the spectrum, this view polarizes religious and scientific views of the world. Rationalists think of "religion" as pertaining to the irrational, imaginary, and non-empirical dimensions of human life, and they hold that as "revelation" religion describes truths otherwise not apparent in the world itself, which are, therefore, subjectivized as belief and faith in a non-empirical order of reality.

Thus, when Trigger characterizes Native American "religions" as both supernaturalistic[78] and belief systems,[79] he extends those terms to include elements of worldview that rationalist scholars think of as non-functional aspects of human life. Since Trigger does not recognize that, in making sense of "religion" in western European settings, both belief and supernaturalism are contested categories, he does not consider whether their application to Native American peoples is appropriate. In Trigger's usage, both belief and supernaturalism become catchwords for Native American worldviews, and both suggest that Native Americans have non-functional relationships with the actual, and "natural" world.[80] To be fair, Trigger recognizes that the thinness of the historical and ethnographic sources understandably requires interpretive caution.[81] But he does not evaluate the ways in which scholars have interpreted those documents, or have supplemented them with others, to estimate Native American motives in contact situations. Instead, Trigger stresses factors that seem to prevent either tribal or comparative study: "The little that we know about these world views suggests that they varied from one region or ethnic group to another and that even adjacent, highly similar world views could, depending on historically contingent situations, structure native interpretations of contact in different ways. From the beginning some interpretations of Europeans were probably more 'rational' than others."[82] Since his essay does not document these variables in contact situations, Trigger's supposition should be noted.

Several observations come to mind about Trigger's views of a very real interpretive problem in accounting for the religious character of Native Americans' pre-contact life, and, therefore, their historical encounter with non-Indians. Without establishing a rigorous understanding of Native American worldviews, his argument—these peoples' utilitarian post-contact behavior provides ample reasons to argue for a universal, meta-cultural, and pragmatic mode of historical explanation—is built in mid-air. Certainly, Trigger's understanding of religious life is ethnocentric. He locates "religion" in a natural, cultural, and supernatural cosmology; he thinks of "religion" as a system of beliefs that culture shields from critical scrutiny. For Trigger, all cultures are opposed to, and constrain, practical reasoning.

Trigger's cosmological commitments must be noted. In his view, "religion" as supernatural and as a belief system refers to an otherwise non-empirical, non-rational world. Culture is equally problematic for Trigger because culture consists of social objectivations which, particularly when grounded in religious supposition, limit the possibility of exercising practical reason. Trigger also makes self-interest foundational, and thus gives the impersonal political and economic aspects of European social life both behavioral and analytical primacy. Unfortunately, his argument does not recognize this implicit perspective, in effect a cosmological bias, nor does he truly test the perspective against the moral and practical trajectories of American Indian life.

Other observations should be noted. Perhaps early contact events, in which Europeans claimed that they were apprehended as gods, and worshiped, were simply the expressions of European bias that Trigger himself warns against.[83] Perhaps Native American "religion" expressed itself in the world in practical ways and in sustenance, technical, economic, political, and social modalities. Finally, in arguing against so-called romantic, idealist, and cultural relativist positions, Trigger seems not to appreciate that they and he share precisely the same ethnocentric assumptions about the nature of Native American religious life. Like them, Trigger does not recognize his ethnocentric assumptions: nature, culture, supernature, belief, and religious irrationality.

The interpretive polarization Trigger posits between scholars who evaluate human life in religious terms, and those who do not, requires careful exploration before we can understand the interpretive limitations of American Indian history. Scholars pursuing qualitative research—to use a neutral term—may actually aim to reconstruct American Indian historical experience in terms that Native Americans themselves might recognize. Others may have less ethnographically precise purposes, aiming instead for a more balanced view of contact history. If Indian history is to be understood in the context of Native American life, then a qualitative perspective that Trigger does not explore, the history of Indian-Indian relations, must be reconstructed. In this sort of social history, scholars will have to engage indigenous meaning as played out among living persons who shape, maintain, and transform their own identity, memory, and history, and to understand those engaged social interactions as religious activities. In these ways, American Indians may have understood the utilitarian, technical, and rational variables as religious, religious meanings that Trigger dismisses as secondary in importance. They may have held that Trigger's variables were actually the means by which they pursued their foremost goal of solidarity between themselves, and between themselves and cosmic beings. In effect, Trigger's materialistic rationalism overlooks, and perhaps denigrates, solidarity as the religious goal of American Indian social life, and a goal native peoples have pursued from time immemorial.

BEYOND SUPERNATURALISM AND MATERIALISM

Given my main argument—that scholars have interpreted Algonkian worldviews in ethnocentric terms—Bruce Trigger's polarization of so-called idealist and rationalist explanations of Indian history seems premature. An idealist explanation, which necessarily attends to the reconstruction of Native American worldviews, is simply impossible until such ethnocentric descriptive strategies are understood and overcome. Such an explanation must seek an understanding that takes Native American cosmologies seriously, must account for human beings' cosmic position vis à vis other beings, and must reconstruct the connection between world-order and the relationships which transpire between human and other-than-human persons. Such an explanation must also account for the religious economy (giving, receiving, withholding) which regulates relations between humans and other persons, and it must construe the ways in which such transactions create, maintain, and transform the skill, knowledge, and power that make human and cosmic identity possible. Until such religious variables are reconstructed, and until their connections are understood, achieving an Indian history will be impossible, for otherwise ethnocentricism will continue to rule the day.

It is important to reflect on the character of ethnohistorians' largely unconscious commitment to a non-Indian cosmology and their tendency to dismiss altogether religious lines of evidence about human meaning and experience. In effect, ethnohistorians tend to reduce religious life, and its historical trajectory as contextualized human meaning, to the unreal, fantastic, imaginary, irrational, and non-functional parts of culture abstractly considered. If my analysis is accurate, and I think that it is, everything remains to be done in understanding the real-world character of Native American religious thought and practice. Bruce Trigger expresses the range of assumptions that have hampered such an understanding in the guise of a rationalism that purports to escape ethnocentrism. Calvin Martin rehearses similar assumptions in ways equally oblivious to their ethnocentric cosmological entailments. At the center of both Trigger's and Martin's confusion rests a pervasive, commonsense notion that reality is constituted objectively, substantively, and subjectively in terms of physicality, emotion, value, and a predominant self-orientation. These assumptions play themselves out in the social sciences' pervasive commitment to objectivity as both method and conclusion. To achieve objectivity, social science holds the subject of its inquiry at arm's length, certain that within the subjective character of changing human meaning lies something that cannot be known but that is true for all times and places. As objective conclusion, social scientists tend to focus not on the human actors, but on second- and third-order abstractions about human behavior, and always disregard human motivation.

A. Irving Hallowell, to whom I turn in the following chapter, articulated the intellectual confusion of what has come to be recognized as the contingent truths of objective ways of studying others' ways of life. In his essay, "Ojibwa Ontology, Behavior, and World View" (1960), Hallowell remarked on the new and fresh concerns of ethnographic inquiry. Hallowell articulated a number of innovations, among them the development of culture and personality studies, national character studies, and Robert Redfield's concept of worldview, "which emphasizes a perspective that is not equivalent to the study of religion in the conventional sense."[84] At the center of Hallowell's methodological exploration lay lessons learned from trying to make sense of Ojibwa persons and their reality system, a task that had occupied him from the 1920s.

Hallowell highlights an ontological issue: the Ojibwa recognize, and non-Indians do not, the existence of persons other-than-human. Hallowell stresses the implications for the social sciences, which focus not on persons and their freighted interactions, but on abstractions about them: "society," "social relations," "social organization." Hallowell was not opposed to human studies that proceed at such abstract levels; he insisted, rather, that the disjunction between human behavior and objectivist methods and results led to a misconstrual of Ojibwa reality. Hallowell writes: "Yet this obviously involves a radical abstraction if, from the standpoint of the people being studied, the concept of person is not, in fact, synonymous with human beings but transcends it." And again: "The study of social organization, defined as human relations of a certain kind, is perfectly intelligible as an objective approach to the study of this subject in any culture. But if, in the world view of a people, persons as a class include entities other than human beings, then our objective approach is not adequate for presenting an accurate description of 'the way a man, in a particular society, sees himself in relation to all else.'"[85] Hallowell recognizes, as I have argued, that projecting Western categories on non-Western peoples is simply "a reflection of *our* subjectivity." Hallowell articulates, moreover, a methodological difference, one that he called a "higher order of objectivity." Such a method could proceed, Hallowell argues, "by adopting a perspective which includes an analysis of the outlook of the people themselves as a complementary procedure."[86] I take this complementary analysis to be the object of Religious Studies, and the interpretive methods that Religious Studies must pursue as its distinctive contribution to the human sciences.

2

Beyond the Supernatural and to a Dialogical Cosmology

One might think that Religious Studies scholars would be less ethnocentric than their counterparts in ethnohistory, but such has not been the case. The problem of religious ethnocentrism that we have reviewed in controversial ethnohistorical interpretations also troubles Religious Studies.[1] Various forms of ethnocentrism will continue to shape our interpretations until three conditions are met. First, scholars must recognize and control the ethnocentric entailments of their own intellectual tradition. Second, Native Americans' religious categories must be reconstructed, including views about cosmological dimensions (perspectives toward time and space) and understandings of humans in relation to cosmic being, power, and exchange. Third, the indigenous categories' influence on Native Americans' historical behavior must be examined.

In a 1983 essay, "The Concept of the Supernatural in Primal Religion," Åke Hultkrantz, a much published scholar of Native American religious traditions, argues that the supernatural describes all religious systems. "Empirical investigations have guided me," Hultkrantz writes, "to the conviction that an assumption of a basic dichotomy between two levels of existence, one ordinary or 'natural,' the other extraordinary or 'supernatural,' conditions man's religious cognition."[2] Hultkrantz's argument is particularly important because he insists on the empirical character of his conclusion as it applies to the ethnographic knowledge of Native American religious traditions. I contend, to the contrary, that Hultkrantz's formulation is, in fact, a widely held assumption about the unconscious existential principles in relation to which we think erroneously that all people shape their lives. For Hultkrantz, and for many others, the supernatural constitutes a supracultural given, coming from on high, to which human symbolic imagination and religious action is directed. Such a system suggests that supernatural beings have agency, and that human beings do not.

Since Hultkrantz forwards a thesis that contradicts directly my criticism of scholars' ethnocentric imposition of alien categories on the Algonkian peoples, in this chapter I focus on two limited purposes. First, I assess Hultkrantz's argument in order to show that he does not demonstrate *empirically* that the supernatural is the "key concept" that informs all religions.[3] Second, because Hultkrantz recognizes that A. Irving Hallowell has long since argued that the "supernatural" does not apply to Algonkian cosmology, I review Hallowell's line of reasoning. In both ways, I demonstrate the need to reconstruct linguistically conditioned religious categories before we begin to ascribe motivations to Native American peoples in their encounter with Europeans.

Hultkrantz insists that human beings live in a cosmic dimension that is only relatively real. This dimension is where a reality of a qualitatively different, supernatural order appears. Hultkrantz's supernatural enjoys "exalted,"[4] "vertical,"[5] superiority over the natural, everyday world: "Its peculiarity does not reside in its unusualness or mysterious character but in the fact that it springs forth from a force or will of another order."[6] Understanding the supernatural as having vertical superiority over human beings, then, entails specific assumptions about the nature of religion and of the religious. These assumptions can include various combinations of the following general characteristics: (1) an idea of theistic transcendence and superiority, or a theocentric view of reality; (2) a concept that human beings are "natural,"[7] imperfect, and, relatively speaking in relation to "supernatural" beings, powerless; (3) the view that religion derives from human belief in a "qualitatively different, mysterious world;"[8] (4) the view that "grace" is a unidirectional flowing of power from on high; and (5) the assumption that prayer as petition flows from a subservient position toward beings who are greater than human beings. While Hultkrantz himself does not articulate such assumptions, they are implicit in his position and are often associated with a supernaturalistic cosmology.

Religious Studies concepts that are related to the idea of the supernatural—the Really Real, the Holy, hierophany, grace, sin, and others like the sacred and the profane—are so commonplace that they seem to need little discussion. In actuality, these ideas are controversial for two main reasons. First, they represent an embattled effort to delineate scholarly turf. Taken in one way, Religious Studies can be understood as an attempt to define what is essential to all religions, and thus to define an intellectual discipline appropriate to their study. No matter how denominated, concern for the supernatural is commonly thought to separate Religious Studies from the sociology, psychology, and anthropology of religion. More particularly, students of religion have often assailed social scientific reductionism because, they contend, social scientists fail to confront religion *qua* the religious, by which they mean those other-worldly experiences often conveyed by the term "numinous," which is defined as "an overwhelming sense of the holy."[9]

The ways in which the concepts associated with the supernatural are handled among historians, anthropologists, and ethnohistorians creates a second reason for interpretive controversy. Although they commonly avoid terms such as "sacred" and "holy," even social scientists have been affected by the terminological quarrel that Hultkrantz brings again to light.[10] On the one hand, a social science literature has emerged which contends that the supernatural-natural dichotomization simply does not fit the ethnographic facts.[11] On the other, as we have seen, the concept of the supernatural is widely used in the social sciences. In either the ethnographic or the sociological case, "supernatural" sometimes has the connotations given it in the study of religions, although its meanings are usually neither clear nor precise. In addition, however, the supernatural often serves the important function of marking the boundary beyond which empirical inquiry cannot proceed.[12]

Mapping the shifts in meaning that the supernatural has undergone in the study of Native American religious thought and practice is far beyond the scope of this study; such a map would need to chart ethnographically the entire continent. But, in Hultkrantz's insistence that the supernatural applies everywhere, it is plain that the comparative and historical study of religious thought and life continues to face a considerable challenge. Whether one seeks to understand religion within or outside the social sciences, the supernatural has become a confused and confusing concept. Whether used to refer to the ultimate(s) of religion, or to those phenomena that the social sciences cannot examine empirically, or to both meanings at the same time, the supernatural as an ostensibly universal category requires ethnographic and terminological reconsideration.

Exploring these issues anew is important for the study of Native American religious traditions, and Algonkian traditions as well. If the concept of the supernatural explains Native American cosmologies, those worldviews could not be holistic, as is so commonly claimed; in a supernatural cosmological system the social, the economic, and the political must be understood as profane.[13] Simply put, the supernatural requires a cosmological hierarchy of human and suprahuman being that contradicts holism. But, if Native American cultures are neither holistic nor supernaturalistic, it would follow that the most commonplace assumptions about the nature of Native American life would be astonishingly wrong. My argument, then, questions the ways in which western European reality postulates have shaped, and even distorted, the ethnographic construction of Native American religious life.

I make two assumptions about the character of religious life that need to be highlighted; both derive from the Algonkian data. First, following the implications of Hallowell's work on the Algonkian-speaking Ojibwa (Anishnaabe),[14] I examine their religious life as related to their ethical theory of otherness. In a cosmos defined psychologically as self and other, and socially as us and them, orientations that are the source of both kinship and tribal identity, ontological and religious questions come necessarily to the fore.[15] At one level, the ontological questions are cognitive: Who are we? Who are we, as compared to them? An adequate view of Algonkian traditions would thus need to reconstruct the ways in which those peoples apprehend the nature and challenge of otherness in individual, sociological, and cosmological terms. Such a perspective makes it possible to reevaluate the ways in which Hallowell and Hultkrantz diverge, and so to recognize that Hallowell describes Ojibwa religious life in dialogical and relational ways, rather than as the belief system Hultkrantz posits.

My second assumption is just as distinctive. The religious question of the other is also behavioral and ethical because the other is both potentially threatening and nurturing: What must we do vis à vis them? According to Mary Rogers Black, Hallowell's student who adds linguistic, psychological, and social detail to develop his theory, the Ojibwa recognize that the world is constituted in terms of persons—human and other-than-human—and so acknowledge that the cosmos is dangerous. Since all persons are powerful to some degree, some persons are very powerful, and since some use power in antisocial ways, uncertainty about the intentions of the other defines a major religious problem that must be worked out in everyday life. Black calls this uncertainty "percept ambiguity," and so emphasizes people's need to position themselves both cautiously and constructively ("respectfully" is the usual contemporary Ojibwa gloss) toward other persons.[16] This religious challenge and opportunity should be located in relations between humans in social life, in human relations with "natural" beings in subsistence activities, and in relations with "cosmological" others in religious life (except, of course, I shall argue that seventeenth-century Algonkians did not separate either "nature" or "culture" from cosmos). When religious life is understood as a theory of powerful human activity directed toward powerful other-than-human persons, rather than human subservience to supernatural others, new light can be cast on both Hallowell's and Hultkrantz's points-of-view. The Ojibwa, like other Algonkian peoples, emphasize their own duty to act responsibly toward others. Hultkrantz overlooks the ethical, relational cast of American Indian life.

Human responsibility regarding themselves and cosmic others is precisely what a supernatural theory of religion misses in the study of Native American religious traditions. The very cosmic principles that define otherness also dictate a rationale for human religious action. Stated in another way, all cosmic systems rest cognitively on existential principles of ontology and ethics.[17] In practice, ontological principles (the ways in which the world exists) dictate normative principles that shape everyday ethical action (the ways in which humans and others ought to act). Both guide human and other-than-human intentionality and behavior. At this level, I make an assumption that rationalist scholars tend to reject: religious principle has an ideological impact on everyday life.

Hultkrantz's supernatural does not account for the ways in which a transcendent/immanent otherness escapes his claimed essential vertical dimensionality. Ojibwa thought and ritual practice posits multiple cosmic dimensions, and these dimensions often intersect in ways that supernatural verticality does not describe. In particular, because Hultkrantz contends that the supernatural is by its very nature vertically superior, his theory of religion cannot account for the responsibility the Ojibwa people exercise in relation to cosmic persons. In

Hallowell's hands, however, religion is understood in far more precise ways. Hallowell contends that Ojibwa religion must be understood in unconventional ways because it has linguistic, perceptual, cognitive, behavioral, and ethical, rather than "exalted," significance. The need to relate constructively with cosmic persons generates the Ojibwa's ethical system. Consequently, I aim to demonstrate that Hallowell's concept of "person" demands a broad rethinking of both pre- and post-contact Native American religious life in order to account for Algonkians' understanding of the world in relational terms.

THE SUPERNATURAL REVISITED

Read carefully, Åke Hultkrantz's essay, "The Concept of the Supernatural in Primal Religions," not only wrongly describes Native American cosmologies, it also subverts the possibility of achieving new, cross-cultural insights about American Indian life. An exalted, vertical superiority does not describe empirically either the Ojibwa or other Native American religious systems. The Ojibwa's case reveals evidence of their long conversation with Catholic missionaries, particularly in the syncretistic being examined in the previous chapter, who came to be called the Great Spirit.[18] Seventeenth-century French Jesuits could find no evidence that Algonkian peoples had any notion of a god, or God, or, for that matter, worship. They did recognize the animate character of Algonkian languages and, consequently, that Algonkian peoples thought, as the Jesuits put it, that various plants, animals, and even "objects" possessed souls just as did human beings. Although the history of Jesuit-introduced "God-talk" has not been documented adequately, the evidence indicates that the priests unified the Algonkians' animate world. Calling their own God-figure "He-Who-Made-All," the Jesuits created a metaphorical bridge between their monotheistic system and the animistic system of the Algonkians. By all indications, however, the Jesuits did not convey successfully a notion of monotheism, and their cosmology, comprised of nature, culture, and the supernatural, likewise remained beyond the Algonkians' recognition. In the long range, sycretistic processes led to a composite figure who combined the known powers of the Algonkian culture hero—often called kitchi manitou—with the centralizing character of the Jesuits' great other. This figure, the Great Spirit, has a still poorly understood history, but, as twentieth-century ethographic work makes clear, the Great Spirit did not attain theistic dominance in the Algonkians' religious view of the world.[19]

As described by anthropologist Ruth Landes, eight domains comprise the Ojibwa dimensional system. At first investigation, these realms appear as a vertical hierarchy as Hultkrantz's argument would require. The Great Spirit, the Creator, exists in the highest realm, but he does not enjoy a position of superiority. Instead, as Theresa S. Smith has shown, the Ojibwa balance high and low.[20]

The metaphor "up is good, and down is bad" does not apply to the Ojibwa religious system.[21] Nor does the Ojibwa's dimension, "the bottom layer of the earth,"[22] have primacy. This is the domain of the great person Shell, who is the Great Spirit's equal. In fact, Shell envisioned the *midewiwin*, a major Ojibwa religious rite, in order to empower the Ojibwa people. In cooperation with the Great Spirit, and with others, Shell brought his vision to reality for the benefit of the human beings who live at the center of this cosmological system. In the origin account of the Ojibwa shaman, Hole-in-the-Sky, the Great Spirit answers Shell's request for assistance:

> "Ho! Thank you for your plan for the Indian. Actually you are just ahead of me, for I was intending a similar thing, practically the same but a little different. This will be good for the Indian. Call all the manitos [personal beings] of Earth; tell them of this that we plan. And I, too, will tell those up there with me."[23]

Hole-in-the-Sky's account of the mediwiwin does not describe the Ojibwa system in terms of a vertical, cosmic superiority. A cosmic differentiation defines the religious situation, but those multiple dimensions do not fit Hultkrantz's supernatural-natural scheme; power/knowledge comes from below, as well as from above, and is, in any case, constituted in the exercise of interpersonal ethics and responsibility. As we shall see, the great persons of all dimensions share personal characteristics with, and give distinctive powers to, human beings. Human beings, furthermore, are bound to these cosmic beings by mutual obligation.

Hultkrantz misses the ontological similiarity of all the personal beings in the Ojibwa cosmos. His argument takes a controversial Western theological category[24] and applies the concept of the supernatural to religious systems that are for all practical purposes non-theistic, or, as is especially revealing in the Ojibwa's syncretistic case, to a religious system that is for all practical purposes non-theocentric.[25] Although Theresa Smith does not address Hultkrantz's theory, her description of this Ojibwa cosmology warrants reflection:

> Surmounting the field of the sky is the hand of Kitche Manitou, the Great Spirit, traditional ruler or, as the Ojibwes would say, *ogimaa* (boss) of the heavens. Kitche Manitou was most often understood as a Creator, 'the master of life' (Brown and Brightman, 1988, 107), who, while seemingly inactive in the day-to-day lives of the Anishnaabeg except as a passive presence or principle, could be invoked through solemn rite. . . . Contemporary Ojibwes view Kitche Manitou as largely interchangeable with the Christian god, and invocations and prayers are offered *up* to both.[26]

Smith's characterization of kitchi manitou shows that we must move with care in defining pre-contact cosmology. The figure, or at least much of its meaning, is clearly post-contact, and the language used to describe him—ruler, boss, creator—departs from commonsense Ojibwa reality in several ways. There is, in the first place, no evidence that the Ojibwa cosmos, even in its post-contact formulation, has its source in a single creator.[27] In the second, the notion of a ruling authority, or even a boss, departs considerably from the consensual character of Ojibwa life. Ojibwa politics proceeds without authority, or duress. Unlike the largely impersonal power politics of Euramericans, Ojibwa politics emerges in the dialogical give-and-take of personality, power, and persuasion. In any case, in his argument, Hultkrantz does not control the historical ramifications of religious dialogue that complicate the Ojibwa's post-contact cosmological picture.

Hultkrantz does begin with a historical survey: "The idea of a dichotomy between ordinary and mysterious, natural and supernatural is of course not new in Western religious thought." Accordingly, he explores the meanings that the supernatural has had for Catholics and Protestants since the eighteenth century. In both theologies (glossing over internal theological differences), the term "supernatural" posits not only the existence of an all-powerful God, but also his radical transcendence. For Protestants, according to Hultkrantz, the concept differentiates "the world as we see it from the world as it really is." For Catholics, however, the term simultaneously values and devalues the world. In Catholic thought, Hultkrantz notes, the supernatural "stands for the gifts of grace which are not natural in man but granted him by God."[28]

Hultkrantz implies, but does not examine, that Christians have extended (at various times and places) the term "supernatural" to several normative frames of reference. In Christian theology, the concept has had wide-ranging ontological, epistemological, and ethical meanings. These meanings should emphasize the crucial factors that must be considered in worldview analysis: all cosmological systems articulate a theory of being and otherness, a way of knowing and/or believing, and a system of value and responsible action. The supernatural posits the differing natures of God and man, and grace as a leavening of imperfect human intellect, and thereby dictates the relative imperfection of human rationality and moral choice. In both Catholic and Protestant contexts, the supernatural has been associated closely with the doctrine of original sin, with notions of theistic transcendence, and with the related idea that the world has been tainted by the Fall. The term "supernatural" has thus expressed as well the sacramental dependence of the created upon the Creator. The natural here and the supernatural have both a vertical and a hierarchal axis; causal relations flow from there to here, and are modified in the merger of man and God in the Incarnation.

None of these people-specific (and shifting) meanings is taken into consideration in Hultkrantz's argument. While Hultkrantz observes that "students in comparative religion, a discipline sprung forth from the Protestant intellectual milieu,"[29] commonly use the concept of the supernatural cross-culturally, he does not evaluate the ways in which they apply the term. He does express a justifiable dissatisfaction with the concept's ambiguous connotations: "On the whole, however, Protestant, Catholic, or atheistic anthropologists, sociologists, and scholars of religion frequently mention 'supernaturals,' 'supernatural power,' and 'supernatural world' without accounting for the philosophical meaning that these expressions might apply."[30] Hultkrantz also defines the heart of the matter: "By 'philosophical meaning' I refer here of course to the world view of the peoples investigated, not to the premises of the scholars concerned."[31] As we shall see, at this level of an empirical accounting for indigenous cosmology, Hultkrantz's theory is most inadequate.

There are other problems, even in Hultkrantz's brief historical survey of the meanings the supernatural has had. In the main, Hultkrantz explains, the term was unnecessary for scholars like E. B. Tylor, James G. Frazier, and Lucien Levy-Bruhl. For Hultkrantz, these scholars and others in the discipline of comparative religion—among them Nathan Soberblom and Gerardus van der Leeuw—subscribed to an evolutionary theory of religion. They thought of the supernatural as an attribute of the 'higher' religions. Hultkrantz notes favorably, however, that R. R. Marett's repudiation of evolutionary theories of religion led to his advocacy of supernaturalism as an attribute of all religion. A critical examination of the early evolutionary theories of religion, however, has demonstrated that they all, Marett's included, suffer from a significant lack of empirical evidence.[32] Strangely, Hultkrantz dismisses the argument of sociologist of religion Robert Bellah. According to Bellah, the dichotomy between the natural and the supernatural can be traced to the first millennium B.C.E. Hultkrantz notes as a "striking fact" Bellah's observation that the notion of world rejection associated with the idea of the supernatural did not exist before that time. Bellah's conclusion that the world-embracing religions subscribe to "an entirely different realm of religious reality," Hultkrantz rejects flatly: "This is, of course, a completely arbitrary point-of-view."[33] In this first historical survey section of his article, Hultkrantz is often dismissive, rather than analytical. He accords Benson Saler's astute study, "Supernatural as a Western Category," a one-sentence, and very misleading nod: "Benson Saler attacks our Western ethnocentric implications of the Western implications in the use of the term 'supernatural.'"[34] In actuality, Saler presents a detailed analysis of the term's philosophical and theological history, and he actively reflects on the problems associated with imposing non-Western terms on peoples who do not recognize such categories. In this historical survey, then, Hultkrantz outlines various theories of the supernatural, but reaches no compelling conclusion about them or their ethnographic applications to empirical cases of indigenous cosmologies.

In his section entitled "The Implications of the Dichotomy," Hultrantz's main concern is to develop the notion that the "supernatural presupposes something of another order, of another kind. It is a deeply qualitative concept."[35] His purpose here is to defend what he considers essential to all religion. Consequently, Hultkrantz is exceptionally critical of Emile Durkheim, who rejected the otherworldly orientation implied by the term "supernatural," and who substituted the terms "sacred" and "profane" in order to account for the religious in human terms. On the one hand, Hultkrantz finds Durkheim's terms very close to the meanings he himself associates with supernatural. On the other, what offends Hultkrantz is Durkheim's claim (in Hultkrantz's words) that "the sacred character of a phenomenon is not inherent, or implied in its intrinsic properties, but added to it. It is society that confers a sacred evaluation to the world of religion."[36] To preserve the integrity of the supernatural category, Hultkrantz denies that social life has a religious character. As we shall see, Native American religious systems are precisely social in conception and practice.

Hultkrantz does recognize the need to proceed cautiously. He quotes Louis Dupré approvingly:

> Sacred reality can maintain itself only by means of an opposition to non-sacred, profane reality. . . . What counts is the opposition itself, not the content which it adopts. The important thing to remember from this is that the term transcendent, so essential for religion, develops dialectically and takes various meanings in different contexts. It is always transcendent in relation to what surrounds it.[37]

Applying Dupré to his argument, Hultkrantz expresses his willingness to put the concept of the supernatural to a similar empirical test: "Thus, in our terminology, the specifics of the supernatural can only be given within the frame of different cultures." Qualitative attributes, like the infinite, powerful, eternal, "and the like refer to specific contents of the supernatural in specific historical religions."[38] Unfortunately, Hultkrantz does not illustrate empirically what these specific variations of the supernatural might be like. In any case, the question must be raised whether the term has any cross-cultural significance if its meaning varies from people to people and its historical significance shifts in time.

In fact, Hultkrantz's definition of the supernatural does not derive from indigenous meanings. He derives his definition from Ernst Arbman:

> In an important, but unfortunately neglected article the Swedish historian of religion Ernst Arbman has postulated that religious man lives in two worlds, both equally real and essentially coexistent in space but totally different in kind, the world of belief and the world of daily experience. The former is the supernatural world, the world of spirits and mysterious powers. However, its peculiarity does not reside in its unusualness or mysterious character but in the fact that it springs forth from a force of will of another order.[39]

Later, Hultkrantz emphasizes the precision of Arbman's claims: "Arbman makes no other attempt to define the supernatural than the general reference that it has a supposed origin in another order of things."[40] But Arbman stresses that this other "order of things" has contingent aspects, a separate reality "of spirits and mysterious powers," and "a force of will of another order."

Two elements of Hultkrantz's application of Arbman require reflection. In the first place, Arbman's contention that the two worlds are "essentially co-existent in space" undercuts the distinctive otherness of "another order of things." At least as Lee Irwin has demonstrated for the native peoples of the Great Plains, the relations between human and other cosmic dimensions are complex.[41] Hultkrantz himself admits that even the quality of transcendence is a culturally conditioned "historical concept." Then, Hultkrantz declares that the supernatural can be "transcendent and/or immanent." He cites several articles of Joseph Kitigawa to the effect "that the early Japanese did not look for another order of meaning behind the natural world. . . . Thus he [Kitagawa] claims that Fujiyama was itself a divine reality and not a symbol of such a reality." Hultkrantz seems to reduce Kitagawa's distinction into irrelevance: "However, from the perspective presented in this article the Japanese believed in a supernatural world, although it was at least partially immanent. The mount Fuji was an instance of this immanence."[42] In actuality, the problem of immanence/transcendence is one issue that the comparative and historical study of Native American religious life must face critically.[43]

Similarly, Hultkrantz seems to move too fast by reducing the definition of "nature," which he considers the necessary contrast to the supernatural, to a concept of "natural laws." By doing so, Hultkrantz finds it easy to criticize scholars who hold different views. As one example, Hultkrantz rejects Diamond Jenness' contention that the existence of "spirits" does not denote an Ojibwa conception of the supernatural. Jenness states the Ojibwa criteria very clearly: spirits "are part of the natural order of the universe no less than man himself, whom they resemble in the possession of intelligence and emotions."[44] This claim that human beings and "spirits" share the same ontology, that a single philosophy of being unites humans and other personal entities, is an important distinction, and one confirmed elsewhere in a variety of Native American contexts. If human beings and other entities share the same ontological characteristics, then Arbman's distinction of "another order" cannot be sustained. Hultkrantz, however, seems to sidestep the issue: "It is obvious that Jenness refers to the same dichotomy that Durkheim disapproved of, namely in relation to the concept of natural laws."[45] In his earlier discussion, Hultkrantz quotes Durkheim to the effect that the supernatural necessarily moves in relation to a contrary idea of a natural order of things: "The phenomena of the universe are bound together by necessary relations, called laws."[46] But Hultkrantz does not appreciate that the objective laws of nature are not easily subsumed under the relational causality that we will see dominates Algonkian ways of thinking.

For this reason, Hultkrantz criticizes both Durkheim and Jenness for apparently denying the existence of "miracles." Hultkrantz quotes Jenness: "At the same time, 'all of them [the spirits] are invisible to human eyes in the ordinary course of life.' They 'may assume any form they wish and make themselves visible whenever they so desire.' "[47] Hultkrantz disagrees and contends that Arbman's view of the supernatural as a "qualitatively different, mysterious world" turns Jenness' position "inside out." Hultkrantz himself contradicts well-established and cross-cultural facts in Native American Religious Studies when he claims that "invisibility and transformation are certainly no abilities of beings belonging to the ordinary world; they transcend the possibilities as we normally know them."[48] Apart from whomever "we" might be, what happens to those human beings who share knowledge, power, ability, and even being with "spirits" and so share their capacity to defy physicality and linear time and space?[49] Hultkrantz's position in fact, denies, rather than disproves, Jenness' insight. Despite Hulktrantz's contention, Jenness did not appeal to "natural laws" as explaining anything of Ojibwa reality.

Considerably later than Jenness, A. Irving Hallowell explored the ontological similarity between "spirits" and human beings. Spirits, he said, "are persons of a category other than human." Stating his position more fully, Hallowell summarizes the ethnographic data: "In the universe of the Ojibwa the conception of 'person' as a living, functioning social being is not only one which transcends the notion of person in the naturalistic sense; it likewise transcends a human appearance as a constant attribute of this category of being." Since "spirits" and human beings share intelligence, power, voice, will, and desire, they are ontologically identical in Ojibwa conception—and in their religious practice. Hallowell was emphatic in identifying the revisionist implications of the Ojibwa conception of the cosmic principle of ontological similarity, implications that have gone largely unexplored in anthropology, history, ethnohistory, and Religious Studies. The idea of "supernatural persons," Hallowell noted, "is completely misleading if for no other reason than the fact that the concept of the 'supernatural' presupposes a concept of the 'natural.' The latter is not present in Ojibwa thought. It is unfortunate that the natural-supernatural dichotomy has been so persistently invoked by anthropologists in describing the outlook of peoples in cultures other than their own."[50] This statement is often quoted, but not often understood. In effect, Hallowell mandates a careful reconsideration of all Native American cosmological systems.

Hultkrantz's response to Hallowell deserves full quotation because it demonstrates not only the logic he brings to bear, but also his failure to relate the concept of the supernatural to any empirical ethnographic case:

> Here again we face the idea that the dichotomy *should* refer to natural laws, an idea that is not necessarily tied to it. What surprises us is that the author avoids dealing with such a dichotomy 'for no other reason' than its reference to natural laws. He does not ponder for a moment the possibility that supernatural may stand against natural in the meaning of 'ordinary.' And how can he be so sure that the idea of something natural does not exist because there is no word for it?[51]

In the first place, Hallowell says nothing about natural laws. By way of contrast, in Christian thought the supernatural is opposed to nature with no necessary reference to natural laws. The same is certainly true in the popular, generalized, nonscientific Ojibwa terms to which Hallowell refers. In the second place, Hallowell cannot be held responsible for not entertaining the notion that the supernatural might be opposed to the ordinary. Such a definition of supernatural in relation to natural laws is peculiar to Hultkrantz. Specifically, Hallowell denies that there is an exalted, other order of reality in Ojibwa life. Furthermore, the posited opposition to ordinary must be extraordinary, not supernatural. Something extraordinary is not different in kind from the ordinary. The extraordinary is merely more than the ordinary. In Hallowell's view, the Ojibwa do not think of, or perceive, other-than-human persons as any more remarkable than themselves.

What is perhaps most disturbing in Hultkrantz's argument is his inaccurate, and therefore misleading, claim that Hallowell's factual material does not sustain his argument. In fact, Hallowell's study provides a rigorous model for a line of inquiry that he called "ethnometaphysics,"[52] and his comprehensive methodology ought to be of interest to all students of Native American religious life and ethnohistory. Hallowell's evidence for the Ojibwa's extended concept of person consists of linguistic, perceptual, cognitive, mythological, ritual, behavioral, and social data. He establishes authoritatively that the personal characteristics of beings who are other-than-human are a matter of direct, practical, and everyday experience. Hallowell is clear: other-than-human persons (whom we locate in an other-than-physical, non-empirical, supernatural dimension by calling them spirits) are active, dynamic presences in the Ojibwa's *behavioral* environment. Moreover, the pragmatic behavioral ground of Ojibwa reality is sustained in critical social discourse in everyday life, as Hallowell explores. In all these ways, Hallowell avoids the problematic concept of belief/faith that is so often associated with the idea of the supernatural. Hallowell locates other-than-human persons as actors in the Ojibwa's everyday life.

A similar distortion emerges in Hultkrantz's discussion of the Ojibwa term *manitou*, a term which he claims refers to "supernatural beings." Although correctly noting that Hallowell does not give the term extended attention, Hultkrantz moves far too quickly in attempting to convince us that supernatural adequately interprets manitou. For example, Hultkrantz admits that manitou "stands for both spirits and humans," but does not recognize that it also applies to stones, plants, animals, moccasins, the Sun, the Moon, and the stars.[53] Hulkrantz does not grasp, moreover, Hallowell's point: since manitou can refer to all sorts of powerful, personal beings, it does not refer to another "order of things." For Hultkrantz, manitou "stands for both spirits and humans endowed with mysterious qualities, a circumstance that seems to indicate that its true meaning is 'other than ordinary,' or 'supernatural.'"[54]

Understanding the Algonkian term "manitou" thus becomes a major nub of the interpretive problem. In defining the terms that govern her study of the Ojibwa, Theresa S. Smith offers a view of manitou that not only differs greatly from Hultkrantz's, but also values Hallowell's findings in a way Hultkrantz does not. Smith is worth quoting at length because she realizes that the term "manitou" refers to a being, and a class of beings, rather than to a cosmological abstraction:

> Manitou(k) refers to the power beings of the Ojibwe cosmos. These beings, upon whom the traditional Anishnaabeg were dependent for their very existence and with whom contemporary Anishnaabeg still relate, are never experienced as impersonal forces. It was A. Irving Hallowell . . . who effectively laid to rest the misconception first promulgated by William Jones . . . that manitou(k) is descriptive of an impersonal power—a sort of supernatural "charge" which may be accessed by vision, dream, or the performance of ritual acts. Hallowell's work among the Northern Ojibwe has proven to be a landmark in the history of Ojibwe studies. Through careful phenomenological study, he ascertained that the Anishnaabe(g) experience of manitou(k) is always at the level of personal relationship. This relationship is further enforced by the use of atisokan(ak) (specialized form of grandfather[s]) as a form of address.[55]

As Hallowell shows for the Ojibwa, power is neither simply mysterious nor ever abstract, impersonal, or supernatural. As Smith demonstrates, power is a demonstrated, relational fact.

Precisely the same over-generalized distortion of indigenous terms for power occurs in Hultkrantz's examination of other Native American concepts, including *maxpe, wakan,*[56] *worak, diyin,*[57] and *na'walaku.*[58] Few of these terms have received careful scholarly examination, let alone an assessment in relation to Hallowell's findings, but several have been established to refer to both humans and other-than-human persons.[59] As a demonstrated ability that applies to all personal action, power shatters the dimensional distinction between nature and the supernatural as another, exalted order of things.

Hultkrantz's brief, two-paragraph discussion of Dorothy Lee's interpretation of California Wintu dimensional categories reveals another case of serious distortion. Lee does declare that among the Wintu "the supernatural is named and can be spoken of."[60] Her statement is not, as Hultkrantz would have it, "sufficient" to unequivocally establish the concept.[61] Lee's study explores what seems to be, from a non-Indian perspective, the Wintu's pardoxical dimensional system. Lee describes the phenomenon she attempts to plumb:

> A basic tenet of the Wintu language, expressed both in nominal and verbal categories, is that reality–ultimate truth–exists irrespective of man. Man's experience actualizes this reality, but does not otherwise affect its being. Outside man's experience this reality is unbounded, undifferentiated, timeless.[62]

Contrary to Hultkrantz's position, then, Lee locates religious meaning not in some derivation of a deterministic, ultimate reality, but in the emerging, microcosmic character of Wintu life: human life "actualizes this reality."

Lee also expresses a conceptual paradox, and her own uncertain role as a translator in relationship to that uncertainty:

> In fact, if 'existence' and 'being' are seen as referring to history, to the here and now, then this reality cannot be said to exist, and the Wintu do not assert its existence or being. Yet I must apply these terms to it, since I have to use the English language.[63]

Significantly, what Lee describes of Wintu categories is the obverse of Hultkantz's claim that the supernatural is opposed to the ordinary. For the Wintu, reality—meaning ordinary reality—is undifferentiated, unpartitioned, immutable. The realm of human beings, however, can become superlative in relation to reality. Human affairs, while participating in the generic givenness of the whole cosmos, can also be differentiated. Indeed, human life embodies this reality in "the here and now."

Wintu language, Lee demonstrates, stresses the paradoxical relationship between the usual experience of a generic whole and the sudden perception of the particular. She gives a series of vivid examples of the Wintu's stress on holism: "When I asked for a word for the body I was given the term *the whole person*. The Wintu does not say *my head aches*; he says *I head ache*. He does not say *my hands are hot*; he says *I hands am hot*. He does not say *my leg*, except extremely rarely and for good reason, such as that his leg has been severed from his body."[64] In other words, the Wintu do not stress the dimensional break required in the natural/supernatural dichotomy. They emphasize the whole rather than the part. As they would put it: normally, I am leg; it is a matter of amazement that, when severed, I can recognize my leg in itself.

Despite Lee's claim that the Wintu can name the supernatural, the phenomena she describes do not meet Hultkrantz's requirement that the supernatural refers to another, vertically superior, order of things. Lee observes the salient conditions that Hultkrantz fails to consider: "If the Wintu starts with an original oneness, we must speak not of identification, but a premise of continuity."[65] The Wintu emphasize not cosmic and social individuation, but "continuity between self and other," thereby highlighting, Lee notes, "the primacy of the unpartitioned whole."[66] Under such cognitive circumstances, then, Lee's use of the terms "natural" and "supernatural" must be open to question. Lee herself admits as much: "If the Wintu offers me an English word in translation for a Wintu one, I rarely have any way of knowing what exactly the word means to him."[67] Lee recognizes, but Hultkrantz does not, that for the Wintu, personal, individuated existence constitutes a cosmological superlative, rather than some separate, higher, or greater reality.

Hultkrantz fails to perceive that neither Lee's data nor her argument fits his dimensional model. He later cites further evidence from a closely related people that explicitly contradicts his claims. Hultkrantz writes: "Walter Goldschmidt, for instance, assures us that the Nomlaki—a branch of the Wintun, another branch are the Wintu—consider the world of 'reality' and the world of the supernatural inseparable, 'so that even the most practical undertaking was circumscribed by ritual.'"[68] In this instance, Hultkrantz contends that Goldschmidt confused "the conceptual distinction between the two worlds with the idea of their interaction in myth and ritual."[69] Rather, the idea of the supernatural blinds Hultkrantz from recognizing the need to explain Nomlaki, and Wintu, religious conception and ritual activity within their own conceptual system.

Understanding Native American views of ritual thus becomes another nub of the matter. If Lee's analysis is correct (apart from her use of inappropriate Western terminology), these peoples stress ritual performance because they understand that ritual consists of those human activities that counter the experience of differentiation; ritual restores cosmic interdependence. Hultkrantz verges on such an insight: "We all know that in primal societies religion is virtually diffused in the cultural life. All thought and activity is more or less guided by religious ideas. The supernatural dimension cuts right through mundane life and *bestows upon* each facet of it a religious or magic sanction. Nevertheless there is still a vertical difference between natural and supernatural."[70] To the contrary (and observing that Hultkrantz here abandons his claim that transcendence is culturally specific), the evidence suggests that verticality is not a dominant dimensional characteristic of Ojibwa (and other Algonkian-speaking Native Americans), Wintu, and Nomlaki life. The same may be true for many other peoples. The data also suggest strongly that religiousness, ritual activity, and supernaturalism need not be equated.

HALLOWELL AND COSMIC INTERSUBJECTIVITY

Åke Hultkrantz's criticism recognizes implicitly that Algonkian studies have come gradually to propose an alternative paradigm by which religious life can be understood in a radically interpersonal way. Since the publication of Hallowell's "Ojibwa Ontology, Behavior, and World View," a broad scholarship has established related insights that sustain his innovative contribution. We can now appreciate the ways in which Algonkian religious traditions in particular, and other Native American religious systems by extension, can be rethought in the manner in which such religious traditions are conceptualized and lived. For these reasons, we must review the characteristics of Algonkian worldview Hallowell identified that provoke him to a more precise understanding of Native American religious life.

Hallowell took a stand that the Ojibwa live in a real world whose logic escapes our own, and also escapes widespread judgments of their primitiveness, superstitiousness, and irrationality. Although calling such a worldview "metaphysical" undercuts Hallowell's argument that the beings of the Ojibwa world (human and otherwise) actually exist in real, everyday, and face-to-face relations, his perspective still gives the study of that tradition an empirical focus that supernaturalistic premises deny. Hallowell notes, for example, that social scientific reifications of human behavior—society, social relations, and social organization—constitute a "radical abstraction if, from the standpoint of the people being studied the concept of person is not, in fact, synonymous with human being but transcends it."[71] Hallowell appreciates the value of "an objective approach," as typified by the mid-twentieth-century social sciences, but he also insists that such an approach has real limitations. As he puts it, "But if, in the world view of a people, persons as a class include entities other than human beings, then our objective approach is not adequate for presenting an accurate description of the 'the way a man, in a particular society, sees himself in relation to all else.'"[72] Hallowell recognizes, as few have before or since, that "categorical abstractions derived from Western thought . . . . are a reflection of *our* cultural subjectivity." Such abstractions are, in a word, ethnocentric. In Hallowell's view, using an "analysis of the outlook of the people themselves as a complementary procedure" could yield "a higher order of objectivity,"[73] although it can be argued that objectivity was not then and is not now an appropriate analytical goal. In the Ojibwa case, Hallowell sought types of data that could reveal the indigenous outlook. Hallowell insists, for one example, that the inclusion of other-than-human persons in the kinship category "grandfather" is a major line of evidence that undercuts a non-Indian tendency to compartmentalize humans and "spirits."[74] In categorizing such beings as relatives, the Ojibwa conflate what we separate.

In a related vein, Hallowell argues that the Ojibwa worldview has cognitive systematicity because of its linguistic character. Here Hallowell observes that Algonkian languages distinguish between entities who are animate, and things which are not. Recognizing that the grammatical distinction was largely unconscious for Algonkian speakers, Hallowell goes to elaborate lengths to show that the distinction has, nevertheless, actual effects in everyday Ojibwa life: "I believe that when evidence from beliefs, attitudes, conduct, and linguistic characterization are all considered together the psychological basis for their unified cognitive outlook can be appreciated, even when there is a radical departure from the framework of our thinking."[75] Hallowell underlines the specificity: the animate in Ojibwa life is not simply a linguistic phenomenon; it also plays itself out in the people's collective observation, thought, experience, and relationships. He criticizes Diamond Jenness, for example, for claiming that "all objects have life"[76] Hallowell shows, to the contrary, that the animate category is not deterministic: "The Ojibwa do not perceive stones, in general, as animate, any more than we do. The crucial test is experience. Is there any personal testimony available?"[77] In all of this, Hallowell always allows the Ojibwa's empirical experience to speak first and last about issues that matter to him as an investigator, but which are, to them, of secondary interest.

Such a sensibility informs Hallowell's interest in myth, first, for its meaning to Ojibwa persons, and second, for the inferences that can be drawn from myth about the "Ojibwa world outlook." At a time when most investigators saw mythology as little more than a record of Native American acts of imagination, which themselves seemed to derive from a generic irrational superstitiousness, Hallowell learned to discriminate Ojibwa thought and religious practice upon its storied basis. As a result, he came to realize that stories embody "living entities who have existed from time immemorial."[78] Hallowell discerns, moreover, that such mythic "persons" become present in talk about them, an awareness that produced complex respect behaviors among the Ojibwa toward mythic narration. Hallowell understands that recounting mythic tradition mattered not only to the Ojibwa, but to the persons of myth as well. Thus, an enduring and little explored legacy of Hallowell's line of reasoning consists in coming to understand that other-than-human persons desire, indeed require, interaction with human beings. Personal and mutual needs bring humans and other-than-human persons into a single, mutually interdependent, reciprocal system.[79]

If these insights into the meaning of Ojibwa narrativity were far in advance of their time, and still remain little explored, Hallowell also argues that the myths "offer basic data about unarticulated, unformalized, and unanalyzed concepts which informants cannot be expected to generalize." As Hallowell reasons, myth texts (especially when heard in the sound of actual Ojibwa life as Hallowell did) were analogous to those language texts that linguists use to derive grammar and linguistic principles.[80] From such a grounded reading, Hallowell learns that the commonplace that myth concerns fictitious and supernatural entities is not true for the Ojibwa. In this way, Hallowell recognizes that the Ojibwa do not distinguish between the natural and the supernatural.[81] This insight leads Hallowell beyond the supernatural categorization he disparages. He declares that the Ojibwa proceed with no reference to objective existence as well: "Above all, any concept of *impersonal* 'natural' forces is totally foreign to Ojibwa thought."[82] Hallowell again raises questions relevant to understanding the limited objectivist methods of the social sciences. Hallowell's enduring contribution, as we shall see, derives from his recognition that the Ojibwa's reality is constituted in the interpersonal give-and-take between themselves and other personal beings.

Hallowell recognizes that the Ojibwa extension of "person" beyond human beings requires conceptual adjustment on our part. Carefully studying cases, among them accounts of the Sun, Flint, the Winds, and Thunder Birds, Hallowell concludes that the Ojibwa do not anthropomorphize such beings.[83] Rather, they combine "naturalistic observation," dream experience (Hallowell wrongly categorizes dreams as subjective experience),[84] and "traditional mythic narrative" in such a way that the combination assumes "the character of a living image."[85] Following yet another line of reasoning, Hallowell shows that the phenomenon he calls "metamorphosis" not only demonstrates that "personal" identity is independent of physical form; transformation is a power that characterizes human as well as other-than-human persons. As with myth, which "is not categorically distinct from the world as experienced by human beings in everyday life," so too with metamorphosis: "In outward manifestation neither animal nor human characteristics define categorical differences in the core of being."[86]

As an expression of power, then, metamorphosis indicates that, while other-than-human persons tend to have greater power than human beings, the pattern is far from absolute. Hallowell observes that, as an indicator of power, metamorphosis "is one of the features which links humans beings with the other-than-human persons in their behavioral environment." He emphasizes that metamorphosis is a "generic property" of all persons, but does not characterize all persons equally. There is a graduation of power within the category of person: "Human beings do not differ from them [other-than-human persons] in kind, but in power." All other-than-human-persons possess power, but only some humans do: "In the case of human beings, while the potentiality for metamorphosis exists and may even be experienced, any outward manifestation is inextricably associated with unusual power, for good or evil." Among humans, such a great power as metamorphosis is always the gift of other-than-human persons. Hallowell drives home his point:

> Speaking as an Ojibwa, one might say: all other persons—human or other than human—are structured the same as I am. There is a vital part which is enduring and an outward appearance that may be transformed under certain conditions. All other "persons," too, have such attributes as self-awareness and understanding. I can talk to them. Like myself, they have personal identity, autonomy, and volition. I cannot always predict exactly how they will act, although most of the time their behavior meets my expectations. In relation to myself, other "persons" vary in power. Many of them have more power than I have, but some have less. They may be friendly and help me when I need them but, at the same time, I have to be prepared for hostile acts, too. I must be cautious in my relations with other "persons" because appearances may be deceptive.[87]

In this line of reasoning, Hallowell reveals that Ojibwa dreams are not only occasions in which humans are empowered. Dream encounters with other-than-human persons also affect the Ojibwa's cognitive orientation. In a dreaming state of consciousness, the Ojibwa have a direct knowledge of others that a supernaturalistic interpretation cannot explain.

If most of "Ojibwa Ontology" proceeds in terms of Hallowell's explication of the religious phenomena of Ojibwa life, his final section, "The Psychological Unity of the Ojibwa World," highlights the interpretive implications of his investigation. In effect, this section articulates a religious logic for which neither a rational naturalism, subjectivism, or supernaturalism can account. Hallowell's premise is straightforward: "Although not formally abstracted and articulated philosophically, the nature of persons is the focal point of Ojibwa ontology and the key to the psychological unity and dynamics of their world outlook."[88] Rather than assign causal significance either to nature or to the supernatural (and by implication to abstracted cultural systems as well), Hallowell lays out an Ojibwa causal logic that focuses on the intentionality, actions, and interactions of persons. The Ojibwa cosmos is so socialized that the people make "no cardinal use of any concept of impersonal forces as major determinants of events." In these terms, Hallowell separates himself from the spiritual/materialist causal controversy reviewed in the previous chapter: "With respect to the Ojibwa conception of causality, all my own observations suggest that a culturally constituted psychological set operates which inevitably directs the reasoning of individuals toward an explanation of events in personalistic terms. *Who* did it, *who* is responsible is always the crucial question to be answered."[89]

Unlike spiritual and materialist explanations, this "personalistic theory of causation," bridges the pragmatic, social morality, and personal behavior.[90] Unlike spiritualists and materialists, Hallowell highlights the pragmatic goals of Ojibwa life, but he describes a pragmatism that is also socially, and therefore, ethically motivated. The Ojibwa category, *pimadaziwin*, articulates a central purposefulness: "Life in the fullest sense, life in the sense of longevity, health and freedom from misfortune." Taken at face value, pimadaziwin seems nothing more than a materialist pragmatism. Hallowell, however, locates its meaning not simply in individual well-being, but in the essential "effective help and cooperation of *both* human and other-than-human persons, as well as by one's own personal efforts."[91] Such cooperation entails "moral responsibilities" as an Ojibwa person strives to achieve pimadaziwin. Ojibwa ethics thus proceeds not in terms of some supernaturalistic ultimacy, and certainly not in terms of the otherworldly orientation that missionaries taught, but in terms of actual relations with other humans and with particular other-than-human persons.

In the Ojibwa's (and unlike a supernatural) cosmos, other-than-human persons have needs that human beings must meet. Hallowell reports that such an ethical system implicates the well-being of cosmic persons, as well as that of the Ojibwa. "Thus we find that the same values are implied throughout the entire range of social interaction that characterizes the Ojibwa world; the same standards which apply mutual obligations between human and other-than-human persons. In his relations with the grandfathers the individual does not expect to receive a blessing for nothing. It is not a free gift; on his part there are obligations to be met. There is a principle of reciprocity implied."[92] Far from being oriented to Hultrkantz's "other order of things," Ojibwa life shares with other-than-human beings common desires and common needs, in short, a common moral situation. Hallowell puts the case succinctly: "The same principle of mutual obligation applies in other spheres in life. . . . The moral values implied document the consistency of the principle of mutual obligations which is inherent in all interactions with persons throughout the Ojibwa world." Pimadaziwin can only be sought "within this web of social relations."[93] The Ojibwa system is not characterized by a world of belief and a world of experience, as Hultrantz requires.

In effect, Hallowell recognizes that the multidimensional character of Ojibwa reality proceeds in terms of social rules that defy the ontologically differentiated principles of supernaturalism. He insists that the Ojibwa system has perceptual, cognitive, behavioral, and ethical regularity; in Hallowell's view, the Ojibwa have no need to appeal, and in fact do not appeal, to a factor of belief or faith to explain their apprehension of reality. Instead, Hallowell recognizes that the multidimensional play of the Ojibwa cosmos transpires in terms of the mutually motivated (and thus interdependent) actions of both human and other-than-human persons. In these complex ways, Hallowell came to appreciate that the Ojibwa world escapes the objective/subjective commonsense reality of non-Indian peoples. In recognizing the pervasive power of metamorphosis, Hallowell in effect demonstrates that the Ojibwa attend to intentionalities expressing themselves in everyday events, rather than to objective, impersonal, or otherworldly considerations. Finally, in his recognition that the Ojibwa cosmos is shaped by a psychological unity, Hallowell establishes an empirical way of reconstructing Ojibwa religious life. He also points to dialogical social conditions that had hitherto escaped views that treat Native American life as spiritual and/or magical. To the contrary, Hallowell lays the groundwork for a new kind of Native American Studies that emphasizes the religious as an interactive, social, and intersubjective field. Although few scholars have noticed, Hallowell shifts the ways in which all Native American thought and behavior ought to be reconsidered.

A DIALOGICAL COSMOS

Hultrkantz does not recognize that Hallowell articulates the philosophical principles of Algonkian worldview in terms that correspond to actual Ojibwa life. In "Ojibwa Ontology, Behavior, and World View," Hallowell lays out his argument in relation to a complex examination of multiple lines of evidence, including linguistics, mythological traditions, dreams, and ritual behavior as they relate to commonsense Ojibwa views of everyday life. Although it was not his stated purpose, Hallowell demonstrates that the main tenets of non-Indian ethnocentricism derive from an inappropriate imposition of non-Indian cosmological categories. He deconstructs those tenets to point the way toward understanding Native American religious realities in innovative and still largely unexamined terms.

Hallowell did not consciously explore the Ojibwa's cosmogony—their accounts of the world's origins—or formally engage their cosmological system, although both levels of meaning express the Ojibwa's philosophy of being. Nor did Hallowell present a coherent treatment of the Ojibwa's dreaming-experience, or their causal understanding of health and illness, or their ideas about human and animal reincarnation, or their theory of ritual. Hallowell discusses such variables, but does not treat them theoretically as individual phenomena, or in systematic relation to each other. Indeed, as religious phenomena, most of these apprehensions of, and engagements with, reality have yet to receive careful scholarly attention. In effect, Hallowell identifies the existential categories by which Native American religious traditions might be studied non-ethnocentrically, and comparatively as well. Hindsight reveals that Hallowell's work on Ojibwa ontology has both deconstructive and constructive implications.

As we have seen, Hallowell's deconstructive moves counter the main thrust of Hultkrantz's argument for a cross-cultural supernaturalism. Because Hallowell demonstrates that the Ojibwa category "person" embraces all types of being, intentionality, desire, purposefulness, compassion, and malevolence, he was able to conclude that Western cosmological notions, particularly the categories of "nature" and the "supernatural," do not fit, represent, or explain the Ojibwa cosmos. Further, because he learned that the intentions and actions of persons structure that cosmos, Hallowell criticizes notions of impersonal, abstract, institutional, supernaturalistic, and social-scientific modes of causality. Hallowell reveals that the interactive, interpersonal, intersubjective Ojibwa causality highlights a precise relational understanding that attends, not to *what* is happening in the world, but to the intent of the person *who* is acting.[94] Hallowell thus rejects the reified categories of social-scientific thought—the economy, politics, and religion—in favor of holistic Ojibwa appreciations of those phenomena in engaged, behavioral terms. In other words, Hallowell highlights abstract categories in their lived modalities—giving and receiving, motivating and persuading, exercising or rejecting responsibility. The precision of Hallowell's thought relocates abstract cultural variables in the ethical purposes of interpersonal behaviors, among them hunting, conducting war, marrying, eating, and healing, which express the contingent meanings of Ojibwa life. If you wish to think accurately about Ojibwa ethnography, Hallowell insists, you must think about the interactions of persons.

Hallowell's 1960 study thus anticipates some of the most important developments in Native American Studies in the late twentieth century. These include a vigorous understanding of the narrative orientations of Native American discourse, the centrality of dream and ritual encounters between human and other-than-human persons, the socio-linguistic cast of all human social life, the essential link between personal and group psychology, and the embodied, relational ground of all religious traditions. In all these ways, Hallowell defines the conscious and unconscious purposes and perspectives of my entire study.

3

Toward a History of Intimate Encounters

Algonkian Folklore, Jesuit Missionaries, and Kiwakwe, the Cannibal Giant

Of course, you have to know what factually happened before you can ask what events mean. But understanding meaning was the goal of "Intimate Encounters," and it broke new ground in listening to oral tradition as a largely untapped documentary resource. While writing my doctoral dissertation at the Newberry Library (at what is now the McNickle Center for the History of the American Indian), I stumbled across a story that led to many more and to new ways of thinking about Algonkian life. Other scholars were aware of these tales of cannibal monsters, and saw them as evidence of mental illness (windigo psychosis) or as records of the effects of environmental marginality and nutritional deficiency.

For me, however, the stories expressed an existential angst because they emerged from the core values of Algonkian life. These stories captured indigenous insights about sociality, insights that proved to be uniform from the Mi'kmaq in Nova Scotia to the Anishnaabe (Ojibwa) of Lake Superior. Although the stories revealed the need to understand Algonkian ethics as a key to reconstructing the peoples' encounter with European newcomers, I was just beginning to think about Native American religious life, let alone its intellectual integrity.

You will see, then, that in listening to these stories I had not yet learned about my own ethnocentric terminological choices. I thought about the stories with ethnocentrism in mind, and voiced a skepticism about the ethnocentric entailments of European documents. I understood that Algonkian life emerged from a distinctive value system that neither missionaries nor scholars understood, and I began to set the record straight. But, clearly, I did not understand the difference between my own (but culturally shared) and Algonkians' views of reality. Time would teach me otherwise.

I had not yet understood that A. I. Hallowell insisted on the cosmological distinctiveness of the Algonkian worldview since I placed plants and animals in "the natural world." Likewise, I characterized the cannibal giants as "forces," as "natural," as well as the anti-social beings they are in the interpersonal Algonkian cosmos. Nor is it useful, I have learned, to represent these beings as "spiritual," a cosmological dimension Hallowell rightly associated with the concept of nature. Other terms, like "faith" and "belief," now give me pause because they undercut the real world, pragmatic, and holistic character of Algonkian religious life.

The historian's attempt to recognize and convey accurately the reality of American Indians' experience in northeastern North America has long foundered on the ethnocentric character of written documentary sources. Because these sources mainly reflect the attitudes of Euramericans, the historian has had to contend with a seeming lack of authentic Indian sources.[1] Historians have emphasized that missionaries, in particular, notoriously biased their records with self-serving, and distorting, justifications. Although seventeenth-century English missionaries have borne the brunt of this recent criticism, French Jesuits have also been closely scrutinized, if only because the priests' published *Jesuit Relations* glowingly report their success among the Indian peoples of New France.

Recent histories have critically assessed the Jesuit-Algonkian relationship. The Jesuits created a mission at Sillery to turn the Montagnais-Naskapi hunting and gathering bands into an agricultural and sedentary people. The newer studies indicate that this Montagnais mission proved disastrous because the Jesuits demanded that the Indians become culturally French. The Montagnais vehemently rejected such expectations and their ridicule of the Jesuits indicates that despite the priests' good intentions, they ethnocentrically ignored the Montagnais' "inferior" cultural values. Read with a critical eye, the *Jesuit Relations* themselves reveal Indians who not only preferred their own way of life, but who also despised the Jesuits as the agents of insidious change. It appears that the Jesuits proved ultimately as destructive for the Montagnais-Naskapi as Puritan programs of directed culture change.[2]

This study assesses issues that defy these generalizations. Jesuit missions to other Algonkian peoples suggest that the Jesuit presentation of French culture and Catholicism was not uniform. As culture bearers, the priests reacted variously to particular Indian peoples at different times and places and, if their goal was to transform Native American cultures, circumstances frequently intervened against them. Another Algonkian mission began in the 1640s among the Wabanaki peoples of present-day Maine. These tribes were already agriculturalists and their reaction to the Jesuits indicate different patterns of culture change. Like some Montagnais-Naskapi, the Wabanaki as often admired the priests as scorned them. Their response to the Jesuits implies that the effects of positive dialogue must be assessed along with those that accompanied hostile polarization.[3] For both Jesuits and Algonkians, subtle interpersonal adaptations grappled with the processes of culture change.[4] Thus the history of culture change in New France must interpret the ethnocentric parameters that influenced both sides of the interaction. Cultural provincialism biased both the Algonkians and the Jesuits, but it also created a limited, interpersonal context for change. This essay plumbs Algonkian folklore for the Indian attitudes that regulated contact, estimates Jesuit recognition of those attitudes, and evaluates some methodological factors that affect the study of adaptation and change. It is very much a preliminary view.

Eastern Algonkian oral traditions expose those communal values that influenced tribal behavior toward Europeans. In a way that is analogous to the role played by the educational institutions of Western society—family, school, and church—these stories had an important value-formative role within individual Algonkian societies.[5] Less abstract than European pedagogy, the tales established the ethics that colored Algonkian culture by revealing values that emerged from the Algonkians' past experience. As such, the tales provide a kind of documentary access to Algonkian social history, as they experienced it. As vehicles of moral education and socialization, then, the stories constitute unique sources for discussing Algonkian reactions to Europeans and, just as important, for evaluating the effects of Western ideas and institutions on core cultural principles.[6] The folk and mythic tales of the Algonkians are nothing if not supple: a seemingly "lost" dimension of colonial history emerges from the evolution of these stories as they gradually accommodated selective elements of Christian cosmology.

Problems of alienation and social conflict centrally concerned the Eastern Algonkians long before the onslaught of the Europeans brought about the more familiar psychological and social dilemmas Indians have faced since the sixteenth century. Recent anthropological and philosophical studies emphasize that the formation of social and religious structures are culturally unique responses to a universal experience of personal and social alienation.[7] Many cultures, European and Algonkian among them, postulate a primeval time free of social conflict and tension when man existed in unity with the world; in this "old time," as the Algonkians would put it, primeval man did not experience what Western philosophers and psychologists refer to as a body-mind differentiation, and so no subjective-objective bifurcation divided his consciousness. Philosophical and religious speculation begins, then, with the introduction of evil into the world: suddenly, world and man were no longer one. When man perceived that beings existed who were inimical to himself, tension replaced the unitary relation linking the human and non-human worlds. In this situation, with a "memory" of that "old time" world not quite lost, alienated man constructed social, religious, and mythological structures to mediate the conflict between the worlds of body and spirit, good and evil. Complicated structures came to define not only the "like me" and the "unlike me" on the sociological level, but also provided avenues of communication bridging the psychological gap between a remembered "ideal" past and the "real" present.[8]

Algonkian folklore explores these abstractions because, for them, as for Europeans, alienation was an urgent problem. The particular tensions felt by the communal Algonkians differed from those experienced by the urbanized societies of the European colonies, yet Algonkian culture did recognize—and successfully—balance the dramatic tensions generated between individualistic impulse and the norm of community-oriented behavior. For the Algonkians, European contact intensified the ancient struggle against alienation and discord with the introduction of new and, at times, contradictory European social views. Nonetheless, there was much common ground between Algonkian and European concerns.

Although objective European conceptual patterns often mistook the more visionary aspects of Algonkian culture for the merely primitive and uncivilized, closer inspection reveals a carefully developed social and religious order of an animistic rather than monotheistic bent appropriate to life in the northeastern forests. It was in fact because of the extremely difficult physical realities of the Algonkian environment that their very survival came to depend on the proper ordering of human attitudes, and they responded to the negative forces of social individuation and personal alienation with the aid of beings who bridged the distances between the human and non-human worlds. Distinct nations of plant and animal beings comprised the natural world for the Algonkians, and the profoundly social behavior of such beings included communication with man. These persons of the other-than-human class, as the Algonkians conceived them, offered human beings models of social cooperation, symbolizing as they did the ethics of political behavior.[9] Thus shamanistic and ritualistic practices, as well as personal totemic bonds with the other-than-human beings, emphasized cooperation within the extended kin group, as well as with other-than-human persons, because cooperation was the norm observed in an animistically charged natural order.[10]

This natural order, as folk and mythic tales indicate, was dominated by cold and brutal Winter. Figuring centrally in Algonkian consciousness, this season pervaded all of Algonkian culture, constituting the milieu that most evoked individual and social values while at the same time putting them to their most severe test. Thus mediation between worlds of body and spirit, or good and evil, fell to the Algonkian cultural heroes who opposed the dread forces of Winter.[11] Gluskap, the central figure of the Wabanaki, Maliseet, and Mi'kmaq "old time," epitomizes such a hero. As the Wabanaki recounted, Gluskap returned one spring to his grandmother's home. She rejoiced to see him, for she had been unhappy: "Grandson," she said, "this has been a very hard winter. A great many of our descendants have starved to death." Gluskap shared her concern for their people and angrily demanded to know where Winter lived. Despite his grandmother's warnings, Gluskap set out to accost him, and after a long march to the north found Winter as a man of ice, living in a house of ice. Winter mocked Gluskap's power and mercilessly allowed him to freeze to death.[12] However, Gluskap revived the following summer and set out to steal Summer from its present captors. He then returned north with his burden until he again reached Winter. This time Gluskap mocked, and with the aid of Summer, finally overcame him.[13]

Another species of being symbolized the antithesis of Gluskap's careful consideration for the welfare and prosperity of his people.[14] Of all the forces that threatened the delicately tuned social order of Algonkian kin groups, none were more powerful, dangerous, or profoundly anti-social than the beings variously named Kiwakwe, Chenoo, or Windigo, the dreaded cannibal giants.[15] The cannibal giant was perhaps the central image of savagery and evil for the Algonkians, combining the most brutal possibilities inherent in man and in the natural order: deepest winter and cannibalism. These creatures revealed to the Algonkians what people were not, and must not be. The stories about cannibal giants, and to a lesser extent, the documented case histories of an associated mental illness, windigo psychosis, are central to understanding Algonkian civilization. More than any other myth or tale, the case of the cannibal giant was the central object lesson demonstrating the urgency behind the core values that civilized Algonkian intercourse and prevented the bands from disintegrating, under even the harshest pressures of the northeastern winter.[16]

The deep psychological significance of these tales for the Algonkian makes it worth the historian's while to trace the evolution of their modifications over the years following contact with French missions, for it is in the stories and myths surrounding the cannibal giant that metaphor most clearly accommodates history. Subtle nuances in folkloric detail can indicate tonal changes in social identity, including altered capacities for good or evil, shifting political and psychological confidence as a people, and the changing moral intervention of powers that provide guidance or deliverance. Algonkian classifications of windigoes reveal these social principles.

There were, first, beings whose natural state was windigo. Although they existed in both male and female forms, these other-than-human cannibal giants were incapable of the affectionate relations enjoyed by Algonkian men and women. Rather, these beings hated each other fiercely, and their meetings produced violent confrontations from which only one cannibal survived. Invariably, the victor swallowed the ice heart of the vanquished, an act that rendered the survivor all the more powerful and fearsome.[17]

Perhaps more frightening to the community at large, however, was the specter of a human being's dissolution into the windigo, or cannibal state. There were several routes into the madness. An evil shaman, for instance, could transform a healthy individual into a vicious, people-hating Kiwakwe either by acting directly against the person or indirectly against the group, usually by depleting the game upon which the group depended, and, in effect, starving the victim into cannibalism. Individuals on vision quests were sometimes tempted by the protection and power a giant might offer; if these favors were accepted, the seeker became possessed. Others simply slid into a windigo state through spiritual dissipation. Such people gradually hardened their hearts toward their kin and degenerated into wild creatures more at home in the forest than in human company.[18] This latter desocialization process was further reinforced by the Algonkian tendency to ostracize deviant persons.[19] Windigoes lost their human status; as one Beaver Indian, who had become a cannibal during a period of famine, put it: "Although I still exist, I cannot any longer consider myself a human being."[20]

Both kinds of windigoes—human and natural—were solitary creatures of the northern forest and as such formed the major exception to the cooperative behavioral norms the Algonkians advocated. The Penobscot word for the giant, Kiwakwe, or "going about in the woods," typified Algonkian response to the anti-social character of the being.[21] All cannibals hated warmth and so preferred the cold forests of the far north; in more southerly regions the cannibal giant's heart of ice prevented him from threatening communities during the summer months. One such giant declared to a lucky group of Maliseet hunters that "this country is too warm for me; I am going to a colder one."[22] Another, a human in the process of becoming a windigo, experienced a "burning sensation" that only snow could relieve.[23]

In his true state the giant was a form easily discerned as "something made of devil, man, and beast in their most dreadful forms." The creature had "wolfish eyes," his hunger for human flesh had so maddened him that he had gnawed away his own lips and shoulders.[24] To further compound his brutal visage, the giant frequently covered himself with balsam pitch and then rolled about in the forest's debris. His size and strength were in direct proportion to his negative spiritual power and were changeable with the fluctuations of his wrath, becoming larger "the angrier he grows."[25] But the most fearsome and threatening aspect of the windigoes was their treacherous ability to neutralize their true physical aspects, assuming at will the posture and physical being of a relative in order to favorably insinuate themselves into a family.[26]

If the Algonkians were perhaps limited to defensive measures against the natural giants, they nonetheless had a clear stake in the prevention of their own members' defection into windigo ranks. Fortunately, the process of disintegration was gradual and recognizable and Algonkian culture developed methods to deliver the individual from so horrendous a fate.[27] A shaman could struggle with the windigo spirit and, if his power was great enough, destroy him.[28] Significantly, such effective shamanistic power was dependent upon the depth of the shaman's concern for the kin group. One typical shaman who successfully overcame a cannibal giant was tribally renowned for his goodness in dealings "with the Indians." The Ojibwa people reported that the shaman Me Sah Ba was "a great man for this world [who] . . . used [the people] good, all like his children anywhere he saw them, and the Indians like this man."[29] Such shamans threatened the windigoes with their social integrity; like such Algonkian cultural heroes as Gluskap, the truly powerful shamans owed their stature to the unusually full development of their interpersonal sensitivities.

Sometimes the task of exorcism was left to a close relative who possessed only ordinary powers. In such an instance, the strength of kinfolk love and faith was put to the test—often, if the kin bonds were strong enough, successfully.

"With non-shamans, assiduous nursing and loving care during the period of melancholia will persuade the sufferer to face life again," Ruth Landes observed of Ojibwa treatment of the affected person.[30] If, however, the kinfolk failed to reintegrate hopelessly deranged persons, the community itself no longer reacted to the victim within the bounds of traditional kin values. Frequently, a family member or friend was at this point faced with the thankless, if necessary, task of killing the patient. Fear of windigo cannibalism was so thoroughly ingrained within the Algonkian psyche, however, that it was not unusual for the afflicted individual to beg for his own destruction.[31]

The case histories of windigo cannibalism, as well as records of the methods for cure, indicate the social significance of this phenomenon for a tightly knit kinfolk society; the stories about the giants amplify the implications of these histories. Tales involving the windigo giant reveal that relations were based on the kinship hunting band for more than economic survival. These relations were in fact the most feasible psychological approach to the harsh environmental realities of the Northeast as well. Algonkians found that face-to-face, intimate relations between relatives were the most effective, if not in fact the only method for bringing about psychological and social adjustments to group behavioral norms and thus ensuring their survival. Algonkian society, miniaturized and physically mobile, scaled its definition of civilized behavior to the limits of the kinfolk relationship—a relationship at once more intimate and more flexible than the class relations of a more socially structured urban society. In the following tales the cannibal giant tested the ongoing integrity of the delicate Algonkian kin relations and his presence warned succeeding generations of the serious consequences of familial indifference.

One story is of special significance for its richly developed detail and its wide distribution among the Algonkians. Morton I. Teicher collected variations from three different Ojibwa groups, and others have been recorded among the Penobscot, Maliseet, and Mi'kmaq far to the east. The Penobscot story that follows capsulizes the essential elements of all these tales:

> A man, his wife and little girl were living far from other people in the woods. They heard someone coming. Suddenly a noise was heard in the smoke hole of the wigwam and looking up they saw a Ki-wa-kwe peering down. The old woman of the wigwam said aloud, "Oh! Your grandfather has come," speaking to her husband. The monster was pleased at this and grew small. He came around and entered the camp. The woman tried to feed him but he would not eat in spite of her coaxing. He said, "I shall meet somebody here and we will fight." Then he sent them away across a lake and he fought with the other Ki-wa-kwe. He had told them to leave the place if he got killed by the other. But he won the fight and when it was over he ate with them, becoming again an ordinary man.[32]

Other versions of this tale possess similar features; all convey the same message. Because the woman did not show her fear of the cannibal giant, but instead greeted him as a long-lost father or grandfather, the startled and amazed giant was forced to consider the more humane possibilities heretofore unknown to him. Thus the subsequent peaceful relationship enjoyed between the giant and the Indian people depended first on the social integrity of the old woman.

> She was a wise and good woman. She took him in, she said she was sorry to see him so woebegone; she pitied his sad state; she brought him a suit of her husband's clothes; she told him to dress himself and be cleaned. He did as she bade. He sat by the side of the wigwam, and looked surly and sad, but kept quiet. It was all a new thing to him.[33]

This socialization process had just begun. When the woman's husband, warned about the cannibal, returned warily to the camp, he too accepted the subdued creature as an honored member of the family.

> He went in and spoke kindly. He said, "N'chilch, my father-in-law," and asked where he had been so long [and the cannibal again] stared in amazement, but when he heard the son talk of all that had happened for years his face grew gentler.[34]

Reacting to the giant with consistent kindness, the Mi'kmaq couple thus encouraged the giant to change himself from within; their behavior provided him with a concrete model of socially considerate relationship never before understood. As an act of exorcism, the Mi'kmaq giant filled a large kettle with tallow given him by the woman, heated it until it was scalding hot, and then drank it down all at once. "He became sick, he grew pale. He cast up all the horrors and abominations of the earth, things appalling in every sense. When all was over he seemed changed." With the Mi'kmaq couple's aid, the cannibal giant had transformed himself; later he ate a great deal of their food, which had previously disgusted him. "From that time he was kind and good. They feared him no more."[35]

Although in the end the effect is the same, the Ojibwa version of this tale includes cautionary variations on the progress of the relationship between the Indian couple and the cannibal giant. In this instance, the giant initially resisted the woman's entreaties, refusing to be addressed as father. "You re not my daughter," he answered. But the Ojibwa woman insisted: "But when I dreamed about you a few nights ago you called me your daughter." This was apparently sufficient to change the giant's mind. He ran up from the river to kiss her and then he went into the house and kissed her children. "He really believes this was his daughter; and this is where the woman beats (bests) him."[36]

But, because the Ojibwa couple, unlike the Mi'kmaq, were not initially inclined to trust and embrace the cannibal giant, the latter's conversion was consequently delayed. When the giant sent the woman to head off her returning husband—"He may be afraid when he sees my tracks"—the uneasy woman decided to conspire with her husband to kill the unsuspecting giant.[37] They returned, however, to find the creature outside the wigwam with their children "sitting on his wrist and [he] was singing to them." The giant rose at once and kissed the abashed father, calling him son-in-law. But this assumption of familial position was only partial; presumably, because of the bad faith still in the air, the giant continued to some extent in his windigo ways, killing nearby Indians and refusing the more human foods offered him by the Ojibwa couple. "When breakfast was ready he says that he'll have his outside where he left his bundle. He always had his meals there till he ate all those Indians he killed." In time, however, the attachment he developed with the Ojibwa couple civilized the cannibal giant: "He was very useful, and now he's a good man. He had been a very bad man at first."[38] It is almost as if the Ojibwa had chosen to inject their own note on the importance of faith. The couple's waverings are implicated in the needless murders committed in the uncertain atmosphere following the initial contact.

The main message is clear. Once transformed, the giants were one and all highly solicitous of their new kin groups, retaining their prodigious powers but now using them solely for the good of the hunting bands. The stories are symbolically consistent on this point: starvation no longer threatened the group that embraced and cured the cannibal. And each cannibal in his turn proved his social fidelity to humanity by testing his newfound moral, as well as physical, strength against other giants. The Mi'kmaq version of this part of the fable is especially vivid:

> One day the Chenoo told them that something terrible would soon come to pass. An enemy, a Chenoo, a woman, was coming like wind—yes on the wind—from the north to kill him. There would be no escape from the battle. She would be far more furious, mad and cruel than any male, even one of his own cruel race, could be. He knew not how the battle would end; but the man and his wife must be put in a place of safety.[39]

The giant of the Ojibwa tale also attacked an adversary, but did not fail to draw an explicit moral from the battle before he went off: "You will see me running on water and the enemy, too, and if you hear me reach the other side, people shall never kill and eat each other any more."[40]

The Mi'kmaq story adds its own telling implication of the positive—and potentially negative—effects of human mediation on the cannibal spirit. In the initial battle the giant succeeded only with the aid of his new relative. "My son-in-law, come and help me," the giant cried. "You have no son-in-law to help you," the female Chenoo mocked.[41] Together, however, man and giant destroyed their common enemy, and in the spring the giant, "with softened soul," went with the couple down the rivers to the sea. Another giant discovered them on the way, however, and their cause was almost lost. The reformed giant had embraced his newfound humanity and no longer cared to fight at all. "I prefer peace," was his quiet response.[42] As the three continued south a final change was to affect the giant, for he "could not endure the soft airs of summer."

> He grew weaker and weaker; when they reached their village he had to be carried like a little child. He had grown gentle. His fierce and formidable face was now like that of a man. His wounds had healed; his teeth no longer grinned wildly all the time. The people gathered round him in wonder.[43]

It is at this point in the Mi'kmaq tale that historical extrapolation may begin in earnest, for this story discusses the religious effect and social significance of the introduction of Jesuit missionaries among the Eastern Algonkian peoples. As the cannibal giant lay dying among the villagers, the Mi'kmaq couple sent for the French priest who lived among them. The giant and the priest were at first antagonistic; the Jesuit "found the Chenoo as ignorant of all religion as a wild beast," while the giant, equally intolerant, "would repel the father in anger." When, however, the giant and priest finally conversed, "the old heathen's heart changed; he was deeply moved." The giant asked to be baptized and died shortly thereafter, shedding at death the first tear of his life.[44]

The consistency of imagery that runs through the various versions of these tales indicates a universal agreement among the Algonkian peoples about the nature of the cannibal giant and of the threat he posed to society; in each version the Algonkians boldly declare the nature of social and spiritual degeneration. The Algonkians knew the civilized man by his concern for the welfare of the people; conversely, the savage was easily recognized by his self-concern and his utter contempt for humanity. The tales' statement about the prevention—or cure—of social deviancy unites these two axioms about human behavior: only a compassionate, trusting response can begin the process of resocialization. Much faith was required on the part of the healer because of the insidious double bind entangling the incorrigibly individualistic or withdrawn person. Because of the obvious—and often dangerous—incompatibility of his behavior with the general community, the iconoclast faced inevitable social rejection, a problem compounded by the fact that his own nature prevented him from ever recognizing his illness.

These tales infer, then, that Algonkians were uneasy and reticent with outsiders.[45] The cannibal giant represented one extreme of this fear, the solitary man who is by nature mutinous, if not in fact plainly murderous. The inclusion of the Jesuit in the Mi'kmaq tale is most revealing in this light, for the priest represents the new possibilities of morally transforming the incorrigibly individualistic Europeans. This breakdown in Algonkian reticence in accepting the priests, along with the obviously transcultural aspect of the priest's relationship with the cannibal giant, who was himself only newly integrated into Mi'kmaq culture, suggests powerful sympathetic impulses between the two peoples which may account for the unusual Jesuit success among the Eastern Algonkians. These impulses—the subtle gives and takes of a mutual spiritual acculturation between the deeply religious Algonkians and French Jesuits—have gone largely underexplored because of a long-standing historical devaluation of folkloric sources. Nonetheless, much of the history of the first years of contact is intimately involved with issues that are perhaps best defined by folklore and metaphor: society's definition, for example, of what constitutes civilized or savage behavior, and how that definition is subject to influences from outside cultures. This is obviously the case with Algonkian-French contact. Both cultures experienced a reorientation in values as intercultural contact deepened and the subtleties of these psychosocial exchanges became embedded in tradition.[46]

Before we can assess the effects of Jesuit-Algonkian contact implied in oral tradition, a range of cultural processes needs to be acknowledged. The metaphorical juxtaposition of Jesuit and windigo occurred under extreme pressure as the Algonkians attempted to make sense of the post-contact world. While it is likely that the cannibal giant existed aboriginally, windigo psychosis may not have been a pre-contact mental disturbance. Devastating ecological crises may have greatly exaggerated the windigoes' social significance to the Algonkians. As famine became a historic social threat to their kin groups, a higher incidence of its related cannibalism became synonymous with windigo traditions.[47] In the seventeenth century the beliefs surrounding the windigo complex affected how Algonkian peoples experienced internal social crisis and how they assessed and responded to the new world order the Jesuits offered.[48]

The conjunction of traditional and Catholic religious systems occurred because of the mutual adaptation of some Jesuits and Algonkians. From the first, the Jesuits observed cannibalistic incidents among the Algonkian people. The early *Jesuit Relations* refer frequently to what seemed to be the astounding acceptance of Christianity by a people who had practiced cannibalism.[49] Such references are never tied to actual reported cases of cannibalism and so are probably cliches the Jesuits used to contrast supposedly decadent aboriginal values with more efficacious Christian grace. In the seventeenth century, there were varied forms of cannibalism and, in time, the Jesuits overcame their initial repugnance and recognized not only the distinct types but also the Algonkian motivations involved. The priests were uniformly against the practice of ritual cannibalism, in which individuals ingested the heart of a distinguished and honored warrior of another tribal group. Such eating of a brave captive's heart "renders them courageous," Father Paul Le Jeune observed in 1636.[50] The Jesuits remained firmly opposed to this practice and it gradually subsided among the Christianized Algonkians.

The Jesuits did, however, distinguish between the ritualistic and famine contexts of cannibalism. When the most sensational outbreak of the century occurred among the Huron after the Five Nations devastated their society in 1649, the Jesuits deplored the incident but granted that it did occur in a time of extreme necessity. "It is true, this is unhuman," Father Ragueneau explained in 1650, but he added that it was

> No less unusual among our savages than among the Europeans, who abhor eating flesh of their own kind. Doubtless the teeth of the starving man make no distinction in food, and do not recognize in the dead body him who a little before was called, until he died, father, son or brother.[51]

Almost as if in the fulfillment of prophecy, three years later the Jesuits recorded in their journal a similar outbreak of famine cannibalism among fugitive Frenchmen.[52] The Jesuits were coming to realize that such incidents were perhaps inevitable considering the extreme harshness of living conditions prevalent in the North America of the day.

The Jesuits noticed other cases which indicate that emotional disorientation, while not necessarily a precipitating factor in cannibalism, could characterize the response of those persons who committed the act; famine cannibalism could produce psychosis out of a profound sense of social guilt. Le Jeune noted two examples of famine-induced cannibalism in 1635. The first involved a group of Montagnais-Naskapi at Tadoussac who had isolated themselves in the woods, for they "do not dare appear before the others because they had wickedly surprised, massacred, and eaten their companions."[53] The second case is even more suggestive, as it involves only the specter of windigo psychosis. An Indian told Le Jeune "that his wife and sister-in-law contemplated killing their own brother." This surprised Le Jeune, and when he asked why they would consider such an act, the man replied: "We are afraid . . . that he will kill us during our sleep, to eat us." Since the French were sharing their food with the Indians, Le Jeune observed that hunger could not be the cause of the man's obsession. "That is true," the Indian answered. "Thou givest us life; but this man is half mad, he does not eat, he has some evil design; we wish to prevent him, wilt thou be displeased at that?" Le Jeune remained perplexed: "I could not consent to his death," he noted, "and yet I believe they had good cause for fear." The Jesuit never found a satisfactory response. Three days later the man tried to kill some Frenchmen, and the governor, "seeing he was mad, had him put in chains, to surrender him to the first Savages that might come along."[54] The man's ultimate fate went unrecorded.

A particularly instructive case of famine cannibalism occurred among the Mi'kmaq in the last quarter of the seventeenth century. While the incident is not tied to windigo giant symbolism, Father Chrestien Le Clercq presents its development in some detail and, as such, it says a great deal about the social tensions and deviance caused by famine among the Mi'kmaq. The winter of 1680 was particularly severe; by January both the Mi'kmaq and the French were starving, and forty or fifty Mi'kmaq had already died. One family group succumbed to cannibalism in order to survive. The man, "unable to endure the hunger which was devouring him alive," decided to kill and eat his wife. Recognizing his intentions, and in order to save her own life, she "put it into his mind" to eat their children instead. "Is it not better," she asked her husband, "that we put to death some of our children, and that we eat them together, in order that I may be able to rear and support the smaller ones who can no longer live if once they come to lose their mother?" This was apparently a persuasive argument; a close relative joined husband and wife in the act, and the family survived the winter.[55]

The ensuing events illustrate the Mi'kmaq's ethical response to cannibalism, even in the supposedly "pragmatic" instances caused by the threat of famine. The couple bitterly reproached themselves for their weakness, internalizing the social ostracism inflicted upon them for their deed. "They could not find tears enough," said Le Clercq, "nor words enough to condemn and to express on their own behalf the enormity of their crime. . . . They imagined that they saw as many executioners as they met Indians; and . . . they travelled the woods day and night without ceasing, seeking everywhere in vain for a rest which they could find no place."

Le Clercq himself reacted to the couple with some sympathy once he understood the depth of their penitence. Considering themselves unworthy to receive the instruction he offered their kinfolk, the family insisted that they could never learn "until this crime was entirely removed and pardoned by God" through the bishop of Quebec. Le Clercq comforted them, explaining that "God has more goodness and compassion for them [than] they had of wickedness and cruelty." Convinced of the priest's power, the couple accepted his religious means to "appease the justice of God and to invite his mercy."[56]

The details of Le Clercq's story, like those reported by Le Jeune, suggest an important feature of the seventeenth-century French-Algonkian relationship. The Eastern Algonkians experienced ecological change and social conflict as a direct result of the settlement of New France in 1608. Two factors operated jointly to threaten the Algonkian kin groups: the economic adjustments the fur trade demanded and the extensive toll taken by the spread of European disease. By the end of the sixteenth century, the fur trade had encouraged the Montagnais-Naskapi in particular to overtrap the limited game resources north of the St. Lawrence River valley. This trade, in turn, exacerbated intertribal rivalries as each group vied vigorously for a monopolistic commercial relationship with the French. Epidemics of European disease then further devastated the Algonkian tribes.

Both trade and disease challenged the communal foundations of Montagnais-Naskapi society. It was not that trade simply made individualistic capitalists of communally oriented hunters. Rather, when the Montagnais-Naskapi added trapping to their subsistence techniques, they deemphasized large-scale multifamily activities, and the extended family became, even more than in the past, the core social group. Mohawk raids made large gatherings more dangerous and the Montagnais-Naskapi became guarded peoples. Both trade and the resulting intertribal competition produced a heavier exploitation of fur-bearing animals and recurrent famine may have been the result, although this problem has not yet been adequately studied. Trade and warfare certainly required defensive adjustments, but these transitional changes in social style were occurring just as new forms of epidemic diseases hit the Montagnais population. The widespread illnesses shook the Montagnais-Naskapi more powerfully, and further undermined social confidence because traditional religious methods of dealing with sickness proved impotent. The shamans' abject failure called into question the very nature of tribal kinship with other-than-human persons, since it was clear that the shamans had no power over the beings who manifested themselves in these new diseases. In the wake of the epidemics, kin groups sometimes dispersed and individuals found sustenance in any manner they could.[57]

While these economic, military, and social problems pushed the Montagnais-Naskapi into an alliance with the French, they can neither alone nor together account for the distinctive Algonkian reaction to the Jesuits. The priests observed the acute effects of post-contact winters on the Eastern Algonkians and the Indians' remarkably persevering hospitality, and they began to comprehend slowly an aboriginal analogue to Christian grace and behavior in the kin-based sociality of the Montagnais-Naskapi. There were no deprived persons among any of the Algonkians so long as any food remained to be shared, and the implications of this example were not lost on the Jesuits. Clearly, a common ethical and spiritual ground existed to be exploited by Jesuit and Algonkian alike. Jesuits before 1650 may have wanted to culturally transform the Montagnais-Naskapi, if only to preserve them from starvation, but the Algonkians countered with their own, cautious ideas about change.

Because European presence thoroughly disrupted Montagnais-Naskapi social life, change did occur. Adaptative social forms emerged from the ethical struggle the Jesuits posed, but the process of change remained traditional. The priests interjected themselves into Algonkian societies, voiced ideas about the nature of the Indians' social crisis, and occasionally became trusted figures whose opinions were, at least, considered. But Jesuit intentions do not explain what actually happened. The Jesuits may have desired radical conversions but their success must be measured through the effective filters of Algonkian values.

Through a fortuitous conjunction of the expectations of Algonkian myth and the active demands of Christian charity, the priests found the means to confirm and strengthen the primacy of social values among the embattled Eastern Algonkians. The priests were able to make a persuasive case for the power of Christian doctrine because they tailored a special interpretation of God to the needs of Algonkian mythic structure. The Jesuits' "He-Who-Made-All" may have hardly resembled either the Yahweh or the Christ of orthodox Christian tradition, but the new conception did fit neatly into the Algonkian philosophy of pervasive and personalized power. The symbol does suggest the sensitivity of Jesuit theological expression, because the Algonkians recognized "He-Who-Made-All" in the Jesuits' personalized presentation.[58]

The integrity of the priests' personal stances defused Algonkian suspicions to such an extent that even the most deeply rooted values were affected, and a process of change began which was formed largely by the credence Algonkians gave to the dialogue. The intercultural struggle began in the 1630s when disease hit the Montagnais-Naskapi. Father Paul Le Jeune "decided to care for the bodies to aid the souls."[59] In 1634 he wintered with the family group of an Indian who had earlier died in the priest's care.[60] Later that spring, Le Jeune found the Montagnais sachem, Manitouchatche, or LaNasse, ill at the mission.[61] Since LaNasse was the first Montagnais to settle his kinfolk near the Jesuit compound, Father Le Jeune embraced the sachem "like a brother." Everyone was startled, but LaNasse preferred the care of Le Jeune and the Jesuits, resisting finally "his own wife, his children, his sons-in-law, his friends and fellow savages, his Manitousiouets, sorcerers, or jugglers, not once but many times, to throw himself into the arms of strangers . . . to die in their faith and in their house."[62] This conversion, a striking variation on the theme of windigo transformation or redemption, with the sachem accepting the ministrations of the moral agents of another culture, is a major key to understanding the accommodation between Jesuit and Algonkian.

This relationship did not, however, extend to the larger population of lay Frenchmen; if anything it revealed to the French priests failings among their own people. When the Montagnais-Naskapi first sought closer relations with the French in 1633, one group, anticipating an Iroquois raid, went so far as to seek asylum. "They wanted to unite, that they might be stronger, but they feared famine in abandoning the chase. They asked us therefore if we would supply them with food." Since the Algonkians were clearly facing economic and social difficulties on all fronts, Le Jeune and the Jesuits proposed a relationship with them modeled on the Christian virtue of charity.[63] But they realized that the larger French society in Canada did not share such sentiments.

As time passed, Le Jeune came to minimize the more pragmatic aspects of Montagnais social motivations and to admire the positive nature of Algonkian kinship bonds. When he proposed to help the Montagnais learn agriculture and Catholic religious practice, a shaman called Le Jeune a liar for promising help without expectation of return. The wisdom of adaptation was not lost on Le Jeune, who was already embarrassed by the transgressions of his own fellow Christians. "When it is necessary to become a Savage with the Savages," he wrote as early as 1633, "one must take his own life and all that he had, and throw it away, so to speak, contenting himself with a very large and very heavy cross for all riches."[64] The Jesuits achieved that detachment and successfully cultivated a Montagnais-Naskapi mission near Quebec. This mission, in turn, ultimately opened the whole of the Algonkian Northeast to the Society of Jesus.

A similar pattern of Christian conversion occurred in the 1640s among the Kennebec Wabanaki farther to the south.[65] Their primary political motivation resembled that of the Montagnais-Naskapi—they wished a strengthened alliance against the threatening Iroquois. But more important, the disastrous impact of European liquor and disease had led them to admire the thriving Montagnais-Naskapi community under Jesuit guidance. Kennebecs who visited the Sillery mission returned repeatedly to their villages with word of the new order created between the Montagnais and the Jesuits. In 1646 the Canadian governor Montmagny approved Kennebec requests for a priest and sent Father Gabriel Druillettes to the Kennebec River in Maine.[66]

Druillettes arrived among this band at an auspicious moment. Another epidemic had killed many Kennebecs the summer before and the shamans were powerless against it. The priest deeply touched the Kennebecs, "winning their souls," the *Jesuit Relation* declared, "through the care he gave their bodies." The fact that some Kennebecs miraculously survived the illness rebounded to the priest's credit.[67] In 1651 the Kennebecs acknowledged their debt to the priest and in a public ceremony declared him one of their own. Like the woman in the tales whose social and moral integrity brought the cannibal giant into the family band, Gabriel Druillettes' behavior assured the Wabanaki that his religious powers were strong and worthy of their respect because they were grounded in his concern for the welfare of the community.

Gabriel Druillettes brought the Society of Jesus closer to the realities of the North American continent. Although North Americans lived on a smaller scale than the urbanized Europeans, Druillettes was able to perceive that native values, rooted in the everyday life of kin groups, compared favorably with the more abstract ideologies of European peoples.[68] Indeed, for both Druillettes and other Jesuits, the Algonkians pointed toward the pristine impulses of Christian ethics in the early centuries after Christ. This Algonkian world beckoned the Jesuits with an intensity that is highlighted by the gradual reappraisal of their own initial judgments of "savagery" leveled against the native peoples. The Society of Jesus, with typical European condescension, began work in Canada assuming their own cultural superiority. The priests' first efforts were bent toward the creation of red Frenchmen and, as educators in the finest schools of Europe, the Jesuits naturally saw formal education as a primary instrument of social change. Algonkians, just as naturally, rejected this seemingly unintegrated system of learning. The Jesuits had wit enough to assess this failure and in time they learned to modify many of the cultural expectations of French tradition. By the 1670s Jesuit appreciation of Indian values had made the priests advocates of Algonkian cultural resistance. The Jesuits clashed with French officials, and ultimately with the Crown itself, against demands for an intensified frenchification program.[69]

The Jesuits came to realize that the issue was not so much the problem of savagery as the ill-conceived notion of frenchification. The priests stood in witness as the catastrophic, demographic, political, and military legacies of European contact destroyed the Huron Confederacy in 1649. They watched as liquor, surreptitiously traded by Frenchmen, thoroughly disrupted the social and religious life of the Montagnais-Naskapi at the mission of Sillery in the 1670s. Despite the subversions of their countrymen—whether in the liquor traffic or in ethnocentric demands for frenchification—the priests held their ground. The Jesuits were ready when large numbers of Wabanaki began to flee to Canada in 1675 seeking refuge from the disastrous effects of King Philip's War.

The early experience of one of the most prominent Jesuit missionaries among these Wabanaki, Sebastien Racle, illustrates in microcosm the acculturative process that occurred between the Society of Jesus and some Algonkians. Racle was thirty-eight years old when he arrived in New France in 1689, and his distinguished career as a professor of rhetoric had not particularly prepared him for the Indian realities of North America.[70] He found himself suddenly surrounded by a bewildering variety of Native American peoples, "which one may almost take," Racle immediately wrote his brother, "for animals as for men." The shock, although profound, was not unusual as an initial reaction to Indian peoples. What is more important is that Racle remained open to the new experience. "It is with these nonetheless, that I must pass the rest of my days," he continued. "It is these people that I must caress, cherish and who must become the object of my cares."[71] These sentiments transcend mere piety; they indicate that Racle confronted his own ethnocentric revulsion and, more important, emotionally oriented himself toward the Algonkians as people worthy of his regard.

Racle's transformation had its own painful struggle. An apprenticeship among the Wabanaki at the St. Francis mission radically altered Racle's early impressions. He was surprised, for instance, that the Wabanaki maintained their inward-looking, extended-family households at the mission. Racle began to learn their language under the bemused tutelage of one of these kin groups. The experience became a rite of passage as Wabanaki manners stripped Racle of his cultural assumptions. "I went there," he wrote, "as a child goes to school." Comparing his situation to the relatively comfortable circumstances of a French schoolboy, Racle admitted that he was intellectually engaged. He learned more than he expected because the Wabanaki language delighted him as much as the classical languages he had already mastered. It "surely has its perfections and is fine," Racle exclaimed of the Wabanaki dialect, and "one is convinced when one considers its economy of expression." The Wabanaki won Racle's affection through the teaching of their language and they, in turn, were impressed by his perseverence in learning it. Racle referred to that particular family as "those of my cabin" and he gave one of the children his own name at baptism. "I love them very much," he wrote his brother. When the time came for Racle to return to the Jesuit college at Quebec, the mother of little

Sebastien," her other children in tow, followed after: "You love us, and you were of our cabin, and you were our father. . . . Why then did you leave us?" "I swear to you," Racle told his brother, "that I could not respond to them except by my tears." Racle concluded: "The Abenaki with whom I lived . . . are the gentlemen of the savages."[72]

This sympathetic integration of Sebastien Racle into Wabanaki social life indicates that there was more to the development of a mutual alliance between the Society of Jesus and the Algonkian peoples than standard historical evidence of economic, social, or religious crises alone can explain. Only an analysis of the conjunction of Algonkian and French culture can suggest the positive context that encouraged both Indian and Jesuit. This meeting of attitudes involved the Jesuits' assumptions of shamanistic responsibility in order to serve the Algonkian people. When the Algonkians began to perceive the Jesuits as individuals with high sympathetic regard for the community at large and as the "shamans" with the greatest apparent power in eradicating post-contact, antisocial evils, they naturally considered carefully the Jesuits' social diagnosis.[73] In doing so, the Algonkians, consciously or not, took their cues from the windigo stories and allied themselves with Jesuit expressions of social power.

The Jesuit priests, then, entered Algonkian traditions sometime during the seventeenth century, performing roles comparable to the benevolent Gluskap, who had seen the tribes through bad years of previous centuries. There are additional cannibal giant stories that indicate the symbolic adjustments. One story states that the Mi'kmaq began to use crosses carved on trees surrounding their villages and band encampments as a means of warding off cannibal giants. The tale notes the strength of the new belief when it reveals that the older, more traditional tribesmen advised the use of the cross as a protective device.[74] Another story, from the Montagnais-Naskapi, suggests that Christian Indians had it in their power to resist even the most dangerous of cannibals with the corresponding implication that perhaps the Montagnais-Naskapi themselves no longer possessed sufficient spiritual power to challenge the giant on their own.[75] Another Montagnais tale explicitly states the degeneration of Indians' spiritual power. When a hunting party failed to kill a giant, one of their members despaired that "we cannot do it [because] our magic power is too weak." With the aid of his guardian spirit, the shaman among them perceived both the giant and a priest coming from the distance toward the camp. The shaman went at once to greet the priest. "We are all going to die here because the witigo has come among us and we cannot kill him," the shaman explained. "But the priest said, 'Oh, no my child, he is not dangerous. We will kill him.'" The priest walked out onto the frozen lake and met the cannibal as he arrived. "The priest raised his crucifix, whereupon the witigo fell dead on the ice."[76]

These stories suggest that once the Jesuits came to appreciate Algonkian communal values, they also came to behave in ways that the Algonkians could recognize within their own cultural terms. As has been noted earlier, only the good man, the individual who had successfully integrated his own personal needs with Algonkian kin-defined ethical norms, could victoriously confront the cannibal giant. Since both shamanistic and individual resistance to the cannibal giant emanated from a profound awareness that the windigo embodied the most terrible anti-social impulses, much was at stake when the Mi'kmaq and the Montagnais-Naskapi declared, through their stories, that the Jesuits finally were more powerful than many native shamans against the forces of the cannibal giant. While the Eastern Algonkians respected and identified with the Jesuits, they found that relationship on the whole atypical of their experience with Europeans. Other Europeans did not develop personal ties with the Algonkians as easily as the Jesuits and, in fact, most Europeans were either a direct or indirect threat to the survival of their communities.

Admittedly, these remarks generalize the Jesuits' impact among the Algonkians to highlight the interpersonal processes that were instrumental between the two peoples. A more detailed view is obviously required to convey accurately the range of interpersonal stances and their effect on culture change. That larger study would assess the continuity of belief among the Algonkians, and it would evaluate the meeting of traditional and Catholic religious symbols. It would also recognize that some Jesuits were more inflexible than the individuals considered here. Nevertheless, a comparison of the "civilized-savage" value structure of the cannibal giant stories with the actual behavior of historic French and Algonkian peoples offers some clarifications for the study of Indian history. The argument that French economic dependence on the Algonkians encouraged good relations, and that, conversely, English and Indian relations faltered because the two peoples competed for the same land base, has dominated discussion of comparative French and English Indian relations. This argument is compelling on the surface, but it says little about the crucially important Indian perceptions of Europeans and, while it does point out the obvious difference between French and English responses, it cannot explain the psychological and spiritual subtleties that lay behind the positive relationships which existed between some Frenchmen and some Indians.

When the cannibal giant stories are admitted as evidence about Algonkian behavior and belief, a different emphasis emerges. The discussion then centers on what actually occurred between particular Europeans and Indians, and the inquiry shifts to how Western institutions and values strengthened and/or undermined Indian communities at any given moment in time. The historic relationship between the Algonkians and the Jesuits raises such methodological issues because, while both Indians and priests adapted willingly to one another, the larger French society, like the English colonies, posed insurmountable economic, political, and military problems for the Algonkians. Mutual acculturation did occur but never smoothly. The structural impact of European institutions on Indian communities remains largely unexplored and the preceding analysis of the impact of one such institution, the Society of Jesus, only suggests the behavioral and ethical issues involved.

Critical readings of European documents with an eye for the ethical concerns of Native American oral traditions illuminates Indian views about culture change. If the Jesuit records indicate a great deal about Algonkian peoples' superficial reactions to Christianity, Algonkian folklore reveals the depth of that response. The Jesuit sources provide rich details about actual face-to-face relations; the folklore remembers the central dynamics of those meetings. Taken separately, each source has its special bias. The Jesuits wished to reassure themselves, and the French public who supported their efforts, that their rocky dialogue with the Algonkians was progressive. The retelling of Algonkian experiences in the windigo tales in turn affirmed the Indians' mythic concerns for social solidarity and, at the same time, applied their history to the embattled present. When oral tradition and written sources converge, Algonkian social processes emerge with the prominence they deserve.

4

The Mythological Sources of Wabanaki Catholicism

A Case Study of the Social History of Power

Looking backward, I can see that "Wabanaki Catholicism" both broke new ground and recapitulated the ethnocentrism that I have come to argue retards Native American Studies. I could already glimpse something of the conclusion to which my studies would move: Algonkians lived within a relational cosmos, a logic that regulated their careful scrutiny of French-Catholic claims to superior religious and social truths. For the moment, I only followed the suggestive lead of the previous essay: if Algonkian oral tradition preserved a pivotal insight about the monstrously anti-social (and thus the threatening character of European contact), it must also record a positive sense of the social.

The stories about Gluskap, it turned out, did value sociality, but with a twist. In reflecting on the cosmic and cultural significance of Gluskap, the Eastern Algonkians celebrated no static, idealized saintliness. Rather, they stressed the dangers of even well-meaning ignorance, the value of horrific mistakes, and the crucial importance of compassionate knowledge—and thus power—wrested from life's adversities. These stories revealed a religious sensibility that focused not on sin and salvation, but on trial and transformation by and through error. Bad things happen by someone's out-of-control agency, these stories declare, and are thus the potential occasions of rectification by reorientation toward the well-being of others.

My language, however, continued to reveal how far I would have to go to comprehend the distinctiveness of Algonkian views of religious life. Algonkians emphasized the religious meaning of the here and now; I thought of religion as transcendent. They stressed religious practicality; I highlighted belief and faith in an unseen spiritual reality. Despite myself, then, I found myself moving toward understanding the Algonkians' powerful ground of religious responsibility toward others: while seventeenth-century Algonkians had ample opportunity to resist, their cardinal insight propelled them toward constructive alliance, a religious socialization of selfish, individualistic, and authoritarian (and thus non-Indian) others. Now I can see that, if Gluskap learned from his mistakes, so have I.

American Indian religions played a vital role in the history of Indian-White relations and this study explores the way mythological traditions worked in one example of that interaction. It focuses generally on the mythological traditions, historical experience, and religious adaptations of the Wabanaki peoples of present-day Quebec, Maine, and New Brunswick.[1] In particular, it outlines the seventeenth-century social crises and exploratory accommodations of the Wabanaki people of the Kennebec River who, in the 1640s and 1670s, sought and harkened to the teachings of Jesuit missionaries in order to resolve the social disorders that beset them. The Kennebecs' subsequent conversion prefigured the religious change of all the Wabanaki peoples who largely remain both Catholic and ethnically distinct to this day. The study therefore searches for the nascent religious principles through which the Wabanaki understood the social implications of Euramerican contact and which allowed them to respond critically even while they urgently reinterpreted their own, faltering traditions.

Kennebec experience, unlike that of the other seventeenth-century Wabanaki, can be reconstructed in unusual detail because of the convergence of several equally important lines of evidence. First, there are many seventeenth-century descriptions of Wabanaki culture and beliefs. Second, mythological and folkloric traditions gathered in the nineteenth and twentieth centuries corroborate and amplify the ideological assumptions that can be glimpsed within the cultural sketches of the early contact period. When they are understood as invaluable records of Wabanaki values—the primary existential postulates of their worldview—mythic and folkloric texts take us to the heart of the Wabanakis' sense of historical process. They document how such charter social values endure in the very fact that *they* direct historical change. Studied in this way, mythological and folkloric accounts permit us to see that the Wabanaki themselves have embedded their sense of historical process in their oral traditions.[2] Third, the *Jesuit Relations* are an unusually rich historical source, not only providing information about specific Kennebec behaviors, but also reporting the Wabanakis' own sense of change in the seventeenth century.[3] Finally, this study benefits from the commentary of Dr. Peter Paul, a thoughtful Maliseet scholar whose linguistic expertise has amplified obscure details of earlier anthropological reports and, as important, has thrown new light on the possible meanings of the events that the Jesuits described.[4] Taken together, these documentary sources make it possible to estimate both the reasons for the Kennebecs' post-contact social crisis and their adaptive purposes in meeting those difficulties through religious change.

The Kennebec experience that emerges from the convergence of these varied sources only partially coincides with the recent revisionist interpretations of Jesuit and Indian contact. The Kennebecs responded so warmly to Catholicism that they seem to support the antiquated view that the Jesuit missions led only to the benevolent transformation of Indian peoples. The newer view that the Jesuits arbitrarily manipulated American Indians' material and ethical cultures, often with dire consequences, does not apply to the Kennebecs' situation. Nor does it appear that the Wabanaki missions triggered a vehement, nativistic backlash, as occasionally occurred in other French missions.[5]

Yet the Wabanakis' unequivocal acceptance of Catholicism does not mean that they either rejected or supplanted their traditional religiosity.[6] Unlike the Montagnais, the Wabanakis' northern Algonkian-speaking neighbors, the Wabanaki did not compartmentalize traditional and Christian beliefs.[7] Instead, Wabanaki Catholicism represents a syncretic intensification of their ancient religious life. Contact with the Jesuits engendered a revitalization of the Wabanakis' mythically given social order, and thus enabled them to adapt creatively to post-contact threats against their mythically grounded identity. In this sense, the Wabanakis' critical response to the Jesuit missionaries supports the developing view that Indian peoples deliberately molded European goals for their cultural modification to their own, long-established purposes.

Seventeenth-century Jesuit missionaries did mistake American Indians' motives, and later Euramerican observers have sometimes compounded their errors. The Jesuits believed that the Wabanakis' enthusiastic interest in Catholicism indicated their admission that they had a religiously deficient tradition.[8] While anthropologists have since outlined the Wabanakis' religiously informed culture, it is still often stated that they, along with other sub-Arctic Algonkian peoples, were extreme religious individualists, lacking any communal rituals beyond the attenuated practices of isolated shamans. Frank G. Speck, the pioneer anthropologist of the Algonkian Northeast, felt that the Wabanaki were so marginally religious that their beliefs must have been degenerate survivals of some more complex religious system.[9] Drawing heavily on Speck, Werner Muller, the historian of religion, came to similar conclusions:

> The Algonquin [sic] tribes which still live in Canada lead the same lives as all other hunters and gatherers of the north, bearers of a nebulous, feebly defined culture; more complex religious and social forms are rendered impossible by the sheer hardness of life.[10]

Such interpretations emerge from an outdated effort to classify religious practices on some evolutionary scale of institutionalized expression. They also derive from an imprecise understanding of the religious adaptations of the Wabanaki since European contact. Speck, for example, gathered evidence about the existence of a complex aboriginal ritual system but, in believing that Catholicism had eradicated and replaced traditional religion, he failed to notice considerable evidence of cultural continuity. As he put it:

> This of course does not mean that the Penobscot [Wabanaki] lacked ceremonial occasions such as installation, greeting, wedding, burial rites and dances. Some of these still exist, but in native concept they are ceremonies of a social rather than a devotional or religious nature.[11]

Although Speck does not recognize the possibility of cultural displacement over time, such surviving ritual forms are not merely social; in fact, in historical context, such rituals remain of religious significance, but they are now located within Catholic liturgical expression. Because they ignore the historical processes that molded post-contact religious beliefs, statements that emphasize the individualized nature of aboriginal ritual seriously distort the actual social character of Wabanaki religiosity.

THE MYTHOLOGICAL PARADIGM

Undeniably, religious power was widely shared within the egalitarian Wabanaki societies. Even well-known shamans found their authority questioned, ridiculed, and sometimes even challenged. But more to the point, while individuals wielded power, power itself was always an instrument for either social good or communal malaise. Legitimate power—whether that of the hunter, warrior, shaman, or any persons engaged in socially productive domestic tasks—existed only for the people's welfare. Power might be abused, but ideally it was sensitive to the needs of the small-scale Wabanaki communities; as their mythology demonstrates, among the Wabanaki community and religious practice were coextensive.

The Wabanakis' experience of post-contact events was rooted in their social ideals—normative values so intense that folkloric accounts record the changing implications of their mythically given religious order. Although concepts of historical periodization may very well violate Wabanaki thought about historical process, distinct types of moral challenge to their social solidarity characterize at least general trends in Wabanaki history, as the oral accounts establish. For example, mythic treatments of the original Wabanaki distinguish between that formative time and all others. Speck also observes that shamanistic traditions fall into three temporal categories: the mythical age, when such powers flourished; the historical period; and a time closely related to the present. Thus, while the Wabanaki themselves may not have thought of temporal categories in linear terms, the idea that their history falls into three general periods has some utility at least in defining particular kinds of moral struggle. Their present time of trouble began at European contact when, suddenly, their ethical order met new problems that tested its integrity. The present era evolved from a middle period in which the Wabanaki explored basic kinship values and applied them to preserve moral unity among their growing and expanding population. This central age rests in turn on a pivotal time of mythic transformation in which the world was cast into its present physical, biological, social, and moral condition. The great persons of the mythical period established the fundamental moral direction of Wabanaki history.[12]

Wabanaki mythology does not describe the creation of the world itself. Instead, the physical world and the various beings who live above, upon, or under it are taken as givens. Yet the myths describe a world that has a dynamism only dimly perceived in the second and third ages. Plasticity formed the world in the mythic age: living presences whose essence as persons was more important than their specific forms enlivened basic matter.[13] The myths do not describe any polarity between good and evil; rather such moral qualities rest only in the singular actions of persons.[14] Nevertheless, the Wabanaki people found the mythic age challenging. Human beings had not yet found their proper place in a world peopled by hostile beings in their plant, animal, and even inanimate guises.[15] Some beings, however, worked for the Wabanakis' well-being, and their altruism grounded the events of the mythic period. This was especially true of Gluskap, the central figure of Wabanaki mythology, whose acts made the world hospitable for the Wabanaki peoples.

Wabanaki mythology describes a system of social dynamics that was quite different from the mythic assumptions of European worldviews. In the Wabanakis' mythic age, men and animals were not cooperative, but they were essentially alike. There was no Wabanaki Adam to name animals, and thus to give human beings dominion over them. In the primary age, men and animals shared the same nature, and they lived with, and married one another, without distinction. Similarly, the Wabanaki had no belief comparable to the Hebraic-Christian fall from grace; human sin did not shatter the amity of the initial world. Gluskap shared no character traits with Adam. Gluskap exposed the evil exercise of power for all to see, and he established an ethical system that could contain it. Adam did neither.

Gluskap taught the Wabanaki that evil came from disordered social relations, and their mythology encapsulated that understanding. Evil power was inherent in the world, and it had to be countered. In a Passamaquoddy account, Gluskap had an evil twin brother, Malsum, the Wolf. Unlike Gluskap, who was born naturally, Malsum thrust himself into the world through his mother's flesh, killing her in the process. Gluskap's first positive act for humankind occurred when he killed his obstreperous brother.[16] In a Penobscot myth, Gluskap had three brothers who were intensely jealous of him, but he vanquished them in games that tested their respective powers.[17]

Orphaned, even Gluskap had to learn the powers of good and evil from his grandmother, Woodchuck, who raised him. Gluskap was an exuberant adolescent, well-intentioned but not always aware of his impact on the world. While Woodchuck easily taught Gluskap to hunt, to fish, and to make snowshoes, she had more trouble with moral concepts. For example, Gluskap carried his concern for his grandmother's welfare to enthusiastic extremes. To make food readily available for Woodchuck, he seized all the animals and trapped all the fish behind a huge weir. Woodchuck appreciated the help but scolded Gluskap for his excesses: if all the animals and fish were dead, she asked, "what will our descendants in the future do to live?" Gluskap repaired his error and learned his lesson. Woodchuck proclaimed proudly: "He will be a great magician. He will do great wonders for our descendants as he goes on."[18] As Speck observed of Gluskap's development, "the extolling of ethical principles and provision for his 'descendants' do not appear at the beginning of his career; a mission develops only with the course of events."[19] In his personal growth, Gluskap dignified the Wabanakis' sense of their own faltering struggle toward responsible power.

Gluskap did become more judicious as he matured. The world was full of beings who did as they pleased without concern for people's welfare. As one tale says of Lox: "Now he was a great magician, though little to other folks' good."[20] Gluskap set about transforming the world and forcing such persons to conform to the moral purposefulness of human activity. He cajoled the giant bird, Culloo, to flap his wings less vigorously to moderate the winds. Gluskap stole tobacco from Grasshopper, who had refused to share it with people. With the help of Summer, Gluskap overcame the worst effects of Winter. He examined the animals to be sure that they could not take unfair advantage of human beings. Some of them, like hostile Squirrel and Beaver, were too large, and Gluskap reduced them to their present size.[21] In all that he accomplished, Gluskap modified the world to human measure.[22]

He did a great deal more. In order to ensure the happiness of the people, Gluskap showed them proper moral conduct, teaching them the rules that should govern their relations with other-than-human persons, as well as with each other. Gluskap taught magnanimity as the primary ethical principle. Seven of his neighbors kidnapped his grandfather and left Gluskap to die. Determined upon revenge, Gluskap caught the culprits, but then he perceived that they were frightened. "Because he is good natured," the myth recounts, "he pities and forgives them."[23] Such social responsibility and freely exercised compassion were the keys to Gluskap's power. The strict rules requiring the Wabanaki to be generous with one another have their source in Gluskap's example. A. Irving Hallowell noted similarly of the Ojibwa that their moral stress on hospitality "is illustrated by the fact that other-than-human persons share their power with human beings."[24] Morality and social mutuality were synonymous for the Wabanaki peoples.

The moral principles of social cooperation that Gluskap taught suffused Wabanaki culture. For example, the Wabanaki derive both their concept of land "ownership" and, indirectly, their social organization, from Gluskap. Among the Penobscots, Maliseets, and Passamaquoddies, one myth relates that once a giant frog held all of the world's water in its belly. When the frog refused to consider the people's plight, Gluskap slew him and released the water, which flows in northeastern streams and rivers. Many of the people could not control their thirst and, rushing into the water, were transformed into aquatic animals—

lobsters, crabs, eels, whales, frogs, yellow perch, and sturgeon. The survivors took the names of their altered relatives' new forms and chose hunting territories adjacent to the new watercourses.²⁵ The extended Wabanaki kinship group—human and animal alike—remained bonded despite persistent differences in outward appearance. The Penobscots used a special word to describe the intimacy that continued to exist between humans and their animal kin: The term *ntu'tem* "my spouse's parents," or in another sense "my partner of a strange race," referred to animal relatives.²⁶ The term also suggests, Dr. Peter Paul observes, the family lines related through intermarriage.

The ntu'tem relationships expressed with everyday immediacy the interests that humans and other-than-human persons shared in the middle age of Wabanaki history. When Gluskap left the world, his power—ktaha'ndo—continued as the "source of dynamics" of Wabanaki life.²⁷ Once Gluskap completed his world transformation for Wabanaki habitation, the world became much less fluid. Yet the myths embody a practical sense of the individual's enduring responsibility for the social welfare of the human group and its animal relatives. Gluskap had not intended to establish a world order in which collective struggle was no longer necessary; rather, "he wanted to show the man that he must not always wait for spiritual help, but do the things with his own labor, only appealing to spiritual power when necessity required it."²⁸ In fact, in the second age, the Wabanaki faced unprecedented tensions as their numbers increased and the people dispersed across the land. Gluskap had demonstrated the fundamental principles of moral solidarity but he "did not recommend any system of organization under which the people might live."²⁹ The Wabanaki found their way in confronting perplexity: in the middle age they learned through trial and error, and with the aid of No-chi-gar-neh, the spirit of the air, to use medicinal plants, to heed the dream spirits of sleep and trance,³⁰ and to wield shamanistic powers of transformation and communication with animals. "You shall be great men among your people," No-chi-gar-neh said to the first shamans, "because your works shall bring great comfort to yourselves [and] also to all your people, for you shall be useful to them."³¹ No-chi-gar-neh also added an ominous admonition that defined the moral parameters of Wabanaki experience:

> Being great, great must be your care in keeping yourselves in this greatness. You must never allow yourselves to become so small as to use your power upon or against your brother on any contention. Do not abuse one another with this power . . . because whoever abuses this power shall lose it.³²

The shamans linked the first and second ages of Wabanaki history. While ordinary people lost much of their power to change form and to speak with other-than-human persons, the *made'olinouk*, the shamans, had power to bridge the resulting void between humans and other persons. The shamanistic relationship with a *baohi"'gan,* or spirit helper, retained and funneled power from the mythical era. The shaman considered a baohi"'gan as part of himself, and such interpersonal solidarity molded shamanistic power, as it had Gluskap's.[33]

The shamans remembered and recorded the Wabanaki cosmos. They recounted the mythic past and through esoteric rituals repaired otherworldly relations. They also integrated the bonds between ordinary and other-than-human persons into the entire ritualistic structure by interpreting the dreams in which such persons appeared. The shaman's medicinal powers stemmed from the same concern for interpersonal relations. The Wabanaki, along with other Algonkians, believed that social disorder caused disease. The shamans either placated or thwarted malevolent persons, or indicated to the afflicted person and his relatives the means to ease some interpersonal affront.[34]

Slowly in the middle age, the institutional structures of the Wabanaki world emerged from this human–non-human sociality that bound man and other persons to mutual responsibility and obligation. Tribal myth, folklore, and practical experience recounted the essential ties between man and other beings and warned of dreadful consequences for failure to respect the integrity of both other-than-human and human persons. Complex prohibitions and a positive sense that the two worlds were intimately connected gave meaning to the Wabanaki food cycle. Ritual surrounded hunting, fishing, and agricultural activities. The Wabanaki explained to the animal or plant that the taking of life was necessary. He carefully prepared himself to hunt, summoning personal power to ensure success, and he ritually acknowledged the life he took.[35] Wabanaki subsistence activities were thus sacral practices; the welfare of the hunting band depended on the proper social orientation of the individual.

CRISIS AND RELIGIOUS ADAPTATION

These religious convictions continued to inform Wabanaki life, even after their present age began with European contact. At the time, the Wabanakis' long-established moral order found itself beset by continuous and cumulative challenge, if only because of the mythological assumption that "every stranger was a potential magical antagonist."[36] While neither European sources nor Wabanaki traditions expose adequately the moral impact of the early contact years on the Wabanaki societies, they do indicate generally the Wabanakis' internal struggle to deal constructively with a greatly expanded world. Both French and English documents report widespread warfare between the Algonkians and the Iroquois of the St. Lawrence River valley,[37] and even among the Algonkians of coastal New England and Atlantic Canada intertribal hostilities predominated.[38] Although these events cannot be precisely reconstructed, Penobscot Wabanaki traditions suggest that internal disagreements were as important as intertribal economic competition for control of the

European fur trade.[39] Until European contact, Penobscot traditions relate, Wabanaki shamans had "never showed among themselves any other kind of feeling only that was kind and brotherly;"[40] thereafter shamanistic rivalries rent the moral unity of the Wabanaki peoples.[41]

In their initial effort to gauge the nature of the European intruders, the Wabanaki chose some noted shamans "to watch the strange people's movements." The selection of these observers unfortunately sparked vicious disagreements among the Wabanaki; shamans who had not been chosen for public service succumbed to jealousy, and they "began to agitate the minds of their friends to discord, each of them having a large influence among the people, [and] the whole country was thrown into different bands." Ignoring their elders who "advised peace and harmony," the disappointed shamans moved aggressively against their rivals, despite No-chi-gar-neh's warning that power abused would be lost.[42] Among the Kennebec Wabanaki the shamans not only used their powers to kill the English settlers of the 1607 Popham colony, they also threatened to inflict sickness on any of their countrymen who collaborated with the newcomers.[43]

The third age of Wabanaki history thus began with the people divided, with intense shamanistic rivalries, and with the fundamental principles of power violated. To their own way of thinking, precisely these departures from tradition made the Wabanaki especially vulnerable to two external contact factors, liquor and disease, which added to the inexorable erosion of the kinship solidarity that Gluskap had taught. Admittedly, the Wabanaki were physiologically incapable of resisting European diseases but, had they been morally united, they might have weathered the crisis of faith that followed. Although many people morally resisted, the traditionalists could not challenge the personal and social disruptions that sickness and drinking unleashed. The illnesses, they knew, were symptomatic of their moral decline, and drinking was a vivid pantomime of the larger, internal social disorders. After European settlement, the Wabanaki became more aware of violations of their mythically based social order and increasingly reeled before the consequences.

Wabanaki religious traditions played a crucial role in defining their experience of post-contact crisis. The religious principles of social solidarity, although honored largely in the breach, still provided the fundamental criteria by which the Wabanaki understood their collective struggle. The Kennebecs realized that European contact directly threatened their charter social values, but they were also uneasily aware of their own responsibility for their shaky moral condition. Shamanistic rivalries abrogated the mythic principles of benevolent power, while many of the people themselves succumbed to self-interested aggrandizement. It is also true that their traditions oriented the Kennebecs toward scrutinizing Europeans for evidence of hostility that may have unleashed the epidemic illnesses that beset them after 1616. The priests of the Society of Jesus figured centrally in this critical assessment of European power.

During the 1630s, the Jesuits began to develop a word-of-mouth reputation among the various Algonkian peoples as the tribes speculated on the priests' nature, and their potential for good or evil. Opinion about their power was by no means uniform, especially among the St. Lawrence Montagnais, who bore the first brunt of missionary contact. Frequently, the priests offended traditional religious beliefs and drew upon themselves the wrath of Montagnais shamans.[44] Sometimes, however, the Montagnais glimpsed within the Jesuits' grasp a kind of power that was as benign as it was potent. Rumors of this second, positive power also engaged the Wabanakis' attention. Early in the 1640s, a few prominent Kennebecs visited the Montagnais mission in Canada, embraced Catholic belief, and returned to their people with an optimistic appreciation of the Jesuits' message.[45] The Kennebecs' interest in the Montagnais missions reflects one aspect of their self-assessment, but their request for their own priest represents their deepening concern. The Jesuits sympathized with the Wabanakis' purposes and sent Father Gabriel Druillettes to winter among them.[46] Although Druillettes catalyzed the Kennebecs' first experiment in cultural adaptation, they themselves deliberately controlled the direction of religious change.

Kennebec Wabanaki society in the 1640s needed to rejuvenate the social integrity which they understood to be the source of healing power, and there was much urgency to their investigation of the priests' putative stature as ritual specialists. While it is unclear what the early Wabanaki converts thought of their new faith, the tribe's intention in asking for a priest in 1646 was serious and practical enough to warrant an abrupt, if temporary, reorientation of lifestyle. Through their Christian kinsmen, the Kennebecs offered to refrain from their usual pattern of winter hunting on their individual family hunting territories and, instead, to remain at their village to evaluate a priest's teachings. This offer to alter residential patterns is remarkable because the Kennebecs could not easily support so many people concentrated in one place; hunting was difficult in February snows, and starvation commonly stalked even the dispersed family groups. The Kennebecs felt, however, that extreme measures were warranted: in the spring of 1646, "a malady which caused vomiting of blood had destroyed a good part of their nation."[47] The Kennebecs' appeal for a priest came from a people who were pushed to the brink of physical and psychic survival.

It was more than fortuitous that Gabriel Druillettes' purposes intersected with those of the Kennebecs. Appreciating the moral crisis that mass sickness created, Druillettes non-verbally communicated his intentions, "winning their souls," the *Jesuit Relations* later said, "through the care he gave their bodies."[48] Druillettes began at once to learn the Wabanaki language, and he visibly attended the sick. Druillettes gave them whatever medical assistance was possible, taught Christianity to the extent that he could verbally communicate, and, only when a death seemed inevitable, would he baptize an Wabanaki. These actions established the priest's credentials: his selflessness was manifest in all that he did. Although the Kennebecs were still unsure about the practical powers of this man, they did not fear him. Unlike many Canadian Indians who had preceded them in exploring the utility of Christianity, the Kennebecs did not identify baptism itself as a killing agent.[49] Among the Wabanaki some of the baptized persons defied Druillettes' medical judgment; that a few survived rebounded to the priest's credit because their families "published everywhere that prayer was good, and that it had cured their children."[50]

Druillettes' ministry was a matter of deliberate design—partly of his own doing and partly the result of the Jesuits' overall experience among the Algonkians. The priests realized that they could win Algonkian allegiance by carefully controlling their personal behavior to express their general, supportive intent. Druillettes, for example, acted confidently as a "master" whenever moral issues of "Christian truths" were involved, and he posed as a thoughtful "scholar" while learning the Wabanaki language and general values.[51] These personal stances lent substance to Druillettes' words after he had learned to speak the Kennebecs' language. While still mute, the Jesuit's seeming spontaneity declared his quiet assurance and underlined his apparent tolerant humility.

Although Druillettes did not understand the mythological criteria the Kennebecs used to judge him, the priest acted as the man of power they expected him to be.[52] Even before his verbal ministry began, the Kennebecs compared him favorably with their shamans. These medicine men and religious leaders, the Jesuit knew, were his only organized opposition. Druillettes shrewdly evaluated the shamans' traditional social roles, and reversed them to his own advantage. Knowing that shamanistic services did not include assiduous nursing (indeed, Jesuits claimed that Algonkians abandoned the terminally ill), and did require payment, the priest lavished care and eschewed grateful gifts. "This man is different from our Jugglers," the Kennebecs marveled. "The latter are always asking, and the former never asks anything; the latter are almost entirely absent from our sick, but the former spends days and nights with them." They noted approvingly that Druillettes was self-effacing; whenever he was given some choice bit of food, "he straightway carries it to our sick."[53]

In this manner Druillettes undermined the prestige of the Kennebec shamans and belief in their powers. He proved himself to be more selfless than the medicine men because the Kennebecs understood that beneficial power rested in manifest social concern. And, although the priest certainly provoked the shamans' opposition,[54] even they succumbed to his presence. One shaman, for example, became sick and sent for the Jesuit, "assuring him that he wished to believe and to pray in earnest."[55] Druillettes spent time with the man and, thinking him to be on the verge of death, baptized him. Sometime later, it occurred to Druillettes to demand the shaman to surrender his "drum and his charms." The man recovered as soon as they were destroyed. The medical effect of the destruction also spelled doom for shamanistic power. Frank G. Speck noted the essential role drums played in shamanistic ritual. The word for "shaman" means "the sound of drumming."⁵⁶ Dr. Peter Paul amplifies Speck's observation in explaining that the root meaning of the word "drum" refers to the act of begging, or beseeching the powers for help. Thus, the Kennebecs freshly appreciated the Jesuit's power. Druillettes' shamanic pose was successful because he identified correctly the Kennebecs' sense of crisis; he also offered seemingly effective techniques that operated within the Wabanakis' most tenaciously held opinions about the religious forces behind their troubles. As the Kennebecs later said of Druillettes: "He is not a man; he is a Nioueskou', that is a Spirit, or an extraordinary Genie."⁵⁷ The testimony of the *Jesuit Relations* is given even more weight in Dr. Peter Paul's observation that the term "Nioueskou'" means one who is blessed or holy.

Druillettes proffered a message that the Kennebecs could recognize. The priest seemed the more remarkable to them in that he acquired their language with more ease than visiting Algonkians.⁵⁸ Although impressive, Druillettes' feat was founded on a thorough knowledge of other Algonkian dialects, and that experience tempered his speech. He frankly declared that he was among the Kennebecs to bring them religious knowledge that they lacked and he insisted ethnocentrically that they must acknowledge the importance of "him who created them" in their daily affairs.⁵⁹

On behalf of "he who created them," and "in token of their goodwill," the priest demanded three things from the Kennebec people. First, he asked that they give up drinking liquor, which they promised to do and, Druillettes said, "have fairly well kept their word." Second, he required them to live peacefully with one another. Within their family groups the Kennebecs lived harmoniously enough but, the priest observed, "as one sees in France, between two cities or hamlets . . . , there may be seen also in this part of our America small envies between the various districts of the Savages." Druillettes further demanded "that they should throw away their Manitou,—or, rather, their Demons, or fantastic charms." Here the confrontation with the shamans aided the Jesuit: "Those who had some of these charms, or Manitous, drew them from their pouches; some cast them away, others brought them to the Father."⁶⁰ These requirements enlivened the Kennebecs' sense of crisis in the 1640s because the concept of a unitary God—He-Who-Made-All—confirmed their belief in pervasive personal power.

Just as concretely, Druillettes identified the Kennebecs' intimations of responsibility for their own social difficulties.⁶¹ The priest explicitly related sickness to sin, and sin he identified with the social disruptions of alcohol. It is a pragmatic measure of the Kennebecs' desperation, and of their appreciation of Jesuit authority, that they accepted their inability to deal with illnesses through traditional means. Druillettes taught them that "He-Who-Made-All" opposed the evil beings who worked through the entire shamanistic power complex. Significantly, Druillettes went beyond condemnation; he also taught them that prayer transformed even death itself into triumph. The Christian Montagnais had warned the Wabanaki that post-contact sickness was an earthly reflection of the hellfire they drew upon themselves forever. Prayer, abstinence from drinking, quiet submission to adversity, and the practice of social restraint were, Druillettes taught, eloquent affirmations of a reestablished religious solidarity which the tribe then lacked.

On his first visit the priest remained among the Kennebecs only during the winter of 1646–47. Yet when Druillettes returned in 1650, he found abundant evidence that his teachings had taken root. Many Wabanaki assured him that prayer was powerful; even in the priest's absence, the Kennebecs continued to recite the prayers that Druillettes had taught them. They, in turn, had taught each other and had invented methods to remember the ritual imagery of Catholicism.[62] Druillettes accepted Kennebec testimony that they were devoted to Christ; in fact, far more complex processes were involved in what the priest saw as their conversion.

It is clear that the Jesuit had engendered a religious revival among the Kennebecs, but their protests of devotion to prayer actually illustrate the way Druillettes reinforced their traditional beliefs. Druillettes may have consciously blended Christian and traditional religious practices. On his 1650 journey, for example, Druillettes' party ran into difficulty and found themselves without provisions. The priest offered a Mass to save them: "The Father, seeing his people in this extreme destitution, had recourse to the God of men and animals,—offering him the sacrifice of his Son in those great forests; and conjuring him by the Blood shed by him for those people, to succor them in their necessity."[63] As the imagery used in this statement powerfully declares, priest and shaman barely differed. Just as Druillettes finished the Mass, a Wabanaki hunter returned with news that he had killed three moose. Uninterested in issues of theological abstraction, the Wabanaki drew the obvious conclusion from Druillettes' behavior as they told their people: "When we were on the point of dying from hunger, he prayed for us; and he who is the master of all the animals gave us meat, more than we needed for the rest of our journey."[64] Nor was this an isolated example of a significant overlap between Jesuit and Wabanaki religiosity. Among the Kennebecs, Christian prayers substantiated traditional hunting values. One old man told the Jesuit: "This winter I have killed four Moose which I hunted down; I have slain two Bears, and put to death a good many small Deer. I think unceasingly of him who made all things; I often speak to Jesus, and he strengthens and comforts me."[65]

Druillettes' teachings undermined traditional shamanism at the same time they produced an evolved form of medical practice; if this was conversion, it was of a remarkably traditional character. Several Kennebecs testified that they continually repudiated the shamans when they tried to cure sick individuals. But more to the point, Druillettes learned that one man received the old shamanistic powers over sickness in new, Christian form. "His people told me," the Jesuit said, "that God often answered the prayers that he offered in behalf of sick persons, or for other purposes."[66] The pattern of religious revelation remained the same. Dreams and visions were as commonplace in Wabanaki experience after Druillettes' preaching as before. The dream symbols did sometimes become symbolically Christian: "Many of these good people," the priest related, "have assured me that their children, dying immediately after Baptism, had appeared to them from Heaven to encourage them to embrace the truths of Christianity."[67]

The indigenous nature of the Wabanakis' response to Catholicism deserves emphasis because their syncretic blending of religious imagery illustrates the voluntary pragmatism that governed all levels of the Wabanaki–French alliance. The Wabanaki missions were products of a fundamental cultural tolerance. Even Druillettes' condemnation of shamanism appears to be a more radical break for the Wabanaki than it actually was. Indeed, the priest's ridicule of shamanistic medicine merely confirmed conclusions the Kennebecs had already reached. The Wabanaki sought a priest in 1646 because it was woefully apparent that their shamans lacked the social integrity necessary to protect their community from cyclical disease; the surviving mythological traditions strongly suggest that the Kennebecs believed that the shamans themselves were responsible for the epidemics.

The religious alliance between the Wabanaki and the French developed because their religious sensibilities were compatible. What the priest identified as demonic forces, the Kennebecs had long recognized as malevolent other-than-human persons who worked through viciously anti-social shamans. When one Wabanaki avowed that Druillettes had driven "away by his orisons the Demon that wished to deprive me of my life,"[68] he merely admitted that prayer was more powerful, rather than different, than traditional medicine. The Kennebecs' conclusion about their situation and Druillettes' potential solution was intellectually conservative: "The Demon has laid waste our Country, because we did not know how we ought to have recourse to Jesus, who is his master."[69]

Druillettes himself had flexible expectations; he did not anticipate that the Kennebecs would become culturally French in accepting Christianity. Rather, he taught them that Christ wished only for their obedience in return for protection against manifold demons. "Thou dost bid us combat and resist the Demons that attack us," the Wabanaki told Druillettes. "They are many in number but their strength is diminishing from day to day, and our courage is increasing."[70] A complex demonology, in fact, became diagnostic of Wabanaki Catholicism: they believed that prayer gave them power to resist the demons of social enmity, of drunkenness, of perverse shamanism, and even of sickness.[71] A single example illustrates how the Kennebecs combined the two traditions of spiritual influences. They told Druillettes: "How many times have we seen persons in the last extremity, whom we thought bewitched, restored to health upon praying to him who is the master of all the Demons!"[72]

Two outstanding factors contributed to the Kennebecs' positive assessment of Jesuit power and underpinned their mutual adaptations. First, the Kennebecs' mythological traditions provided them with a clear view of the purposes and pitfalls of power. In this light, the devastating events of the early seventeenth century did not lead the Kennebecs toward repudiating their religious beliefs. To the contrary, they concluded only that their difficulties derived from the abuse of power, and they believed that the negative effects of such violations might be repaired. Second, their mythology defined the personal characteristics of socially constructive men of power. From this perspective Gabriel Druillettes' behavior conformed closely to the Kennebecs' expectations. In sum, the Kennebecs' traditions predisposed them to a pragmatic assessment of the religious realities that Druillettes concretely addressed.

THE RELIGIOUS ALLIANCE CONSOLIDATED

While the interaction of the Kennebecs and Gabriel Druillettes established substantial common ground, it did not lead directly to their conversion, even in the manner of their temporary religious reorientation of the 1640s and 1650s. Until 1675, neither the Jesuits nor the Kennebecs were prepared to explore their mutual religious interests. In the interim, the Jesuits learned a good deal about the practical limits of missionization, and the Kennebecs' communal crisis intensified. When the dialogue reopened in the 1670s, the Jesuits were ready to acknowledge the legitimacy of the Kennebecs' religious concerns in a manner that permitted flexible adjustment. The Kennebecs were also more inclined to take practical steps to begin social and religious reform because their consistently negative relations with the settlers of New England aggravated their internal differences. If their mythology predisposed the Kennebecs to evaluate the social consciousness of Europeans, that scrutiny also made the French seem unusually warm allies. By the third quarter of the seventeenth century, as their relations with New Englanders deteriorated, the Wabanaki turned increasingly to the Jesuits in an effort to comprehend and adjust to abrasive contact conditions.

The second stage of the Kennebecs' exploration of Catholicism came as an accidental effect of war. In 1675, extreme English phobic reactions to Indians inflamed a local conflict between the Wampanoag tribe and Plymouth Colony into a regional confrontation between Algonkians and Englishmen generally. Pressed by racist incidents and by arrogant English demands for their political subservience, the Wabanaki peoples found themselves fighting a defensive war. Most Wabanaki, and especially the Kennebecs and the Penobscots, sought uselessly to create an acceptable neutrality for themselves; failing to do so, many actually chose exile over involvement in the fighting. The misfortunes of war thus made the fugitive Wabanaki the nucleus of a burgeoning Jesuit mission.[73]

As it turned out, the French could not give the Wabanaki refugees much help. The summer of 1676 was a very hungry time. Yet the mutual acquaintance of the Wabanaki and the French created the basic foundation for a relationship that endured until the conquest of Canada in 1760: the nexus of shared religious expression bonded the Wabanaki-French alliance. In seeking refuge, said Father Jacques Vaultier piously, "they thus advanced, without realizing it, towards their own blessedness, in coming to the missionaries, who could not have gone to them in their own country."[74]

Actually, these Wabanaki were at first highly ambivalent about the mission. Having fled English violence, only to confront Jesuit demands that they repudiate their religious convictions and embrace the uncertain comforts of Catholicism, the exiles must have thought twice about the move to Canada. Their perplexity was probably severe; most of the refugees were elderly, and they would have chosen to leave their home territory as the least disruptive, and therefore the most attractive, response to the disastrous war. The Jesuits noted the Wabanakis' "impassive" and even "averse" attitudes to their teachings, but they also wondered aloud how "in a very short time there were few of them who did not come most regularly to the Church, night and morning."[75] It may be supposed that the aged Wabanaki responded as politely as they could, since they realized that they had no means to support themselves. But the Jesuits could provide too little support, and the Wabanaki gave considerable energy to voluntary Catholic activities. The Jesuits insisted that there was a marked change "in the morals of the majority of them," and pointed to the Wabanakis' rejection of shamanistic healing rites although many were ill in the summer of 1676. The missionaries also observed hopefully an uncharacteristic sobriety among the Wabanaki newcomers; although drunkenness was "their greatest failing, almost all of them usually abstained from it."[76]

Despite these promising indications, the Jesuits hesitated to baptize the Wabanaki at Sillery. They carefully tested the Wabanakis' resolve and inculcated whenever they could "a veritable Dread" of profaning their baptism and "of losing its graces."[77] Only young children and a few older persons were baptized, but the Jesuits included among them the Wabanaki sagamore Pirouakki. The headman's gentleness, judicious management of his people, and eloquence seemed to the priests excellent qualities of Christian persuasion among his people.[78]

The thirty Wabanaki refugees left the mission for their winter hunting in November 1676. A few Wabanaki returned the following spring, however, and the permanent mission began. The continuing war between the Wabanaki and Massachusetts provided one motivation for this new migration, but it is also probable that favorable reports from the first visitors contributed to the Wabanakis' positive esteem of the Jesuits. With a determination which amazed the priests, the Sillery Wabanaki traveled persistently between Maine and Quebec as they had in the 1640s, telling their relatives what they had learned of Christianity.[79]

At Sillery, the Wabanaki fell under the care and supervision of Father Jacques Bigot, who developed a thorough regimen of work and prayer to occupy the neophytes. The priests felt that it was unusual for Indian people to show such willingness to embrace Catholic and French ways; at least, the Jesuits repeatedly noted their docility. The Wabanaki catechumens aided Bigot in his regular duties, teaching each other, chiding backsliders, and providing for the community's material needs. One Wabanaki man, for example, took charge of teaching the young boys the catechism, Catholic prayers, and church music, while a woman was similarly responsible for the girls.[80]

For the Wabanaki, conversion meant a fundamental social revitalization, and they usually settled at Sillery in extended family groups. Relatives and friends of newcomers taught them the daily routine and the important rituals, and prepared them for baptism. These responsibilities were onerous because the Jesuits carefully examined each neophyte over an extended period. In general, the priests accorded the Wabanaki Christians unique praise: "We have never seen savages say their prayers with more sedateness and devotion, or whose Singing had been more touching or more harmonious." "There have been none," Bigot added, "who have prayed as devoutly as these."[81]

The *Jesuit Relations* indicate that the Wabanaki reacted more profoundly to Catholicism in the 1670s than they had in the 1640s. There is evidence that in both decades the Wabanakis' motivations were at base similar: they interpreted Catholicism within traditional religious understandings, and Jesuit warnings about the evil activities of demons struck a responsive chord. Catholicism also seemed efficacious in ensuring the success of the Wabanakis' hunting economy; probably no alien religion could have been encompassed unless it addressed the well-established mechanisms of reciprocal relations with animal persons.[82] Christianity dealt with chronic problems, like the impact of European diseases, by emphasizing the complex social dynamics that the Wabanaki had always recognized as the psychosomatic component of both individual and social malaise.

It appears that Catholicism addressed, or perhaps focused, the anxieties of Wabanaki life in the last quarter of the seventeenth century. Indian people feared Jesuit threats that they faced eternal damnation. It may be that their lives promised them too little hope, or Jesuit portrayals of hellfire were too reminiscent of the northeastern torture complex for Catholic symbols of damnation to be ignored. Whatever the reason, for the Wabanaki, as for other contemporary American Indian peoples, hell became a palpable reality that Jesuit pictures vividly conveyed.[83] Verbal and graphic depictions of unrelenting torment were a central part of missionization: the Wabanaki themselves hastened to show new arrivals visual evidence of the fate that awaited the recalcitrant.[84]

Trepidation about life after death, and about the right or wrong conduct that might win either relief or everlasting pain, characterized the Wabanaki experience at Sillery. That pervasive fear manifested itself on all levels of

Wabanaki life: birth, sickness, work, the need for social harmony, all were issues of intense concern.[85] One Wabanaki family, which the Jesuits considered exemplary, illustrates their heightened emotional experience at the mission. Two of the young men fell fatally ill (an extremely common event), and Jacques Bigot told them that they "must accept everything from the hand of God."[86] This family had a difficult time adjusting to the deaths because they worried that the young men were not animated by the appropriate Christian resignation which Bigot demanded. "Alas," they said of one of the sick men, "we fear for him because after his baptism He manifested some Chagrin at His illness."[87] Such scrupulous anxiety also typified these Wabanakis' struggle with their personal grief. After the young man's death, his grandmother and mother "Regarded As a great sin the Cries that Their Sorrow caused them to Utter from time to time."[88] The Jesuits aggravated these psychological confusions, because they regarded self-inflicted mortifications as proof of Christian virtue, and the women forcibly attempted to suppress their emotions.[89] When given permission, Bigot observed: "They treat Their Bodies so harshly that I have been surprised at it, and have often been alarmed at the Blows of the discipline that I have heard when they had withdrawn secretly to some Spot remote from their Cabins."[90]

The need for the Wabanaki to atone continually for their past offenses to placate the spiritual forces of vengeance which attacked them and their self-mortifications suggest how deeply they had internalized their own responsibility for post-contact cultural upheaval. This rationale, it should be observed, was embedded in Wabanaki traditions that related social discord to illness; the Jesuits deliberately affirmed this over-weaning sense of guilt to ensure Wabanaki submission to Christian order. The priests taught the Wabanaki a prayer that expresses the psychological uncertainties with which they grappled: "Jesus, may I see you in heaven; may I never be damned. Keep me from anger, from evil speaking, and from drunkenness. Save me from the evil Spirit."[91]

In entering the Canadian missions, the Wabanaki acknowledged their individual and collective stand against impending communal chaos. The Wabanaki found Catholicism attractive because its diagnosis of the severe problems that beset them seemed in accord with their mythological traditions about moral struggle. The war with the English in 1675–77 had thoroughly disrupted their hunting and agricultural economy, and the Jesuits offered them a community base that was far removed from the hostilities. But Catholicism also encouraged the Wabanaki to foster among themselves a reinvigorated tribal order because it provided them both a religious and a social critique of insidious alcoholism that traditional values alone had been unable to contain or eradicate.[92]

Still, the Wabanaki did not simply accept the Catholicism that the Jesuits presented. The rigid moral requirements of the missions provoked opposition, as did some of the diseases the priests could not prevent. Traditionalists hostile to the new way of life sometimes ridiculed and maltreated the Christians.[93]

These confrontations usually occurred over issues involving social changes that seemed unwarranted. The missionaries insisted on monogamy, for example, and although the Wabanaki generally agreed, one person asserted "that all those people would return to acadia if they were treated thus."[94] Similarly, diseases continued to devastate the Wabanaki, and the Jesuits reported that the older people, "both men and women, who hate Christianity, have represented to the christians that the reason why so great a number of them died at Sillery was, because they prayed."[95] This reasoning rested on an emerging conviction that European religious practices were directly responsible for the Wabanakis' gradual demise. Like the Montagnais who founded Sillery, the Wabanaki shared a profound sense that disease had a religious etiology. Unlike the first generation of Wabanaki in contact with Europeans, however, who remembered vividly the mythological warnings about the anti-social source of disease, the Sillery traditionalists were inclined to blame the Jesuits, rather than their own divisive tribal condition.

Yet the Christian Wabanaki had powerful forces of moral persuasion on their side because as the reputation of the Jesuit mission grew conversion to Catholicism followed kinship lines. The rare person accepted, or rejected, Christianity in isolation from his fellows. Entire families arrived from Maine and chose to settle permanently in New France. By June 1681, nearly a hundred Wabanaki had moved to Quebec, and in 1683, a new Wabanaki mission was established on the water route to the Kennebec.[96] By 1689, 600 Wabanaki resided in the Canadian missions.[97] The Wabanaki villages near French centers of population became what their summer villages had been long before European contact, the physical locus of economic and political life and the seasonal center of communal religious expression.

The voluntary nature of the Wabanaki migrations highlights the flexible cultural response of the Jesuit missionaries. Although the French government officially demanded a program of forced culture change to create red Frenchmen, the Jesuits advocated a much less radical policy.[98] They recognized that Catholic symbols embraced much of the Wabanakis' ingrained religiosity and they were therefore content, despite disgruntled political officials, to translate their liturgy into the Wabanaki language, and thus to supplement the aboriginal song and dance cycle. With Jesuit connivance, the Wabanaki remained culturally distinct.

The traditional character of Wabanaki Catholicism derives from their intellectual, as well as their emotional, assessment of both formative religions. It is sometimes stated that American Indian peoples responded to Catholicism mainly because the liturgy appealed to their aesthetic sense of color and sound.[99] This argument often begins with the statement that American Indians did not appreciate the theological distinctiveness of Christianity. In the Wabanakis' case, such statements threaten to devalue their discriminating sense of Catholicism as a system of vitally effective power. The argument relates, in fact, to colonial Puritan opinion that Catholics and Indians shared a deluded investment in perverse idolatry.[100] The Reverend John Williams, who witnessed a mission Mass in 1704, expressed the enduring image of the Catholic Wabanakis' mindless religious expression: "So I went in and sat down behind the door," Williams wrote, "and there saw a great confusion instead of gospel order. For one of the Jesuits was at the altar saying Mass in a tongue unknown to the savages, and the other between the altar and the door saying and singing prayers among the Indians at the same time saying over their Pater Nosters and Ave Marias by tale from their chaplets, or beads on a string."[101] Stunned by the differences in religious expression, Williams did not appreciate that the actual appeal of Catholicism for the Wabanaki lay in the manner it encompassed the search for communal well-being, which had always been the goal of their religious activity. While the Jesuits consciously worked within the Wabanakis' ceremonial sensibilities, there was more to mission ritual than met with eye or ear. Social life in the missions centered on the daily and weekly Mass, but the impact of Catholic symbolism pervaded all of Wabanaki culture: "He-Who-Made-All" ensured success in hunting, in agriculture, and in warfare. Patron saints, the use of medals and crucifixes as personal power objects, the placement of chapels in the fields, and community prayer—all represent elaborations of the traditional Wabanaki belief in a cosmos organized by conflicting, personalized powers.

MYTH AND HISTORICAL PROCESS

The Wabanakis' highly critical, and essentially conservative, response to Catholicism is reflected in a wide variety of traditional accounts that further indicate the evolution of their religious beliefs. While it is still uncertain whether the aboriginal Algonkians believed in a supreme deity, by the twentieth century the Wabanaki acknowledged a Great Being who, in their usage, combines traditional attributes and the powers of the Christian Holy Spirit.[102] Similarly, they recognize an evil spirit, and their concept of the underworld, originally peopled with several classes of hostile beings, is now associated with their idea of hell.[103] There is some evidence that shamanism and Catholicism have continued to be seen as antithetical systems of power. Although shamans still operated in the nineteenth century, and in the present as well, their powers now seem to be relatively divorced from the processes of community life.[104]

Perhaps the most dramatic evidence of Wabanaki responses to Catholicism, and of their overall response to Euramerican contact, is found in accounts about Gluskap. Taken together, these syncretic mythological treatments indicate the basic flexibility of Wabanaki traditions, but they also emphasize a fundamental conviction that Gluskap remains at the center of Wabanaki history.[105] One creation myth observes that the Great Spirit "made Adam out of earth but he did not make Gluskabe." Instead, "Gluskap made himself out of dust that was kicked up in the creation of Adam," although he could not speak until the Great Spirit "opened his lips." The Great Spirit may have been responsible for the creation of the world, but he heeded Gluskap's advice about its ultimate arrangement.[106] Another account asserts the basic equality between Gluskap and Christ: in a contest of power Gluskap matched Christ's magical feats.[107] A Mi'kmaq and a Penobscot source ascribe Gluskap's creation to Christ, but their assessment of Gluskap's character is in harmony with mythological traditions. The Mi'kmaq example has Gluskap as Christ's first created being who then fabricates as always the Mi'kmaq's moral order. It also describes Adam, who is second-man, as the father of both European peoples and of evil in the world.[108] In the Penobscot case, Gluskap derived his strength from the Great Being, who made him responsible for teaching the people: "I will be thy teacher," the Great Being said, "and you will be their teacher."[109] Such mythological accounts demonstrate the Wabanakis' sense of the compatibility between Catholicism and their traditional religion. Dr. Peter Paul also explains the harmony between traditional beliefs and Catholicism when he reports that Gluskap was just like Jesus: they were both sent to improve the people's understanding of right and wrong and they both had similar missions for human well-being.

The mythological and folkloric accounts further expose the moral problems which Europeans posed, and which elicited the Wabanakis' religious and social adaptation. Penobscot traditions describe the racial differentiation of human beings and record Gluskap's prophecy that European peoples would compete for the Wabanakis' land and that the Wabanaki themselves would face many temptations. But Gluskap also anticipated the Wabanakis' adjustment to Christianity. The Europeans "will show you the things that caused the death of the Great Spirit," Gluskap declared, "and he will teach you to bow down to these things; and bow you may; but never forget that the Great Spirit is in the air, in the sun, moon, and in all things which your eyes can see—Here the teachings of Klose-kur-beh ended."[110] In departing this world, Gluskap apparently admitted the primacy of the Christian God, but there is still a widespread belief in Gluskap's continued existence and in his promise to return at some future time of need.[111]

Although this study of Wabanaki Catholicism has emphasized the reconstruction of their historical experience with the French Jesuits in the seventeenth century, the contribution of both mythological and folkloric traditions to that interpretation warrants further discussion. Historians often complain about the lack of authentic Indian voices in the overwhelming mass of Euramerican documents. Practically speaking, the information about mythically derived value orientations which Wabanaki traditions provide suggests that there is a body of peculiarly Indian testimony that still awaits study. The sheer extent of that literature is tremendous, including myth cycles and extensive collections of folklore, to say nothing about the vast number of anthropological treatments of religious culture and innumerable studies of specific rituals. If historians have found it difficult to separate themselves from the ethnocentric documentation of Indian-White relations, and if they have only begun to explore these uniquely Indian documents, it is also true that such sources represent the as yet untapped wealth that challenges us.[112]

The Wabanaki example of religious adaptation suggests the utility of a broad integration of American Indian traditions in historical work. Without the inclusion of their own sense of history expressed in their mythology and folklore—and this discussion of Kennebec religious change only suggests some possibilities—the Wabanaki response to European contact appears to be simply devastating and frantically accommodating. Like other Indian peoples, the Wabanaki were pushed to the brink of physical and moral survival. The Kennebecs had well-developed ideas about the causes of their crisis and about the religious techniques that might win respite from these difficulties. We can say, in general, that the continuity of Wabanaki pre- and post-contact history derives from their mythic, social traditions. Both the *Jesuit Relations* and Wabanaki folklore focus on the social principles of religious images of power. Combined, they make the Wabanakis' creative adaptations of central historical importance.

One of the most important contributions that American Indian traditions can make to our understanding of Indian experience is, then, the realization that those traditions created ethnocentric boundaries that tempered Indian-White relations. Seventeenth-century American Indian cultures were inward-looking, and their mythological traditions defined parameters of belonging and not-belonging. While Wabanaki traditions were parochial, they also permitted limited dialogue with foreigners. These Wabanaki oral traditions oriented them toward dealing with outsiders in ways which critically assessed both the moral character of the European strangers and encouraged their socialization. The inclusion of oral sources, therefore, directs the historian to examine intercultural activity as American Indian peoples themselves valued the exchange. Although the traditional accounts used in this study are without exception written documents, they are much closer to the actual tenor of Indian life than the official records which are the mainstay of Indian-White relations. Some Euramerican observers like the Canadian Jesuits did leave accurate descriptions of Indian life and behavior, entirely apart from the invariable fact that their emphases in those accounts are culturally skewed. The orally derived documents of the Wabanaki make such Euramerican descriptions of even greater value because they urge the historian to establish a balanced behavioral context within which the cultural foibles the priests expressed can be recognized and used to reassess comparative cultural problems in Indians' history.

The socially normative role that Wabanaki traditions played in their religious and cultural adaptation suggests further new, interdisciplinary historical concerns in the study of American Indian struggles. The mythic principles of

Wabanaki sociality provide a perspective on historical causality that is often lacking in Euramerican treatments of Indian history. Ethnological evidence strongly demonstrates that the Algonkian-speaking peoples did not have a materialistic sense of causality: they never asked *what* the causes of events were. Instead, they inquired systematically about *who* was responsible, and that is an essentially religious inquiry.[113] For the Wabanaki, this sense of social causality, and their concept of mythic power deriving from Gluskap's impeccable concern for people, were synonymous. Wabanaki mythology thus established a causal baseline that exposes their core cultural values[114] and, therefore, the direction of their history. Finally, the Wabanaki example of religious change suggests that neither tribal motivations nor European influences can be understood unless the perceptual, cognitive, and value orientations of Indian peoples inform the study of their particular historical experiences. The challenge of this larger task of plumbing American Indian realities demands an earnest dialogue among religious scholars, anthropologists, and historians.

5

Discourse and the Accommodation of Values

Toward a Revision of Mission History

By the early 1980s my research agenda had been set. My working hypothesis—that Algonkians oriented to reality in rigorously relational ways and that Euramericans did not—then engaged my attention. Algonkian stories of cannibal monsters, and especially the rich tales of transformer Gluskap, revealed the core values that informed Algonkian sociality and shaped their discernment of equally transformative, but manipulative, European newcomers. Neither victimization nor colonialism could explain the complexity of the encounter as it actually transpired in cooperative and conflicted relationships. While other scholars emphasized power relations and nativistic resistance (Ronda, Jaenen), I began to reconstruct the give-and-take of religious discourse.

I had begun to understand that what missionaries called "religion," and associated with Church, sacred texts, and ecclesiastical laws and social roles, had little to say about Algonkians' religious lives. Even missionaries began to temper their harsh dismissal of Algonkians as socially, linguistically, and religiously deficient. Learning Algonkian dialects and negotiating meaning with shockingly proud and incomprehensibly confident native peoples led the priests (if not other Europeans) to glimpse the ethical codes that Algonkians valued and expressed.

In a long conversation at the Newberry Library, Robert Berkhofer (see 1969) also affirmed my instinct to focus on the behavioral intersection of Algonkian and missionary sociality. Berkhofer pointed to a then emerging perspective—the sociology of knowledge—for methodological guidance, particularly for recognizing the unspoken social codes negotiated in all attempts at communication. In this way, what I had learned about Algonkian sociality led to a more nuanced understanding of missionization. At a time when historians and ethnohistorians argued either for or against missionaries as either positive or negative colonial agents (both views relegated native peoples to a passive and victimized position), my socio-linguistic perspective helped me to reconstruct missionization in the actual conversations and interactions in which religious meanings are always negotiated.

The success of new interpretations of Christian missions among Native American peoples depends on the quality of the documentary data and our ability to achieve an understanding rooted in Indian as well as Euramerican worldviews. We need sources that expose American Indian thought, and we require a cross-cultural hermeneutics capable of explaining Indian and missionary responses to each other. The need is clear, but achieving both goals is not always possible. Given the paucity of documents for many of the missions, it has been difficult to reconstruct the daily give-and-take out of which mission institutions developed. As a result, our understanding of recent theoretical developments has been thwarted. Historians have established the general patterns of mission history, but much remains to be understood about the interplay of Indian and missionary motives as they were expressed in particular mission situations.[1]

Only in the most general terms do we know that the personalities of the missionaries, their expertise in native languages, and their sensitivity to Native American values played a vital role. Similarly, it is only now becoming clear that Native Americans understood the encounter in traditional religious terms. They assessed missionaries for attributes that characterized their own religious practitioners, borrowed theological ideas and ritual practices selectively, and always followed practical purposes of their own.[2]

In brief, because we have come to recognize that missions were invariably attempts to achieve cross-cultural communication—missions had to express some agreement between Indians and missionaries—a new hermeneutical imperative has emerged. An ideal history of the missions would be able to reconstruct the process of religious dialogue, and sketch the motives for religious change, as a deliberate negotiation. In other words, a religious history of Christian missions seeks an understanding of religious communication as a crucial event in its own right. It also attempts to discover within the reconstructed dialogue the empathetic and ethnocentric factors that channeled shifting agreement and disagreement.

This chapter examines one situation in which detailed documents and interdisciplinary concerns with the study of religion intersect. It reconstructs the encounter during the early 1630s between Jesuit missionaries in New France and several Montagnais people who first drew the priests' concerted attention. In particular, the Canadian *Jesuit Relations* make it possible to attain what Clifford Geertz has termed a "thick description" of what Peter Berger would call the intersection between divergent sociologies of knowledge.[3] In time, the Montagnais chose to enter a mission village at Sillery, and this early dialogue exposes the misunderstandings that had first to be resolved. The *Jesuit Relations* relate a familiar scene: eager, idealistic, and self-assured missionaries were bent on convincing highly skeptical Native Americans to leave their errant ways for the truths of Christian and European life. The documents also show that communication between them was troubled because both parties found it difficult to discriminate between verbal and non-verbal behavior, between what was said and what was meant, between what was heard and what was understood. In this particular instance, rich sources, communication theory, and the sociology of religion can be brought together.[4]

There is no better illustration of the complexity of religious dialogue than that provided in the early *Jesuit Relations*. The *Relations* of 1632, 1633, and 1634 expose both the relative importance of communication and the critical techniques necessary to identify and read behind missionary bias. It is often stated that the *Jesuit Relations* were written with such partisan purposes that they are next to useless as historical documents capable of explicating the Indian point-of-view. It is known, for example, that the *Jesuit Relations* were published in France with the explicit purpose of celebrating missionary valor and of soliciting financial support for the Jesuits' work in Canada. From all appearances, they were successful in achieving those goals. It remains to be proven, however, that they consciously distorted the actual encounter between the Jesuits and Native American peoples. The Jesuits certainly expressed their own point-of-view, but their opinions also indicate how and why they both failed and succeeded in communicating with Native American people.

The *Relations* of 1632, 1633, and 1634 are particularly useful in exploring the problem of bias because they were written by a single man, Paul Le Jeune, superior of the Society of Jesus in New France. It is important to note that he wrote what became the first *Relation* simply as a report to his superior in Paris, without intending that it be published. Similarly, Le Jeune was unaware that his first letter had been published when he wrote the second *Relation*. He may have seen the book before he sent his 1633 account to Paris, but he did not have time to edit the diary he had already largely prepared. The *Relation* of 1634, however, was written with publication in mind. While the first two *Relations* were simply diaries in the form of letters, the *Relation* of 1634 was divided into chapters and was much more comprehensive in its treatment of Canadian affairs.[5]

Le Jeune himself assured his readers that his account was as faithful to the facts as it could be. In 1633, as if aware that his superiors would scrutinize the validity of his observations, Le Jeune introduced a note of caution. He wrote: "I have been told many different things about the customs of these tribes; we shall have time enough to learn how true they are."[6] A year later, he offered much more assurance. In the opening pages of the *Relation* of 1634 he explains that, in addition to the chronological arrangement used before (in this case, added to the end), his topical description of Montagnais people was based on direct experience. "All that I shall say regarding the Savages," Le Jeune wrote, "I have either seen with my own eyes, or have received from the lips of natives, especially from an old man very well versed in their beliefs, and from a number of others with whom I have passed six months with the exception of a few days, following them into the woods to learn their language."[7]

Another significant factor that allows a critical comparison of these early *Relations*, and that makes it possible to examine them for possible bias associated with publication, is Lucien Campeau's discovery of Paul Le Jeune's original manuscripts for the editions of 1632 and 1634. Campeau concluded after exhaustive comparison that few editorial changes were made to the handwritten text. He thus assures us of the printed integrity of Le Jeune's voice. As the following discussion indicates, Le Jeune made his personal bias a major theme of all the *Relations* he wrote. We would be unable to identify either the unshakeable elements of the priest's confidence, or his sometimes considerably confused judgments, if his manuscripts had been significantly altered.[8]

Le Jeune's outspoken style exposes his struggle against prejudice in learning how to communicate with the Montagnais, the Native Americans who first occupied the Jesuits' attention. More than this, Le Jeune's first three *Relations* are so candid that they quote Montagnais individuals at length about concerns that were certain to startle ethnocentric French readers. As a result, we can establish that the Montagnais, as well as the priests, had to contend with prejudice and their vocal objections indicate that Indians also found the encounter disturbing.

Since everything depended on their ability to communicate, language study occupied the Jesuits from the beginning of their work in New France. The task was difficult. In the first place, the priests had no reliable teachers. Some French individuals had learned something of Native American languages. It soon became apparent, however, that these men were hostile and unreliable; moreover, the Jesuits feared that they were morally unsuitable for the task. The interpreters worked among the tribes to further French commerce, and many demonstrated that they preferred a relatively footloose life among the Indians to close supervision by the Church. More seriously, the interpreters were not trained linguists, and their ability to communicate was hampered by the fact that a hybrid language, a patois of several Indian and French dialects, had become standard in Canada. While this mixed language served the purposes of trade, it was hardly able to convey either the complexities of Indian thought or the subtle mysteries of Roman Catholic faith and dogma. Still, the first Jesuits developed crude dictionaries, and a few Indians had been sent overseas to learn French. Then, just as this first experiment began, English traders seized temporary control of Canada in 1629.[9]

When the Jesuits returned to New France in the summer of 1632, they made a simple dictum the basis of their approach. "Faith," Paul Le Jeune contended, "enters by the ear."[10] The Jesuit superior declared from the outset that "any one who knew [the Indian] language could manage them as he pleased."[11] Since the dictionary they had inherited from their predecessors proved inadequate, the priests turned for assistance to a Christianized Montagnais who had been educated in France. Although Pierre Antoine Pastedechouan had lost much of his ability to speak Montagnais during his years away, by 1632 he had recovered the language so that he spoke it as well as French. But Pierre proved to be as intractable as the interpreters who worked as fur traders.[12]

Le Jeune thought that the man had reverted to barbarism and called him a renegade and the "Apostate." In actuality, Pierre was one of the first Native

Americans to be caught between cultures, and his experience illustrates that something more than language competency would be needed to communicate cross-culturally. Pierre stayed long enough among the French to learn a very real fear of the Christian God, but not long enough to replace his emotional ties to Montagnais ritual practice. Besides, during the three years in which the English controlled Canada, he had no choice but to somehow readjust to Montagnais life. When the Jesuits returned, Pierre attempted to live among them as they urged. Unfortunately, by that time everyone distrusted him. Ignorant of Montagnais hunting methods, scorned by his Indian wife, chided by the Jesuits for moral backsliding, Pierre met ridicule even from the kinfolk on whom he depended. Le Jeune explains: "He gave up Christians and Christianity, because he could not suffer the taunts of the Savages, who jeered at him occasionally because he was Sedentary and not wandering, as they were; and now he is their butt and their laughingstock."[13] Pierre Antoine was, in short, at home neither among his relatives nor among the French.

Although Le Jeune complained that Pierre was undependable, the priest learned enough Montagnais from him to appreciate something of the long-range challenge. Even only with intermittent study (which happened whenever Pierre sought temporary refuge from his kin), Le Jeune came to understand the need for linguistic relativism. In the 1620s, Father Charles Lalement considered the Montagnais language deficient and incapable of expressing spiritual ideas, but Le Jeune soon suspected that his judgment was premature. "This language is very poor and very rich," Le Jeune wrote after the first winter of study. "It is poor; because, having no knowledge of thousands and thousands of things which are in Europe, they have no names to indicate them. It is rich, because in the things of which they have a knowledge, it is fertile and plentiful."[14] So impressed was the priest that he came to a new appreciation of Montagnais humanity: "People may call them Barbarians as much as they please, but their language is very regular."[15] He also learned that, since the Montagnais had a consensual society, eloquence would be a prerequisite of religious persuasion.

During his first year of language study, Pierre Le Jeune achieved many cultural insights that provide a glimpse into the documentary potential of all the *Jesuit Relations*. This reconstruction is possible only because the priest adopted a characteristic writing style. Throughout the *Relation* of 1633, Le Jeune reported his observations with careful attention to detail. He as often expressed his judgments of what he saw. These statements range from surprised approval to shocked contempt of Montagnais customs and, therefore, reveal the boundary between Le Jeune's preconceptions and Canadian realities. As famous as it has become, Jesuit cultural relativism was not born full grown.

The depth of Le Jeune's 1633 report is remarkable. On the surface, the *Relation* recounts the historical situation of Canada in 1632–33, reporting the details of French and Indian commercial alliance, describing intertribal war with its attendant anxieties, and sketching starkly the famine that afflicted the Montagnais. At a second level, the *Relation* catalogues the manifold cultural differences that complicated Montagnais relations with the French. Le Jeune notes that the Montagnais rejected authoritarian government and scorned the coercive methods the French used to achieve social order. The priest also reveals that, while the Montagnais had substantial military and economic purposes for seeking an alliance with the French, their goals went far beyond strategic considerations. The Montagnais sought the kind of religiously grounded solidarity with the French that they enjoyed among their own relatives. They expected mutual courtesy and hospitality. Le Jeune observes that the Montagnais were disappointed because French economic individualism seemed to make such an alliance impossible. Although he felt that the Montagnais were profligate and grasping, the priest also sensed that Montagnais contempt for French notions of property might be justified. The Indians accused the French of loving their property: "When you refuse anything to a Savage, he immediately says *Khisakhitan*, 'Thou lovest that,' *sakhita, sakhita*, 'Love it, love it;' as if they would say that we are attached to what we love, and that we prefer it to their friendship."[16] During this first year, then, Le Jeune discovered that the Montagnais were unimpressed with his assumption that the French were economically and politically superior.

He found that the Montagnais were as religiously self-assured, but here the priest was less inclined to compromise. All was superstition, and especially dreams because these often urged the Montagnais to kill the French on sight. It mattered little that Indians insisted on the reality of their dreams despite Le Jeune's protest that he would be able to prove their folly after he learned the Montagnais language. Le Jeune admits that he scoffed at such beliefs and is equally candid about his failure to convince the Montagnais that their assumptions about reality were ridiculous. The priest was simply told that "all nations had something especially their own; that, if our dreams were not true, theirs were; and that they would die if they did not execute them."[17] "The savages agree very readily with what you say," Le Jeune wrote, "but they do not, for all that, cease to act upon their own ideas."[18]

The priest did sense with some optimism that the Montagnais had a knowledge of God, and he specifically argued against common reports to the contrary. He said too that they had some confused sense of the existence of the soul. He was more alarmed with Montagnais shamans, taking seriously the possibility that they could communicate with the devil. While the average Montagnais seemed willing to converse about religious realities, the shamans proved intransigent. When Le Jeune denounced the use of music and song in curing rituals, he was ignored. "That is very good for you people," one shaman rejoined; "but, for us, it is thus that we cure our sick." Admitting that he did not really know what he called Montagnais "secrets," Le Jeune declared at the end of his 1633 *Relation*: "Time is the father of truth."[19]

Time had lessons to teach. In 1633–34, Paul Le Jeune confronted the fact that effective communication was more than a function of spoken language.

During that winter, Le Jeune placed himself in a situation that made him totally dependent on the good will of the Montagnais. The priest decided that he needed to travel with a Montagnais band in order to learn their language. Significantly, he thought that linguistic competence would make dialogue possible. Reading between the lines of the *Relation* of 1634 makes it clear that Le Jeune was largely unaware that the Montagnais had their own code of proper social discourse. Since the priest did not recognize the existence of this social code, it is equally apparent that Le Jeune continually flouted Montagnais expectations concerning proper behavior. He thereby effectively communicated his social incompetence. Under such circumstances, the priest had considerable difficulty impressing the superiority of Christianity on his Montagnais critics.

Le Jeune thought that the Montagnais would accommodate themselves to his cultural expectations. He hinted to Pierre Antoine that he wished to spend the winter with him, knowing full well that the decision had to be made by Pierre's brothers. The brothers discussed the possibility, and Carigonan, who was a shaman, visited to extend their invitation. Carigonan told Le Jeune "that he loved good men, because he himself was good, and had always been so from his early youth." Moreover, the shaman indicated that he was interested in Le Jeune's religion, asking him "if Jesus had not spoken to me about the disease which tormented him. 'Come,' said he, 'with me, and thou wilt make me live now, for I am in danger of dying.'"[20]

In responding, Le Jeune made a series of mistakes that would trouble him all winter. The priest immediately rebuffed Carigonan's offer in a way which non-verbally communicated that he considered the shaman not only a rival but also "a very impudent fellow."[21] Although Le Jeune apparently understood that the four brothers and their families constituted a single band, he treated Carigonan's offer as though it came from him alone. "I refused him as gently as I could," Le Jeune wrote.[22] He also observed that Carigonan resented the rejection "because he saw that I cared more for my host, his younger brother, than I did for him."[23] Le Jeune then approached Pierre Antoine and changed his hinted desire into three demands. He required that the band remain on the north side of the St. Lawrence River, that Carigonan be excluded from the hunting party, and that Pierre would teach him the language.

Le Jeune later claimed that the brothers were faithless in that they did not fulfill any of his conditions. In fact, Le Jeune himself had failed to understand the social values of Montagnais life. Under the winter famine conditions that prevailed—conditions Le Jeune had described at length the year before—it would have been suicidal for the Montagnais to limit themselves to the territory that the missionary insisted upon. It would have been equally disastrous to attempt hunting without the ritual skills of Carigonan. Finally, Le Jeune's expectation that Pierre Antoine would teach him the language indicates that he knew little of the band politics to which he and the interpreter would have had to adjust. Since Pierre was a misfit by Montagnais standards, he found it wise to conform. In particular, Pierre protected himself from the hostility of his relatives by allying himself with Carigonan. Le Jeune had aroused the shaman's hostility, so Pierre had to keep his distance lest he offend his mentor.[24]

Starting out on the wrong foot as he did, it quickly became plain to all the Montagnais that Le Jeune was even more incompetent than Pierre Antoine. The priest was dead weight in a situation where the margin for survival was slim. Le Jeune refused to adapt and, with the exception of providing some food that helped at the beginning of the journey, contributed nothing to the band's resources. In fact, the opposite was true. Since the band camped in no less than twenty-three places throughout the winter, much labor was expended in travel.[25] Everyone shared the burden, except for Le Jeune. As he himself admitted: "All the Savages made sport of me because I was not a good pack horse, being satisfied to carry my cloak, which was heavy enough; a small bag in which I kept my little necessaries; and their sneers, which were not as heavy as my body; and this was my load."[26] The priest also demonstrated that he could not be trusted, as on the day when he wandered off the trail leading to the next camp. In his panic at being lost, Le Jeune abandoned a young child who had fallen into his care.[27]

To compound an already bad situation, Le Jeune continually communicated his contempt for the people on whom he depended. The priest was a master of ridicule. He constantly badgered the Montagnais, especially for their religious orientation to hunting, which to their mind ensured their survival. For example, Le Jeune intruded against Montagnais wishes in the most sacred of their ceremonies: "I had always shown my amusement at this superstition."[28] Le Jeune witnessed a shaking tent ritual in which a Montagnais shaman consulted with other-than-human persons on whom the band depended for good health and successful hunting. The priest reported that he had been "forbidden to speak; but as I had not vowed obedience to them, I did not fail to intrude a little word into their proceedings. Sometimes I begged them to have pity on this poor juggler [shaman], who was killing himself in this tent; at other times I told them they should cry louder, for the Genii had gone to sleep."[29] Le Jeune often pretended respectful interest to get the Montagnais to reveal their religious secrets. The Montagnais understood his actual motives because the priest frequently laughed at their religious claims in order to make "them see that the mysteries of the sorcerer were nothing but child's play."[30]

Le Jeune felt that he could shame the Montagnais into heeding his teachings. He could not have been more mistaken. The priest's combative temperament drew continual fire from Carigonan, who bore the brunt of Le Jeune's testy criticism. "I did not lose any opportunity . . . ," the Jesuit wrote, of "exposing the senselessness of his superstitions. Now this was like tearing his soul out of his body; for, as he could no longer hunt, he acted the Prophet and Magician more than ever before."[31]

In all of these confrontations, the Montagnais defended the integrity of their religion. Invariably, they turned the table on the priest. "Thou art an ignoramus, thou hast no sense," they answered.[32] Le Jeune felt that he had learned very little of the Montagnais language, but he managed to understand a variety of Montagnais insults. Among these, the following tell a significant story: "Shut up, shut up, thou hast no sense"; "He is proud"; "He is haughty"; "He looks like a Dog."[33] In effect, the Montagnais applied considerable social pressure to stem the priest's abrasive behavior, but he failed to comprehend the meaning of their insults.

It is significant for understanding the deliberate character of Le Jeune's provocations that the priest knew that the Montagnais shunned all direct expressions of anger. In fact, he noted that they feared that an angry person had so lost control that he might threaten the lives of his kin. As Le Jeune put it: "I have only heard one Savage pronounce this word, *Ninichcatihin*, 'I am angry,' and he only said it once. But I noticed that they kept their eyes on him, for when these Barbarians are angry, they are dangerous and unrestrained."[34] It is all the more remarkable, therefore, that Le Jeune needled Carigonan at every opportunity. Le Jeune noted that the shaman prided himself on his ability to control his temper. Carigonan "is more haughty than any other Savage," Le Jeune claimed, but noted that "it is true also that he often restrains and governs himself by force, especially when I expose his foolishness."[35]

Carigonan held his own against the Jesuit's taunts because he successfully demonstrated to his relatives that the priest did not share their values. On the one hand, for example, Le Jeune openly accused the shaman of being covetous in the extreme. On the other, Carigonan knew that the priest shared individualistic French notions of private property and he exposed Le Jeune's selfishness for all to see: "I had nothing that he did not ask me for, often taking my mantle off my shoulders to put it on his own. Now as I could not satisfy all his demands, he looked upon me with an evil eye; indeed, even if I had given him all the little I had, I could not have gained his friendship, because we were at variance on other subjects."[36] Despite the fact that Le Jeune had come to admire the sharing that typified Montagnais attitudes toward property, he did not sense the telling criticism that Carigonan consistently lodged against him.

One day, after the priest promised to help the Montagnais improve the material circumstances of their lives, Carigonan openly scoffed: "See how boldly this black robe lies in our presence." Stung by this declaration, Le Jeune asked for an explanation. "Because," said Carigonan, "we never see in this world men so good as thou sayest, who would take the trouble to help us without hope of reward, and to employ so many men to aid us without taking anything from us." "If thou shouldst do that," he added, "thou wouldst secure the greater part of the Savages, and they would all believe in thy words."[37] The Jesuits eventually understood Carigonan's challenge; for the moment, Le Jeune continued to hold his personal property tightly. The Montagnais wanted the priest to share his tobacco, but he held out: "The Sorcerer was so annoying in his demands for it, that I could not endure him; and all the others acted as if they wanted to eat me, when I refused them."[38]

The mutual distaste between the priest and shaman became hotly political as the winter passed and famine conditions set in. Le Jeune attempted to persuade the Montagnais to repudiate their shaman but had little success. Two reasons explain the priest's failure. First, since he did not understand the Montagnais' kinship politics, he did not sense that he had branded himself an outsider. Second, Pierre Antoine (whom Le Jeune badgered no less than he did Carigonan) did all in his power to undermine the Jesuit's religious claims. Both of these factors operated on one occasion when the Montagnais were particularly hard pressed for food. Since Carigonan had not located game, the Jesuit convinced the band members to pray to his God for assistance. A very successful hunt followed immediately. Unfortunately, Le Jeune so offended the Montagnais that Pierre Antoine and Carigonan were able to argue that the priest actually endangered their welfare.[39]

Although he claimed that his prayers had assisted them in the hunt, Le Jeune showed great disdain when the Montagnais prepared to celebrate in their traditional manner. They held what Le Jeune called an "Eat-all" feast, a ritual which subsequent ethnological reports show was an essential religious act of Montagnais culture. Simply put, the Montagnais consumed a large quantity of food at the feast in order to honor the animals who had given their lives and to maintain good relations with the animals' master. Le Jeune knew something of the Montagnais' religious understanding of these acts, but he still attacked the ritual directly. "God," he declared, "forbids such excess."[40]

Disgusted with this interference, Pierre Antoine told the others "that God was angry because they had something to eat." Le Jeune then compounded his original error. He threw meat to the dogs even though he knew that he would thereby offend the animals. Le Jeune describes the Montagnais' horrified reaction: They "commenced to cry out against me, saying that I was contaminating their feast, that they would capture nothing more, and that we would die of hunger. When the women and children heard of this afterward, they looked upon me as a very bad man, reproached me disdainfully, and saying that I would be the cause of their death; and truly, if God had not granted us anything for a long time, I would have been in danger of being put to death for having committed such a sacrilege, to such an extent does their superstition go."[41] Thereafter, whenever hunting went badly, Pierre pointed his finger at Le Jeune's ill-will. "The God who is sorry when we eat," he told the frustrated hunters, "is now very glad that we have not anything to dine upon."[42]

Throughout the *Relation* of 1634, Paul Le Jeune castigated Carigonan and Pierre Antoine for their hostility. To his mind, they were religious adversaries who perversely opposed him; he thought that they feared the superiority of Christianity. The opposition of Carigonan and Pierre was real enough, but Le

Jeune's detailed description of his encounters with them reveals that they had good reasons for their enmity. Both shaman and ex-Christian knew that Le Jeune's religion threatened to disrupt Montagnais life. In his self-assured refusal either to respect Montagnais religion or to adjust to their social mores, Le Jeune revealed, albeit inadvertently, the ethnocentric assumptions with which both the Jesuits and Indians would have to deal.

But Montagnais resistance against Jesuit arrogance is not the whole story. It is significant that even in this first close contact, dialogue between the priest and some Montagnais began to create the possibility of eventual mutuality. For example, Mestigoït, the band headman, held himself aloof from the altercations that surrounded Le Jeune. Just as important, in his dialogue with Mestigoït, Le Jeune refrained from his usual ridicule; instead, he maintained careful relations with the headman, who responded tolerantly to the priest's inability to adapt to Montagnais life. Both men were also pragmatic in matters of religion. Since they avoided sparring on theological issues, they spent many hours comparing French and Montagnais cultures. These discussions make the *Relation* of 1634 the first comprehensive account of Montagnais material culture, religious values, and social behavior.

The discourse with Mestigoït that Le Jeune recorded also highlights more positively the same issues of communication that polarized Le Jeune's relations with Carigonan and Pierre Antoine. Mestigoït urged the priest to relax, advising him when he fell sick to overcome the psychological trauma of the Montagnais hunting lifestyle. "Do not be sad," Mestigoït counseled; "if thy sickness increases thou wilt die." Mestigoït urged Le Jeune to respond to adversity as the Montagnais did: "See what a beautiful country this is; love it; if thou lovest it, thou wilt take pleasure in it, and if thou takest pleasure in it thou wilt become cheerful, and if thou art cheerful thou wilt recover."[43] In addition to attempting to ease the Jesuit's psychosomatic reactions to culture shock, the headman promised to approach Le Jeune with a comparable flexibility: "I will believe thee when thou shalt know how to speak; but we have now too much trouble in understanding each other."[44] In his behavior toward the priest, moreover, Mestigoït also indicated that successful communication involved more than linguistic competence.

In the end, while Le Jeune admitted that he spoke Montagnais poorly, he did not grasp the fact that his social indiscretions had turned most of the Montagnais against him. Still, his *Relation* of 1634 indicates that he had achieved a remarkable grasp of the structure of the language, even if his speech remained as confused as his behavior. In one of his chapters, Le Jeune detailed what he had learned of Montagnais grammar. He even observed that Montagnais differed from European languages in its basic assumptions about the nature of reality.

Specifically, Le Jeune described (without appreciating its implications) what is now called the linguistic category of the animate. The Jesuit noted that the Montagnais categorized as persons entities Europeans regarded as mere things—hail, for example. Le Jeune did not know it, but this discovery held the key for understanding what he could only regard as the Montagnais' superstitious actions. The Montagnais considered communication not only vital among human beings, but also among themselves, the animals, and many other-than-human persons. Throughout the *Relation* of 1634, the Jesuit described many instances where the Montagnais reacted to the natural world in such a personalistic manner. For them, ritual and hunting were essentially acts of communication. But for the priest the animate features of Montagnais thought remained a linguistic category rather than a reflection of their ontology and an explanation of the religious character of their life.[45]

The *Jesuit Relations* thus reveal how the study of communication can throw new light on the clash and accommodation of values that occurred within the missions. Specifically, Le Jeune's focus on dialogue highlights the questions of religious reality that were actually at contest between him and the Montagnais. Here it is necessary to appreciate that religion encompasses a good deal more than belief. Indeed, the idea that belief constitutes the core of religion can be dangerously misleading because it limits our attention to what may seem to be ineffable matters of faith. Of course, belief is an important aspect of religion, but as Carigonan declared to Le Jeune, faith is grounded in an entire worldview, which gives belief everyday substance.

This matter of mutual meaning, therefore, is the element of the cross-cultural encounter for which historical interpretations of the missions ought to strive. Increasingly, scholars of religion, who draw on the methods and findings of several disciplines, have recognized that religion is closely bound up with metaphysical, cognitive, psychological, and social realms of meaning. In this interpretative light, it can be seen that religion not only structures the most basic temporal and spatial orientations of people, but also encapsulates their existential and normative assumptions about the character of reality. Religions can thus be seen as deeply satisfying cognitive and social systems. Although people are often disconcerted by symbolic disorder or outbreaks of evil, they also recognize a crucial connection between their metaphysical assumptions about the nature of world order and the values they actually draw upon in any troubled historical situation. In the way in which they think and act, people apply the totality of their experience to create and maintain meaningful order in the world.[46] Here we can grasp the fact that both Paul Le Jeune and the Montagnais were hard at work attempting to achieve what Wilfred Cantwell Smith has long since advocated as the premier goal of cross-cultural religious study. At issue, for the Montagnais, Le Jeune, and the historian of religion who needs to reconstruct and explain their cross-cultural encounters, was the challenge of discovering truths that could be accepted by people from two or more cultures.[47] Given such a task, it is not surprising that intercultural communication was highly controversial, and the study of it has remained methodologically challenging.

6

Montagnais Missionization in Early New France

The Syncretic Imperative

Just as I had hoped, Religious Studies gave me new ways of thinking about Native American religious life and, therefore, missionization and religious change. All three shifts in understanding are reflected in "The Syncretic Imperative." In the first place, I bring together scholarly perspectives which suggest that culture and religion can be reconstructed concretely as contingent human meanings. Second, Sam D. Gill created comparative ground for the study of religious life because he demonstrates that "religion" ought to understood as a process, and hence as a speech act (whether verbal or non-verbal does not matter), a performative emphasis that conjoins human and cosmic meaning. And, at last, I began to understand Hallowell's critique of Western ethnocentrism and his hard-won conviction that Algonkian people (and others) must be understood in the orientational terms of their actual lives.

"The Syncretic Imperative" tests these insights in a close reading of the Jesuit Relations *which chronicled French-Montagnais relations in the 1630s. I began to hear distinctive Algonkian voices. I began to understand the myriad ways in which neither missionaries nor historians comprehended the distinctive terms of Algonkian realities and therefore misinterpreted Algonkian peoples' views of contact and change. Neither the priests nor scholars understood (as I argue in Chapter Eight) that Algonkians reasoned from a complex tradition (which focused on the social ethics of change) about a socially troubled present reality, and toward a morally sustainable future. Accordingly, for the first time I repudiated the category "belief" for its failure to encompass the practical and concrete Algonkian discriminations about religious reality and the religious views of the French. In a related way, in my continuing effort to reconstruct the Algonkians' day-to-day reasoning, I came to see their attempt to build bridges from the core truths of their tradition toward those of the French. The category "conversion," I concluded, not only emphasizes erroneously an ethnocentric outcome to religious change, it also blinds scholars to the intercultural discriminations by which Algonkians sought to understand, to extend, and to preserve tradition.*

The Montagnais kin groups that entered the Canadian mission at Sillery in 1639 throw significant light on the process of religious change. The *Jesuit*

Relations richly document the Montagnais' culture, and describe in detail their struggle to comprehend Catholicism.[1] As a result, it is possible to achieve an Indian history grounded in the reality assumptions of a particular Native American people. The Montagnais demonstrate that when religious change is described as conversion, both Native Americans' role in missionization and their syncretic intentions are missed. The Montagnais resisted Jesuit teachings for the better part of ten years, but some of them settled at Sillery for their own reasons. The challenge remains to reconstruct the reasoning by which some Montagnais adopted what appears to be the radically alien lifestyle the missionaries offered.

To begin with, it is useful to ask how we can achieve the insiders' view of missionization. The answer consists in identifying the common theoretical ground that has emerged between Religious Studies and several social science and humanistic disciplines. A good place to start is Susanne K. Langer's *Philosophy in a New Key*.[2] Langer heralded what might be thought of as a radical humanism focusing on meaning as an empirical, cross-disciplinary field of inquiry. Although Langer is seldom cited in social science literature or, for that matter, in the study of the humanities, the problem of meaning she highlighted has received concerted attention in the postwar era.

There are a number of examples of an emerging methodological focus on meaning. One can cite the interdisciplinary study of symbol, myth, and ritual. Equally fruitful lines of investigation have emerged in the philosophy of language, sociolinguistics, cognitive anthropology, and the sociology of knowledge, as well as social and ethnic history. Taken together, these collaborations have brought home the need for an ethnohistorical investigation which assumes that history has alternative causal explanations in cross-cultural situations.[3]

The Montagnais-Naskapi relationship with the French is a case in point. A quick review of the histories of seventeenth-century Canada suggests that the Montagnais story is so familiar that alternative explanations are not needed. The Montagnais were among the first northeastern Native Americans to experience regular contact with Europeans. They were pioneers in developing commercial, political, and military alliances with the French. They were also among the first to regret the negative impact of European contact. After 1633, when the French reestablished their base at Quebec, the Montagnais began to find themselves commercially displaced, subject to Iroquoian harassment, and politically subordinate to the French. To make matters worse, overtrapping led to a dramatic decrease in Montagnais food resources, and winter famines became commonplace. European diseases also took a heavy toll. Finally, in this situation of apparently massive cultural dissolution, the Montagnais capitulated in despair to the Jesuit missionaries who promised salvation.

Briefly put, it is the primary goal of this chapter to establish the way in which these causal variables intersected with the Montagnais understanding of French Catholicism. What is particularly relevant here is what the priests and the Montagnais saw as salvation. Historians have rightly emphasized the practical concerns of both parties, but they have also taken European pragmatism as the Montagnais' norm. It appears that the Montagnais had nothing to lose and everything to gain from a privileged relationship with the French. The alliance certainly made economic, political, and military sense. That some Montagnais apparently accepted what we have come to think of as ideological colonization is more difficult to comprehend. The history of the Montagnais has revealed some of the factors governing their reaction to the Jesuits, but these do not tell the whole story. Post-contact crisis posed problems with which the Montagnais had to grapple, but their own religious, philosophical, and social tradition channeled their conservative response.[4]

RELIGION AND MONTAGNAIS EXISTENTIAL ASSUMPTIONS: PERSON, POWER, GIFT

Despite the fact that the Jesuits never really understood Montagnais motives, their annual *Relations* expose the reasoning of the Montagnais. The *Jesuit Relations* are extraordinary documents because they present accurate ethnological descriptions of Montagnais life. Moreover, they are invaluable because they not only record what the Montagnais had to say, but also describe how they acted. In these ways, the missionaries have provided unparalleled documentary access to Native American experience. What remains misleading in the Jesuit texts, however, are the religious assumptions by which the Jesuits judged Montagnais culture. If the French priests eventually embraced something resembling cultural relativism, they still contended that the Montagnais lacked those qualities we call religious.

The Jesuits' religious anthropology merits attention because, try as they did, the priests could not relegate the Montagnais to irreligious savagery. At first, the priests held only that they were called to bring the Montagnais what they lacked. The Jesuits thought of the Montagnais as religiously deficient: they lacked knowledge of God and his written revelation, as well as the dogma and ritual that properly belong to institutionalized religion. Under the circumstances, the Jesuits faced a clear-cut, if difficult, task. After two years of work among the Montagnais, Father Paul Le Jeune described missionization pragmatically, although, as will be clear from the following discussion, he did not grasp the Montagnais' understanding of power: "The more imposing the power of our French people is made in these Countries," the priest declared, "the more easily they can make their belief received by these Barbarians, who are influenced even more through the senses than through reason."[5]

The priests had concluded that the Montagnais were as satanically misguided as they were ignorant. The *Jesuit Relations* catalogue a wide variety of Montagnais delusions: in common with other Native American peoples, the

Montagnais were trammeled by strange stories, were led by shamanistic charlatans, and were perversely dependent on dreams. In time, the Jesuits felt that all of Montagnais culture evinced religious backwardness and degradation. But, at the same time, much of Montagnais life defied condemnation.

Jesuit relativism began in the recognition that the Montagnais lived by a pervasive value system that set the stage for their Christian enlightenment.[6] The priests were forced to recognize that, however superstitious the Montagnais seemed, they had intractable notions of right and wrong. The more closely the priests looked, the more they admired the social values that the Montagnais professed. In the end, and as clear evidence of the limitations of their anthropological thought, the Jesuits created the paradoxical image of the noble savage—people who were naturally good but religiously and civilly backward, people who were, in short, inexplicable in either rational or moral terms. Of course, the Jesuits were left with God's will as the bottom line.

The problem of cross-cultural anthropology remains. If the field of religious studies is fundamentally concerned with confronting and making sense of cultural otherness, we need to recognize at the outset the rational impediments to understanding that cultural differences have always imposed.[7] In effect, a primary requirement for understanding the course of the Montagnais' religious change is to confront the meaning "otherness" itself had in particular historical situations. We must begin with the recognition that what we gloss as religion may not describe Montagnais reality. There is, for example, the commonplace notion that Native American religions are holistic, inseparable from what we think of as the linguistic, political, economic, and social aspects of culture. Such a view may be useful in highlighting genuine differences in religious outlook, but it also creates a real problem that eludes our empirical concerns. If religion is so pervasive, the end effect is that religion as a category may disappear. There is now considerable interdisciplinary agreement that religion is not simply another part of culture. One could cite Peter Berger as providing evidence of the religiously grounded nature of socio-cultural reality systems.[8] In a complementary interpretation, Clifford Geertz contends that religion has to do with world creation, maintenance, and transformation. Geertz defines the major challenge: "The notion that religion tunes human actions to an envisaged cosmic order, and projects images of cosmic order onto the plane of human experience is hardly novel. But it is hardly investigated either, so that we have very little idea of how, in empirical terms, this particular miracle is accomplished."[9]

Sam D. Gill adds a major qualification that focuses our attention on the historical role of religion: religion is that activity by which people continually take responsibility for the meaning of the worlds they in fact create. As such, religion has no necessary feature or mandatory content. As Gill puts it:

> We will consider as religious those images, actions, and symbols that both express and define the extent and character of the world, espe-

cially those that provide the cosmic framework in which human life finds meaning and the terms of fulfillment. We will also consider as religious those actions, processes and symbols through which life is lived in order that it be meaningful and purposive.[10]

Given this common emphasis on the relation between religion and cultural meaning, confusing religion with particular aspects of culture should no longer be troubling. Religion is nothing more, nor less, than that human activity through which people assign responsibility for meaning, worldly and otherwise.

There are other problems that an existential, activity-oriented view of religion avoids. Much of what we ordinarily consider integral to religion is inapplicable to Montagnais (and other Native American) reality. If A. Irving Hallowell was correct in rejecting the terms "supernatural" and "spirit," contending as he did that they did not fit Algonkian experience, then Montagnais-Jesuit dialogue faced tremendous hurdles.[11] Applied to the seventeenth century, Hallowell's point means that what the Jesuits thought of as the transcendental nature of religion was simply not relevant to the Algonkian peoples, who emphasized the immanent character of religion. As one shaman declared in 1637, the only life he cared for was the life of this world.[12]

Another Montagnais shaman expressed this difference in orientation to Father Le Jeune during the winter of 1633–34. "Thy God," he replied, "has not come to our country, and that is why we do not believe in him; make me see him and I will believe in him."[13] Such statements were commonplace; the Montagnais continually insisted that it was obvious that Christian revelation had been addressed to the French. In 1637 Makheabichtichiou tellingly made the point: "The son of God did not love our country, . . . for he did not come here, and did not say anything to us about all that."[14] Le Jeune protested in this instance that Jesus had not been born among the French either, but they had still come to accept him. Moreover, the priest urged Makheabichtichiou to give rational assent to Christian teachings. The Montagnais answered in typical terms: "I have nothing to say against all this," he answered, "for I have not been taught anything to the contrary."[15] Yet another man declared: "I do not know him . . . , if I could see him, I would thank him."[16] For their part, the Montagnais felt that they had religious knowledge sufficient to meet their needs and appropriate to their situation.

In effect, then, the idea of belief or faith in some sacred and transcendental otherness which we commonly associate with religion was not particularly relevant to Montagnais interests. From this point of view French religion at first seemed absurd. The Montagnais found it incomprehensible that the missionaries believed in a transcendent God. "Thou hast no sense," the Montagnais accosted Paul Le Jeune in 1634, "how canst thou believe in him, if thou hast not seen him."[17] On another occasion a shaman declared flatly: "When I see him, I will believe in him, and not until then. How believe in him who we do not see?"[18]

Nor were the Montagnais theistically oriented, which accounts for Le Jeune's shocked dismissal of their religious attitude as "ingratitude." As the priest put it: "although they believe that the [Culture Hero] Messou has restored the world, that Nipinoukhe and Pipounoukhe bring the seasons, that their Khichikouai teach them where to find Elks or Moose, and render them a thousand good offices,—yet up to the present I have not been able to learn that they render them the slightest honor."[19] The priest did not comprehend that what mattered to the Montagnais was concrete experience, and he did not understand that rituals attached to hunting ensured proper relations with these mythological beings. The Montagnais' religious discrimination was everyday and practical.

Still, the religious outlook of the Montagnais people was systematic, and that system channeled their evaluation of the Jesuits' religious claims. While they did approach religious change pragmatically, they made largely unconscious and usually unarticulated assumptions about the character of reality. Three ideas are central to Montagnais reality assumptions, as they were to all Algonkian-speaking Native Americans. These are the concepts of person, power, and gift, which dominated their perception, cognition, and social behavior.[20]

Hallowell cited as evidence for Algonkian interest in religious immanence the fact that for them the idea of person was not limited to human beings. Likewise, in the 1630s, Paul Le Jeune learned from his study of the language that European ways of thinking did not apply to the Montagnais. In particular, the idea that the world was constituted by persons, human and otherwise, rather than by nature or natural forces, was central to Montagnais thought.[21] Le Jeune discussed this reality assumption in detail and, although his writings provide ample evidence, he never truly understood that the idea of person had more than intellectual implications. The concept actually organized the Montagnais' social world, a world that had as much to do with action as with thought. For them, the Sun, Moon, winds, thunder, plants, minerals, and even man-made objects were all potential persons.[22] As Le Jeune put it, "the Savages persuade themselves that not only men and other animals, but also other things are endowed with souls, and that all the souls are immortal."[23]

Montagnais life concerned itself with maintaining positive relations with these other-than-human persons. The Jesuits discovered that all human abilities, and particularly the abilities to hunt, to practice medicine, and to wage successful war, depended on right relations with these entities. For example, the shaman's power to cure and to kill derived from them. The Montagnais name for shaman—*Manitouisiouekhi*—means "those who are acquainted with the Manitou, with him who is superior to men." The shaman, accordingly, fasted in order to seek power from various classes of persons. Le Jeune reported that the Montagnais "gave the name Manitou to all Nature superior to man, good or bad."[24]

In discussing this personalistic sense of causality that the Montagnais shared with other Algonkians, Hallowell was also emphatic that, as a necessary result, any idea of impersonal cause was foreign to their thinking.[25] Thus, the idea of power was closely related to the Montagnais' concept of person. In fact, the word for power—manitou—was also synonymous with the concept of person, human and otherwise, and whether used in a positive or a negative sense. There were persons of both kinds. Another way of thinking in these terms is to acknowledge that for the Montagnais history included the actions of both human and other-than-human persons. Moreover, their sense of causality, linked as it was to personal intent, was not at all concerned with the abstract causal forces—economic, political, military, and even medical—by which we impersonally explain their experience.[26] Thus, the net effect of the ideas of person and power was to lead the Montagnais to ground their value judgments upon how people acted. Montagnais thinking, and the social values their rationality sustained, was behaviorally precise.

The idea of gift was intimately related to the first two concepts because it defined the criteria by which the Montagnais assessed personal motives. Sharing, gift giving, and reciprocity identified the ideal characteristics of powerful people and so allowed the Montagnais to decide ethical issues of personal and social responsibility. For the Montagnais, kinship, or its absence, defined trust or distrust. The Jesuits identified what they saw as Montagnais vices, especially those that affected relations with dangerous and feared outsiders. These included ungratefulness, deceitfulness, treachery, and revenge. The priests also came to appreciate the normative values which derived from Montagnais religion and which shaped their internal social life. These social virtues consisted of good-naturedness, peacefulness, patience, compassion, hospitality, and generosity. In these negative and positive ways, the Montagnais emphasized the moral implications of a world comprised of unrelated and related persons. For them, it was cosmologically given that power ought to be used to help other people.[27]

A mythically grounded rule of responsible reciprocity regulated the relations between all classes of people.[28] For example, as the Montagnais understood it, they prayed to the Master of the Game, asking for help in feeding their families. When the prayers were successful, the animals heard and answered the plea. The hunter in turn generously helped his kinfolk and paid respect to the bones of the animal. Mutuality, generosity, and cooperation were not only the basic values of Montagnais social life, but also the very means used to maintain proper relations with the persons of the larger world. The dominant role ritual played in all of their activity reflected this central concern for proper relationships.[29]

Although these ideas are properly understood as the fundamental existential assumptions of the Montagnais worldview, they were not mere abstractions. Rooted as they were in the language, the concepts affected the Montagnais' perceptual and cognitive style and thereby shaped the pragmatism the Montagnais applied to Jesuit religious claims. It is significant that these criteria explain

Montagnais estimations of the French as people. In the first place, the French continually violated the rule of reciprocity.[30] Not only did they hold tenaciously to their private property, they sometimes even refused to share food.[31] Sharing was an imperative for the Montagnais, and group opinion carried considerable weight in maintaining contempt for the French. Given French notions of property, the Montagnais concluded that they were unlikely to be friends, thinking, Paul Le Jeune declared, "that we do not wish to ally ourselves with them as brothers, which they would very much desire."[32]

This uncertainty about French political intentions (best understood in light of Montagnais skepticism about French social ethics) highlights the contrast between different modes of Montagnais and European pragmatism. In a provocative essay that examines Hallowell's characterization of Algonkian thought, anthropologist Mary Black raises issues that help explain Montagnais motives in the 1630s.[33] Her findings can be summarized as follows: the Algonkian category of person was too general to fit all situations. Hallowell stressed that Algonkians were highly discriminating in their recognition of other-than-human persons; in particular, he noted that many persons had the ability to shift bodies. Also, in one situation a bear (for example) could be simply an animal; in another, the bear could turn out to be a shaman in disguise.

Black underlines Hallowell's conclusion that Algonkians acted cautiously toward all potential persons. Algonkian speakers could only judge the personal character (and power for good or ill) of entities linguistically classed as animate according to how they acted in particular situations. It follows that Algonkians had to assume that reality was not always as it seemed. Moreover, since power was unevenly distributed, it behooved Algonkians to act cautiously for fear of being disrespectful toward potentially dangerous persons. Black calls this phenomenon "percept ambiguity" and, as we shall see, it goes far to explain the kind of anxiety the Montagnais experienced in dealing with the post-contact crisis of the 1630s.[34]

RELIGION AND CRISIS

Whether explained in Montagnais or European terms, the decade of the 1630s was a time of mounting crisis. When the French returned to Canada in 1633, the Montagnais felt little concern for the future. Between 1633 and 1635 they showed generalized contempt for French culture. The colonists were ineffectual in making a living off the land, and consistently demonstrated that they did not share Montagnais social values. Not surprisingly, the Montagnais concluded not only that French religion had little to offer, but also that it was probably dangerous. As a result, they resisted baptism. Nevertheless, events of those years began to undercut Montagnais confidence. Their hunting economy began to fail as the beaver became depleted and disease attacked young and old alike.

In 1636–37, the Montagnais began to hedge their bets religiously. While they had faced the fact of growing crisis, they had also decided that they could do something about the situation. The numbers of baptisms increased from 22 in 1635 to 115 in 1636.[35] These numbers fail to convey the whole story, however, because more and more the Montagnais themselves sought baptism for their children, partly because they thought of the sacrament as a potentially powerful medicine. As significantly, dying adults also began to ask to be baptized.

The Montagnais had become increasingly despondent—an emotional state that they had always seen as a primary cause of disease.[36] For this reason, the Montagnais had begun to react fearfully to the possibility that the Jesuits' hell truly existed. In 1637, for example, they asked what was causing so many deaths, saying that "since the coming of the French their nation was going to destruction."[37] They repeatedly lodged such complaints against the French but, in fact, a growing belief in hell paralleled serious disruptions in Montagnais social life. The Montagnais worried that they might have drawn trouble to themselves.

By all indications, the Montagnais were truly uncertain where to place the blame. Several cases of windigo cannibalism indicate the way in which the Montagnais internalized their own responsibility for the crisis. The number of human windigoes threatening the Montagnais in this decade reflects the Indians' sense of ethical malaise. Windigoes were at once a mythological symbol of anti-social savagery and a human psychotic condition.[38] In 1636, for instance, a powerful other-than-human person warned the Montagnais that a cannibal would attack and eat them if they attempted to settle near the French.[39]

It is also significant that their war with the Iroquois made the Montagnais even more anxious and impelled them to seek a closer alliance with the French. The Montagnais annually fielded small war parties, but these were insignificant when compared with Iroquoian military strength. To make matters much worse, the French not only refused to side with the Montagnais, but also criticized traditional war itself. The Montagnais were perplexed when the Jesuits accused them of bloodlust and decried their war feasts as rank savagery.[40] The priests also criticized the dreams and visions in which other-than-human persons aided the Montagnais against the enemy.[41] Throughout the 1630s, the situation deteriorated to a point where the Montagnais became militarily impotent. In 1637, for instance, Paul Le Jeune accosted one headman. The Jesuit warned him of defeat because the war party's shaman had blasphemed against the Christian God. Disaster did occur and Le Jeune later confronted the shaman publicly, declaring "that he had been the cause of their defeat."[42]

By 1638, some Montagnais concluded that the priests had power on their side and sought baptism as a symbolically potent expression of solidarity with the French. Many of the Montagnais deliberately camped near French settlements, apparently hoping that an alliance would help solve their economic, political, military, and even social problems. Fear of baptism was still common, but the number of cures associated with the sacrament began to increase. As evidence that the French priests were seen as more powerful than traditional medicine men, one shaman, Pigarouich, destroyed his ritual paraphernalia and accepted baptism. The following year the Jesuits noted that calamities like a smallpox epidemic seemed to attract more and more of the Montagnais.

In the short term, the Montagnais took Christian claims seriously for three main reasons. First, given the ambiguous nature of power, they came to see the Jesuits as religious specialists comparable to, and more capable than, their own shamans. Second, although they remained distrustful of baptism, they came to see it positively. The sacrament not only healed in some cases, it also ensured continued contact between living and dead Montagnais. Third, the person(s) of Jesus and He-Who-Made-All reinvigorated the traditional hunting economy, based as it was on reciprocal relations between human and animal persons. In all of these ways, Catholicism made sense in traditional terms. Each of these factors deserves discussion.

Montagnais assessment of the Jesuits' personal character shaped their overall reaction to the new religious system. From the first, the Montagnais appreciated that the priests were religious specialists and responded with appropriate caution. Still, during the first years of contact, the Montagnais held to their contemptuous view of the French, not in the least because of their relations with the priests. The Jesuits were rude and discourteous. They were incompetent in the vital matter of making a living and, when visiting among the Montagnais, were utterly dependent on Indian willingness to care for them. As significantly, the priests acted in selfish ways. The Jesuits appeared to expect that the Montagnais ought to provide for them, while they showed themselves unwilling to share.[43]

It took many years for the Jesuits and the Montagnais to reach mutual understanding, largely because the Montagnais distrusted their own religious practitioners.[44] Although the shamans were essential to group survival, they often acted in ways that threatened well-being.[45] The shamans could and did use religious means to inflict sickness and even to kill.[46] As Le Jeune expressed it in 1637, "I hardly ever see any of them die who does not think he has been bewitched."[47] In this regard, the Jesuits also seemed dangerous, even to the extent of being the cause of bad weather.[48] In fact, the Montagnais claimed that old-time Indians had warned that the Jesuits would come and kill them.[49] The Montagnais accused the priests on several occasions of using their power to murder them. As the Montagnais searched for the cause of epidemic illness, they frequently accused the French, and especially the Jesuits, of making them sick.[50] Then too, the priests encouraged the Montagnais to understand that their God, He-Who-Made-All, was vengeful.[51] They often observed that particular Montagnais individuals apparently fell sick, or died in brutal ways, because they had acted disrespectfully toward the Christian God.[52]

In effect, the Jesuits' actions and teachings kept the Montagnais off balance. Much of the priests' behavior horrified them. Jesuit brashness seemed to violate the need for respect between humans and other powerful persons. On many occasions the priests ridiculed the powers of the Montagnais world, pitting themselves against other-than-human persons and the shamans as they did so. On one such occasion, Le Jeune noticed that the Montagnais had thrown eels into the fire and asked them why. "Keep still," they replied, "we are giving the devil something to eat, so that he will not harm us."[53]

Jesuit criticism also made the Montagnais uncertain about Christian power. For example, the priests often scoffed at the revelations the Montagnais received in dreams. Eventually, they made a crucial distinction between those dreams in which demons attacked would-be Christians and those that were mere superstitions. For the short term, the mixed message may have confused the Montagnais, but it is not surprising that they began to compare the priests to their shamans. The Jesuits took it upon themselves to interpret dreams for Montagnais, thereby displacing the shamans in one of their most important functions. In one conversation, Le Jeune confronted the shaman Pigarouich for refusing to give up his belief in dreams.[54] Most important, the priests acted with an impunity that effectively communicated their powerful confidence.[55] So great was their self-assurance that they frequently urged the Montagnais to kill their shamans.[56] The net effect of Jesuit behavior was to convince many Montagnais that the priests were not only equivalent to the shamans, but also more powerful.[57] In 1637, Makeabichtichiou told his countrymen that "those who believe in God are protected against sorcerers."[58]

Ultimately, the priests adapted their behavior toward the Montagnais in ways that communicated genuine concern, and this benevolence fit the traditional criterion of generosity. Since rational argument proved ineffective in convincing the Montagnais of Christian truths, and since the Indians were easily alarmed, the Jesuits cultivated more humane methods. To prove their benevolent power, the Jesuits devoted themselves to Montagnais well-being. They provided food, took in orphans, nursed and cured the sick. The Montagnais could understand charity, as Paul Le Jeune stressed more than once:

> To convert the Savages, not so much knowledge is necessary as goodness and sound virtue. The four Elements of an Apostolic man in New France are Affability, Humility, Patience and a generous Charity. Too ardent zeal scorches more than it warms, and ruins everything; great magnanimity and compliance are necessary to attract gradually these Savages. They do not comprehend our Theology well, but they comprehend perfectly our humility and our friendliness, and allow themselves to be won.[59]

In effect, the priests began to operate within the kin values central to Montagnais life and, in so doing, defused Montagnais criticism.[60] Moreover, they mediated between the Montagnais and the colonial government, thus showing that they aimed at creating an effective and genuine alliance between equals.

The tension between caution and trust regulated other aspects of the Montagnais' scrutiny of Catholicism. Baptism produced a terrified kind of uncertainty because it seemed to be the priests' preferred way of killing. The Jesuits never did eradicate entirely the Montagnais' fear of the sacrament, but Indian religious pragmatism gave them the means to abate it. Unwittingly, by baptizing only the dying, the Jesuits achieved an unexpected opening. The Montagnais were told that baptized persons went to heaven.[61] Since the Jesuits insisted that heaven and the traditional land of the dead were different places, the living relatives of the dead found themselves confronting a dilemma. Traditionally, the Montagnais stressed the maintenance of proper and reciprocal relations with dead kin.[62] The result was that some Montagnais, particularly parents who had lost a loved child, sought baptism as a way to ensure continued contact.[63]

Other Montagnais also hedged their bets. Some sought baptism as a means to deal with disease, since the Jesuits apparently cured many individuals.[64] Still others, worried that Jesuit threats of eternal damnation might be real, sought to avoid hell even at the cost of present death.[65] As one man put it: "Many of their nation had this idea, that baptism is injurious to life, but that it is a good thing with which to protect oneself from the fires with which we threaten them."[66]

In perceiving the Jesuits as shamans, and in overcoming their fear of baptism, the Montagnais were not repudiating traditional religious practice. They took Jesuit criticism seriously because, while they were inclined to blame the French for their troubles, they also worried that they themselves might have been at fault. The traditional religious system provided no easy answers to everyday problems, but it did require that the Montagnais do everything in their power to identify and rectify error. Frank G. Speck identified this issue of responsibility, at least as it pertained to hunting: "Failure on the chase, the disappearance of game from the hunter's districts, with ensuing famine, starvation, weakness, sickness, and death, are all attributed to the hunter's ignorance of some hidden principles of behavior toward the animals, or to his willful disregard of them."[67] Since crisis was so pervasive in the 1630s, the Montagnais had to heed missionary criticism, at least to the extent of examining themselves for personal responsibility for the deepening crisis.

It is true that the Jesuits spent far more time condemning Montagnais life than approving it, but still much of what they had to offer made sense in traditional terms. Nowhere was this truer than in the intersection of Catholicism and hunting. Hunting stood at the very heart of Montagnais religious life, as the Jesuits realized, even though they called Montagnais prayers ridiculous. It seemed both naive and superstitious to call upon the animals to give their lives.[68] In 1634, Paul Le Jeune noted that the Montagnais could not understand why the French prayed: "'Ask him,' they say to me, 'for Moose, Bears, and Beavers; tell him that thou wishest to eat.'"[69] To ask for food was the most common Montagnais prayer, and seemed to the missionaries nothing short of self-serving.[70] Nevertheless, the priests realized that the Montagnais needed prayers in the 1630s.[71] The Montagnais faced disaster in the collapse of their hunting economy. Time after time, the shamans proved incapable of improving hunting and the Jesuits saw a basic opportunity.

As early as the winter of 1633–34, when Paul Le Jeune wintered with one family band, the Montagnais began to hear that the shamans were responsible for their troubles. Le Jeune lost no opportunity to urge the Montagnais to redirect their prayers from the Master of Game to He-Who-Made-All.[72] Praying to Jesus seemed to help. Jesus himself began to appear in dreams to promise a successful hunt.[73] Le Jeune relates one instance when two Montagnais reported that Jesus offered to aid them: "I have seen thy Manitou, and I thy Jesus. . . . Oh what a good year he promised us! What Beavers, what Elks!"[74] The Jesuits were undoubtedly dismayed when the two men stipulated that Jesus expected tobacco in return for his assistance. Here again we have persuasive evidence that the Montagnais did not need to repudiate basic reality assumptions in order to embrace Christianity. At first uncertain as to the value of the Jesuits' religious contentions, the Montagnais could experiment as needed. In this case, the result was gratifying: Jesus turned out to be a hitherto unknown, but extremely powerful, Master of the Animals.

THE SYNCRETIC IMPERATIVE

To acknowledge that the Montagnais had a distinctive way of thinking is to begin to appreciate the complex forces that governed their exploration of Catholicism. In the first place, we must note the cognitive heterogeneity of Montagnais life. The Jesuits were well aware of such differences: "It is, indeed, true" wrote Paul Le Jeune, "that these people have not all the same idea in regard to their belief, which will some day make it appear that those who treat of their customs are contradicting each other."[75] Although the ideas of person, power, and gift structured the Montagnais' overall tradition, the tradition itself was possessed unevenly. The Montagnais did have an egalitarian society. Still, some knowledge was the special preserve of women, of men, of children, hunters, and shamans.[76] Age, experience, and social role defined the way in which individuals had access to the tradition. Those factors also shaped the kinds of concerns groups of people had with Catholicism.

At the level of social life (which, given the consensual character of Montagnais society, was paramount), the Montagnais evaluated French claims, bringing to bear both existential assumptions and practical experience. In other words, missionization can be understood best as a discourse between Montagnais individuals and the priests.[77] As a central feature of this dialogue, however, the Montagnais also had to evaluate collectively the Jesuits' often shocking statements. One necessary result frustrated the priests: try as they might, they found it extremely difficult to persuade individuals who feared family ridicule to listen to them.[78]

Given this religious heterogeneity, the idea that the Montagnais converted to Catholicism is too simple to encompass the complex intellectual, ethical, and social decisions they had to make to bridge their own cultural differences and to find common ground with the French way of life. If, as the evidence suggests, conversion did not take place as we have thought, it may be that we mistakenly see religions as dogmatically incompatible and exclusive in their deistic orientation. Such was the Jesuit view. The priests expected that the Montagnais would scuttle and abandon their tradition. There is no evidence, however, that even those who entered the mission at Sillery ever understood—at least until it was too late—that Catholicism posed a radical threat. Rather, the Montagnais learned piecemeal what the Jesuits considered acceptable and what they considered evil and sinful.

In the end, as at the beginning, the missionaries and neophytes saw religious dialogue in opposed terms. The Jesuits thought of conversion as a goal, an end point, an object to be won. The Montagnais, on the other hand, could not see where the Jesuits were leading. In any case, the Montagnais were impelled by both continuing crisis and a failure of traditional religious techniques. It was no coincidence that Paul Le Jeune contended that "fear is the forerunner of faith in these Barbarous Minds."[79] Terrified they were, and the Montagnais had to pay closer attention than the priests to the practical implications of religious change. The Jesuits demanded, but the Montagnais weighed their options and decided what did or did not make sense.

The Montagnais continued to understand themselves and the French in terms of the categories of person, power, and gift. One might say, for example, that they came to think of Jesus and Mary as additional other-than-human persons, admittedly very powerful persons who offered daily assistance. In 1626, the Jesuits reported that the Montagnais had associated the person Jesus with the person of the Sun.[80] In an analogous way, some Montagnais thought of the Christian Holy Spirit, whom the Jesuits pictured as a dove, as the equivalent of the great person Thunder.[81] The Montagnais continued to reach from the known to the unfamiliar. In 1637, the Jesuits noted that the Montagnais applied the term "manitou" to both God and the devil.[82] In a similar fashion, the Christian idea of a personal creator had some impact. When asked who had created the world and human beings, one shaman expressed uncertainty. It seems that the Montagnais had some vague idea of a high god they began to associate with the Jesuit creator.[83] Such a figure did not replace, however, the culture hero, Messou, the restorer.[84]

It can be said even that this God—He-Who-Made-All—made functional sense. At least there is no evidence to suggest any conflict occurred between the Montagnais' idea of a world organized by many plant, animal, and other personal powers and the Jesuit concept of a Creator God. As time went by, He-

Who-Made-All served to unify and focus the Montagnais cosmology of powerful persons. In fact, the Jesuits blithely adjusted their theology to fit Montagnais presupposition. Paul LeJeune wrote:

> I told them that this great Captain [He-Who-Made-All] overwhelms us with blessings,—it is he who gives us light with the Sun, who maintains for us the fish with the waters, and the animals with the land; it is he who forms our bodies in our mothers' wombs, who creates our souls by his word.[85]

Whatever the Jesuits claimed about the preeminence of the Christian God, nothing in Montagnais religious practice constituted a dogmatic creed. So the fundamental problem with the term "conversion" has to do with the assumption that to convert is to change traditions, to shift religious direction. Admittedly, such an assumption does seem warranted when it is applied to cross-cultural situations. But conversion has another, related meaning which stresses the idea of *giving assent*.

This second meaning has considerable implications for understanding the syncretic direction of the mission process. Instead of thinking of conversion as radical ideological change from one religion to another, conversion can be seen as a process of rediscovery. As a result of their contact with Catholic religious powers, and from their ritual use of Catholic symbols, the Montagnais converted themselves. In other words, they came to reexperience and thereby revitalize the basic religious truths of their traditional life. The Montagnais world continued to be charged with personal presence and human and other-than-human persons remained bound by mutual obligation.

Whatever we may think of the colonial implications of missionization in other settings, the Montagnais controlled the process during the 1630s. Since the Jesuits never really understood the Montagnais religious system, they could not eradicate it. The Jesuits, like the Protestant missionaries in New England, demanded religious change without understanding the cultural processes involved. For the Montagnais, who attempted to live out the contradictions of Jesuit demands, mission life posed few choices, but some of these allowed them considerable freedom. They could leave the missions, and many did. They could submit and accept the view of some of the catechists that life had become loathsome. They might also attempt to make sense of Christian religiosity in order to end the considerable cognitive dissonance missionization produced. Ultimately, they could try to integrate old and new, as did the Montagnais who first lived at Sillery. As it turns out, these "Christians" failed to strike such a balance and paid the highest cost. This was the eventual tragic fate of Sillery.

7

Baptism and Alliance

The Symbolic Mediations of Religious Syncretism

To make sense constitutes the motivation behind the syncretic imperative. I had learned that the process rather than the outcome of religious change warranted close attention. Syncretism is always a logical engagement with alien meanings, not simply an act of bricolage, a cobbling together of bits and pieces of disparate symbolic elements. Rather, syncretism extends the meanings of tradition in relation to conservative processes of assimilation. Driven by indigenous rationality, syncretism could never be controlled by missionaries whose ethnocentrism prevented them from understanding the integrity of Algonkian life.

In "Symbolic Mediations," I continued to listen to the Montagnais voices of the late 1630s, and their symbolic meanings and acts of ritual responsibility began to engage my attention. I also become more confident in reading (Brown and Vibert) Jesuit descriptions of Algonkian behavior with an eye and an ear for the subtleties of Algonkian views. Unlike most studies of these early French missions, I consciously kept the missionaries and their intentions in the background, and chose, instead, to place Algonkian motivations front and center. By this time, I had become convinced that the category "conversion" was much too static a term for the dynamic and creative processes captured better by the neutral term "religious change."

As importantly, this essay demonstrates that I had come to understand Hallowell's injunction that intellectual ethnocentrism dominated all facets of Native American studies—including anthropology, history, and Religious Studies. I had internalized and begun to extend Hallowell's cardinal insights that cultures encapsulate distinctive philosophies of being, systematic ways of thinking, and closely related ethical principles that regulate the ways in which various beings understand themselves and the character of their self-interested and other-oriented relations. In a related insight, I could now see the dramatic ways in which the Algonkians' worldview departed from the hierarchical, monotheistic, and dependent principles of French-Catholic cosmology. The course of religious change, it turned out, was far more complicated than missionaries and historians have appreciated. I could see, moreover, that the Montagnais themselves made religiously divisive, and thus culturally dysfunctional, choices.

Studies of Christian missions among Native Americans must seek to understand the symbolic transmission of religious knowledge as grounded in controversial conversations about the nature of reality. Because the *Jesuit Relations* richly detail the baptisms of Canadian Montagnais between 1632 and 1642, it is possible to isolate the major symbolic factors that initially impeded and then facilitated religious dialogue. The initial barriers to religious change included the terrifying cultural devastation of epidemic disease, a burgeoning fear of witchcraft as an inverted form of shamanism, and a closely related conservative ambivalence toward French missionaries. In ritualistic terms, the Montagnais of the 1630s were within a liminal period "betwixt and between" an increasingly dysfunctional tradition and the uncertain advantages of cultural adjustment to the demanding and critical French.

Anthropologist Victor Turner has shown for the African Ndembu that such disordered periods elicit two ritual responses.[1] The first reaction is diagnostic: a no longer viable community needs to plumb the causes of crisis. The second is redressive: the people need to counter the forces of entropy and to reconstitute themselves symbolically through decisive religious action. Turner's depictions of cultural states of liminality make it possible to link religious and social change. He demonstrates that thinking of society in only structural terms—the economic, political, social, and ideological patterns of ethnohistory—misses the motive force, particularly the community's rejuvenating goal of ritual activity, which drives cultural change. Historical adjustments, Turner shows, have a ritual character as people stand beyond their once steady-state world, critically confront the core values that lay behind the factual cultural order, and, having thus reassessed social malaise, take normative control of the world at large.

In the shaky world of the Montagnais of the 1630s, that ritual imperative meant placating the offended animal and hostile human others whose anger had brought starvation, sickness, and death at the hands of enemies. While the Montagnais resembled other peoples who have highly complex ritual means of divination and redress, their use of ritual in the 1630s reflected their growing uncertainty and social anomy.[2] Ritual seemed not to work. Over the decade, it became increasingly obvious that the future could not be known with certainty, and responsible action seemed futile. In this situation (defined by the very relational disorders with which ritual always grapples), some Montagnais turned to the French in search of ritual techniques that might avert catastrophe. It was more than fortuitous that the primal French ritual, the sacrament of baptism, highlighted just those symbols of social solidarity and cooperation that the Montagnais sought. Baptism opened paths to a new life of positive relations with animals and with other humans, demonstrably improved hunting, smoothed reciprocal relations with the French, and so promised to assist the Montagnais against threatening Indian enemies. Ceremonial baptisms, so often followed by equally solemn burials, created relationships between French godparents and Montagnais godchildren and channeled concrete examples of economic alliance. Thus, the Montagnais came to appreciate the constructive purposes of the French.[3]

A few words about methodology will illustrate the aims of this study. I consciously treat elements of French and Montagnais cultures as symbolic, that is, as having an immediate and vital relationship to other elements in each cultural system of meaning; a change in meaning would therefore shift the entire system. Symbol systems are meaning systems and, in this case, were rooted in Jesuit and Montagnais religious values. But it is crucial to realize that symbol systems are much more than ways of thinking about life. Embedded in Montagnais and French religious practice, symbols were the very means by which both the French missionaries and the Montagnais adapted. By shifting their symbolic story to suit the changing facts, the Montagnais in particular sought to ensure their survival. A symbolic integration of their tradition with that of the French was the eventual result, but achieving a symbolic "fit" required controversial individual and collective efforts. For the Montagnais, as for the priests, this was gut-wrenching work. Thus, in my view, symbols comprise the technology of Montagnais religious change.[4]

This chapter examines baptism as the way in which the Montagnais moved from one state of being to another. Two kinds of evidence map this transition. The first has to do with the existential symbolism of the Montagnais worldview, principles encapsulated in oral tradition and practiced in ritual. The second line of evidence is drawn from the *Jesuit Relations*. Since the *Relations* is the focus of this study, I have taken care to distinguish between Jesuit descriptions of Montagnais behavior (descriptions that can be evaluated in relation to the ethnographic record) and the priests' judgments of Montagnais motives in embracing Catholicism. My concern here is to estimate the ways in which the Montagnais symbolized baptism and thereby to reconstruct the religious reasons that led some of them to settle at the mission village which came into being at Sillery, near the French post of Quebec.[5]

Montagnais cognitive and value assumptions, not examined in detail in this study, form the background from which to assess this people's religious adaptation. The symbolic factors that shaped Montagnais reactions to the French can be summarized quickly here.[6] First, the Montagnais shared with other Algonkian-speaking people three linked existential categories. For them, the primary category of "person" embraced plants, animals, natural forces, and cultural artifacts, as well as human beings. Since all persons had sentience, will, and voice, the Montagnais held that the second category, "power," was never impersonal. Rather, causality was distributed broadly, if differentially, among all people. The symbolic interdependence among various classes of people was structured in terms of the normative value of reciprocity. This final category, "gift," falling on an ethical continuum from sharing to profit, described not only the central religious ideal of Montagnais reality but also the challenge of daily living. At one level, human beings and other-than-human persons were bound by webs of ritual exchange. At the same time, the value of sharing shaped every facet of Montagnais life, including their social, economic, and political relations. And, of course, the entire range of meanings attached to exchange shaped Montagnais relations with the French.[7]

Ideological flexibility characterized the Montagnais symbol system. Since power was cosmologically central, it followed that Montagnais religion was both non-deistic and non-dogmatic. The workings of power mattered to them, not the abstract theology (and the overarching intentionality of God) which characterized Jesuit Catholicism. As a result, Montagnais assessment of Jesuit reality claims was shaped neither by belief nor by intellectual considerations. As we shall see, some Montagnais accepted baptism because they became convinced that the Jesuits wielded power and came to sense that the priests put Montagnais welfare before all else.

This process must also be summarized. Jesuit teachings made sense because they symbolized God as He-Who-Made-All. While the Jesuits failed to communicate the Christian distinction between humanity and divinity, the missionaries' He-Who-Made-All taught the Montagnais about a new, paramount other-than-human person. As a result, the priests revealed the existence of a "Master" of creation who seemed more powerful than any of the great persons in the traditional Montagnais world. Since the post-contact era was characterized by cultural upheaval, epidemic illness, and social disintegration, the Montagnais scrutinized not only Jesuit reality claims but also their behavior, seeking clues to their intentions. Not surprisingly, anxiety channeled this process of evaluation, since the Montagnais assumed that the priests, like traditional power holders, might use their power in destructive ways. It can be said, in fact, that Montagnais resistance to Jesuit teachings stemmed from this basic symbolic ambivalence, since power itself was ethically neutral. Not surprisingly, many Montagnais attributed the increase in post-contact disease and death to the sacrament of baptism.[8]

Still, there was much in Jesuit Catholicism which fit the reality assumptions of the Montagnais world. Although the priests were monotheistic and stressed the superior, otherworldliness of heaven, they also scrutinized the everyday world for the workings of both God and the devil. Their theory of grace corresponded to the Montagnais category of power. For example, in noting a dramatic increase in the number of baptisms from twenty-two in 1635 to over a hundred in 1636, Paul Le Jeune attributed what he saw as conversions to a vow the priests had made to the Virgin.[9] The direct result, Le Jeune observed, was that the Montagnais no longer resisted the baptism of their children; moreover, the elderly "are likewise beginning to wish to die Christians, asking for baptism when they are sick, in order not to go down into the fires with which they are threatened."[10] Writing to enlist the support of pious French people for the missions, Le Jeune lost no occasion to stress not only that "Grace produces many results" but also that it is "elevated above the forces of nature."[11]

The Jesuits' symbolic appreciation of grace as power also created the criteria by which they and the Montagnais could make sense of God's will. Like the traditional Montagnais power persons, God (and his saints) intervened on earth, both helping those who deserved assistance and chastising those who acted in anti-social ways. If the Jesuits stressed the absolute transcendence of God, and thus insisted on the profanity of the world, they also affirmed his immanence in the affairs of human beings. The missionaries felt that they were doing his work and so identified the Montagnais' other-than-human persons with demons who undermined their efforts.

Given this correspondence between Jesuit and Montagnais realities, their discourse had an urgent religious purpose, because the Montagnais were grappling with ultimate issues, particularly the increasing pain of post-contact life and the meaning of death. For most of the 1630s the Jesuits baptized only the dying and so fed Montagnais fears that the priests were the real cause of their troubles. There was a widespread awareness that the mounting numbers of deaths correlated with French settlement, and the Jesuits were therefore distrusted. But when directly confronted with the actuality of their own death or that of a close relative, many Montagnais hedged their bets. Thinking in terms of the vital symbols of traditional power, the Montagnais concluded that if baptism could kill, it might also cure. Such was the controversial nub of the conversation.

The symbolic tension between baptism as good or bad medicine played itself out in hundreds of situations, many of which were chronicled in the Jesuits' annual *Relations*. For most of the 1630s the Jesuits baptized isolated individuals, desperate adults ready to try anything, and children whose parents were consumed with anxiety. The Jesuits contended that baptism always healed the soul and, sometimes, the body.[12] Moreover, they deliberately increased the tensions impelling the Montagnais' religious pragmatism. In the Jesuit view, power was not merely a characteristic of the religious world; it was also symbolically polarized between good and evil. So they taught the Montagnais that heaven, the realm of God and goodness, contended against hell, the realm of devils. The Jesuits used graphic depictions of hell to illustrate the fate "of those who would not believe." Realizing that it would be years before the Montagnais even began to appreciate the complexities of Catholic religious dogma, Le Jeune declared that pictures of hell "are half the instruction that one is able to give the Savages."[13] Hellish symbols soon dominated Montagnais dreams.

Since they held that "fear is the forerunner of faith,"[14] the Jesuits made baptism the main symbolic vehicle by which the French offered the Montagnais religious safety as well as a political, economic, and military alliance. From the first, they exacted promises that if baptized children survived, they would be educated among the French. Some baptized children were actually surrendered, although often with reluctance. Others who had not been baptized were accepted by French foster parents because they hoped to Christianize them, and sometimes because their relatives could not care for them, a kindness the Montagnais appreciated.[15] In other instances, prominent French people became the godparents of baptized Montagnais, effectively demonstrating that baptism extended the bonds of social solidarity. Baptism thus operated like many traditional native rituals that aimed to create and maintain alliances among all classes of people. Moreover, French godparents reserved the right to name the newly baptized, and again French custom meshed with Montagnais tradition. Changing one's name had always been a powerful way to declare a personal transition.[16]

In a similarly fortuitous accident, the Jesuits came to communicate in ways that characterized traditional benevolent men of power. For example, the Jesuits ceremoniously buried those Montagnais who died baptized.[17] It was a matter of some importance in the mid-1630s that the priests permitted the Montagnais to bury grave goods with the Christian dead. In this way, the Jesuits not only communicated their concern but also conveyed cultural tolerance, even respect,[18] although they tried to dissuade the Montagnais.[19] Le Jeune explained the Jesuits' rationale: "If these poor, ignorant people were refused the privilege of placing in the graves of their dead their few belongings to go with them to the other life, they say, they would also refuse to allow us to approach their sick."[20] The Jesuits also taught that the baptized went to heaven rather than to the traditional land of the dead. As a result, the sacrament became a powerful inducement to parents who wished to maintain contact with their dead children.[21]

Moreover, the governor of New France, Charles Huault de Montmagny, attended such funerals, surrounded by his official retinue, and invited the grieving Montagnais kin to cement their relationship with the Jesuits by accepting their guidance. In insisting that baptism created a special brotherhood, the French affirmed the value of closer relations and underlined their conditions for them. The Montagnais came to understand that the burial of their relatives in consecrated ground was an important symbolic gesture, reserved only for those willing to embrace the French religion. Their request that their unbaptized dead be accorded the same honor was denied.[22] The Jesuits insisted that the unbaptized had no value to the French. He-Who-Made-All loved the baptized and drew them to him. All others were condemned to eternal flames.

In all this the Montagnais heard mixed symbolic messages, but even by the middle of the 1630s the Jesuits had taught some of them to react cautiously. The Montagnais could see that the priests were the equivalent of their shamans. Their caution stemmed from a traditional fear of power wielders. But they could also see that the priests had their welfare in mind. In 1636, for example, an old woman chided a shaman who opposed the baptism of his child. These people, she said, "give and ask [for] nothing; thou knowest how they care for the sick, let them go on; if this poor little one dies, they will bury him better than thou couldst."[23] While the Jesuits emotionally abused sick Montagnais by portraying the tragic consequences of damnation, they also held out hope to them. They terrified the sick and the dying with the eventuality of endless suffering only because they were convinced that they offered real help.

Again, Montagnais tradition supported Jesuit claims. Disaster on the scale of the epidemic illnesses of the 1630s had to be explained. Tradition required the Montagnais to assess their responsibility for all the deaths. The Jesuits inadvertently made the same point. They said that God permitted the Montagnais to die because they were sinful and unwilling to accept him. He used demons as agents of punishment. It said everything to the Montagnais that not only were their shamans powerless over the new diseases but also that the Jesuits insisted that God protected Christians against shamanic malevolence. For adults who accepted baptism, the conclusion was persuasive: because the shamans were in league with demons, they had to be repudiated.

The Montagnais understood that the blessings of power required reciprocity on their part and so interpreted their developing relationship with the Christian God. In 1636, Paul Le Jeune recorded a controversial baptism that illustrates the ways in which the Montagnais came to surrender to the reciprocity He-Who-Made-All demanded. Attikamegou, "the Prince," had called a missionary to baptize his dying infant son over his wife's vociferous resistance. After much argument, the priest suggested that "if she would believe God could perform this wonder, her son might recover."[24] The woman acquiesced to the baptism but declared that she would do so only if the Jesuit could cure her son.

Attikamegou, for his part, contended that he believed that "he who made all can cure him." Others enjoined Attikamegou to urge his wife: "Consider well if thou believest," he warned. "For, if thou liest in thy heart, God will not cure thy child."[25] The woman was further tested when the Jesuit asked them to surrender their son if he lived. Balking again, she gave in when the priest explained that he wanted the child only to instruct him, and then not until he was six or seven years old. "They were then assured that, if they believed that God was powerful enough and good enough to restore life to their child, he would do it." So it happened, and everyone "was struck dumb with amazement."[26] Attikamegou appreciated his debt, as he warned his wife, "Take care of this child, and see that thou dost not prevent him from being instructed some day; for the death which was to have killed him would fall upon thy head."[27]

Such threats were often made and had a telling effect on the still reluctant majority of the Montagnais. Paul Le Jeune devoted an entire chapter of his 1636 *Relation* to the divine punishment of those who resisted or maligned the Christian faith. These people included members of a band with whom Le Jeune wintered in 1632–33. Mestigoït, his host, drowned; Carigonan, the shaman, was burned alive; and Pierre Antoine Pastedechouan, "the Apostate," starved in the midst of plenty. Since others died just as miserably, and the Jesuits lost no occasion to stress such evidence of God's just retribution, the Montagnais learned continually the price of irreverence. "The death of these men," Le Jeune contended, "renders the others more pliable and more disposed to grant us what we desire from them."[28] "The goodness of God . . . little by little casts fear into these souls."[29] Le Jeune also fully appreciated that the Montagnais' mixed fear and respect of Christianity reflected the growing power of the French.[30]

This mixture of religious fear and the need to achieve an economic and military alliance came to characterize Montagnais policy toward the French after 1637, as can be seen in the case of Makheabichtichiou.[31] The headman of a small Montagnais band, Makheabichtichiou had all the prerequisites for leadership: strength, skill in war, and a persuasive speaking style. Seeking close ties with the French, he soon discovered that the French governor, as Paul Le Jeune wrote, "only granted his more intimate friendship to those who were instructed in our belief." Having gotten "a flea in his ear,"[32] Makheabichtichiou submitted to Jesuit education. Le Jeune personally led him through the biblical account of the Creation, of Adam and Eve, of the Virgin birth, and of Christ's death. To this Makheabichtichiou replied, honestly but without fervor, "I have nothing to say against all this, for I have not been taught anything to the contrary."[33]

Realizing that biblical symbols were too abstract for his pupil to grasp, Le Jeune began to draw on everyday experience to prove the existence of good and evil and to justify God's wrath. "These arguments," observed the priest, "made some impression upon his mind." For Makheabichtichiou, hell began to become palpable:

> "This life," said he, "is very short, the other very long, since it has no end; to be sad without consolation, to be hungry and to eat only serpents and toads, to be thirsty and drink nothing but flames, to wish to die and not be able to kill oneself, and to live forever, for an eternity, in these afflictions—it is upon that that I think sometimes; thou wouldst do me a great favor to baptize me soon."[34]

He had also to overcome his fear that baptism would kill him, but in time he concluded that he did not "want to go into the fires."[35]

Then Makheabichtichiou became so ill that his relatives "looked upon him as dead." The Jesuits nursed him, and he promised not to have recourse to the shamans. When Makheabichtichiou recovered, both he and his relatives contended that the Jesuits' "knowledge of God had cured him." In short, in order to gain the favor of the French, Makheabichtichiou was willing to forego those Montagnais customs that offended the priests. He assured Le Jeune that he would no longer use a sweat lodge to ensure good hunting, and that he would no longer believe in dreams, consult shamans, or participate in ritual feasts.[36] For Makheabichtichiou, and for many other Montagnais, it was easier to repudiate traditional religious practice to meet French demands than it was to comprehend and embrace the symbols of Jesuit Catholicism. As Le Jeune put it, "The dread of punishment is beginning to gain such an ascendancy over their minds that, although they do not soon amend, yet they are little by little giving up their evil customs."[37]

Given the value of an alliance with the French, Makheabichtichiou accepted the long period of testing that the Jesuits imposed. The trial proved difficult, as he himself told Le Jeune: "I do really wish to embrace your belief, but you give me two commandments which conflict with each other; on the one hand you forbid me to kill, and on the other you prohibit me from having several wives; these commandments do not agree."[38] In fact, Makheabichtichiou remained so attached to his wives that he came to have critics among the French. They contended that he was interested in Catholicism only because he wished to court another, younger woman and so replace his wives. He never did find a way to divorce his wives and was never granted baptism, despite his persistent request. Eventually, at least according to the Jesuits, his refusal would lead the Christian Montagnais to expel him from the village at Sillery and would result in his terrible death among the Wabanaki with whom he sought refuge.[39]

In the short term, however, Makheabichtichiou lost no opportunity to curry favor with the French by defending them and the Jesuits among the Montagnais. The result was factional strife, whether or not one accepts Le Jeune's contention that some Montagnais were jealous of Makheabichtichiou's close connection with the French.[40] For instance, speaking at one general council, Makheabichtichiou advocated embracing French customs. Arguing against Makheabichtichiou's pretensions to leadership and in favor of a traditional course of action, the shaman Pigarouich[41] declared that there were five things that he would never give up: his love of women, dream divination, ritual feasts to win the favor of the powers, and hatred of the Iroquois. Finally, he also emphasized that he would always believe in his shamanic power.[42] As time would show, Pigarouich would abandon much tradition, but in allying himself with the Jesuits, he continued to affirm his shamanic power.

The occasion of this council gave Le Jeune an opportunity for a comprehensive rebuttal. He declared that only one wife was permitted, observed that demons delighted in the natives' ritual feasts, and scoffed at shamans because they could not cure disease. The Black Robe had always ridiculed the Montagnais' belief in dreams; now he expanded his condemnation: "The devil meddles with your imaginations in the night; and, if you obey him, he will make you the most wicked people in the world." Le Jeune's final point, concerning the Montagnais' war with the Iroquois, proved more acceptable. For some time the Montagnais had speculated whether Christian prayers could help them be victorious over the Iroquois, and Le Jeune urged them "to kill them all."[43] On this and other occasions, it seemed to some Montagnais that the Jesuits had the advantage of greater knowledge and therefore greater power. The priests constantly expounded a complex and intellectualized symbol system, the meaning of which non-literate Montagnais could only partially discern. Since the Montagnais were more concerned with correct religious practice than with belief, they were often at a loss to counter many of the priests' claims. Le Jeune described one such encounter: "The most prominent one among them, having heard me very attentively, replied that, as to their [traditional] doctrine, they did not have so much certainty about it, nor were they greatly attached to it."[44]

Since Pigarouich was the established shaman of Makheabichtichiou's band, his assessment of Catholicism is particularly revealing of the Montagnais' overall religious purposes. Like Makheabichtichiou, Pigarouich was much concerned with using the Jesuits to bolster his own political position among his people. But the people urged the Jesuits to "hold out firmly against this sorcerer, [saying] that he was feared in the cabins, and that he would oppose us." And attack him the priests did. Le Jeune accused him of being an imposter, challenging him to call spirits in the ritual of the shaking tent. Le Jeune stressed that the devil feared the missionaries: "I shall make him confess his impotence against those who believe in God; and I shall make him confess that he is deceiving you." Intimidated, Pigarouich failed to meet Le Jeune at the appointed hour for the rite of the shaking tent. "His people said among themselves that he was afraid, that he had no courage; some of them were astonished, and wondered at our belief; others said the French were greater sorcerers than they were."[45]

Several days later, Pigarouich approached Le Jeune in private. He not only was flustered when his Montagnais relatives discovered him there but grew afraid when the priest told them that "in France they put Sorcerers and Magicians to death."[46] In short, Pigarouich, like the other Montagnais, "began . . . to consider us greater Sorcerers than himself." But he did not immediately acquiesce to Jesuit power. Rather, he boldly described his shamanic responsibilities, inviting the Jesuits to demonstrate how such activities were misguided. He also told Le Jeune that three or four years earlier he had had a dream of the Jesuits' house, which had cured him of a serious illness. In fact, he said that on other occasions when he was ill, the same dream symbol had made him better.[47]

Like his relatives, Pigarouich submitted to Christian instruction and even came to promise "that he would no longer consult the Demons, and that he would refrain from other things [Le Jeune] had prohibited." Le Jeune contended that Pigarouich's was "the faith of fear and servility," but Pigarouich actually took Christianity seriously.[48] The fact that he was willing to examine Jesuit claims reflects the growing uncertainty that epidemic sickness had produced. The Montagnais were beginning to feel that real shamans no longer lived among them.[49] Given both the medical and the ecological emergency of the time, it is not surprising that Pigarouich, in Le Jeune's words, "requested us earnestly to teach him what must be sung to cure the sick, and to have a good chase, promising us to observe it exactly."[50] To his own way of thinking, Pigarouich was attempting to build a symbolic bridge between the old system of religious practice and the new, a bridge that he hoped would lead to solutions to real problems. Nevertheless, Pigarouich knew that the Jesuits were single-minded, and for that reason he destroyed his ritual paraphernalia in 1637.[51]

Pigarouich was not granted baptism until 1639. In the meantime, he pragmatically explored the power that He-Who-Made-All offered. For example, he told the Jesuits that God had protected him in a battle against the Iroquois. His companions, who had scoffed when Pigarouich had urged them to pray, fell dead or wounded all around him. Because he prayed and made the sign of the cross, however, Pigarouich escaped unscathed. The few other survivors remained indifferent when Pigarouich called upon them to ask God to grant them success in hunting. Still acting the part of shaman for his fellows, Pigarouich prayed, "Thou who hast made the birds, I have need of them; thou canst give me some if thou wilt; if thou will not, it does not matter; I shall not cease to believe in thee." Again making the sign of the cross, Pigarouich led his people to game. From the Jesuits' point-of-view, Pigarouich became an exemplary force, leading his people to conversion. Although in fact much ridiculed by them, and severely tested by God when his wife, children, and brother were stricken with a fatal illness, he persevered in his devotion.[52]

Makheabichtichiou's and Pigarouich's interest in Catholicism marked the opening of a period in which many Montagnais adults accepted baptism and also began to construct a closer alliance with the French. In 1637, for example, Makheabichtichiou led a headman to the Jesuits, asking for an introduction to the governor. The headman reminded the governor that, years before, Champlain had promised the Montagnais that the French would help them create an agricultural settlement. He said that the possibility had been much discussed in tribal councils and that some of the Montagnais had resolved to live near the French. He outlined three factors for their consideration: the Montagnais' interest in and need of Jesuit teaching, their intensifying war with the Iroquois, and the serious depletion of their game.

With the governor's permission, Le Jeune reminded the Montagnais that Champlain's offer had an important condition that they had forgotten, namely, that they "would give their children to be instructed and reared in the Christian faith."[53] This condition proved controversial. Some Montagnais again raised the old fear that the Jesuits were responsible for the ever-increasing death rate among them. Others contended that since the French remained in good health, "it must be that they know something which preserves their nation." Accordingly, one man offered the Jesuits his two sons, but the priests were not yet prepared to care for them.[54] Nevertheless, two families, led by Etinechkaenat and Nenaskoumat, began to clear land.[55] In effect, the Montagnais closest to the French and therefore to the threatening Iroquois were clearly expressing their willingness to abide by the terms that the French imposed on any alliance.[56] In accepting the small house the Jesuits provided, they told Le Jeune that he was now of their nation and that they were going to tell everywhere that they were also of ours."[57]

The Montagnais resolution was immediately put to the test, because all those who accepted Jesuit instruction fell sick, and many died.[58] Nenaskoumat, one of those most interested in both instruction and village life, illustrates the problems that the new life posed. As soon as he decided to settle with the French, his family was stricken: "An old woman, a relative, who managed his household, was taken off in a few days; his own wife and two of his children died before his eyes; some of his kindred and relations who were living with him were carried off at the same time."[59] Then he too became sick. "It was," said Paul Le Jeune, "enough to crush the spirit of a Giant, and to revive the ideas that many of the Savages had entertained, that to intend to become a Christian was to consent to depart from this world."[60]

But Nenaskoumat remained steadfast and was granted a ceremonial baptism attended by the leading Frenchmen. His godfather named him Francois Xavier.[61] A week later he reported an awesome vision:

> I saw myself surrounded by a great light; I saw the beauties of Heaven, of which thou tellest us; I saw the House of that great Captain who has made all. I was in a state of delight which cannot be expressed. This suddenly disappearing, I lowered my eyes toward the earth, and saw a frightful gulf which paralyzed me with fear. It seemed to me some one was saying to me, "Do not go there!"

Since the Jesuits feared the devilish delusions of dreams, they threatened François Xavier with damnation if he lied about the content of the dream. But his protests won them over. This willingness to acknowledge the workings of grace in the spontaneous religious life of the Montagnais was a major factor in the founding of the mission at Sillery. François Xavier survived a three-month illness and became a major influence among the Montagnais seeking a full association with the French.[62]

François Xavier exemplifies the new Christians of Sillery because most of them were struck with a usually fatal illness, and they invariably accepted their situation as the will of God. But François Xavier also attributed his recovery to God's will and so urged the others who were sick to ask for mercy. It also helped that the French offered attentive nursing in their new hospital. But gratitude toward the French cannot explain the Montagnais' newfound resigned determination.

The details recorded in the *Relations* reveal that the Christian Montagnais developed a terrified aversion to the world. One woman, convinced that she must accept baptism, warded off a demon with prayers.[63] One new Christian declared that he hated his sick body and did not fear death. He clearly was driven by guilt: "He preaches to his own people, reproaching them for their vices and their ingratitude with a freedom that consoles us; and the best of it is that he first accuses himself, publicly, of having formerly committed the sins that he reproves in them."[64] Still another man saw "frightful people" around him just before he died. Others were filled with great remorse for having resisted baptism, and their extreme mortification testifies to the genuineness of their sentiment. One of them, although recovering from terrible burns and stricken with disease, refused to eat the meat his relatives brought him. For Le Jeune these experiences were providential, inasmuch as the Montagnais' acceptance of Christianity had come as "a very sudden change."[65]

Le Jeune recorded other telling details that demonstrate how convinced of the Jesuits' power these Montagnais had become. One priest observed a sick woman shifting from delirium to quiet as he prayed for her recovery.[66] The Montagnais "even recognized that, in the case of some, God denied them at death the baptism they had ridiculed during life."[67] In other words, the Montagnais had begun to attribute their troubles to their own irresponsibility, particularly in refusing to accept baptism. Four families stricken at Sillery "concluded that they must believe in God and have recourse to his goodness."[68] For many, fear remained the basis of their faith. Many Montagnais were convinced, for example, that Le Jeune himself had inflicted smallpox on a man he had threatened with God's retribution.[69]

Because of the prevalence of smallpox and other diseases, more and more Montagnais accepted baptism after 1638. Those who survived their illnesses began to draw apart from those who clung to tradition. As a result, they entered yet another cycle of liminal uncertainty as everyday life became controversial to them. The Christian Montagnais began to scrutinize their traditions for the workings of evil demons. They refused to participate either in war feasts or in any occasion that had a ritual character.[70] They even began to adopt courtship customs that the Jesuits considered more decorous. Francois Xavier and others refused to permit traditionalists to marry their daughters.[71] All meetings with non-Christians began to be feared as occasions when the temptation to sin was great.[72] In the background, watching and judging, the Jesuits constantly reminded the Christian Montagnais that God wished to try their faith.[73] Le Jeune himself could barely contain his wonder over their transformation: "Grace is very strong which overturns the customs of the country, bridles the laws of the flesh, and combats self interest."[74]

In 1640 the Christian Montagnais assembled at Sillery to form a new social and political organization and in doing so tried to restructure the values of solidarity. Their first resolution, adopted with distinctly untraditional purpose (they "hardly ever contradict one another," Le Jeune wrote),[75] was to drive away all open enemies of Christianity. Pigarouich led the way in condemning the non-Christians, particularly those with two wives. Noel Negabamat, who conceded that the French cared for Christians and traditionalists alike, still concluded that "we all ought to unite in one and the same belief." Another headman, Jean Baptiste, spoke last: "I believe," said he, "that the only means of restoring your nation, which is going to destruction, is for all to assemble and to believe in God."

One traditionalist alone objected, appealing to the patriotism of the Montagnais: "As for me, if I were related to the French as you are who have received their belief, I would not be willing, however, to offend my countrymen."[76] But the Sillery Christians remained firm in their desire to forge a new symbolic cultural order more in tune with the French. They named Jean Baptiste the headman of Sillery and gave him and two subordinates religious and political responsibilities. They also chose a "Captain of Prayers" and appointed two others to lead the young men.[77] Then the women were called to the council and informed that they had to mend their ways: "It is you women . . . who are the cause of all our misfortunes,—it is you who keep the demons among us."[78] All of this received Jesuit approval: "This is part of the sermon of these new Preachers, who . . . are so much the more wonderful as they are new and very far removed from the Savage methods of actions."[79]

The Christians at Sillery had, however, institutionalized a basic cultural confusion. In taking responsibility for the quality of their community life, they created a political system that mixed the techniques of achieving the traditional goal of consensus with the coercive measures of French society. On the one hand, they openly reproved each other for their moral failings and publicly did penance;[80] on the other, they dealt harshly with the recalcitrant. In 1640, for instance, food was withheld from one young girl who had refused to tend her father's nets. For another, two young boys who were late for prayers had hot cinders thrown on their heads and received warnings that they would get worse the next time.[81]

In 1641 a council of the Christians decided that sinners ought to be imprisoned. Those traditionalists who still lived circumspectly at Sillery heard this resolution with some dismay, countering that it was a violation of Montagnais values. The Jesuits agreed: "It is well that the Savages feel these ardors, but we must not yield to all their desires; the customs of a people do not change so soon,—it is necessary to proceed with skill, gentleness, and patience."[82] Still, the new Christians persisted. The relatives of one young man imprisoned for drunkenness even argued that his punishment should be twice as severe because he was not Christian; they declared that they would "entirely renounce" their kin ties if he persisted.[83] It would seem that the Christian Montagnais could forge the new forms of solidarity only on the ashes of the old.

Although the Montagnais formulated these policies themselves, they were wholly dependent upon the Jesuits for guidance. The meaning of much that was asked was not at all clear to them. Besides receiving personal guidance in private meetings and at confession, the Montagnais sought the priests' advice on many daily concerns: "if they shall go hunting in such a place, if they shall take medicine, if they shall have a sweat, if they shall dance, if they shall marry."[84] There is much in these queries to suggest that even the Christians retained traditional religious concerns. One man, for example, asked whether it was a "great sin to dream something wrong at night, although even in dreaming one should resist it."[85] Many others found in Christianity an affirmation of the religious character of hunting: "It is a very common practice with the Christians to fall upon their knees as soon as they have killed some animal, and to thank God for it upon the spot."[86]

The Christian Montagnais of Sillery were among the first Native Americans in the Northeast to experience the end of an ancient way of life. That end was dramatic but not sudden. For the better part of ten years, the Montagnais were pioneers in forging a new religious and social order. Their experiment in social engineering was constructed firmly on traditional assumptions concerning reality. The Jesuits brought them an awareness of powerful new other-than-human persons who offered real assistance in return for moral obedience. This exchange was familiar to Montagnais ways of thinking and acting. What was new was the intensity of the relationship. He-Who-Made-All turned out to be a punishing God, particularly quick to condemn those who rejected his guidance.[87] Ridiculing the traditionalists' continuing fear of baptism, the Christians declared: "It is not faith that exterminates us, but our sins, and especially your unbelief; it is you who cause your own death, retaining the Demons in your midst by your wicked acts."[88] Accelerating Iroquois attacks, diminishing game, and ever more deadly diseases drove home the need for action.

The Montagnais took religious action. The Christian Montagnais illustrate the importance of religious symbols in sustaining particular ways of life, in justifying the existing symbolic social order. But traditional Montagnais were not so slavish; they comprehended that power could be abused as well as extended in affirmations of solidarity. It was this insight that shaped Montagnais scrutiny of the Jesuits and their power.

The decade of the 1630s was, in the terms of symbolic anthropology, a liminal period. With their traditional economic, political, and military world shaken up, the Montagnais found themselves adrift. They wavered between adherence to their failing tradition and hopeful examination of the uncertain religious claims of the French. Their religious uncertainty drove them to adapt. At the beginning of the decade, they used baptism to associate themselves with a new power in the sky and with his agents on earth. Significantly, their conception of power itself did not change; Christian power merely emerged as a new manifestation of the ancient category of person. Similarly, symbolic bonds of economic alliance with French priests and colonists constituted a rechanneling of the mythic principle of gift. In these ways, Montagnais tradition survived. But toward the end of the decade, Christian baptism also became the Montagnais' preferred vehicle by which to transform tradition. By accepting the sacrament of baptism, the Montagnais extended their cosmological system, adding heaven, hell, and purgatory (as well as the idea of a European place of origin) as ultimate life destinations arrived at through human responsibility and choice. At the end of the 1630s, the Montagnais had internalized the Jesuit theory of sin to such an extent that continuing crisis over which they had little or no control implied their overwhelming guilt.

The Christian natives came to trust the priests, at least, even while they learned through the new symbols of sin that they themselves violated the reciprocity that the powers required. That they came to respect He-Who-Made-All does not indicate that they understood the deistic character of Catholic theology. To the contrary, the Montagnais reacted to crisis, feared painful oblivion, and urgently attempted reform. Theirs was never a formal religion of dogma and abstract principle, but rather one of symbolic action shaped by the demands of the moment. Pragmatism remained a trait even of the Christian Montagnais, who adapted some Catholic symbols to their ancient religious practices in order to deal with real and novel problems.

In hindsight, we can see that Montagnais applications of Christian symbolism did not work from the beginning. In their devotion to He-Who-Made-All (in reporting what they saw as the workings of grace among the Montagnais, the Jesuits did not exaggerate), the Christians erred on the side of excess. They accepted Jesuit claims that baptism cleansed them of sin and justified their existence, but they also heard too keenly the priests' warning against backsliding. The threatening Jesuit God became terrifyingly real in the ongoing calamities of the 1640s. Like the Jesuits, the Montagnais themselves failed to appreciate both the powerful hold traditional religious fears had on them and the ways in which the priests amplified these fears. The integration of Montagnais and Catholic symbolism did not work.

As an immediate result, and as a measure of the religious anxiety that Catholicism greatly intensified, the Montagnais borrowed coercive behaviors from the French which flouted the traditional value of solidarity. The new religious order thus produced as many problems as it resolved. In the first place, Jesuit Catholicism stressed self-abnegation, even mortification, and thus undermined individual mental and emotional well-being; the Montagnais began to flagellate themselves and to fast excessively. Far worse, individuals struggling with biculturalism found themselves estranged from family and friends. The new Christians of Sillery began to pull away from Montagnais traditionalists, who resisted the new symbolic order, and found themselves caught between the demanding French and the offended, conservative Montagnais; moreover, the Sillery Christians, divided even among themselves and confronting opposition on all sides, embroiled themselves in unceasing controversy. In the end, the socially divisive impact of perceived sin and guilt undercut the Montagnais' attempt to use Catholic ritual to renew their communal solidarity.

8

The Solidarity of Kin

The Intersection of Eastern Algonkian and French-Catholic Cosmologies

Since the preceding essays (including those written for this volume) have engaged some of the major issues troubling Native American history, I now focus on the scholarship on northeastern missions. Because the French left such a rich record of their encounter with the Eastern Algonkians,[1] a substantial literature has developed since the 1970s on these missions. This work has had somehow to grapple with the nature and meaning of the Native American response to what is now commonly thought of, as Francis Jennings has put it, as the invasion of America.[2] With varying degrees of success, these studies have had to account for the religious character of Native American cultural life, a problem of ethnographic reconstruction, and for Native American people's religious dialogue with the missionaries, an historical challenge.

To review these issues in relation to the history of Eastern Algonkian missionization, I focus initially on the work of James Axtell, who contends that these peoples converted to Christianity. To suggest an alternative way of studying religious change, I revisit the ways in which oral tradition can be assessed to identify new ways of reasoning about Algonkian religious history. Finally, I recapitulate the interpretations explored in this volume to suggest that Algonkian peoples reasoned in their own way about the religious claims of the French. In all of this, I argue that conversion poorly describes the complex processes of religious change.

As will become clear, scholars have not achieved a cross-cultural understanding of missionization, an achievement that both ethnographic and historical reconstruction requires. The enduring problem centers on the fact that ethnohistorians have not understood Native American religious traditions, have in fact often dismissed "religion" as offering an explanation of contact events, and have, instead, championed materialist and rationalist ways of explaining intercultural relations. Such interpretations tend to marginalize Native Americans' understanding of their own history, as well as their distinctive assessments of the European encounter. The rationalist interpretation, in particular, locates Native

Americans in the superstitious and nonsensical places to which missionaries usually consigned them. Some rationalist historians allow for Native Americans in contact history only to the extent that they apparently submitted to the technological, economic, and political workings of European life. We must, therefore, consider the ways in which the religious dimension of Algonkian history has been misunderstood, ignored, or dismissed as causally irrelevant.

Understanding religious change continues to trouble scholars, as the 1993 publication of *Conversion to Christianity: Historical and Anthropological Perspectives on a Great Transformation* reveals. In his overview essay—"World Building and the Rationality of Conversion"—editor Robert Hefner surveys the many ways in which theorizing about ostensibly universal but enduringly local forms of Christianity has defined the colonial dilemma now troubling scholars. Hefner describes this need to discriminate between universalizing and indigenizing Christianities as a central interdisciplinary problem engaging anthropology, sociology, history, theology, and Religious Studies.[3] Hefner recognizes that political and economic systems have come and gone, but contends that the world religions, Christianity among them, have survived:

> *They are the longest lasting of civilization's primary institutions.* Their genius lies in their curious ability to renounce this world and announce another, more compelling and true. They relocate the divisive solidarities of language, custom, and region within a broader community and higher Truth. They do so ideally, of course, and it goes without saying that the ideal may be, and routinely is, ignored or violated by those who would use the Truth for other ends.[4]

The problem of religious truth remains central to understanding an emerging world order, either from the points-of-view of missionaries, who attempted to impose cultural and religious change, or in appreciating the enduring cultural realities of people who made sense of Christianity as they themselves pleased. The problem has been, of course, that missions have often produced counterintuitive results that undercut Hefner's position. In the seventeenth-century Northeast, indigenous peoples followed their own religious views of the world, and sought to preserve an inward-oriented and distinctive social identity, no matter the universalizing claims of Christianity.

Essayist Peter Wood defines this conceptual conundrum in his afterword to the *Conversion to Christianity* volume: "Conversion to Christianity means different things to different peoples and entails divergent social consequences."[5] Wood rejects the conclusion that Christianity has a universal meaning:

> The essays in this volume clarify some of the variables, such as the social position of those who embrace the new religion, their motives, the receptivity of their communities to intellectual innovation and other forms of change, and—what is not quite the same thing—the

mutability of their cultures. . . . On the evidence at hand, the variations do not offset each other. Differences in the *process* of conversion seem, to the contrary, to lead to differences in the *results*. The Christianity that conversion produces in different human communities is complexly diverse.

Both contemporary anthropology and theology, Wood observes, share "a radical skepticism that Christianity has intellectual content or social consequences that transcend cultural differences."[6] He notes that the essays in *Conversion to Christianity* "seem to accept without cavil" the idea that in understanding religious change "the local perspective is the primary reality." The essays contend that "religious meaning is to be found first of all in the exegetical accounts of religious participants." The essayists also agree that any claim that indigenous peoples have converted to Christianity must be proven by those who take such a position, rather than by those who react skeptically.[7] Upon reflection, Wood's propositions can lead to a view of religious change that complicates the unidirectional religious processes and outcome heralded in the volume's title: conversion as a great transformation. The consensus is remarkable: interdisciplinary work on religious change must focus on indigenous perspectives, purposes, and experiences.

THE QUESTION OF CONVERSION

Although productive lines of investigation have emerged, most of the literature on the Native American encounter with Catholic missionaries fails to meet Wood's interpretive propositions.[8] In the first place, historians have not taken the local perspective as the primary reality. In the second, little effort has been made to understand the ways in which Native Americans discriminated Catholic truth claims. Finally, while historians often argue that Native Americans converted to Christianity, they have not proven their case. Each of these claims is telling. Taken together, they amount to a tremendous failure to make sense of cultural encounter from the perspectives of all the participants. This failure to achieve Wood's conditions suggests that scholarly accounts of the so-called conversion of Eastern Algonkians must be reassessed.

Applying Wood's propositions, such a reassessment suggests that scholars have failed for a variety of reasons, which emerge in the reasoning of James Axtell, who alone offers a comprehensive overview of religious change.[9] On the face of it, Axtell seems sympathetic to Wood's criteria. In his first interpretation of missions—"The European Failure to Convert the Indians: An Autopsy"—Axtell details a Native American resistance against both Christianity and European civilization."[10] In another essay—"Some Thoughts on the Ethnohistory of Missions"—Axtell identifies another "interpretive problem that has not been handled particularly well by ethnohistorians or by historians of religion. And that is, What are the criteria for judging the success or failure of a missionary program?"[11] Axtell's affirmative answer to his final question—"Were Indian Conversions Bona Fide?"[12]—seems to align him with scholars who contend that Christian missions amount to a great, appropriate, and even inevitable transformation. As we shall see, Axtell begins with the stated purpose of a balanced presentation of the mission encounter, ostensibly arguing for a dialogical parity of Native American and missionary points-of-view, and ends with an interpretation that proclaims the ultimate truth of the Christian mission.[13]

In "The European Failure to Convert the Indians," Axtell opens with a foundational European ambivalence. While Recollet missionaries felt that American "savagery" precluded even the possibility of conversion, the early Jesuits, particularly Paul Le Jeune, articulated a more optimistic view. In this period, the Recollets and Jesuits agreed about the task at hand: Native Americans must be civilized before Christianity could be conveyed successfully. In Axtell's view, the Jesuits were well prepared for the task, if only because the French did not compete with Native Americans for land. Since the French focused on the fur trade, their success "depended wholly upon the well-being and friendship of the Indian trappers and middlemen." As Axtell puts the case: "To secure the trust and allegiance of their Indian partners required a tactful blend of cultural toleration, personal flexibility, and endurance."[14] In this way, Axtell seems to recognize that the missionaries' success depended on their ability to locate themselves within Native American value systems, but he stresses missionary, not Native American, adaptability.

Axtell argues that the Jesuits had several strengths in "the contest of conversion." The Jesuits were able to adjust to indigenous ways of life, and thus to win Indians' trust. Then, too, the Jesuits were cultural relativists; without giving up their claims of ultimate religious truth, the Jesuits compromised with Native American sensibilities to establish common ground.[15] "In large measure," Axtell writes, "the Jesuits' success was gained not by expecting less of their converts, as the English accused, but by accepting more."[16] Axtell notes other factors: the Jesuits were, as "the intellectual shock-troops of the Counter-Reformation," well-prepared to "attack heresy and paganism" with "classical, patristic, and Biblical" arguments.[17] In addition, the Jesuits were trained linguists whose finely tuned ears positioned them well "in the Indian Babel of the New World."[18] Axtell also argues that Catholic liturgy engaged Native American peoples subjectively: "Catholicism embraced the human emotions." As he puts it, "the Catholic's trademark was the Mass, which appealed to the communicant's senses with candles, bells, vestments, incense, and the familiar sonorities of Latin chants and responses." These "affective ceremonies" "appealed to the Indians' practical intelligence."[19] Moreover, Catholicism accorded with Indian "belief," particularly its doctrine of good words and virtuous living, but Axtell does not establish how such suppositions informed Native American ways of life.

For all of these advantages, Axtell observes that after two centuries the missionaries admitted their defeat. Axtell is not impressed with the usual explanation of the failure as the result of the "inevitable results of contact with European culture": disease, war, alcohol, "and the immoral example of false Christians."[20] Axtell acknowledges these external forces, but prefers to "emphasize the traits within Indian culture itself that impeded first the civilizing and then the Christianizing attempts of the Europeans."[21] What follows, however, continues to stress missionary views of the encounter. First, the Jesuits soon came to realize that their efforts to educate Indian peoples failed for lack of both money and students. The Jesuits learned that "Indian boys 'love[d] liberty' and 'abhor[red] restraint' of any kind, which fostered a healthy sense of pride in their status as junior hunters and warriors."[22] European education, Axtell concludes "was, in short, the wrong method for the wrong people at the wrong time."[23]

Axtell observes that Indians also created obstacles to the Jesuits' conversion program. The first was language. The second was the native shaman: "Pitting one kind of magic and power against another, the priest sought to win the people's allegiance to Christianity by discrediting the symbol and spokesmen of their native religion."[24] At this level, Axtell again gives the Jesuits the advantage, having as they did "printed truths,"[25] "a scientific understanding of Nature," "and an unrelenting questioning of the habitual (which no cultural practice can long survive)." In these ways, the Jesuits undercut the shamans' standing, but not without resistance. "Native customs," Axtell writes, "enjoyed a long life well after many of the Indians had accepted the form if not the spirit of Christianity. Priests were ridiculed, insulted, berated, threatened, and even killed by pagan factions, and their new converts were subjected to similar indignities."[26] Axtell quotes one Jesuit to the effect that the missionaries had more trouble keeping Indians than in converting them in the first place. And no wonder. Axtell shows that a main source of conflict arose between Jesuit and Indian notions of sexuality, and quotes another Jesuit on the enormity of this clash: "'It is this that prevents most of the infidels from accepting the Faith, and has caused some to lose it who had already embraced it.'"[27] Axtell identifies still more stumbling blocks: Lenten fasting, burial customs, competition among Christians, the Christian work week, and the threat of hell. "All these practices and more," Axtell writes, "seemed simply unreasonable to a people who had been raised in a religious tradition that was better adapted to the natural and social world in which they lived."[28] Axtell notes that, while Indian sachems, speakers, and shamans raised objections to these practices, most responded with passive-aggressive resistance: Indians seemed to agree with missionary pronouncements in order not to disagree. Axtell concludes that Native Americans' polite resistance "was an outgrowth of the basic Indian toleration of other religions and the correspondent wish to pursue their own."[29]

In a second essay, Axtell criticizes ethnohistorical interpretations of the missions. Axtell frames a central question: "What are the criteria for judging the success or failure of a missionary program?"[30] Without considering that the question itself might be unduly partisan—the real question concerns whose criteria one attends to—Axtell observes that not only do most writers fail to ask the question, "they just plunge in and with an unarticulated set of assumptions proceed to judge the mission efforts from the perspective of the missionaries." The missiological side of such literature,[31] Axtell avows, judges missions "a semi-success, but the judgement leaves the reader in doubt as to the criteria being applied, as well as the historical value of such a conclusion."[32]

Axtell claims that such scholars pursue inappropriate interpretations. For their part, "lay historians" do not differ much from church historians or missionaries. They simply peer over the missionaries' shoulders, albeit in a skeptical manner: "almost invariably their judgments have been negative because, while they still tend to take the missionary goals as the standards for judgment, they switch focus in the end to assume that the results in the native society being *acted upon*—passively—are more important."[33] Axtell contends that such historians suffer from counter-cultural tendencies, tend to weep with natives "over their loss of cultural integrity" and to curse missionary intolerance and coercive measures. Moreover, these historians "no longer share the Christian belief that pagans and infidels should be converted," and they emulate anthropologists' cultural relativism in bending "over backwards for the natives without performing the same gyration for the Europeans." As a result, "the historians writing mission history have come up with the wrong conclusion for reasons that are more than half right."[34] As I read their arguments, however, these scholars are not nearly so partisan. Axtell's purposes seem polemical because he condemns, but does not closely assess, these historians' arguments: "Thus far, historians have judged the missionaries by the missionaries' criteria, but then have judged the Indians only from their *own* contemporary perspective as champions of the underdog, defenders of the weak, and protectors of the ethnic enclave." Arguing for what is ostensibly a more balanced treatment, Axtell proposes another perspective: "But if we ask whether the *Indians*, from *their* point-of-view, were successful or not in adopting or adapting Christianity, I think we arrive at a somewhat different measure of success."[35]

Most everyone would agree that the telling point is whether or not the adoption or adaptation of Christianity conformed to Indian purposefulness. Rather than reconstruct how Native Americans assessed Christian truth claims, however, Axtell reasons from an outcome that no one, either Native or Euramerican, could have foreseen: "The elemental fact of ethnic survival is all-important in assessing the success or failure of mission efforts from the native perspective."[36] The question of missionary success, then, relates to missionaries and Native Americans in different ways. "Therefore," Axtell writes in a variation of the victimization theory, "we should judge the European colonial cultures in *offense* terms, as societies on the muscle." Thus, Axtell reverts to the methodology he supposedly abhors: using hindsight to look over the missionaries' shoulders. Conversely, Axtell disclaims, "we should judge the Indian cultures in *defensive* terms, largely because they were tolerant of other people and their religions and were, in fact, the targets of the European invasions."[37] In other words, Axtell holds that historical hindsight holds the key to understanding the Indian perspective toward missionization: "How effective were they [Native Americans] in accepting only as much of the Europeans' offerings as helped them to survive and prosper in their own terms?"[38] Again, those terms are slighted in favor of a overly generalized theory of resistance:

> By now it will be obvious that my suggestions rest on one large assumption, namely, that cultures should be free to define their own goals, set their own course, and to survive in any way they can—and that ethnohistorians should honor those rights in their scholarship as well as in everyday life. If one culture tries to infringe the rights of another, we are at least allowed, if not obligated, to condemn the practice. But we should first see how successfully the invaded group defended its own terrain and turned what may at first glance appear to be a social defeat into a cultural victory. In our histories as in our own world, underdogs often do need champions. But I suspect that they possess more cultural resources and stronger instincts and capacities for survival than even their friends tended to allow.[39]

Because Axtell does not reconstruct how Indians understood Christianity, he falls back to the position of moralizing that he otherwise criticizes.

By far the most complex and controversial statement of Axtell's treatment of conversion appears in his essay "Were Indian Conversions Bona Fide?" In this study, Axtell backs away from his two earlier essays. He reports that Native American experience, as well as "the history of Christianity around the world,"[40] led him to correct his earlier view that many Indians had not converted. This essay continues to criticize other scholars, now for casting aspersions "on the quantity, quality, and longevity of native conversions." Axtell seeks to displace two results of such revisionistic conclusions. First, he says, missionaries are depicted either as evil colonialists or as naive fools. Second, Indian converts are treated as "hapless victims," or "Br'er Rabbits of the forest."[41]

Axtell understands conversion as a moving away *from* one tradition and *to* another. He writes that many Indians "were capable of taking the decisive step *from* their old religions *to* the new, without deceiving themselves, the missionaries or us."[42] For this reason, Axtell takes a critical stance toward three scholars—David Blanchard,[43] Cornelius Jaenen,[44] and Bruce Trigger[45]—because they question conversion as a viable description of religious change. They emphasize, instead, "the tenacity of native traditions and the gullibility of French missionaries."[46] Axtell summarizes these scholars' respective points-of-view. Blanchard suggests that the Mohawks of Caughnawaga played French against English for their own advantage. Blanchard says, also, that Mohawk Catholicism amounted to a "protective coloration" behind which the Mohawks hid their traditional values. In addition, they "did not relinquish their traditional religion and beliefs but merely 'modified their religious practices and developed a syncretistic system of ritual that yielded the desired affect [sic].'"[47]

According to Axtell, Cornelius Jaenen takes a different route to the same conclusion: Jaenen cites apostasy, backsliding, economically motivated baptisms, "the childish attraction of colorful ceremonies," the lack of a native clergy, competing religious orders, "and, of course, the existence of syncretism, the 'incorporation of pagan and pre-Christian elements' in Catholic Indian belief and ritual." For all these reasons, Jaenen concludes that "Jesuit success 'was not always as sincere a case of acculturation as the missionaries hoped it would be. Rather, it was often a mere addition of Catholicism as a cultural overlay.'"[48] For his part, Axtell reports, Trigger doubts that the Jesuits were able to convey "an accurate understanding of Christianity" to Native American peoples. Trigger observes that "an anthropological understanding of social typology" reveals a cultural gulf between Native Americans, who were organized in egalitarian terms, and the French, who lived in a hierarchical and coercive society. Until Indians made the social transition, Trigger argues, conversion was not possible.[49] In short, Axtell concludes that the new interpretive wisdom holds that there were a few Indian converts, "but many, perhaps most, of them were not even made in good faith."[50]

As he had earlier, Axtell argues that the revisionists are polemical and incorrect.[51] He thinks that such revisionism is related to colonial rivalries between Catholics and Protestants, but he does not connect this claimed inheritance to the scholars in question. As before, Axtell also tars these scholars with an ideological brush, but again without linking his assertions with their interpretations. Two types of historians disturb the present interpretive stance, Axtell avows. There are, first, "those of a secular, agnostic, or atheistic disposition for whom religion, past or present, is largely irrelevant." Second, some historians are "of a 'liberal,' anti-Establishment, or pro-underdog persuasion who think—or rather hope—that inscrutable Indian protagonists and 'patriots' have an infinite capacity for putting one over on the white man."[52]

Then, for a space, Axtell accords the revisionists room to breathe. "Whatever its source," he writes, "the new iconoclasm has something to be said for it." Axtell admits that many northeastern Indians "were not given adequate instruction in the Christian mysteries, morally tested to ensure that their outer lives reflected their inner grace, or sustained by established churches, sacraments, and ecclesiastical discipline."[53] This admission quietly introduces religious matters around which Axtell's argument revolves: the challenge of teaching Christian doctrine (which, we might observe, is a troublesome act of translation between differently constituted worldviews, especially when one is doctrinal and the other is not) consists of an education in "mysteries." The real test of conversion is evidence of "inner grace," and sacramental efficacy. Seemingly oblivious to his own critique of Trigger's concern for understanding the ways in which cultural differences may have shaped the encounter, Axtell has it that effective missionization must be weighed in the successful application of institutional and authoritarian arrangements.

Axtell proceeds immediately with a litany of limitations: Jesse Fléché baptized Mi'kmaqs with no instruction (here, apparently, sacramentalism had no causal effect), and he notes the existence of "beggarly hypocrites who would grunt assent to the missionaries' preachments as long as they were offered a pipe of tobacco, a nip of brandy, a new shirt, trading advantages at the company store, or military protection." Axtell again notes the retarding effect, here more positively than earlier, of a Native American polite reticence that amounted to "masterly dissembling, even over long periods."[54] Axtell returns to details used earlier to prove that Native Americans did not convert to Christianity. If Native Americans "fell from grace," it was not because they were "fickle and irresolute." Rather, they felt "an understandable desire to cling to familiar cultural habits."[55] For all of that, Axtell asserts rather than documents the steady endurance of Native Christianity, to which claim he assigns four reasons.

For readers who might have become confused by this close reading of Axtell's argument, his own criteria, and ours, require that any argument for or against conversion must be made within Native American understandings of reality, and in terms of actual Native American responses to Catholic truth claims. Axtell's four reasons do not meet this requirement because they all focus upon the missionaries rather than upon Native Americans. As he sees it, because "the first two generations of missionaries were well qualified for the task of conversion," they ensured "the good faith of their native converts."[56] Thus, he first surveys the missionaries' linguistic gifts, their motives and stamina, and their astuteness in smelling a rat. In the midst of this catalogue of missionary prowess, Axtell returns to the subtle and ultimate direction of his argument: the missionaries remembered, "as should we—that *bona fide* conversion *was* a matter of the heart, a secret transaction between the self and the soul." The missionaries, like historians since, realized that "cultural reform and 'right living'" could be assayed only in "outward behavior" of supposedly Christian Indians, but such an assessment Axtell does not undertake.[57]

Axtell's second reason is not so clear, but seems to be a variation on the first: missionaries knew how to respond when their "listeners balked or wavered," particularly by playing on Indian credulity. If even limiting themselves to teaching only "the essential articles of faith" proved inadequate, the missionaries used clocks, predictions of eclipses, the stench of burning sulphur, lodestones, compasses, prisms, and the printed page to declare their power.[58] In this regard, Axtell does not reconstruct the ways in which missionary audiences may have heard, agreed, "balked or wavered," let alone been persuaded by the wonders of non-Indian science. Axtell declares that the third key to understanding missionary success was due to the missionaries' high standards, but this claim does not (particularly in relationship to the French Jesuits) receive convincing detail. Finally, the missionaries persevered by establishing effective institutions, particularly churches "symbolizing the place of the new religion in the natives' lives."[59]

Having taken the stand that the missionaries controlled the direction and content of conversion, Axtell then attacks what is for him the nub of the revisionists' agenda. Not only do the "new skeptics" doubt "the sincerity of their [Native Americans'] conversions," they resort "to the hobgoblin of 'syncretism'" to explain what really happened.[60] Axtell's stance about syncretism is unambiguous: "In the hands of the new critics, syncretism is a red herring dragged across the discussion of the quality of native conversions." For Axtell, the problem is that historians have no way of ascertaining the conscious or unconsciousness character of Indian responses.[61] Axtell is willing to recognize syncretism, but in a limited way that fits his argument that Native Americans could only acquiesce to Christian claims of ultimate truth: "The Jesuits, for example, were well aware of a certain amount of syncretism on the part of their *neophytes*, less often of their *converts*. In fact, they approved, encouraged, and initiated the moderate use of it in order to ease the Indians' transition to the new faith." Axtell includes among these missionary-supported syncretisms traditional naming and adoption ceremonies, feasts, and dreams that the priests assigned Christian purposes. Moreover, "tobacco sacrifices were made to the new God rather than to local deities; Christian sacramentals—rings, medals, crosses, rosaries, and relics—assumed the instrumental function of traditional charms and amulets. And in the most significant replacement of all, Jesuit priests accepted the spiritual mantle of shamans, conjurers, and healers until they could educate the natives in the true office of a Catholic priest."[62] For their part, Native Americans were propelled to syncretism for emotional, rather than thoughtful purposes: "The native sought some carryover because they bore expressive rather than instrumental value and helped the natives maintain their social identity as Indians."[63]

Axtell insists on two clarifications in understanding syncretism, whatever that process may have been. "First, the missionaries dominated the conversion process, monitoring every stage and guarding the gates of admission." The net result was that "pagan" elements were effectively contained: "They were translated piecemeal as isolated elements rather than religious complexes or systems, and it was the missionaries who allowed them to pass." In time, as they gained the upper hand, missionaries increasingly "defined the relevant concepts, delineated the proper stages of spiritual growth, installed the new pantheon, and set appropriate moral standards." Ultimately, Axtell states, Christianity, like other world religions, proclaims a dogmatic position "intolerant of other visions of the world." "The alternative perspectives offered by tribal religions, which feature a host of local deities concerned mainly with particular communities and their environments, have no validity in the eyes of those who worship a supreme deity of universal proportions."[64] At this point, Axtell stakes out methodological ground for a religious understanding of conversion:

> The new skepticism errs also in reducing religion, in the manner of cultural materialists, to a mere epiphenomenon of socio-economic realities. Indians in the Northeast 'converted,' the critics believe, because they were forced to take on protective coloration by the harsh realities of imperial subjection. This assumption is misleading in three ways: (1) it is unwarrantedly reductionist and belied by countless historical examples, (2) it confuses the social functions of conversion for *groups* with its *emotional* and *intellectual* meaning for *individuals*, and (3) it confuses the *explanation* of conversion with the *validity* or *quality* of the results.[65]

In these terms, Axtell highlights the essential need to understand religious change in Algonkian terms.

In the end, Axtell aligns himself with missionaries everywhere: "As history has shown many times over, the true 'meaning and spirit' of Christianity were accessible to all kinds of people universally, regardless of the societies from which they came." In the Northeast, Native Americans "turned to Christianity because that world religion satisfied new emotional needs and intellectual hunger." Although Axtell provides no evidence about these new needs, his conclusion warrants extensive quotation:

> Those needs were created by the advent of the European strangers, their marvelous technology, and their deadly diseases. The ablest native minds could simply not explain—much less predict—the origins of white men and black, the geographies of continents beyond their own 'island on the turtle's back,' the lethal etiology of smallpox, the arts of metallurgy and papermaking, alphabetic literacy, or lunar eclipses. Nor could native societies control even their own circumscribed worlds as before. The invaders put so much pressure on native America, some of it deliberate, some inadvertent, that traditional culture was sooner or later thrown into disarray. Understandably, Indians whose lives were most affected by the colonial juggernaut were the likeliest candidates for conversion. For Christianity (and its attendant culture) offered answers to their most urgent questions, balm to their frayed emotion, and techniques of prediction and control to replace those they had lost.

Under the conditions of such victimization, much of it derived from the weakness of their own cultural condition, Native Americans "placed themselves under the spiritual tutelage of the black-robed spokesmen for a greater God."[66]

Axtell's ultimate claim is a theologically biased position, not a reasoned conclusion rooted in a careful understanding of either the religious character of Native American life or the peoples' actual historical engagement with missionaries. Much of the argument rests on flimsy assertions, particularly the claims that religious change consisted of individual conversion (the seventeenth-century Eastern Algonkian had a decisively communal religious orientation), and that historians who have attempted other, more culturally responsive explanations, are little more than methodological charlatans. But most telling of all is Axtell's unfounded claim to have engaged the cross-cultural discourse of missionization in Native American terms.

Religious discernment derives from a particular kind of reasoning that happens in particular times and places. In the life experience of Eastern Algonkian peoples, the missionaries' religious claims made sense (or not) in the time and place of their pronouncement—and negotiation. On the St. Lawrence River in the 1630s, as we have seen in Chapters Five, Six, and Seven, what the Jesuits had to say had meaning for the Montagnais in a variety of complex ways. To the extent that they perceived these ways, the Jesuits responded with innovation, telling arguments, and adaptation. Such flexibility had its limits, however. Seventeenth-century French missionaries understood very little about the Algonkian ways of reasoning that led to what they described as a perverse, even demonic, resistance to Christian religious and cultural truths. The Montagnais in conversation with the French were engaged in acts of making sense, and they did so necessarily within the logical patterns of their own way of reasoning. Algonkians reasoned *from* tradition, *about* Catholic religious claims, and *for* their own reasons.

Certainly, the Montagnais had their own ways of understanding reality. In the Jesuits' view, for individual Montagnais to "convert" required a move from one traditional, deluded order of reality to another, higher order of truth. But little in the historical record suggests that the Montagnais recognized the cultural revolution the Jesuits proposed to implement. Some Montagnais did accept the rite of baptism, the meaning of which they understood in complementary ways: baptism was a means of establishing, securing, and processing a relationship with French allies. Baptism was also understood as a kind of medicine, a rite that invoked the healing intervention of a figure the Jesuits called "He-Who-Made-All."

For their part, the Jesuit missionaries operated naively. They contended, erroneously, that the Montagnais lacked any real or systematic view of reality. They insisted that the Montagnais had no idea of a true God, which was accurate, but does not equal the priests' claims that the Montagnais were irreligious. They warned the Montagnais that they were duped by demons, and so engaged in superstitious ritual acts. They also claimed that baptism, and the other sacramental interventions of the Church, had divine and transformative power. As a result of such positions, the Jesuits had extreme difficulty in comprehending Montagnais reasons for rejecting or accepting baptism. The priests' understanding of the complexities of the social and religious change they demanded was correspondingly simplistic. In George Tinker's argument, missionary policy was necessarily genocidal because the early Jesuits aimed to kill what they saw as religiously aberrant customs in order to save the person.[67] The Montagnais responded in the moment without apprehending the long-term implications of the priests' cultural colonialism.

Most significantly, Axtell fails to apprehend Native American modes of thinking. To contend that Native Amerians made sense of Christianity from the perspective of their "practical intelligence" and in the ways in which Catholic rituals engaged their senses and emotions offers no explanation of either intelligence or emotionalism. Such a claim actually demeans Native American ways of thinking, and defies what has increasingly been appreciated as the bodily basis of all knowledge.[68] Nor does Axtell's proposition that conversion consisted of a substitution of "local deities concerned mainly with particular communities" for a "supreme deity of universal pretentions"[69] stand up to scrutiny. Native Americans were not theists, did not subscribe to an hierarchical arrangement of either the cosmos or their social life, and were little inclined to submit to the abrasive claims that linked Christian morality to what most Algonkians thought of as the bizarre, authoritarian forms of French social life.

Axtell unsuccessfully compares Native American and European religions because he has not examined critically the categories scholars use to describe religion. Terms such as God, worship, spiritual, natural, cultural, and supernatural cannot be applied to Native American religious traditions; at least, such terms ought not be applied without empirical justification. Axtell contends that spiritual or supernatural power, supernatural talismans, and a monotheistic belief in an "ultimate being" characterized Native American religious orientations to the world. Then, ironically, Axtell writes that Native Americans did not make a distinction between natural and supernatural.[70] He notes similarly that prior to contact, Indians had no heaven and no hell.[71] While Axtell says that each Native American group had a religion consisting of ritual designed to affect humans and nature, he reduces the complex functions of myth to rationalizing ritual. He also reduces ritual to acts that mobilize "supernatural powers."[72] Mythographer William Doty argues, to the contrary, that the so-called Gods of myth may be transcendent, but they do not negate "ordinary personhood" and are nothing like "the *totaliter aliter* (absolute otherness) of deity in Western theology."[73] While Axtell does seem to recognize that their distinctive "voice-and-ear" world gave Native Americans a dynamic social outlook—"their own religious and moral ethos"—he does not study the principles of their worldviews.[74]

Axtell misunderstands Native American religions in part because he relies on Anthony F. C. Wallace's study *Religion: An Anthropological View*. In Wallace's definition, "religion is based on supernaturalistic beliefs about the nature of the world which are not only inconsistent with scientific knowledge but also difficult to relate to naive human experience."[75] Wallace's objectivist stand is paradoxical because he studied with A. Irving Hallowell, who discovered that Algonkian-speaking peoples' religious lives are linguistically grounded, and so escape dismissal as mere belief systems.[76] The Algonkians' category of the animate grammatically highlights the personal character of entities (including those entities non-Indians call Gods) that Euramericans designate merely as inanimate.[77] Wallace, like Axtell, acknowledges the animistic character of Native American religions, but neither attend to the ways in which the animate category of "Person" belies the language of supernaturalistic belief and gives Native American life perceptual, cognitive, linguistic, and behavioral integrity.[78]

Thinking in supernaturalistic terms also fails to account for the ways in which Native American religious life proceeds. The theory of the supernatural posits an ultimate macrocosm in relationship to a microcosm that is, by derivation and comparison, only relatively real. In missionary teachings, the Fall taints creation. Northeastern Algonkian myth, however, does not concern itself either with the creation of the world or with a prescient creator. Rather, Algonkian myth describes a cosmos where, in the beginning, human beings share the same nature and language with animals, plants, "natural" "forces," and even "artifacts," all of whom are engaged actively in shaping the world, particularly in mutually beneficial ritual activities.

While Christianity and Algonkian religious orientations both constitute theories of cosmic and worldly otherness, they differ greatly in emphasis. Algonkians recognize a system of otherness that stresses dimensional continuities among all classes of persons. If power (manitou) creates a practical hierarchy of personal stature (some beings are more powerful than others), human beings themselves stand at every level because they too have power, and some humans even have great power. In Christianity, on the other hand, the supernatural enjoys vertical superiority over both nature and culture. God and humans have radically different natures. Grace comes exclusively from on high. Worship and prayer denote submission.[79]

In attending to the effects of religious action including speech, rather than to written, dogmatic, and faith positions about the world's character, Algonkian religious thought emphasizes reciprocity between persons, and especially human responsibility. Described in myth as constructive sharing, reciprocity shapes daily life in the give-and-take of every sort of ritual. If the category "power" differentiates personal entities who otherwise share the same manner of being, then the category "gift" becomes the central ethical trajectory of Algonkian religious practice. Positive, powerful others share; negative, powerful others withhold. In these ways, the Algonkians' analogues to evil and sin (and their analogues to savagery and civilization) highlight anti-social behavior. Thus, seventeenth-century Algonkian peoples all shared the same social orientation in understanding and working with the religious challenge of achieving solidarity between human and cosmic persons. Algonkians brought that mythic tradition to the process of making sense of French claims about their universal religious and cultural truths.

AN INTERSECTION OF WORLDVIEWS

As a conclusion drawn from studying Algonkian religious traditions, as well as from reconstructing their seventeenth-century encounter, I argue that Eastern Algonkian relations with French missionaries led to religious change, but not to conversion as a type of change. The main problem with conversion is that it stipulates a particular and singular outcome to religious encounter. To describe Eastern Algonkian religious change as conversion is to fail to understand that change itself is a process, and particularly a process of discerning, negotiating, making, and adapting religious meaning. The category "conversion" is intimately related to the pervasive view that Native American history proceeds in terms of victimization and cultural decline, and in terms of non-Indian views of a universal, progressive, and Christian history. Algonkians were not simply victims, however, and they did not lose their distinctive worldview as a result of contact with either Europeans or the Catholic religious tradition.

The concept of conversion is a dehumanizing reification that overlooks, denies, and dismisses the Algonkians' historical agency. Conversion claims that Native Americans came to agree with pervasive and aggressive critiques of their lifeways. Conversion denies that either pre- or post-contact Native American life had or has systematic and intellectual integrity. Conversion contends that Native Americans themselves perceived the superior truth claims of Christianity as a series of overarching theological and cultural propositions about reality. Conversion claims that Native Americans repudiated their religious traditions, and thus their ways of perceiving, thinking, valuing, and acting. Conversion concludes that Native Americans turned away from ancient truth, and moved toward a system that offered them a morally superior, and intellectually more effective, way of understanding the world. Conversion stipulates that Christianity proclaims a new, universal truth by which Native Americans could understand an unprecedented, post-contact world. In all these ways, conversion is a problematic way of describing religious change. As an ethnocentrically charged but multivalent category, conversion fails utterly to understand the distinctive and integral character of Native American life both before and after contact. It is appropriate, therefore, to consider the ways in which Algonkian and French-Catholic views of the world came to intersect as a result of Algonkian ways of making sense.

As Ramsey MacMullen has shown in the case of Greco-Roman conversion to Christianity, changes in religious practice do not necessarily constitute a rejection of tradition, an acceptance of a superior religious philosophy, or the adoption of a more effective ethical practice. MacMullen quotes R. W. Bulliet's conclusion about medieval conversion to Islam: "As conversion progresses, the new religion becomes in its social dimension increasingly like the old."[80] Bulliet's insight applies equally to Algonkian responses to Catholicism. In the Algonkians' case, a deeply rooted philosophical conservatism informed their discourse with the missionaries and shaped their critical adjustment to Catholic truth claims.

The idea that Algonkians accepted Christianity wholesale as a "religion" and as a "system" just does not make sense in the immediate, pragmatic, everyday, non-dogmatic, relational, and non-theistic emphases of Algonkian life. When they first met French missionaries, Algonkians had no word, concept, category, or abstraction even roughly analogous to the non-Indian category "religion." That is one reason, of course, why the early missionaries judged that Algonkian people were linguistically and intellectually deficient. The philosophical and ethical integrity of the Algonkian world (with which missionaries dealt without a clear understanding of that world) did not consist of premises, doctrines, or beliefs. To the extent that missionaries contended for such foundational propositions, Catholic "religion" could not easily translate. Eastern Algonkians were interested in achieving a viable social life in relation to disruptive European newcomers, but not at all in disembodied, abstract, philosophical, or theological truth.

Despite all the linguistic and intellectual impediments, aspects of Christianity came to make sense to Algonkians as we have seen in Chapters Three to Seven. This process affirmed the essential relevance of traditional ways of understanding and valuing the world. While it is highly doubtful that missionaries succeeded in conveying their theism (including the creation of the world, its subservient, creaturely, and essentially sinful character, and its prophesied meaning in the will and purposefulness of an ultimate and authoritarian God), Algonkians soon came to accept at least some of the persons of the Catholic cosmos. They did so because He-Who-Made-All came to them in dreams offering protection, healing, and access to the animals upon whom their hunting lives depended. In Algonkian experience, then, the missionaries' "God" made himself known in their daily life, and he did so in ways that fit traditional cosmological assumptions. The He-Who-Made-All of Algonkian dreams and ritual entered into intimate, mutual, and reciprocal relations with the people. There is no evidence that in interacting with the Algonkians he claimed preeminence.

Algonkian oral tradition reveals the intellectual trajectory of their reasoning about Catholicism. Tradition continued to locate the people in a meaningful cosmic order, and without the distinguishing cosmic hierarchy of being that the

French missionaries attempted to promulgate. Without positing the existence of greater and lesser beings in the world, Algonkians recognized that various beings embodied and expressed power in negative and positive ways. Algonkians apprehended religious, cultural, and historical meaning not in some abstract notion of cosmic order, but in the emergent, purposeful, intersecting, and sometimes conflicting actions of persons. In these pragmatic ways, Algonkians construed the missionaries' claims of superior religious truth in the everyday events of their own world.[81]

As we saw in the Wabanaki chapters, Algonkian accounts of the beginning-time stressed either the kin-orientation or the anti-social selfishness of various beings. Algonkians also highlighted personal responsibility between human beings and between human beings and other-than-human persons as the only way to explain world order and disorder. As a result, Algonkian oral tradition articulated a philosophical system that had cosmological, rather than merely local, significance. In other words, the Algonkian cosmos was constituted as the interpersonal, intersubjective moral order we explored in Chapter Two. This order subsumed what social scientists consider impersonal causality (mechanical, economic, political, and institutional) under a relational way of thinking. As became clear in the historical chapters of this study, Algonkians recognized anti-social behavior as the antithesis of their moral order. As might be expected, since human beings commonly assess the unknown in terms of the known, Algonkians tested Europeans' humanity (that is, Europeans' capacity to act constructively as persons) and found many of them wanting. Far from converting to a European authoritarian and impersonal cultural system, nothing in the Eastern Algonkians' relations with the French changed their confidence in their relational world order. Without such an assessment of the relational constitution of the Algonkian's cosmos their self-motivated and self-referential purposes cannot be appreciated.

The opening chapters of this book (Introduction and Chapters One and Two) argue that scholars have not recognized these alternative ways in which Algonkian life has proceeded. A deep-seated source of this failure lies in western European pretensions of cultural and religious superiority (complex claims to civilization) and the related position that Native Americans were culturally and religiously inferior (claims of primitivism). This tension between the two claims—belied both by Euramerican injustice and by Algonkian social civility—has received considerable scholarly attention and is widely understood as a false, inaccurate, and self-serving dichotomy.[82] In addition, these chapters have also argued that scholars should acknowledge what has been a largely unrecognized misunderstanding: scholars have imposed intellectually ethnocentric judgments because of the inappropriate assumptions they make about the nature of religious life. Overly abstract understandings of religion have judged Native Americans as undeveloped, illogical, and superstitious, and even dupes of Satan. In making sense of these claims of cultural and religious inferiority, scholars have followed two inappropriate interpretive paths. The first simply rejects the real-world relevance of "religion" as non-empirical, imaginary, non-utilitarian, and, therefore, non-objective. The other path, ostensibly more responsive to Native American sensibilities, takes a subjectivist route toward explaining Native American religious life. This approach, which self-styled rationalist objectivists marginalize and/or dismiss as romantic, tends to describe Native American religious life as belief, worship, and spiritual. Most tellingly, the opening chapters demonstrated that the tension between the objectivist and subjectivist approaches do not constitute a simple, or even logical, polarization. Subjectivist scholars also think in overly abstract terms—nature, culture, and the supernatural, for examples—and objectivists share precisely the same categorical assumptions in opposing materiality and spirituality. Thus, I have argued that not only is there an unexamined intellectual complicity between only apparently polarized interpretations, but that both positions have failed to engage Native American life in its own terms.

My introduction also reflects on the ways in which these tensions have affected my own work and my emerging understanding of other perspectives. Even while I continued to exercise a range of inappropriate and ethnocentric terminology, I began to move toward another understanding. The process began simply because Algonkian stories captured my imagination. The stories about the cannibal giants and Gluskap taught me that seventeenth-century Algonkians had a systematic, precise, and subtle view of social reality that non-Indians seemed not to have noticed. The same stories pointed to a confident Algonkian critique of European newcomers. Algonkians could see that French ethical claims and their social individualism, coercive politics, and profit-driven economics moved in contradictory directions. Tellingly, these stories, so often dismissed as quaint folklore and as non-historical, attend to the moral rather than the factual conditions of the Algonkians' encounter with the French. The stories articulate a relational logic that cuts two ways. On the one hand, the stories associate the French with an ancient understanding of anti-social evil. On the other, the tales record a process of the Algonkians reflecting about the internal effects of contact in challenging, and even undercutting, the kinship solidarity among the peoples themselves. In these stories, Algonkian tradition grapples with history. It is not known when these stories began, but their concerns reverberate with both ethnographic and historical evidence. The stories suggest the moral trajectory of Algonkian religious history: Algonkians used religious dialogue to turn inward and revitalize social relations and to turn outward and hold at bay threatening forms of French social behavior.

As we have seen in the historical chapters of this study (Chapters Three to Seven), Algonkian oral tradition served the peoples well. As their stories urged, Algonkians scrutinized not only French religion and culture, they also struggled to adjust their internal and external relationships accordingly. Although the early French found it hard to grasp, seventeenth-century Algonkians had an ethical system that was quite capable of leading them to the social and religious adaptations they needed to make. Some of the French missionaries responded to Algonkian sociality, even while their writings indicate an extreme difficulty in understanding how such uncivilized peoples (the French word *sauvage* means people of the woods) could be ethical without either the leadership of God or of an authority-wielding king.[83] In effect, some French missionaries adapted to Algonkian life without understanding its religious character. As a result, they did not clearly understand Algonkian motivations in their mutual dealings.

There are several reasons why the Algonkians responded conservatively to the French. First among those reasons was the value they placed on community life. In this regard, French sociality struck the Algonkians as irreligious because the French were rude, acquisitive, and individualistic.[84] Second, Algonkian ways of reasoning in relational terms fully allowed them to see that French sociality was in many ways antithetical to their own way of life. Third, both the Algonkians and the French saw the world as an expression of religious intentionalities (manitou for the Algonkians, spirit for the French) emerging in contemporary events. In a related vein, fourth, Algonkians and missionaries understood both disease and the anti-social behavior induced by the liquor trade in religious ways. Finally, because some French adjusted to Algonkian social mores, Algonkians' sense of self-confidence was affirmed in everyday life. All told, then, these observations suggest that whatever they made of Catholicism, Algonkians did so in their own distinct ways and for their own reasons.

We can first glimpse a religious sociality operating among Algonkians even in the poorly documented sixteenth century. Their initial encounters with European voyagers will probably always remain beyond satisfactory reconstruction. But, as we saw in Chapter One, historians have argued for and against a religious understanding of this contact period, and for and against a explanation in terms of economic rationality. We can do better. Father Chrestien Le Clercq recorded in the 1680s an account of a sixteenth-century, indigenously motivated case of religious change among the Mi'kmaq of the Miramichi River in what is now the northeastern section of the province of New Brunswick. While there is no way to affirm the factuality of the Mi'kmaq tradition Le Clercq documented, its details are congruent with the Algonkians' way of reasoning in relational terms.

By way of historical context, we know that in the early sixteenth century the French appeared from nowhere. They traded with Mi'kmaq people. They raised large crosses on prominent seashore sites. The French departed as suddenly as they had appeared. Although Le Clercq does not recognize this historical context for the religious movement he describes, he records details that document a religious response to the immediately devastating effect of first contact. Epidemic illness overwhelmed the Mi'kmaq peoples. Some of the Mi'kmaq began to dream of a person who offered help via a cross he revealed to them. This intervention helped the Mi'kmaq to counter the illness that beset them. The Mi'kmaq also began to use the healing cross to affirm and extend relationships between their geographically dispersed social groups. These Mi'kmaq placed a special value on the dream-person's gift of the cross, and their descendants remembered this religious history in the second half of the seventeenth century. Some historians have noted variously these facts, but have not explained them.[85] Understanding these facts in Algonkian terms is possible, however, when one focuses the Algonkians' religious sociality upon them. Such a focus demonstrates the value of integrating Religious Studies with the interdisciplinary work of ethnohistory. The task is to compare Le Clercq's record of Algonkian oral tradition with new relational insights about the Algonkians' religious life. As we saw in Chapter One, such a overlap of perspectives is not easily achieved given the long tradition of ethnocentrically misinterpreting Algonkian religious life.

The Mi'kmaq and French reasoned about the cross in distinct and yet complementary ways. French explorers and fishermen used crosses for pragmatic, political, and religious purposes. Practically, the large coastal crosses the French erected served as navigational devices. They were traffic signs leading French ships through the Gulf of St. Lawrence and toward the dangerous mouth of the St. Lawrence River. The crosses were also more than signs. The French consciously erected the crosses as a political symbol of God-given power. In this sense, the cross embodied the religious legitimacy of French civilization, and the right, even the responsibility, of the French to colonize and to proselytize. In addition, the cross expressed for the French the world-emergence of Christian civilization and a French national certainty about their religious and political place in the developing new order. Finally, in its most basic sense, the cross projected cosmic religious meaning operating in the world: the divine-human Incarnation of Jesus Christ, a hierophany that shattered the categorical distinction between divinity and humanity, and a self-sacrifice that offered salvation of an otherwise sinful world. For the French, these overlapping and sometimes conflicting meanings of the cross made the colonization of Acadia and New France a religious history.[86]

For the sixteenth-century Mi'kmaq of the Miramichi River, the cross had pragmatic, political, and religious meanings as well. As with the French, it is difficult to distinguish between the religious character of Algonkian life and its social, economic, and political expressions. The appearance of the French set the stage for the Mi'kmaqs' appropriation of an alien symbol that also indicates the ancient religious holism of their sociality. The French struck the Mi'kmaq as a sudden revelation of a new intentionality now expressing itself in the world. While language differences kept the French and the Mi'kmaq from communicating verbally, the economic behavior of the newcomers spoke eloquently, if non-verbally. The new beings (the Mi'kmaq were probably uncertain whether the French were ethical persons, as we saw in Chapter Three) were not the bearers of gifts, and so were not altruistic. But the French were interested in exchange. In this give-and-take, the religious history of the Algonkian-French encounter began, particularly because the crosses the French erected soon came to play a religious role in Mi'kmaq life.[87]

The French also brought disease, and there is some evidence that the Mi'kmaq understood that line of transmission.[88] The Mi'kmaq also had their own way of reasoning about disease. Because the new illnesses were devastating and, since the Mi'kmaq had no impersonal theory to explain them, they had to be understood in other ways. For the Mi'kmaq, widespread and unprecedented illness could only be understood relationally. Either the diseases were caused by their own ethical irresponsibility against some offended being or beings, or a new and terrifying anti-social intentionality had entered the Mi'kmaq world.

Le Clercq shows that the Mi'kmaq came to link disease both with alien malevolence and with the need to revitalize their religious relations with cosmic beings, just as later Algonkians reasoned. As had always been true, dreaming showed the Mi'kmaq that another being offered protection in return for a new relationship between himself and the people. As a sign of that solidarity, the being offered a cross to express his care and to extend his powerful purposefulness. The Mi'kmaq, in turn, created new religious expressions of sociality to give witness to the new identity the relationship created. Le Clercq documents that the Mi'kmaq countered disease with the cross, they recentered social identity upon the cross, and they used the cross to express their confidence in their relations with other Mi'kmaq people.[89]

Monseigneur Saint-Vallier, the bishop of Quebec, wrote another account of the Mi'kmaq's oral tradition about the cross.[90] Saint-Vallier adds compelling details about how the cross came to reverberate symbolically throughout Mi'kmaq life. In Saint-Vallier's text, the Mi'kmaq testified that they had received not one cross, but three. In this version, famine beset the Miramichi Mi'kmaq, and the people resorted to ritual means to seek an explanation from the various beings of their world. As in Le Clercq's book, however, the explanation came in a dream in which a being offered assistance: "One of the oldest of them saw in a dream a young man who, in assuring him of their approaching deliverance through the virtue of the Cross, showed him three of these, of which he declared that one should serve them in public calamities, the other in deliberations and councils, and the third in voyages and perils."[91] Thus, in this instance the cross denominates the three most important social domains of Mi'kmaq life before and after French contact: disease and other threatening events, domestic affairs, and diplomatic and military relations.

Although Le Clercq and Saint-Vallier differ in their descriptions of the dream-gift, they agree that the cross came to suffuse Miramichi Mi'kmaq life. The cross had totemic significance in expressing the compelling relationship that gave these Mi'kmaq their protected identity. Le Clercq and Saint-Vallier agree that the Mi'kmaq painted the cross on their bodies and clothing and used it to protect the unborn. They also note that the cross designated the respected status of the Miramichi headman, the wisdom of solemn public assemblies, and the responsible commission given to ambassadors sent to visit neighboring peoples. They also document that the cross expressed the value of solidarity at the center of Mi'kmaq homes, identified the resting places of their dead, stood at the bows of their canoes, and marked Miramichi territory and its prominent fishing and hunting places. In all these ways, the Miramichi Mi'kmaq used the cross to witness the relationship that gave every level of their sociality a religious meaning.[92]

The French authors do not indicate the identity of the person who gave the Mi'kmaq the cross. While some controversy developed among the French about whether their cross indicated that the Mi'kmaq had actually been visited by the apostles in ancient times, or by God himself, or by early French missionaries,[93] Le Clercq presents evidence that suggests that the Mi'kmaq may have associated their dream benefactor with the Sun. In the first place, Le Clercq insists that the Mi'kmaq as a whole had traditionally "worshiped" the Sun. In the second, Le Clercq documents that the seventeenth-century Mi'kmaq drew an analogy between the Sun and the being the missionaries introduced.[94] Whatever his identity, the Mi'kmaq clearly thought about him and the meaning of his gift in the logical terms that continued to inform their relational religious life in the seventeenth century and beyond.

Such a relational understanding of the Miramichi cross points to an Algonkian social and religious logic that construed missionary teachings in ways historians have not recognized. Indeed, historians have misinterpreted Algonkian responses in one of two ways. First, they have over-stressed the agency of the French priests as dominating the relationship. Second, they have not recognized that Algonkians judged the priests' claims of religious power by the integrity of the missionaries' social behavior and in their practical relevance in meeting the religious needs of everyday life—in curing disease, in hunting, and in diplomatic and military relations. It is certainly true that, at least before the 1670s, the priests were self-consciously insistent that Christian Algonkians must become culturally French. But the effects of such colonialism must be weighed against the Algonkians' principled religious response.

Historian James Ronda has led the way toward reconstructing the complex social dynamics of the missions.[95] In focusing on the history of the Montagnais mission of Saint Joseph at Sillery, for example, Ronda demonstrates that the Jesuits' plans far outstripped the priests' ability to cope with social and cultural change. Sillery attempted to institutionalize the priests' fervent conviction that, if the Algonkians could be made sedentary, if they could be made to eschew their hunting lifestyle and to accept an agriculturally based village life, Christianity would flourish. Despite promising early financial support, the course of poor economic, military, and medical conditions, as well as the Algonkians' cultural conservatism, undercut the priests' high hopes. More tellingly, the priests used Saint Joseph to impose severe cultural changes upon those Montagnais who made the effort to ally themselves with the French. No facet of Montagnais life remained uncriticized. No Montagnais values escaped trenchant ridicule. For a time, as I document in Chapter Seven, the Montagnais themselves attempted to coerce compliance with French cultural expectations, particularly in attempting to ban customs that had to do with ritual life, domestic manners including sexual habits, polygamy, and divorce, and political and military relations. As Karen Anderson has shown, the world-rejecting and French culture-embracing Jesuit missionaries understood the ways in which the social permissiveness of Algonkian lifeways precluded the male-centered, authoritarian family life they envisioned as normative for all Christians. Anderson may have overstated the extent to which the priests were successful in implementing their misogynist vision, but the priests certainly attacked traditional gender-identity and gender-complementarity among those Montagnais who attempted to adapt to Sillery Christianity.[96] For a variety of reasons, then, Saint Joseph failed to establish the Jesuits' dream of a new world order. Although some Montagnais made every effort to adapt and even to conform, many, perhaps most, remained skeptical.

External factors also played a decisive role that undercut the Montagnais effort to reason pragmatically in their traditional religious terms. Saint Joseph never developed an agricultural base to support the Montagnais population. All Montagnais thus remained dependent on their traditional hunting economy, and therefore their religious relations with animals, because their trade with the French required a steady supply of furs. The mission itself faced enemies within and without. Despite providing its residents with the services of the Hospital nuns, European diseases became endemic. Accelerating warfare with the Five Nations threatened the mission and killed prominent Montagnais leaders throughout the 1640s and 1650s. Coupled with these constraining economic and military factors, a 1656 fire consumed the priests' residence, the chapel, and most of the surrounding village. By the 1660s, French farmers replaced the Montagnais population. Sillery, in short, failed to meet either French or Montagnais expectations.

The Montagnais of Sillery also used their syncretic understanding of Catholicism in ways that the priests could not have foreseen, but in ways that followed the relational logic of the Miramichi Mi'kmaq in the sixteenth century. Although both external and internal factors led to the collapse of Saint Joseph, the "Christian" Montagnais also played a crucial role for a time in the ways in which other Eastern Algonkian peoples responded to post-contact realities. In effect, the Sillery residents mediated among the French authorities, the missionaries, and Algonkian peoples throughout the Northeast. They carried the message that the French offered new, adaptive possibilities for Eastern Algonkian peoples. The French sought economic and military cooperation and Algonkians up and down the St. Lawrence River and its tributaries began to explore that offer of alliance for its short- and long-term advantages. The Saint Joseph

Montagnais also articulated new forms of intertribal solidarity and intertribal identity. These Montagnais proposed a religious solidarity: they reported far and wide that the Jesuits offered nothing less than revitalized social values, successful hunting, powerful religious assistance in military defense against the Iroquois, and even persuasive explanation of and protection against the devastating new diseases. As long as Sillery endured, its residents carried this complicated, controversial, and enticing message throughout the Northeast, west to the Algonkins of Trois Rivieres, east and north to the Montagnais of Tadoussac and the tributaries of the Saguenay River, and south to the Kennebec Wabanaki in the borderlands between New France and New England. These people listened to, and questioned, the new proposals in ways that made sense for themselves.[97]

Historians understand the importance of reconstructing the Algonkians' modes of thought in these complicated interactions with the French, but achieving that perspective has been elusive. For example, Robert Conkling—"Legitimacy and Conversion in Social Change"—essayed the impact of Sillery's hinterland missionization in a manner that suggests that the Jesuit and other missionaries transformed radically the Algonkians' religious orientation. To his mind, the missionaries' behavior, particularly their ability to cure postcontact diseases, made it possible for the priests to usurp shamanistic roles in Algonkian communities and so to convert the people. "By its very nature charismatic authority permits a sudden break with tradition," Conkling writes, "The power of a charismatic figure is so extraordinary that his decrees supercede the rules of tradition on which all leaders, in ordinary times, rely." What charisma permits and what it accomplishes are very different things, however. Conkling seems to recognize that internal factors also shaped the Algonkians' responses to missionary claims. Conkling notes that charisma, that is, the ability to shape persuasively the course of cultural innovation, "was part of the aboriginal system," but he does not reconstruct the traditional logic of that system. At the same time, Conkling contends that the priests held the upper hand: "The major instigators of this transformation, however, were not aboriginal leaders but the missionaries." Conkling, unfortunately, moves too quickly and without documenting his main claims:

> It is clear that an important element in this case of social and religious change was not just dominance but legitimate dominance. The power of the French missionaries was not just a fact, it was a fact that was conceded to be right and proper by the Wabanaki, because the missionaries met the Wabanaki's own idea of charismatic qualification for an authoritative role in their society. It is this which explains the profound conversions of many of these Indians, who remain steadfast Catholics today, and their ready acceptance of a new orientation towards external regulation.[98]

For Conkling, Jesuit and shaman clashed because they proposed conflicting alternatives. The shamans' charisma declined, while that of the missionaries grew, as the priests proposed social and cultural innovations appropriate for the new times. Conkling writes: "At stake in the competition between the shamans and the missionaries was not just the superiority of one sort of curer or politician over another, but an entire world or Reality." In Conkling's view, religious conversion involved "new ideas about magic charms, cures, dreams, precognition, and divine wrath: the Indians could see that some ideas were no longer very useful in the manipulation of reality."[99] In Chapters Three to Seven, I have argued and documented to the contrary that old ideas continued to make sense.

A major conceptual fallacy, indeed an ethnocentric commitment, pervades the ways that Conkling and other ethnohistorians describe Algonkian religious change as conversion, and even Ronda's view that the Algonkians resisted Christian colonization. All of these scholars fail to understand Algonkian religious life in its own terms. They all contend that Algonkian religious ways of understanding the world paralleled that of the monotheistic Jesuits. They confound Algonkian "spirits" with local "deities." They assume that Jesuit notions of God easily translated into ostensibly closely related Algonkian views of the cosmos. They think that Algonkian and Jesuit disease theory differed. They claim that Algonkians came consequently to reject a traditional religious system that post-contact conditions rendered ineffectual and even dysfunctional. They tend also to assume that, given Indians' perceptions of missionary powers, Algonkians accepted new forms of religious authority and social hierarchy. None of these conclusions are warranted, as a review of Kennebec Wabanaki Catholicism reveals.

The Kennebec case examined in Chapters Three and Four shows that Eastern Algonkian peoples made religious adjustments to Catholicism in ways that fit their own changing needs. Indeed, the Jesuit account of Gabriel Druillettes' relationship with the Kennebecs indicates the many ways in which he worked within, rather than sought to replace, Algonkian reality assumptions. Druillettes did not describe a new theistic and authoritarian cosmology. To the contrary, he revealed a cosmic figure—He-Who-Made-All—who affirmed the personalistic character of the Algonkian world system. Druillettes made no attempt to criticize Kennebec views of reality. Instead, he ascribed their considerable troubles in the 1640s to their own irresponsibility, a relational disorder that, when rectified, could lead to the healing of disease, the resolution of social discord, the affirmation of kinship solidarity, and the nurturing support of He-Who-Made-All. Most tellingly, Druillettes did not simply undermine the powers of religious specialists; rather, he revealed another great person who offered the Kennebec people, including the religious specialists, the power that they needed.

Later Jesuit accounts are not nearly so detailed in revealing the give-and-take that certainly continued between the Eastern Algonkians and the missionaries living in their communities. Algonkians did not accept uncritically either missionary or French authority. They did not repudiate tradition, as their vital oral tradition in the twentieth century attests.[100] That dynamic tradition articulates a millennial confidence that belies conversion as a simple historical outcome. The post-contact era did bring changes, even to the extent that the Algonkians' culture hero, Gluskap, apparently withdrew as an active presence in Algonkian life. The oral tradition also relates two other conditions that belie the hasty conclusion that Eastern Algonkians radically converted to Catholicism. First, Gluskap's teachings still inform the ongoing cultural solidarity of Eastern Algonkian ways of life. Second, the people remember Gluskap's promise to return at some future time of need.

In effect, any effort to reconstruct the relationship between Eastern Algonkian peoples and Catholic missionaries must recognize an innate and principled conservatism to indigenous views of the world. Long before European contact, language and tradition gave Algonkians an effective way of reasoning about the world as constituted in the interaction of morally purposeful actors. Accordingly, Eastern Algonkians scrutinized Catholicism from a position of confidence, and embraced only so much of Catholicism as made sense to themselves. Seen in such a way, the Eastern Algonkian used Catholicism to bolster traditional truth, ensure the survival of tradition, and affirm tribal solidarity as the overarching religious ideal.

Notes

MAKING SENSE—RELIGIOUS STUDIES AND ETHNOHISTORY

1. See Selected Bibliography: Axtell; Comaroff; Fabian; O'Brian and Roseberry.

2. See Anthony F. C. Wallace, *Religion: An Anthropological View* (New York: Random House, 1966). For a critical examination, see Morton Klass, *Ordered Universes: Approaches to the Anthropology of Religion* (Boulder: Westview, 1995).

3. Ninian Smart, *Worldviews: Crosscultural Explorations of Human Beliefs*, 2nd ed. (Englewood Cliffs, NJ: Prentice Hall, 1995).

4. I do not mean to suggest that there is an orthodox, uniform way in which to study Native American religious traditions. Among many suggestive approaches, see the Selected Bibliography: Peggy V. Beck and Anna L. Walters; Joseph Epes Brown; Walter Holden Capps; Denise Lardner Carmody and John Tully Carmody; Vine Deloria, Jr.; D. M. Dooling and Paul Jordan-Smith; Armin W. Geertz; Sam D. Gill; John Grim; Howard L. Harrod; Åke Hultkrantz; Lee Irwin; John D. Loftin; Joel Martin; Daniel Merkur; Jordan Paper; Melissa A. Pflug; Theresa S. Smith; Ruth M. Underhill; Christopher Vecsey; Jace Weaver; and Ray A. Williamson.

5. Although many of his religious categories are inappropriate—supernatural and magic, for example—the possibility of understanding cultures as they are existentially and ethically principled is given compelling detail in Thomas Blackburn, ed., *December's Child: A Book of Chumash Oral Narratives* (Berkeley: University of California Press, 1975), 43–48. See also A. Irving Hallowell, "Myth, Culture and Personality," *American Anthropologist* 49 (1947): 544–556; Katherine Spencer, "Reflections of Social Life in the Navaho Origin Myth," *University of New Mexico Publications in Anthropology*, 3 (Albuquerque: University of New Mexico Press, 1947); idem, "Mythology and Values: An Analysis of Navaho Chantway Myths," *Memoirs of the American Folklore Society*, 48 (Philadelphia: American Folklore Society, 1957).

6. See Lee Irwin, "Introduction," Special Issue: "To Hear the Eagles Cry: Contemporary Themes in Native American Spirituality," *American Indian*

Quarterly 20 (1996): 309–328; Lee Irwin, "Native Voices in the Study of Native American Religions," *European Review of Native American Studies* 12 (1998): 25–40. See the Selected Bibliography for Native American Studies perspectives: Thomas Biolsi and Larry J. Zimmerman; Jennifer S. H. Brown and Elizabeth Vibert; Donald L. Fixico; Frederick E. Hoxie; Devon A. Mihesuah; and William R. Swagerty.

7. An important strain of that struggle can be seen in the emergence of American Indian social history, including ethnic and women's history. See, for example, works in the Selected Bibliography focusing on the Canadian-American Northeast: Karen Anderson; Carole Blackburn; Colin G. Calloway; Carol Devens; Gregory Evans Dowd; Mona Etienne and Eleanor Leacock; Rebecca Kugel; Melissa Meyer; Daniel K. Richter; Richard White. See also Peter Nabokov; "Native Views of History," in *The Cambridge History of the Native Peoples of the Americas: North America*, ed. Bruce G. Trigger and Wilcomb E. Washburn (Cambridge: Cambridge University Press, 1996), part 1, 1–60.

8. A good place to start is Robert F. Berkhofer, Jr., "Cultural Pluralism Versus Ethnocentrism in the New Indian History," in *The American Indian and the Problem of History*, ed. Calvin Martin (New York: Oxford University Press, 1987), 35–45.

9. See Eric Wolf, *Europe and the People Without History* (Berkeley: University of California Press, 1982); Denys Delage, *Bitter Feast: Amerindians and Europeans in Northeastern North America, 1600–64* (Vancouver: University of British Columbia Press, 1993).

10. Robert F. Berkhofer, Jr., "The Political Context of a New Indian History," *Pacific Historical Review* 40 (1971): 357–382. For recent overviews of ethnohistory and cognate fields, see Melissa L. Meyer and Kerwin Lee Klein, "Native American Studies and the End of Ethnohistory"; and Richard White, "Using the Past: History and Native American Studies," in *Studying Native America: Problems and Prospects*, ed. Russell Thornton (Madison: University of Wisconsin Press, 1998), 182–243. See also James A. Clifton, ed., *The Invented Indian: Cultural Fictions & Government Policies* (New Brunswick, NJ: Transaction, 1996).

11. Alfred Crosby, *The Columbian Exchange* (Westport, CT: Greenwood, 1972); William Cronon, *Changes in the Land: Indians, Colonists, and the Ecology of New England* (New York: Hill and Wang, 1983); William W. Fitzhugh, *Cultures in Contact: The Impact of European Contacts on Native American Cultural Institutions, A.D. 1000–1800* (Washington: Smithsonian Institution, 1985); Wright J. Lietch, *The Only Land They Knew* (New York: The Free Press, 1981).

12. Anthony F. C. Wallace, *The Death and Rebirth of the Seneca* (New York: Random House, 1972).

13. Edwin Oliver James, *Creation and Cosmology: A Historical and Comparative Inquiry* (Leiden: E. J. Brill, 1969); Robin W. Lovin and Frank E. Reynolds, eds., *Cosmogony and Ethical Order: New Studies in Comparative Ethics* (Chicago: University of Chicago Press, 1985); David MacLagan, *Creation Myths: Man's Introduction to the World* (London: Thames and Hudson, 1977); Barbara C. Sproul, *Primal Myths: Creating the World* (San Francisco: Harper & Row, 1979).

14. See, for example, Robert Berkhofer, Jr., *The White Man's Indian: Images of the American Indian from Columbus to the Present* (New York: Knopf, 1978); Robert E. Bieder, *Science Encounters the Indian, 1820–1880: The Early Years of American Ethnology* (Norman: University of Oklahoma Press, 1986); Helen Carr, *Inventing the American Primitive: Politics, Gender and the Representation of Native American Literary Traditions, 1789–1936* (New York: New York University Press, 1996); Richard Drinnon, *Facing West: The Metaphysics of Indian-Hating and Empire-Building* (New York: New American Library, 1980); Bernard W. Sheehan, *Seeds of Extinction: Jeffersonian Philanthropy and the American Indian* (New York: Norton, 1973).

15. I do not mean to suggest that Turner achieved successfully an explication of African religious points-of-view, but only that his work has been an important step in that direction. See his *Dramas, Fields, and Metaphors: Symbolic Action in Human Society* (Ithaca, NY: Cornell University Press, 1974); *Drums of Affliction: A Study of Religious Process among the Ndembu of Zambia* (Ithaca, NY: Cornell University Press, 1981); *The Forest of Symbols: Aspects of Ndembu Ritual* (Ithaca, NY: Cornell University Press, 1970); *The Ritual Process: Structure and Anti-Structure* (Chicago: Aldine, 1969); *Schism and Continuity in an African Society: A Study of Ndembu Village Life* (Manchester: Manchester University Press, 1957).

16. See Selected Bibliography.

17. George E. Tinker, *Missionary Conquest: The Gospel and Native American Cultural Genocide* (Minneapolis: Fortress, 1993).

18. Thomas C. Parkhill, *Weaving Ourselves into the Land: Charles Godfrey Leland, 'Indians', and the Study of Native American Religions* (Albany: State University of New York Press, 1997).

19. Henry Warner Bowden, *American Indians and Christian Missions: Studies in Cultural Conflict* (Chicago: University of Chicago Press, 1981), 17, 23, overstates pre-contact religious change as proselytizing and historical adaptations as a matter of conversion.

20. For a study of the historical shifts in oral tradition, see Armin W. Geertz, *The Invention of Prophecy: Continuity and Meaning in Hopi Indian Religion* (Berkeley: University of California Press, 1994).

21. Vine Deloria, Jr., *For This Land: Writings on Religion in America* (New York: Routledge, 1999); James Treat, *Native and Christian: Indigenous Voices on Religious Identity in the United States and Canada* (New York: Routledge, 1996); Jace Weaver, *That the People Might Live: Native American Literatures and Native American Community* (New York: Oxford University Press, 1997).

22. See particularly Robert L. Hall, *An Archaeology of the Soul: North American Indian Belief and Ritual* (Urbana: University of Illinois Press, 1997); Howard L. Harrod, *Becoming and Remaining a People: Native American Religions on the Northern Plains* (Tucson: University of Arizona Press, 1995).

23. See Wilfrid Cantwell Smith, "Comparative Religions: Whither and Why?" in *The History of Religions: Essays in Methodology*, ed. Mircea Eliade and Joseph M. Kitagawa (Chicago: University of Chicago Press, 1959), 31–50; and reprinted with his "Objectivity and the Humane Sciences: A New Proposal," in Wilfred Cantwell Smith, *Religious Diversity*, ed. Willard G. Octoby (New York: Crossroad, 1982), 138–180.

24. My interest in their respective views of "religion" shape this discussion. Each study is also valuable in many ways my brief treatment cannot assess.

25. Peggy V. Beck and Anna L. Walters, *The Sacred: Ways of Knowledge, Sources of Life* (Tsaile, AZ: Navajo Community College, 1977), 3–4.

26. Ibid., 4.

27. Ibid., 3.

28. See Robert Torrance, *The Spiritual Quest: Transcendence in Mythology. Science. and Religion* (Berkeley: University of California Press, 1994), for an argument that encountering the unknown is the very process of cosmic and cultural being.

29. For an alternative reading of the term "spiritual," see Lee Irwin, "Introduction," 311.

30. Jess Byron Hollenback, "Mysticism Among the Oglala Lakota: The Visions of Black Elk," in his *Mysticism: Experience, Response, and Empowerment* (University Park: Pennsylvania State University Press, 1996), 305–443.

31. For comparative discussion, see Jane Hubert, "Sacred Beliefs and Beliefs of Sacredness," in *Sacred Sites Sacred Places,* ed. David L. Carmichael et al. (London: Routledge, 1994), 9–19; Colleen McDannell, *Material Christianity: Religion and Popular Culture in America* (New Haven: Yale University Press, 1995).

32. Sam D. Gill, *Native American Religions: An Introduction* (Belmont, CA: Wadsworth, 1982), 11.

33. See Selected Bibliography: Classen; Classen, Howes and Synott; Eilberg-Schwartz; Gill; Johnson; Porteous; Rodaway; and Stoller.

34. See, for example, Clifford Geertz, *Local Knowledge: Further Essays in Interpretive Anthropology* (New York: Basic, 1983).

35. Clifford Geertz, "Religion as a Cultural System," in *Anthropological Approaches to the Study of Religion*, ed. M. Banton (London: Tavistock, 1971), 1–46.

36. While writing Chapters Three and Four, I was aware of an enormous problem (whose resolution I then avoided as a major project in its own right) which has been only partially addressed in Algonkian scholarship in particular and Native American Studies in general. That problem has to do with the complex history of representation that lies behind the written oral tradition of Native American peoples. For examples of the issue, see James Wherry's introduction to Joseph Nicolar, *The Life and Traditions of the Red Man* (Fredericton: Saint Anne's Point Press, 1979 [1893]), ix–xvi; and Parkhill's *Weaving Ourselves into the Land*.

37. For a practical discussion of this ethnohistorical technique, the so-called direct historical approach, see Russell J. Barber and Frances F. Berdan, *The Emperor's Mirror: Understanding Cultures through Primary Sources* (Tucson: University of Arizona Press, 1998), 26–27, 265–266, 273.

38. See Chapter Three, notes 25, 28, and 45, where I cite Leland as one source from which I derived the notion that cannibals are beastly and wild. On Leland, see Parkhill, *Weaving Ourselves into the Land*.

39. Blackburn, *December's Child*, 43–88.

40. Kenneth M. Morrison, "The Cosmos as Intersubjective: Native American Other-than-Human Persons," in *Indigenous Religions: A Companion*, ed. Graham Harvey (London: Cassell, 2000), 23–36.

41. Lynn C. Brun, "Capturing Souls: An Interpretation of Mohave and Quechan Warfare," M.A. thesis (Tempe: Arizona State University, 1993); John Robert Lindamood, "The Quest for Solidarity: The Category of Gift in Apache Religious Systems," M.A. thesis (Tempe: Arizona State University, 1989); Kenneth Hayes Lokensgard, "Medicine Bundle Persons: Blackfoot Ontology and the Study of Native American Religions," M.A. thesis (Tempe: Arizona State University, 1996); Mary R. Schulte-Dwan, "The Category of Person in the Hopi Cosmos: A Non-Supernatural Interpretive Model," M.A. thesis (Tempe: Arizona State University, 1999).

42. See Selected Bibliography: Theresa S. Smith.

43. See Selected Bibliography: Pflug.

44. Maureen Trudelle Schwarz, *Molded in the Image of Changing Woman: Navajo Views on the Human Body and Personhood* (Tucson: University of Arizona Press, 1997).

45. John Fulbright, "Hopi and Zuni Prayer Sticks: Magic, Symbolic Texts, Barter, or Self-Sacrifice?" *Religion* 22 (1992): 221–234.

46. Kenneth M. Morrison, "Sharing the Flower: A Non-Supernaturalistic Theory of Grace," *Religion* 22 (1992): 207–219.

47. Blackburn, *December's Child*, 65–66, documents that "the assumption of a personalized universe" is held throughout the western United States.

48. Marie Mauzé, "The Concept of the Person and Reincarnation among the Kwakiutl Indians," in *Amerindian Rebirth: Reincarnation Belief among North American Indians and Inuit*, ed. Antonia Mills and Richard Slobodin (Toronto: University of Toronto Press, 1994), 177–191; and Michael Harkin, "Person, Time, and Being: Northwest Coast Rebirth in Comparative Perspective," in ibid., 192–210.

49. Ann Fienup-Riordan, "The Real People: The Concept of Personhood among the Yup'ik Eskimos of Western Alaska," *Etudes/Inuit/Studies* 10 (1986): 261–270; idem, *Eskimo Essays: Yup'ik Lives and How We See Them* (New Brunswick, NJ: Rutgers University Press, 1990).

50. Harvey, ed., *Indigenous Religions*.

51. In subtitling his *The Ritual Process: Structure and Anti-Structure*, Victor Turner explicitly turns his analysis from structural-functional ways of thinking about culture to ways that stress social, religious, and, therefore, ideological processes.

CHAPTER 1. THE STUDY OF ALGONKIAN RELIGIOUS LIFE

1. See the Selected Bibliography for this literature.

2. Calvin Martin, ed., *The American Indian and the Problem of History* (New York: Oxford University Press, 1987), 6.

3. Ibid., 7.

4. See Selected Bibliography.

5. See Roy Harvey Pearce, *Savagism and Civilization: A Study of the Indian and the American Mind* (Berkeley: University of California Press, 1988 [1953]); Robert Berkhofer, *The White Man's Indian: Images of the American Indian from Columbus to the Present* (New York: Knopf, 1978); Thomas C. Parkhill, *Weaving Ourselves into the Land: Charles Godfrey Leland, "Indians," and the Study of Native American Religions* (Albany: State University of New York Press, 1997).

6. Alfred Goldsworthy Bailey, *The Conflict of European and Eastern Algonkian Cultures, 1504–1700: A Study in Canadian Civilization*, 2nd ed. (Toronto: University of Toronto Press, 1969 [1937]).

7. As quoted in Bailey, *Conflict*, ix.

8. Ibid., 5.

9. Ibid., 9.

10. See Wilcomb E. Washburn and Bruce G. Trigger, "Native American Peoples in Euro-American Historiography," in *The Cambridge History of the*

Native Peoples of the Americas: North America, eds. Bruce G. Trigger and Wilcomb Washburn (Cambridge: Cambridge University Press, 1996), part 1, 99–100; Bruce G. Trigger, "Alfred G. Bailey—Ethnohistorian," *Acadiensis* 18 (1989).

11. Bailey, *Conflict*, 20.

12. Ibid., 47, 84, 91, 97, 101–113. In my estimation, Bailey's discussion of mythology as a way toward understanding Algonkian points-of-view about contact events is his most important contribution to Native American Studies. See especially his chapter "Mythology," ibid., 157–191.

13. Ibid., 47.

14. For an argument about the importance of studying Native American cosmogony, particularly for controlling non-Indian ethnocentric assumptions, see Sam D. Gill's chapter, "The Place to Begin," in his *Native American Religions: An Introduction* (Belmont, CA: Wadsworth, 1982), 15–38. See also Christopher Vecsey, *Imagine Ourselves Richly: Mythic Narratives of North American Indians* (San Francisco: Harper, San Francisco, 1991).

15. Gill is again relevant. See his chapter, "Symbols in Action," *Native American Religions*, 59–82; and idem, *Native American Religious Action: A Performance Approach to Religion* (Columbia: University of South Carolina Press, 1987). See also N. Ross Crumrine and Marjorie Halpin, eds., *The Power of Symbols: Masks and Masquerade in the Americas* (Vancouver: University of British Columbia Press, 1983).

16. Bailey, *Conflict*, 75.

17. Ibid.

18. Ibid., 80, 97, 128, 134, 142.

19. Ibid., 81, 99. But Bailey also expresses some ambivalence about the category "magic." He writes: "The relationship between magic and religion is the subject of much controversy and there is no need to enlarge upon it here. Both systems have sprung from the same human impulse which is based upon the psychology of wish-fulfillment. If magic is a means of coercing personal beings and impersonal powers either to benefit oneself or relatives, or to inflict injury upon an enemy, and if religion is the belief in personal supernatural beings who control departments of nature and who require to be supplicated in order that they might grant conditions favourable to life, then the two, magic and religion, appear to have existed side by side and to have supplemented each other in eastern Algonkian culture." Ibid., 141.

20. Ibid., *Conflict*, 133.

21. Diamond Jenness quoted in ibid., 133–134; my italics. See Diamond Jenness, *The Indians of Canada*, National Museum of Canada, Bulletin 65, Anthropological Series, 15, 6th ed. (Ottawa, 1963), 169–170.

22. Calvin Martin, *Keepers of the Game: Indian-Animal Relationships and the Fur Trade* (Berkeley: University of California Press, 1978).

23. In Bishop's view, Martin's methodological problem consists of misreading the historical data to suggest that Native Americans were despiritualized before European contact, went through a phase of relationship with Christianity in which they developed a "mongrel" religion, and later "reverted to more pristine beliefs and practices concerning nature." Charles A. Bishop, "Northeastern Indian Concepts of Conservation and the Fur Trade: A Critique of Calvin Martin's Thesis," in *Indians, Animals, and the Fur Trade: A Critique of Keepers of the Game*, ed. Shepard Krech, III (Athens: University of Georgia Press, 1981), 39–58; quotations at 41 and 44.

24. Bruce G. Trigger, "Ontario Native Peoples and the Epidemics of 1634–1640," in *Indians, Animals, and the Fur Trade*, ed. Krech, 19–38; quotations at 36.

25. As Theresa Smith observes, while contemporary Ojibwa people use the terms "Anishnaabe, Anishnaabeg," they are also extended to the central Algonkian peoples who are not discussed in this study. Because of this lack of clarity, I retain the term "Ojibwa." *Island of the Anishnaabeg: Thunderers and Water Monsters in the Traditional Ojibwe Life-World* (Moscow: University of Idaho Press, 1995), 6.

26. Martin, *Keepers*, 6.

27. Rodney Needham, *Belief, Language, and Experience* (Chicago: University of Chicago Press, 1972). Needham argues that an examination of anthropologists' use of "belief" reveals that the term has no technical precision, particularly because it often masks a failure to reconstruct the epistemological character of "belief."

28. See Kenneth M. Morrison, "The Cosmos as Intersubjective: Native American Other-than-Human Persons," in *Indigenous Religions: A Companion*, ed. Graham Harvey (London: Cassell, 2000), 23–36.

29. In discussing the religious character of Ojibwa and Dakota responses to the French, Bruce M. White notes that "descriptions often assert that these Indian groups called the French *esprits*, or spirits." White observes that the question of the accuracy of this characterization is a question of translation. He carefully reconstructs the appropriate terminology—manido for the Ojibwa and *wasicun* for the Dakota. See "Encounters with Spirits: Ojibwa and Dakota Theories about the French and Their Merchandise," *Ethnohistory* 41 (1994): 369–405; quotation at 369.

30. Martin, *Keepers*, 20.

31. Bailey, *Conflict*, 6. Quoted in ibid., 8. See the following series of reworked articles that suggest the ways in which the early trade proceeded in terms of exchanges of symbolic value, rather than the utilitarian ways that Bailey supposed: George R. Hamell, "Strawberries, Floating Islands, and Rabbit Captains: Mythical Realities and European Contact in the Northeast during the Sixteenth and Seventeenth Centuries," *Journal of Canadian Studies* 21 (1987): 72–94; idem, "Trading in Metaphors: The Magic of Beads:

Another Perspective upon Indian-European Contact in Northeastern North America," in *Proceedings of the 1982 Glass Trade Bead Conference*, ed. Charles F. Hayes, III (Rochester, NY, 1983), 5–28; Christopher L. Miller and George R. Hamell, "A New Perspective on Indian-White Contact: Cultural Symbols and Colonial Trade," *Journal of American History* 73 (1986): 311–328. See also Calvin Martin, "Four Lives of a Micmac Pot," *Ethnohistory* 22 (1975): 111–133.

32. Martin, *Keepers*, 8.

33. Although Martin apparently accepts A. Irving Hallowell's argument that it is ethnocentric to interpret Algonkian religious life in terms of gods, nature, and the supernatural, he does not adjust his own interpretation accordingly. He opens his prologue, "The Paradox," with a quotation from a mid-nineteenth-century text by Peter Jones. For Jones, the Ojibwa lived in a subjective world of "'imaginary deities'" in that, when they need life-assistance, they appeal to "'the god who presides over the deer, the bear or the beaver'" or "'to the god of the waters.'" Peter Jones, *History of the Ojebway Indians; with especial reference to Their Conversion to Christianity* (London: A. W. Bennett, 1861), 64, as quoted in Martin, *Keepers*, 1.

34. Martin, *Keepers*, 33.

35. Murray and Rosalie Wax, "The Notion of Magic," *Current Anthropology* 4 (1963): 495–503.

36. A. Irving Hallowell, "Ojibwa Ontology, Behavior, and Worldview," in *Teachings from the American Earth*, ed. Dennis Tedlock and Barbara Tedlock (New York: Liveright, 1975), 158.

37. See ibid., 196, note 33. Murray Wax, "Religion and Magic," in *Introduction to Cultural Anthropology: Essays in the Scope and Methods of the Science of Man*, ed. James A. Clifton (Boston: Houghton Mifflin, 1969), 225–242; quotation at 235. Quoted in Martin, *Keepers*, 33–34.

38. Martin, *Keepers*, 34.

39. Hallowell, "Ojibwa Ontology," 158.

40. Martin, *Keepers*, 34–35.

41. Martin, *Keepers*, 35.

42. Ibid., 34–35.

43. Ibid., 69-70.

44. Ibid., 70.

45. Ibid.

46. William C. Sturtevant, "Animals and Disease in Indian Belief," in *Indians, Animals, and the Fur Trade*, ed., Krech, 182, thinks that Martin misunderstands A. Irving Hallowell's Algonkian ethnography.

47. Hallowell, "Ojibwa Ontology," 154, 168–169.

48. Martin, *Keepers*, 72.

49. Ibid. Reuben Gold Thwaites, ed., *The Jesuit Relations and Allied Documents*, 73 vols. (New York: Pageant, 1959), 3: 133; 4: 203.

50. Martin, *Keepers*, 72.

51. See Robert L. Hall, *An Archaeology of the Soul: North American Indian Belief and Ritual* (Urbana and Chicago: University of Illinois Press, 1997), 48–67.

52. Martin, *Keepers*, 72. Martin's copious note (202–203, note 8) cites sources that reveal a long history of ethnographic misinterpretation of Algonkian religious life.

53. See the discussion of Hallowell in the following chapter.

54. Martin, *Keepers*, 74.

55. See ibid., 33, for the methodological need to achieve an emic, or indigenous, perspective. The terms I isolate for critical attention are pervasive throughout the text.

56. Ibid., 113–115. See Frank G. Speck, *Naskapi: The Savage Hunters of the Labrador Peninsula*, 2nd ed. (Norman: University of Oklahoma Press, 1977 [1935]).

57. Martin, *Keepers*, 115. See A. Irving Hallowell, "Bear Ceremonialism in the Northern Hemisphere," *American Anthropologist* 28 (1926): 1–175.

58. Martin, *Keepers*, 115–117. See John Witthoft, *The American Indian as Hunter* (Harrisburg: Pennsylvania Historical and Museum Commission, 1967); and Adrian Tanner, *Bringing Home Animals: Religious Ideology and Modes of Production of the Mistassini Cree Hunters* (New York: St. Martin's, 1979).

59. William C. Sturtevant, "Animals and Disease in Indian Belief," in *Indians, Animals, and the Fur Trade*, ed. Krech, 177–188 questions Martin's reconstruction of Algonkian disease theory. See Martin's response: "Comment," ibid., 189–196.

60. See Shepard Krech's "Introduction," ibid., 1–10.

61. Dean R. Snow, "*Keepers of the Game* and the Nature of Explanation," ibid., 65.

62. Bruce G. Trigger, "Early Native North American Responses to European Contact: Romantic versus Rationalistic Interpretations," *Journal of American History* 77 (1991): 1195–1215.

63. For Trigger's nominal recognition of the value of "romantic" interpretations, see ibid., 1195–1197, 1199–1200, 1204–1206, 1214. Trigger also observes: "The total corpus of documentary evidence that religious beliefs played an important and widespread role in influencing native behavior is in fact very limited." Ibid., 1204.

64. Ibid., 1195–1196, 1198.

65. Ibid., 1200.

66. Ibid., 1199.

67. Trigger summarizes what he sees as a fit between the archaeological data and George Hamell's archaeological and ethnographical characterization of

sixteenth-century Native American religious worldviews (ibid., 1205), and cites his own work (1206). On Hamell's views, see this chapter, note 31.

68. See subsection "First Perceptions," ibid., 1201–1206.

69. See subsections "Seventeenth-Century Pragmatism," and "Cognitive Reorientation," ibid., 1206–1209; 1210–1213.

70. Martin, *Keepers*, 19.

71. Trigger, "Early Native Responses," 1215.

72. Although Trigger does not identify my argument as "romantic," he does reduce it to subjectivity: "Kenneth Morrison *believes* [my italics] that early in their encounter the Abenakis . . . inferred from European behavioral patterns that the Europeans might be the cannibal giants of their mythology." Ibid., 1202. Trigger does not refer to the extended argument reprinted in Chapter Three of this volume. Instead, he cites the very brief discussion of the cannibal giant in my book *The Embattled Northeast: The Elusive Ideal of Alliance in Abenaki-Euramerican Relations* (Berkeley: University of California Press, 1984), 67–68. I have never argued that the Wabanaki thought that "Europeans might be the cannibal giants of their mythology." I reason, to the contrary, that both the mythical figure of the cannibal giant and its appearance in everyday life gave Algonkians the ethical criteria by which they could judge constructively European claims of superiority.

73. Gill, *Native American Religions*, 10–11.

74. Trigger, "Early Native Responses," 1199.

75. Ibid., 1195.

76. A. Irving Hallowell, "Some Psychological Characteristics of the Northeastern Indians," in *Man in Northeastern North America*, ed. Frederick Johnson, Papers of the Robert S. Peabody Foundation for Archaeology, 3 (Andover, MA, 1946), 195–225.

77. A. G. Bailey recognizes the individualistic challenge to social solidarity that fur trade capitalism posed for Mi'kmaq society in the early seventeenth century. See Bailey, *Conflict*, 91–95.

78. Trigger, "Early Native Responses," 1201, 1203, 1205, 1206, 1209, 1211, 1212.

79. Ibid., 1195, 1197, 1199, 1206, 1210, 1212–1215.

80. For an extended discussion which concludes that the dichotomy between religious and practical life wrongly describes one Native American group, see Lowell John Bean, *Mukat's People: The Cahuilla Indians of Southern California* (Berkeley: University of California Press, 1972).

81. Trigger, "Early Native Responses," 1196.

82. Ibid., 1213.

83. James Axtell does not seem to recognize this bias. See his "Those Poor Blind Infidels," in his *The Invasion Within: The Contest of Cultures in Colonial North America* (New York: Oxford University Press, 1985), 7–22.

84. Hallowell, "Ojibwa Ontology," 142.
85. Robert Redfield, "The Primitive World View," *Proceedings of the American Philosophical Society* 96 (1952): 30. Quoted in Hallowell, "Ojibwa Ontology," 143–144.
86. Hallowell, "Ojibwa Ontology," 142–143.

CHAPTER TWO. BEYOND THE SUPERNATURAL AND
TO A DIALOGICAL COSMOLOGY

1. For a critical assessment of Religious Studies in general, and Native American religions in particular, see Sam D. Gill, "The Academic Study of Religion," *Journal of the American Academy of Religion* 62 (1994): 965–975.
2. Åke Hultkrantz, "The Concept of the Supernatural in Primal Religion," *History of Religions* 22 (1983): 231.
3. Ibid., 231, 253.
4. Ibid., 239.
5. Ibid., 250.
6. Ibid., 239.
7. I note that Hultkrantz insists on "nature" as a cosmological category. Ibid., passim. Some general observations are in order. Hultkrantz does not study Native American cosmological systems per se. Nor does he account for a "cultural" cosmological dimension. Both the categories "nature" and "culture" warrant close ethnographic and cross-cultural examination if this terminological quarrel is to be resolved. In the case of the Yoeme (Yaqui) of northwestern Mexico and Arizona, a complex dimensional system reflects continuity between pre- and post-contact cosmologies. In the post-contact period of their history, the Yoeme recognize a human domain, the "Pueblo," and worlds associated with Jesus, Mary, and Satan, "heaven" or "Glory," "hell," and "purgatory." In addition, the pre-contact "unitary" world of the Yaqui became differentiated: the "*Yo Ania*," the Ancient and Honorable realm; the "*Sea Ania*," the Flower world; the "*Huya Ania*," the Forest world; the "*Tukia Ania*," the Dream world; and, the "*Tenku Ania*," the Night world. See Kenneth M. Morrison, "Sharing the Flower: A Non-Supernaturalistic Theory of Grace," *Religion* 22 (1992): 207–220.
8. Hultkrantz, "Supernatural," 244.
9. Jonathan Z. Smith and William Scott Green, eds., *The Harper Collins Dictionary of Religion* (San Francisco: HarperSanFrancisco, 1995), 804.
10. See Benson Saler's magisterial study: *Conceptualizing Religion: Immanent Anthropologists, Transcendent Natives—and Unbounded Categories*, ed. H. G. Kippenberg and E. T. Lawson, Studies in the History of Religions, 56 (Leiden: E. J. Brill, 1993).
11. Morton Klass, *Ordered Universes: Approaches to the Anthropology of Religion* (Boulder, CO: Westview, 1995), 25–33, questions supernaturalism

from the perspective of the social sciences. See also the works Hultrantz references: "Supernatural," passim.

12. See Peter Berger's argument that sociologists "must rigidly bracket . . . any questions of the ultimate truth or illusion of religious propositions about the world." *The Sacred Canopy: Elements of a Sociological Theory of Religion* (New York: Doubleday, 1967), v. Anthropologist Walter Goldschmidt (see the discussion to follow) is a good case-in-point. As Hultkrantz notes, Goldschmidt argues that the Nomlaki (Wintuan speakers) do not distinguish between the supernatural and other domains of reality. In fact, Goldschmidt characterizes these people as "animistic," a concept to which Hultkrantz does not refer. In his discussion of Nomlaki religious life, nonetheless, Goldschmidt immediately uses supernatural and magic to refer to the non-empirical referents of the Nomlaki religious system. See Walter Goldschmidt, "Nomaki," in *Handbook of North American Indians: California*, ed. Robert F. Heizer (Washington: Smithsonian Institution, 1978), 8: 345–346.

13. See Mircea Eliade, *The Sacred and the Profane: The Nature of Religion* (New York: Harcourt Brace Jovanovich, 1959) and his *The Myth of the Eternal Return or, Cosmos and History* (Princeton: Princeton University Press, 1954).

14. On the usage of Ojibwa/Anishnaabe-Anishnaabeg, see Chapter One, note 25.

15. A. Irving Hallowell, "The Self and Its Behavioral Environment," in his *Culture and Experience* (Philadelphia: University of Pennsylvania Press, 1955), 75–111.

16. Mary B. Black, "Ojibwa Power Belief System," in The *Anthropology of Power: Ethnographic Studies from Asia, Oceania, and the New World*, ed. Raymond D. Fogelson and Richard N. Adams (New York: Academic, 1977), 141–151. On the contemporary use of the term "respect" among the Ojibwa, see Theresa S. Smith, *Island of the Anishnaabeg: Thunderers and Water Monsters in the Traditional Ojibwe Life-World* (Moscow: University of Idaho Press, 1995).

17. Thomas C. Blackburn, ed., *December's Child: A Book of Chumash Oral Narratives* (Berkeley: University of California Press, 1975), 63–80.

18. For Hultkrantz's view on the influence of Christianity on one part of northeastern Algonkian religious life, see his "The Problem of Christian Influence on Northern Algonkian Eschatology," in his *Belief and Worship in Native North America*, ed. Christopher Vecsey (Syracuse: Syracuse University Press, 1981), 187–211.

19. Besides the documentation I provide in later chapters, see Jordan Paper, "The Post-Contact Origin of an American High God: The Suppression of Female Spirituality," *American Indian Quarterly* 7 (1983): 1–24; Michael Pomedli, "Beyond Unbelief: Early Jesuit Interpretations of Native Religions," *Studies in Religion* 16 (1987): 275–287; Jacques Rousseau, "Persistances païennes chez les Amérindiens de la Forêt boréale," *Cahiers des Dix* 17 (1952):

183–208. In his essay "The Structure of Theistic Belief," *Belief and Worship*, ed. Vecsey, 27, note 7, Hultkrantz observes: "In his stimulating account from 1855, the German explorer Kohl says that the word for the Great Spirit, *Kitsche Manitou*, sometimes ('zuweilen') was no *nomen proprium* of a single being but an appellation of a whole class of great spirits (Kohl 1859a, 1: 86)."

20. Smith, *The Island of the Anishnaabeg*, 44–47.

21. The commonsense metaphor, "up is good and down is bad," suggests that the concept of the supernatural is linguistically shaped, at least in English. See George Lakoff and Mark Johnson, *Metaphors We Live By* (Chicago: University of Chicago Press, 1980), 14–33.

22. Ruth Landes, *Ojibwa Religion and the Midewiwin* (Madison: University of Wisconsin Press, 1968), 98.

23. Ibid.

24. See Benson Saler, "Supernatural as a Western Category," *Ethos* 5 (1977): 31–53.

25. Thanks to Melissa Pflug for suggesting this useful distinction.

26. Her italics. Smith, *Island of the Anishnaabeg*, 44–45, quoting Jennifer S. H. Brown and Robert Brightman, eds., *The Orders of the Dreamed: George Nelson on Cree and Northern Ojibwa Religion and Myth, 1823* (Winnepeg: University of Manitoba Press, 1988). Smith's argument thus seems to recognize the syncretistic figure of the Great Spirit, but does not treat it as a historical development. See Jordan Paper (note 19) and my remarks on the meaning of kitchi manitou as the hard-won, compassionate power of the Wabanaki culture hero, Gluskap (Chapter Four). The Jesuits translated kitchi manitou based on their understanding of the term. In Eastern Algonkian thought, kitchi is an Algonkian superlative—in this case, it refers to power as achieved through trial-and-error, and as a most refined and compassionate quality, a power directed toward the well-being of others. Recognizing the term as a superlative, the Jesuits translated kitchi as great, and they knew that manitou referred to a powerful being and so translated the term as spirit. It also helps to understand the need to reconstruct the history of the Great Spirit in noting that the seventeenth-century evidence indicates that other Algonkian peoples were not theists, that they equated the Jesuits' significant other with the person of the Sun, and that the Jesuits unified for a time the many persons of the Algonkian cosmos with their trope "He-Who-Made-All." For Jesuit efforts to comprehend the religious systems of Native Americans, see Pomedli, "Beyond Unbelief." For a rich mid-nineteenth-century discourse on the Great Spirit, see Denys Delage and Helen H. Tanner, trans. and eds., "The Ojibwa-Jesuit Debate at Walpole Island, 1844," *Ethnohistory* 41 (1994): 295–321.

27. See Christopher Vecsey with John F. Fisher, "The Ojibwa Creation Myth," in Vecsey's *Imagine Ourselves Richly: Mythic Narratives of North American Indians* (San Francisco: HarperSanFrancisco, 1991), 64–93.

28. Hultkrantz, "Supernatural," 232.

29. Ibid.
30. Ibid.
31. Ibid., 233.
32. Jan de Vries, *Perspectives in the History of Religions,* trans. Kees Bolle (Berkeley: University of California Press, 1977); Anthony F. C. Wallace, *Religion: An Anthropological View* (New York: Random House, 1966), 48–49.
33. Hultkrantz, "Supernatural," 232–234.
34. Ibid., 236. See Benson Saler, "Supernatural as a Western Category."
35. Hultkrantz, "Supernatural," 237.
36. Ibid. 241.
37. Ibid., 240–241.
38. Ibid., 241.
39. Ibid., 239.
40. Ibid., 240.
41. See Lee Irwin, *The Dream Seekers: Native American Visionary Traditions of the Great Plains* (Norman: University of Oklahoma Press, 1994).
42. Ibid., 241, note 42.
43. See Selected Bibliography: Howard L. Harrod.
44. Diamond Jenness, *The Ojibwa Indians of Parry Island: Their Social and Religious Life.* National Museum of Canada, Bulletin 78 (Ottawa, 1935), 29. Quoted in Hultkrantz, "Supernatural," 243.
45. Hultkrantz, "Supernatural," 243–244. For a more detailed discussion of Durkheim in this regard, see Saler, "Supernatural as a Western Category," 34–37.
46. Emile Durkheim, *The Elementary Forms of the Religious Life* (London: George Allen & Unwin, 1954), 24ff., as quoted and cited in Hultkrantz, "Supernatural," 237.
47. Jenness, *The Ojibwa Indians of Parry Island*, 29. Quoted in Hultkrantz, "Supernatural," 243.
48. Hultkrantz, "Supernatural," 243–244.
49. See Hallowell's discussion of metamorphosis, "Ojibwa Ontology, Behavior, and Worldview," in *Teachings from the American Earth: Indian Religion and Philosophy,* ed. Dennis Tedlock and Barbara Tedlock (New York: Liveright, 1975), 158–164.
50. Ibid., 144, 151, 158.
51. Hultkrantz, "Supernatural," 244–245; my italics.
52. Hallowell, "Ojibwa Ontology," 143.
53. Father Paul Le Jeune noted as much in the mid-1630s: "They have different Verbs to signify an action toward an animate or toward an inanimate object; and yet they join with animate things a number of things that have no souls, as tobacco, apples, etc." Reuben Gold Thwaites, ed., *The Jesuit Relations and Allied Documents,* 73 vols. (New York: Pageant, 1959), 7: 23.

54. Hultkrantz, "Supernatural," 245. See index entry—"Supernatural beings"—in Bruce G. Trigger, ed., *Handbook of North American Indians: Northeast* (Washington: Smithsonian Institution, 1978), 15: 920.

55. Smith, *Island of the Anishnaabeg*, 6–7. See also Theresa A. Smith, "Calling the Thunder, Part One: *Animikeek*, the Thunderstorm as Speech Event in the Anishinaabe Lifeworld," *American Indian Culture and Research Journal* 15 (1991): 19–20; idem, "Ojibwe Persons: Toward a Phenomenology of an American Indian Lifeworld," *Journal of Phenomenological Psychology* 20 (1989): 130–144.

56. For the complex meanings of *wakan*, see James R. Walker, *Lakota Belief and Ritual*, ed. Raymond J. Demallie and Elaine A. Jahner (Lincoln: University of Nebraska Press, 1980). See also Raymond J. Demallie, ed., *The Sixth Grandfather: Black Elk's Teachings Given to John G. Neihardt* (Lincoln: University of Nebraska Press, 1984), 80–82, for discussion.

57. John R. Farella, *The Main Stalk: A Synthesis of Navajo Philosophy* (Tucson: University of Arizona Press, 1984), 67, reflects on the meaning of *diyin*: "Diyin contains both bidziil and bahadzid, 'power' and 'danger,' It is helpful to view this as a continuum. All beings in the universe, whether they are in the realm of diyinii, human beings, natural phenomena, or what ever, can be placed on this continuum and differentiated according to the particular knowledge and concomitant power they possess."

58. Hultkrantz's discussion of the Kwakiutl term *nawalak* is a case of unnecessary distortion. Later in the text he observes: "Boas states that the Kwakiutl, in spite of their very clear theoretical distinction between natural and supernatural, could not clearly differentiate between events that were ordinary and others that were caused supernaturally." Hultkrantz, "Supernatural," 250. In this instance, Hultkrantz cites Franz Boas, *Kwakiutl Ethnography* (Chicago: University of Chicago Press, 1966), 162. It should also be noted that Benson Saler had reported (and, given his citation of Saler, Hultkrantz had read) that Franz Boas' translation of the term was inappropriate. See Saler, "Supernatural as a Western Category," 44, note 6, in which he cites Werner Cohen, "What is Religion? An Analysis for Cross-Cultural Comparisons," *Journal of Christian Education* 7 (1964).

59. See "Power," in Sam D. Gill and Irene F. Sullivan, *Dictionary of Native American Mythology* (New York: Oxford University Press, 1992), 242, for discussion and references to additional power concepts. It is significant that Hultkrantz does not collate his discussion of Native American power concepts with major anthropological findings. See, for example, Fogelson and Adams, *The Anthropology of Power*.

60. Dorothy Lee, "Linguistic Reflection of Wintu Thought," in *Teachings from the American Earth*, ed.Tedlock and Tedlock, eds., 140.

61. Hultkrantz, "Supernatural," 246.

62. Lee, "Wintu Thought," 130.

63. Ibid.
64. Ibid., 134; Lee's italics.
65. Ibid., 138.
66. Ibid., 139.
67. Ibid., 136.
68. Walter Goldschmidt, *Nomlaki Ethnography*, University of California Publications in American Archaeology and Ethnology, 42 (Berkeley and Los Angeles: University of California Press, 1951), 348; Walter Goldschmidt, "Nomlaki," in *Handbook of North American Indians*, ed. Heizer, 8: 345; Hultkrantz, "Supernatural," 249.
69. Hultkrantz, "Supernatural," 249.
70. Ibid., 249–250; my italics.
71. Hallowell, "Ojibwa Ontology," 143.
72. Ibid., 144; quoting Robert Redfield.
73. Ibid., 144; Hallowell's italics.
74. Ibid., 144–145.
75. Ibid., 147.
76. Ibid., 174, note 10.
77. Ibid., 148.
78. Ibid., 150.
79. For an excellent case study, see Ann Fienup-Riordan, *The Nelson Island Eskimo: Social Structure and Ritual Distribution* (Anchorage: Alaska Pacific University Press, 1983).
80. Hallowell, "Ojibwa Ontology," 151.
81. One of the great issues overlooked in all of this cosmological discussion is the plain fact that Algonkians, and probably other Native American peoples, do not entertain a category comparable to non-Indian notions of "culture," meaning the world of human creation. While Algonkians operated consciously out of a sense of world-responsibility, and so created the world in their interactive activities with other-than-human persons, their "cultural" activity participated in a pattern set down by the culture-creating gifts of their culture hero (and other mythic persons). Such gifts became, therefore, an ideal pattern to which human behavior ought to conform. In the Ojibwa world, "culture" is given in the formative period of creation mythology, and in the ongoing interaction of human and other-than-humans in the recitation of myth, in fasting, in dreaming, and in ritual performances in which the distance between humans and others is either bridged or managed in positive ways.
82. Hallowell, "Ojibwa Ontology," 151; Hallowell's italics.
83. Ibid., 154.
84. In dreams, the Ojibwa encounter and interact with other-than-human persons. See Irwin, *The Dream Seekers*.
85. Hallowell, "Ojibwa Ontology," 154–155.
86. Ibid., 159.

87. Ibid., 168.
88. Ibid.
89. Ibid., 170; Hallowell's italics.
90. Ibid., 171.
91. Ibid.; Hallowell's italics.
92. Ibid., 172.
93. Ibid., 173.

94. See Lakoff and Johnson, *Metaphors We Live By*, 185–238 for a critique of the "myth" of objectivity and of subjectivity. See also Nick Crossley, *Intersubjectivity: The Fabric of Social Becoming* (London: SAGE, 1996); Kathleen M. Haney, *Intersubjectivity Revisited: Phenomenology and the Other* (Athens: Ohio University Press, 1994); Dennis Tedlock and Bruce Mannheim, eds., *The Dialogic Emergence of Culture* (Urbana and Chicago: University of Illinois Press, 1995). See also Chapter Five, note 4.

CHAPTER THREE. TOWARD A HISTORY OF INTIMATE ENCOUNTERS

1. For discussion of Indians in colonial America, see William N. Fenton, Lyman H. Butterfield, and Wilcomb E. Washburn, *American Indian and White Relations to 1830: Needs and Opportunities for Study* (Chapel Hill: University of North Carolina Press, 1957); Bernard W. Sheehan, "Indian-White Relations in Early America: A Review Essay," *William and Mary Quarterly* 26 (1969): 267ff.; James Axtell, "Ethnohistory of Early America: A Review Essay," *William and Mary Quarterly* 35 (1978): 110–144; Wilcomb Washburn's comments on the moral perplexities are important—"Moral History of Indian-White Relations: Needs and Opportunities for Study," *Ethnohistory* 9 (1957): 55ff.

2. For these views, see Alfred Goldsworthy Bailey, *The Conflict of European and Eastern Algonkian Cultures, 1504–1700*, 2nd ed. (Toronto: University of Toronto Press, 1969 [1937]); Cornelius J. Jaenen, *Friend and Foe: Aspects of French-Amerindian Cultural Contact in the Sixteenth and Seventeenth Centuries* (New York: Columbia University Press, 1976); idem, "Amerindian Views of French Culture in the Seventeenth Century," *Canadian Historical Review* 55 (1974): 261–291; James P. Ronda, "The European Indian: Jesuit Civilization Planning in New France," *Church History* 41 (1972): 385–395; idem, "The Sillery Experiment: A Jesuit-Indian Village in New France, 1637–1663," *American Indian Culture and Research Journal* 3 (1979): 1–18; idem, "'We Are Well As We Are': An Indian Critique of Seventeenth Century Christian Missions," *William and Mary Quarterly* 34 (1977): 66–82.

3. This study complements Robert Conkling, "Legitimacy and Conversion in Social Change: The Case of French Missionaries and the Northeastern Algonkian," *Ethnohistory* 21 (1974): 1–24. See also Peter Duignan, "Early Jesuit Missionaries: A Suggestion for Further Study,"

American Anthropologist 60 (1958): 725–732. I have reviewed some of these problems in comparative history. Kenneth M. Morrison, "Native American History: The Issue of Values," *Journal of Ethnic Studies* 5 (1978): 80–89.

4. Processes of culture change in New France have attracted recent study. See Leo-Paul Desrosiers, *Iroquoisie* (Montreal: Institut d'Histoire de l'Amérique Française, 1947); George R. Healy, "The French Jesuits and the Idea of the Noble Savage," *William and Mary Quarterly* 15 (1958): 143–67; Marcel Trudel, "La Recontre des Cultures," *Revue d'Histoire de l'Amérique Française* 18 (1965): 477–516; Bruce G. Trigger, "Champlain Judged by His Indian Policy: A Different View of Early Canadian History," *Anthropologica* 13 (1971): 85–114; and idem, *The Children of Aataentsic: A History of the Huron People to 1660*, 2 vols. (Montreal: McGill-Queen's University Press, 1976). For some of the theoretical approaches that can be applied to ethnohistorical problems of culture change, see H. Pertti and Gretel H. Pelto, "Intracultural Diversity: Some Theoretical Issues," *American Ethnologist* 2 (1975): 1–18; Anthony F. C. Wallace, *Culture and Personality*, especially chapter 4, "The Psychology of Culture Change" (New York: Random House, 1961), 120–163; Social Science Research Council, "Acculturation: An Exploratory Formulation," *American Anthropologist* 56 (1954): 973–1002; Florence R. Kluckhohn, "Dominant and Variant Value Orientations," in *Personality in Nature, Society and Culture*, ed. Clyde Kluckhohn and Henry S. Murray, 2nd ed., rev. (New York: Knopf, 1967), 342–357; and in history, Robert Berkhofer, *A Behavioral Approach to Historical Analysis* (New York: The Free Press, 1969).

5. Paula Gunn Allen, "The Mythopoeic Vision in Native American Literature: The Problem of Myth," *American Indian Culture and Research Journal* 1 (1974): 14–16.

6. See A. Irving Hallowell, "Temporal Orientations in Western Civilization and in a Pre-literate Society," *American Anthropologist* 39 (1937): 647–670; and Gordon M. Day, "Oral Tradition as Complement," *Ethnohistory* 19 (1972): 99–108.

7. In philosophical anthropology, see the work of Martin Buber, *I and Thou* (New York: Charles Scribner's Sons, 1958); and his development of the phenomenological concept of the "between" in his "Dialogue," in *Between Man and Man* (New York: Macmillan, 1965), 1–39. Robert Redfield's "Civilization and the Moral Order," in his *The Primitive World and Its Transformations* (Ithaca, NY: Great Seal, 1957), 54–83 is important. Bertell Ollman's *Alienation: Marx's Conception of Man in Capitalist Society* (Cambridge: The University Press, 1970) clarifies social relations in Marxian thought. See also W. Goldschmidt, "An Ethnography of Encounters: A Methodology for the Enquiry into the Relation Between the Individual and Society," *Current Anthropology* 13 (1972): 59–78.

8. Claude Levi-Strauss, *The Savage Mind* (Chicago: University of Chicago Press, 1966); Clifford Geertz, "Religion as a Cultural System," in

Anthropological Approaches to the Study of Religion, ed. Michael Banton (London: Tavistock, 1966), 1–46. For literature discussing Native American worldviews, see Dennis Tedlock and Barbara Tedlock, eds., *Teachings From the American Earth: Indian Religion and Philosophy* (New York: Liveright, 1975); and Walter Holden Capps, *Seeing With a Native Eye* (New York: Harper and Row, 1976).

9. A. Irving Hallowell, "Ojibwa Ontology, Behavior, and World View," in *Teachings from the American Earth*, ed. Tedlock and Tedlock, 168–173.

10. A. Irving Hallowell, "Myth, Culture and Personality," *American Anthropologist* 49 (1947): 544-556.

11. See the Ojibwa stories "Nanabushu and Windigo" and "Windigo and Misabe" and the Cree tales "Wesakaychak and the Cannibal" and "The Culture Hero and the Cannibal," all in Morton I. Teicher, *Windigo Psychosis: A Study of a Relationship between Belief and Behavior Among Indians of Northeastern Canada* (Seattle: University of Washington Press, 1960), 25–26, 33, 34, 35, respectively. On Gluskap, see "Glouseclappe," in Claude Melançon, *Légendes Indiennes du Canada* (Montreal: Éditions du jour, 1967), 15–18.

12. "Gluskabe Overcome by Winter," in Frank G. Speck, "Penobscot Tales and Religious Beliefs," *Journal of American Folklore* 48 (1935): 44.

13. "Gluskabe Steals Summer and Overcomes Winter," Speck, "Penobscot Tales," 46–47; and see the Passamaquoddy story, "How the Master Found the Summer," in Charles G. Leland and John D. Prince, *Kuloskap, the Master* (New York: Funk and Wagnalls, 1902), 210–212.

14. The culture hero intervened against cannibals in other tales. See "Whiskey-Jack Man and Tseqa'bec Marry the Daughters of the Cannibal Woman," in Frank G. Speck, "Montagnais and Naskapi Tales from the Labrador Peninsula," *Journal of American Folklore* 38 (1925): 6; "Tseka'bec, the Swing, and Two Beautiful Cannibal Girls," ibid., 15; "Tseka'bec Marries the Daughter of a Cannibal," ibid., 26–27; and see note 12.

15. Kiwakwe (Penobscot), Chenoo (Mi'kmaq and Passamaquoddy), Gugus (Mi'kmaq), Windigo (Montagnais-Naskapi, Ojibwa, Cree), Atsen (Montagnais-Naskapi).

16. Harold Franklin McGee, Jr., "The Windigo Down-East, or the Taming of the Windigo," in *Proceedings of the Second Congress, Canadian Ethnology Society* (Ottawa: National Museum of Man, Mercury Series, 1975), 1: 110–132.

17. See Speck's remarks in "Penobscot Tales," 13; and "Kewkwe, the Cannibal Giant," ibid., 81–82; "The Story of the Great Chenoo, as Told by the Passamaquoddies," in Charles Leland, *The Algonquin Legends* (Boston: Houghton Mifflin, 1884), 246–247. Leland states that the "female Kewhqu is more powerful than the male," ibid., 247. See "Atsen, the Cannibal Giant," in Speck, "Montagnais and Naskapi Tales," 11; "Ketpusye'genau," in Elsie Clews Parsons, "Micmac Folklore," *Journal of American Folklore* 38 (1925): 56–59;

"Gugus Duel," ibid., 59–60; "Kiwakw," in W. H. Mechling, *Malecite Tales*, Canada, Department of Mines, Memoir 49 (Ottawa: Government Printing Bureau, 1914), 75–77.

18. Teicher, *Windigo Psychosis*, 5–6.

19. Frank G. Speck, "Ethical Attitudes of the Labrador Indians," *American Anthropologist* 35 (1933): 565–566.

20. Quoted in Raymond D. Fogelson, "Psychological Theories of Windigo 'Psychosis' and a Preliminary Application of a Models Approach," in *Context and Meaning in Cultural Anthropology*, ed. M. E. Spiro (New York: The Free Press, 1965), 79.

21. Speck, "Penobscot Tales," 13.

22. Leland, *The Algonquin Legends*, 233.

23. Ibid., 252.

24. Ibid., 233.

25. Speck, "Penobscot Tales," 14.

26. Speck, "Penobscot Tales," 66; Speck, "Montagnais and Naskapi Tales," 11; Parsons, "Micmac Folklore," 59. In the nineteenth-century case histories, windigo cannibalism was "usually directed against members of the individual's immediate family." Teicher, *Windigo Psychosis*, 5.

27. In "The Girl Chenoo," a young man became the instrument through which the girl was changed into a cannibal. When she refused his offer of marriage, "she roused all that was savage in him and he gave up his mind to revenge." Leland, *The Algonquin Legends*, 251. See also Speck, "Montagnais and Naskapi Tales," 6; Horace P. Beck, "Algonquin Folklore from Maniwaki," *Journal of American Folklore* 60 (1947): 259–264; and "Taken-from-guts," Frank G. Speck, "Some Micmac Tales from Cape Breton Island," *Journal of American Folklore* 28 (1915): 61ff.

28. Teicher, *Windigo Psychosis*, 32–33.

29. "Me Sah Ba and the Windigo," Teicher, *Windigo Psychosis*, 19. Another story, "Windigo and the Indian," tells of a "kind-hearted man" who struggled and won against a windigo who was his own brother to save a stranger. Ibid., 19. These two stories, and the others later quoted extensively, indicate the source of power of the individual who could overpower the cannibal giant. They do not indicate that this was the source of shamanistic power in general. See Ruth Landes, *The Ojibwa Woman* (New York: Norton, 1971), 178–226, for a discussion of shamanistic power. Speck observed that the "conjurer can become the arch-criminal or the benefactor in his social sphere, according to the motives that govern him." "Ethical Attributes of the Labrador Indians," 560.

30. Quoted in Teicher, *Windigo Psychosis*, 59.

31. Ibid., 5.

32. Speck, "Penobscot Tales," 14.

33. "The Chenoo," Leland, *The Algonquin Legends*, 234.
34. Ibid., 235.
35. Ibid., 235–236.
36. "Giants: Why People Do Not Eat Each Other Nowadays," Teicher, *Windigo Psychosis*, 22.
37. Ibid.
38. Ibid.
39. "The Chenoo," Leland, *The Algonquin Legends*, 238.
40. Teicher, *Windigo Psychosis*, 23.
41. "The Chenoo," Leland, *The Algonquin Legends*, 240.
42. Ibid., 242–243.
43. Ibid., 244.
44. Ibid.
45. The Jesuits report that the Algonkians held strangers in contempt. See, for example, Reuben Gold Thwaites, ed., *The Jesuit Relations and Allied Documents*, 73 vols. (New York: Pageant, 1959), 16: 201. Cited hereafter as JR. They also state that the attitude changed in the Montagnais-Naskapi mission village at Sillery. JR, 20: 89.
46. Recently, the argument that windigo cannibalism has a nutritional base has attracted some attention. See Vivian J. Rohl, "A Nutritional Factor in Windigo Psychosis," *American Anthropologist* 72 (1970): 97–101; and Jennifer Brown's response, "The Cure and the Feeding of Windigoes: A Critique," *American Anthropologist* 73 (1971): 20–22.
47. Charles A. Bishop, "Ojibwa Cannibalism," paper presented at the 9th International Congress of Anthropological and Ethnological Sciences, 1–20.
48. Bishop, "Ojibwa Cannibalism," 14. See also Harold Hickerson, *The Chippewa and Their Neighbors: A Study in Ethnohistory* (New York: Holt, Rinehart and Winston, 1970), and his "Fur Trade Colonialism and the North American Indian," *Journal of Ethnic Studies* 1 (1973): 15–44, for a discussion of the social and cultural effects of rapid economic change.
49. JR, 14: 147; 18: 111; 21: 115; 25: 161.
50. Ibid., 10: 27. For Paul Le Jeune's life and an astute evaluation of the *Jesuit Relations* as a source, see Leon Pouliot, "Paul Le Jeune," in *Dictionary of Canadian Biography*, ed., G. W. Brown (Toronto: University of Toronto Press, 1966), 1: 453–458.
51. JR, 35: 21.
52. Ibid., 38: 179–181.
53. Ibid., 23: 29.
54. Ibid., 23: 31–33.
55. Chrestien Le Clercq, *New Relation of Gaspesia, with the Customs and Religion of the Gaspesian Indians*, ed. William F. Ganong (Toronto: The Champlain Society, 1910), 112.
56. Ibid., 112–115.

57. Bishop, "Ojibwa Cannibalism," 58; see also Eleanor Leacock, "The Montagnais 'Hunting Territory' and the Fur Trade," *American Anthropological Association Memoir*, 78 (1954); Calvin Martin, "The European Impact on the Culture of a Northeastern Algonquian Tribe: An Ecological Interpretation," *William and Mary Quarterly* 31 (1974): 3–26; and Fred Eggan, "Northern Woodland Ethnology," in *The Philadelphia Anthropological Society, Papers Presented on Its Golden Anniversary*, ed. Jacob W. Gruber (New York: Columbia University Press, 1967), 107–124.

58. JR, 11: 123.

59. Ibid., 6: 11.

60. Ibid., 6: 115.

61. Thomas Grassman, "Joseph Manitougatche," *Dictionary of Canadian Biography*, 1: 487–488.

62. JR, 5: 93.

63. Ibid., 6: 143; and see especially Chapter 5, "Of the Good Things which Are Found among the Savages." See also ibid., 16: 103; 25: 111. On the role of the Hospital Nuns, see ibid., 19: 25; and Kenneth M. Morrison, "That 'Earthly Paradise': The Experience of the Canadian Ursulines: A Review Essay of Dom G. Oury's *Marie de l'Incarnation*," *American Review of Canadian Studies* 4 (1974): 76–77; Jaenen, "Amerindian Views of French Culture," 270.

64. Ibid., 5: 169.

65. G. F. G. Stanley, "The First Indian 'Reserves' in Canada," *Revue d'Histoire de l'Amérique Française* 4 (1950): 182.

66. On the impact of liquor, see André Vachon, "L Eau-de-vie dans la Société Indienne," Canadian Historical Association, *Report* (1960), 22–23. This paragraph, and the following, summarize Chapter 4: "The Rebirth of the Dream: The Creation of the French/Abenaki Alliance, 1630–1689," in my "The People of the Dawn: The Abenaki and Their Relations with New England and New France, 1602–1727" (Ph.D. diss., University of Maine, Orono, 1975), 88–118.

67. JR 31: 187, 199.

68. On the Jesuits' optimistic reaction to North America, see Healy, "The French Jesuits and the Idea of the Noble Savage," 143–167.

69. Cornelius J. Jaenen deals at length with this conflict. See "The Relationship between Church and State in New France, 1647–1685" (Ph.D. diss., University of Ottawa, 1962).

70. For the extensive literature on Sebastien Racle, see my "Sebastien Racle versus New England: A Case Study of Frontier Conflict" (M.A. thesis, University of Maine, Orono, 1970), and Thomas Charland, "Sebastien Rale," *Dictionary of Canadian Biography*, 2: 542–545.

71. Racle to his Brother, October 30, 1689, letter #1, Houghton Library, Harvard University.

72. Racle to his Brother, August 26, 1690, letter #2, Houghton Library, Harvard University.

73. Father Jacques Bigot, for example, asserted that he functioned in a shamanistic role among the Wabanaki. JR 63: 107. Bailey, *Conflict*, emphasizes the destructive effect of the meeting. André Vachon, "L'Eau-de-vie dans la Société Indienne," 22–32, and Calvin Martin, "European Impact on the Culture of a Northeastern Algonquian Tribe," 20, assert that the Jesuits' success depended on their undermining of traditional shamans. Martin goes further in asserting that the Mi'kmaq apostatized in accepting Christianity and European trade and that they repudiated traditional values and religious belief. See 21ff. Martin amplifies this argument in his *Keepers of the Game: Indian-Animal Relationships and the Fur Trade* (Berkeley: University of California Press, 1978).

74. Leland, *The Algonquin Legends*, 249.

75. "The Cannibal Mamiltehe'o, 'He who has a hairy heart,'" in Speck, "Montagnais and Naskapi Tales," 19–20.

76. "The Witigo or 'Cannibal,'" Speck, "Montagnais and Naskapi Tales," 211, also printed in Teicher, *Windigo Psychosis*, 38–39.

CHAPTER FOUR. THE MYTHOLOGICAL SOURCES OF WABANAKI CATHOLICISM

1. For basic ethnological information on the Wabanaki societies, see the articles by Philip K. Bock, Vincent O. Erikson, Dean R. Snow, and Gordon M. Day in *Handbook of North American Indians*, ed. Bruce G. Trigger (Washington, DC: Smithsonian Institution Press, 1978), 15: 109–122; 123–136; 137–147; 148–159.

2. For important interpretative orientations on the study of myth, see: Alfonso Ortiz, "Some Concerns Central to the Writing of 'Indian' History," *The Indian Historian* 10 (1977): 17–22; Kees W. Bolle, *The Freedom of Man in Myth* (Nashville, TN: Vanderbilt University Press, 1968); Mircea Eliade, *The Sacred and the Profane: The Nature of Religion*, trans. Willard R. Trask (New York: Harcourt Brace, 1959); Clifford Geertz, *The Interpretation of Cultures* (New York: Basic, 1973); G. Van Der Leeuw, *Religion in Essence and Manifestation*, 2 vols. (Gloucester, MA: Peter Smith, 1967 [1938]), 2: 591–670.

3. A word should be added on the usefulness of the *Jesuit Relations* for the Indian history of the Northeast. The *Relations* were written, as might be expected, with the purpose of convincing potential French supporters that their mission program met with success. At the same time, the Society of Jesus used the *Relations* as a vehicle for exploring the difficulties of Christianization and how Indian affairs applied to the interests of New France as a whole. The Jesuits therefore included a great deal of detailed information about the actual behavior and speech of both the Indians and the French. Expressions of personal and collective bias that colors the Jesuits' estimation of reported behavior are

also useful: they show the ethnocentric assumptions with which Indian peoples contended. Leon Pouliot, "Paul Le Jeune," in *Dictionary of Canadian Biography*, ed. G. W. Brown (Toronto: University of Toronto Press, 1966), 1: 453–458 provides a critical overview of the writing of the early *Relations*. See also his *Étude sur les Relations des Jésuites de la Nouvelle France (1632–1672)* (Paris: Studia Collegii Maximi Immaculatae Conceptionis, V, 1940).

4. All references in the text to Dr. Peter Paul refer to conversations he had with Andrea and Daryl Nicholas. His observations have added significantly to already published data, and I am delighted to be able to include them here.

5. Alfred Goldsworthy Bailey expresses the older view in *The Conflict of European and Eastern Algonkian Cultures, 1504-1700*, 2nd ed. (Toronto: University of Toronto Press, 1969 [1937]). For recent reactions, see Cornelius J. Jaenen, *Friend and Foe: Aspects of French-Amerindian Cultural Contact in the Sixteenth and Seventeenth Centuries* (New York: Columbia University Press, 1976); idem, "Amerindian Views of French Culture in the Seventeenth Century," *Canadian Historical Review* 55 (1974): 261–291; James P. Ronda, "The European Indian: Jesuit Civilization Planning in New France," *Church History* 31 (1972): 385–395; idem, "The Sillery Experiment: A Jesuit-Indian Village in New France, 1637–1663," *American Indian Culture and Research Journal* 3 (1979): 1–18; idem, "'We Are Well As We Are': An Indian Critique of Seventeenth Century Christian Missions," *William and Mary Quarterly* 34 (1977): 66–82; James Axtell, "The Failure to Convert the Indians: An Autopsy," in *Papers of the Sixth Algonquian Conference, 1974*, ed. William Cowan (Ottawa: Carleton University, 1975), 274–290. For the literature dealing specifically with the Wabanaki, see Robert Conkling, "Legitimacy and Conversion in Social Change: The Case of the French Missionaries," *Ethnohistory* 21 (1974): 1–24; and Kenneth M. Morrison, "Towards a History of Intimate Encounters: Algonkian Folklore, Jesuit Missionaries, and Kiwakwe, the Cannibal Giant," *American Indian Culture and Research Journal* 3 (1979): 51–80.

6. As Calvin Martin, *Keepers of the Game: Indian-Animal Relationships and the Fur Trade* (Berkeley and Los Angeles: University of California Press, 1978), 152, contends for other Algonkian peoples.

7. Jacques Rousseau, "Le Dualisme des Peuplades de la Forêt Boréale," in *Acculturation in the Americas, Proceedings of the 29th International Congress of Americanists*, ed. Sol Tax (Chicago: University of Chicago Press, 1952), 2: 118–126; and his "Persistances Païennes chez les Amérindiens de la Forêt Boréale," *Cahiers des Dix* 17 (1952): 183–208.

8. Jaenen, *Friend and Foe*, 12–40; Olive P. Dickason, "The Concept of l'homme sauvage and the Early French Colonialism in the Americas," *Revue Française d'Histoire D'Outre-Mer* 58 (1977): 5–32.

9. Frank G. Speck, "Penobscot Shamanism," *Memoirs of the American Anthropological Association* 6 (1919): 238–288.

10. Werner Muller, "North America," in *Pre-Columbian American Religions*, ed. Walter Krickeberg et al., trans. Stanley David (London: Weidenfeld and Nicholson, 1961), 152.

11. Frank G. Speck, "Penobscot Tales and Religious Beliefs," *Journal of American Folklore* 48 (1935): 1–107.

12. See ibid., 34–35; Speck, "Penobscot Shamanism," 254–255.

13. Charles G. Leland, *The Algonquin Legends of New England or Myths and Folklore of the Micmac, Passamaquoddy and Penobscot Tribes* (Boston: Houghton Mifflin, 1884), 31, 180–181; John Dyneley Prince, *Passamaquoddy Texts*, Publications of the American Ethnological Society, 10 (New York: n.p., 1921), 27, 35. This was also true of the Ojibwa: A. Irving Hallowell, "Ojibwa Ontology, Behavior and World View," in *Teachings from the American Earth: Indian Religion and Philosophy*, ed. Dennis Tedlock and Barbara Tedlock (New York: Liveright, 1975), 141-178.

14. Bailey, *Conflict*, 135.

15. Joseph Nicolar, *The Life and Traditions of the Red Man* (Fredericton, NB: St. Anne's Point Press, 1979), 21.

16. Leland, *The Algonquin Legends*, 15–17.

17. Frank G. Speck, "Penobscot Transformer Tales, dictated by Newell Lion," *International Journal of American Linguistics* 1 (1918): 187–244.

18. Ibid., 184–194; Speck, "Penobscot Tales and Religious Beliefs," 6.

19. Speck, "Penobscot Tales and Religious Beliefs," 6.

20. Leland, *The Algonquin Legends*, 183.

21. For the myth texts from which these details have been drawn, see Speck, "Penobscot Tales and Religious Beliefs," 40–49; Speck, "Penobscot Transformer Tales," 187–216; Leland, *The Algonquin Legends*, 28–30, 62–74, 111–120. For extended studies that examine how myth and folkloric texts can be used to establish worldview postulates, see Thomas C. Blackburn, ed., *December's Child: A Book of Chumash Oral Narratives* (Berkeley and Los Angeles: University of California Press, 1975); Melville Jacobs, *The Content and Style of an Oral Literature: Clackamas Chinook Myths and Tales* (Chicago: University of Chicago Press, 1959); Katherine Spencer, *Mythology and Values: An Analysis of Navaho Chantway Myths* (Philadelphia: American Folklore Society, 1957); Victor Barnouw, *Wisconsin Chippewa Myths and Tales and their Relations to Chippewa Life* (Madison: University of Wisconsin Press, 1977).

22. Speck, "Penobscot Tales and Religious Beliefs," 8, 10.

23. Prince, *Passamaquoddy Texts*, 31; Leland, *The Algonquin Legends*, 60.

24. Hallowell, "Ojibwa Ontology," 47.

25. Speck, "Penobscot Tales and Religious Beliefs," 42–43; for the Passamaquoddy version, see Leland, *The Algonquin Legends*, 114–119; and for the Maliseet account, see Frank G. Speck, "Malecite Tales," *Journal of American Folklore* 39 (1917): 480–481.

26. Frank G. Speck, *Penobscot Man: The Life History of a Forest Tribe in Maine* (Philadelphia: University of Pennsylvania Press, 1940), 203.

27. Speck, "Penobscot Shamanism," 240; Frank G. Speck, "Game Totems among the Northeastern Algonkians," *American Anthropologist* 3 (1890): 66.

28. Nicolar, *Life and Traditions*, 83.

29. Ibid., 65.

30. On ritual specialists who interpreted dreams, see Speck, "Penobscot Shamanism," 268–273.

31. Nicolar, *Life and Traditions*, 83.

32. Ibid.

33. Speck, "Penobscot Shamanism," 249–253. On the shamans' "guardian spirits," see Garrick Mallery, "Fight with the Giant Witch," *American Anthropologist* 3 (1890): 66.

34. Speck discusses shamanistic responsibility for causing illness but denies shamans a significant role in healing: "Penobscot Shamanism," 259. While many illnesses were treated, as Speck observes, by women herbalists, he also admits that seventeenth-century sources indicate that the shamans were medical specialists. Ibid., 266. See also Frank G. Speck, "Medical Practices of the Northeastern Algonquians," *Proceedings of the Nineteenth International Congress of Americanists* (Nendeln, Liechtenstein: Kraus Reprint, 1968 [1915]), 307–313. Dr. Peter Paul notes that the Wabanaki discovered the use of calamus root after the introduction of European diseases.

35. Speck, "Penobscot Tales and Religious Beliefs," 23; Calvin Martin, "The European Impact on the Culture of a Northeastern Algonquian Tribe: An Ecological Interpretation," *William and Mary Quarterly* 31 (1974), 13; Chrestien LeClercq, *New Relation of Gaspesia, With the Customs and Religion of the Gaspesian Indians*, ed. William F. Ganong (Toronto: The Champlain Society, 1910), 176–177, 214.

36. Frank G. Speck, *Naskapi: The Savage Hunters of the Labrador Peninsula*, 2nd ed. (Norman: University of Oklahoma Press, 1977 [1935]), 122; and see idem, "Penobscot Tales and Religious Beliefs," 5; idem, "Penobscot Shamanism," 257; Prince, *Passamaquoddy Texts*, 65.

37. Bruce G. Trigger, "Trade and Tribal Warfare on the St. Lawrence in the Sixteenth Century," *Ethnohistory* 9 (1962): 240–256.

38. For the intertribal warfare among the coastal Algonkians, see articles by Lucien Campeau, Thomas Grassman, W. Austin Squires, and D. C. Harvey in the *Dictionary of Canadian Biography*, 1: 69; 500–501; 526–527; 529–530; 604.

39. Nicolar, *Life and Traditions*, 95–126.

40. Ibid., 106.

41. On rivalries between shamans, see Speck, "Penobscot Shamanism," 243; for individual tales see ibid., 280–281, 282–283.

42. Nicolar, *Life and Traditions*, 106–108. Mi'kmaq traditions also record shamanistic jealousies attending European contact. See the story quoted by Bailey, *Conflict*, 185.

43. For the English evidence, see Samuel Purchas, "Purchas, His Pilgrimes," in *The Sagadahoc Colony*, ed. Henry O. Thayer (Portland: The Gorges Society, 1892), 88. As early as 1611, the Wabanaki shamans told the French that their powers were waning. Reuben Gold Thwaites, ed., *The Jesuit Relations and Allied Documents*, 73 vols. (New York: Pageant, 1959), 2: 77. Hereafter cited as JR.

44. Ronda, "'We Are Well As We Are,'" 76–77; Jaenen, "Amerindian Views," 274–275.

45. JR, 24: 61–63, 185; 25: 117–21.

46. Ibid., 29: 69–71.

47. Ibid., 28: 203.

48. Ibid., 31: 187.

49. Ibid., 8: 251; 9: 9.

50. Ibid., 31: 187.

51. Ibid., 31: 185–187.

52. See Lucien Campeau's remarks on the Wabanakis' recognition of Druillettes' power: "Gabriel Druillettes," *Dictionary of Canadian Biograghy*, 1: 281–282. See also Martin, "European Impact on the Culture of a Northeastern Algonquian Tribe," 20, who states that the "missionary was successful only to the degree that his power exceeded that of the shaman." Andre Vachon, "L'Eau de Vie dans la Société Indienne," Canadian Historical Association, *Report* (1960), 22–32, makes a similar argument. It is striking that Father Jacques Bigot, a later Wabanaki missionary, considered that he played a shamanistic role in Wabanaki society. JR, 63: 107. See also Chapter Three.

53. JR, 31: 203.

54. Ibid., 31: 193–197.

55. Ibid., 38: 37; and see 37: 251–253.

56. Ibid., 31: 197; Speck, "Penobscot Shamanism," 240–241.

57. JR, 37: 253.

58. Ibid., 31: 187. For estimations of Jesuit facility with Indian languages, see Victor Egon Hanzeli, *Missionary Linguistics in New France: A Study of Seventeenth and Eighteenth Century Descriptions of American Indian Languages* (The Hague: Mouton, 1969); and Frank T. Siebert, "The Penobscot Dictionary Project: Preferences and Problems of Format, Presentation and Entry," in *Papers of the Eleventh Algonquian Conference*, ed. William Cowan (Ottawa: Carleton University, 1980), 115–124.

59. It may be that the Kennebecs identified "He-Who-Made-All" with No-chi-gar-neh, the Spirit of the Air. In 1650, the Kennebec sagamore greeted Gabriel Druillettes as follows: "I see now that the great Spirit who commands in

the Skies is pleased to regard us with favor, since he sends us back our Patriarch." JR, 37: 249.

60. Ibid., 31: 189–193.
61. Ibid., 31: 199–201.
62. Ibid., 38: 27.
63. Ibid., 37: 245.
64. Ibid., 37: 251.
65. Ibid., 38: 21. Martin, *Keepers*, 144-149 argues to the contrary that Christianity undermined traditional man-animal relationships among the Algonkian peoples.
66. JR, 38: 23.
67. Ibid., 38: 25. One possible reason that dreaming continued to play a significant role in post-Christian Wabanaki life is that the religious specialists who interpreted dreams did not wield their powers selfishly. "The informants agree," Frank G. Speck noted, "that the dreamers were harmless in their behavior towards other men, they never inflicted injury, sickness, or misfortune on rivals, as we find the *made'olinu* so frequently doing." "Penobscot Shamanism," 269.
68. JR, 37: 251.
69. Ibid.
70. Ibid., 38: 33–35.
71. Ibid., 38: 35–37.
72. Ibid., 37.
73. Kenneth M. Morrison, "The Bias of Colonial Law: English Paranoia and the Abenaki Arena of King Philip's War, 1675–1678," *New England Quarterly* 53 (1980): 363–387.
74. JR, 60: 233.
75. Ibid., 60: 233–235.
76. Ibid., 60: 237–239.
77. Ibid.
78. Ibid., 60: 239–241.
79. Ibid., 62: 259–261. Thomas M. Charland, *Histoire des Abénakis d'Odanak (1675–1937)* (Montreal: Éditions du Lévier, 1964), 15–25.
80. JR, 62: 49. On the optimistic French view of the Indians, see George R. Healy, "The French Jesuits and the Idea of the Noble Savage," *William and Mary Quarterly* 25 (1958): 143–167.
81. JR, 62: 47–49.
82. For a different view, see Martin, *Keepers of the Game*.
83. See generally François-Marc Gagnon, *La Conversion par l'Image: Un Aspect de la Mission des Jésuites auprès des Indiens du Canada au XVIIe Siècle* (Montreal: Bellarmin, 1975).
84. JR, 62: 43.

85. For the psychological background, see A. I. Hallowell, *Culture and Experience* (Philadelphia: University of Pennsylvania Press, 1955), chapters 14–15.

86. JR, 62: 29.

87. Ibid., 62: 31.

88. Ibid., 62: 31–33.

89. Ibid., 62: 37.

90. Ibid., 62: 45.

91. Ibid., 62: 43.

92. For suggestive treatments of seventeenth-century Indian reactions to alcohol, see Vachon, "L'Eau de Vie," and R. C. Dailey, "The Role of Alcohol among North American Indian Tribes as Reported in the Jesuit Relations," *Anthropologica* 10 (1968): 45–59.

93. JR, 62: 33.

94. Ibid., 62: 35.

95. Ibid., 62: 39. For folkloric evidence of continuing Jesuit-shaman tensions, see Elsie Clews Parsons, "Micmac Folklore," *Journal of American Folklore* 38 (1925): 90–91; and Charles G. Leland and John D. Prince, *Kulóskap, the Master: And Other Algonkin Poems* (New York: Funk & Wagnalls, 1902), 242–243.

96. JR, 62: 25, 109; 63: 27ff.

97. G. F. G. Stanley, "The First Indian 'Reserves' in Canada," *Revue d'Histoire de l'Amérique Française* 4 (1950): 178–210.

98. G. F. G. Stanley, "The Policy of 'Francisation' as Applied to the Indians during the Ancien Regime," *Revue d'Histoire de l'Amérique Française* 3 (1949): 333–348.

99. Axtell, "Failure to Convert the Indians," 280; Rousseau, "Le Dualisme Religieux," 122.

100. Kenneth M. Morrison, "'The Wonders of Divine Mercy': A Review of John Williams' *The Redeemed Captive*," *American Review of Canadian Studies* 9 (1979): 56–62.

101. John Williams, *The Redeemed Captive*, ed. Edward W. Clark (Amherst: University of Massachusetts Press, 1976), 61.

102. Speck, "Penobscot Tales and Religious Beliefs," 4; John M. Cooper, "The Northern Algonquian Supreme Being," *Primitive Man* 4 (1933): 41–112; William Jones, "The Algonkin Manitou," *Journal of American Folklore*, 28 (1905): 183–190; Paul Radin, "Monotheism among American Indians," in *Teachings from the American Earth*, ed. Dennis Tedlock and Barbara Tedlock, 219–257; Åke Hultkrantz, *The Religions of the American Indians*, trans. Monica Setterwall (Berkeley and Los Angeles: University of California Press, 1979), 15-26.

103. Speck, "Penobscot Tales and Religious Beliefs," 5, 19.

104. Speck, "Penobscot Shamanism," 246, note 1; Fannie Hardy Eckstorm, *Old John Neptune and Other Indian Shamans* (Portland, ME: Southworth-Anthoensen, 1945).

105. Jeanne Guillemin, *Urban Renegades: The Cultural Strategy of American Indians* (New York: Columbia University Press, 1975), 102–110, provides a compelling treatment of Gluskap's enduring importance to contemporary Mi'kmaq peoples. For a different point-of-view, see Wilson D. Wallis and Ruth Sawtell Wallis, "Culture Loss and Culture Change among the Micmac of the Canadian Maritime Provinces, 1912–1950," in *The Native Peoples of Atlantic Canada: A Reader in Regional Ethnic Relations*, ed. Harold F. McGee (Toronto: McClelland and Stewart, 1974), 142.

106. See text in Speck, "Penobscot Tales and Religious Beliefs," 9.

107. Bailey, *Conflict*, 188; Frank G. Speck, "Some Micmac Tales from Cape Breton Island," *Journal of American Folklore* 28 (1915): 60–61; and see "Gluskabe Creates Himself and Competes with the Creator," in idem, "Wawenock Myth Texts from Maine," *43rd Annual Report of the Bureau of American Ethnology* (Washington: U.S. Government Printing Office, 1928), 180–181, 186.

108. Parsons, "Micmac Folklore," 88–89.

109. Nicolar, *Life and Traditions*, 10.

110. Ibid., 27, 30–32; and see Helen Keith Frost, "Two Abenaki Legends," *Journal of American Folklore* 25 (1912): 188–189.

111. Edward Jack, "Malecite Legends," *Journal of American Folklore* 8 (1895): 194; Silas T. Rand, *Legends of the Micmac* (New York: Longnass, Green, 1894), 229; Speck, "Penobscot Tales and Religious Beliefs," 6; Guillemin, *Urban Renegades*, 109.

112. The Newberry Library, Center for the History of the American Indian, Bibliographical Series, ed. Francis Jennings (Bloomington, Indiana, 1976–), surveys these types of literature.

113. Hallowell, "Ojibwa Ontology," 152.

114. For a suggestive review of the importance of values to the appreciation of holistic cultural organization, and therefore to the process of historical change, see Leslie A. White, "Values and Cultural Systems," in his *The Concept of Cultural Systems: A Key to Understanding Tribes and Nations* (New York: Columbia University Press, 1975), 141–146.

CHAPTER FIVE. DISCOURSE AND THE ACCOMMODATION OF VALUES

1. For an introduction to the literature on missionization among Native Americans, see James P. Ronda and James Axtell, *Indian Missions: A Critical Bibliography* (Bloomington: Indiana University Press, 1978). For a general

overview, see Henry Warner Bowden, *American Indian and Christian Missions, Studies in Cultural Conflict* (Chicago: University of Chicago Press, 1981).

2. See the literature on the Jesuit mission at Sillery: Alfred Goldsworthy Bailey, *The Conflict of European and Eastern Algonkian Cultures, 1504–1700: A Study in Canadian Civilization*, 2nd ed. (Toronto: University of Toronto Press, 1969 [1937]); Cornelius Jaenen, "Amerindian Views of French Culture in the Seventeenth Century," *Canadian Historical Review* 55 (1974): 261–291; James P. Ronda, "The European Indian: Jesuit Civilization Planning in New France," *Church History* 31 (1972): 385–395; idem, "'We Are Well As We Are': An Indian Critique of Seventeenth Century Christian Missions," *William and Mary Quarterly* 34 (1977): 66–82; idem, "The Sillery Experiment: A Jesuit-Indian Village in New France, 1637–1663," *American Indian Culture and Research Journal* 3 (1979): 1–18.

3. Peter L. Berger, *The Sacred Canopy: Elements of a Sociological Theory of Religion* (New York: Doubleday, 1967); Clifford Geertz, "Thick Description: Toward an Interpretive Theory of Culture," in his *Interpretation of Cultures* (New York: Basic, 1973), 3–30.

4. Although there is no overall theoretical orientation to the religious study of communication, a number of recent works raise questions that are relevant to the historical reinterpretation of interaction in the missions. For my general theoretical and interdisciplinary orientation, see Kenneth M. Morrison, *The Embattled Northeast: The Elusive Ideal of Alliance in Abenaki-Euramerican Relations* (Berkeley and Los Angeles: University of California Press, 1984), 1–11. In addition to the literature cited there, the following works emphasize the close relationship among language, social codes, and communication and how these ultimately affect the reconstruction of conflicting and overlapping senses of meaning. Taken together, these works suggest that the study of the conscious and unconscious elements of speech acts can identify how the competing abstractions peculiar to each worldview come home, and are made concrete and personable. See, among many others, David Silverman, *Reading Castaneda: A Prologue to the Social Sciences* (London: Routledge & Kegan Paul, 1975); Susan K. Langer, *Philosophy in a New Key*, 2nd ed. (Cambridge, MA: Harvard University Press, 1951); Erving Goffman, *Interaction Ritual: Essays on Face-to-Face Behavior* (Garden City, NY: Doubleday, 1967); Keith H. Basso and Henry A. Selby, eds., *Meaning in Anthropology* (Albuquerque: University of New Mexico Press, 1976); Dell Hymes, *Foundations in Sociolinguistics: An Ethnographic Approach* (Philadelphia: University of Pennsylvania Press, 1974); Ben G. Blount, ed., *Language, Culture and Society: A Book of Readings* (Cambridge: Winthrop, 1974); Roy Turner, ed., *Ethnomethodology: Selected Readings* (Middlesex: Penguin Education, 1974); Pier Paulo Giglioli, ed., *Language and Social Context: Selected Readings* (Middlesex: Penguin Education, 1972); Richard Baumann and Joel Sherzer, eds., *Explorations in the Ethnography of Speaking* (Cambridge: Cambridge University Press, 1974); Paul Ricoeur, *Interpretation*

Theory: Discourse and the Surplus of Meaning (Fort Worth: Texas Christian University Press, 1976); Mary Louise Pratt, *Toward a Speech Act Theory of Literary Discourse* (Bloomington: Indiana University Press, 1977); Kenneth Burke, *A Grammar of Motives* (New York: Prentice-Hall, 1945); Robin Horton and Ruth Finnegan, *Modes of Thought* (London: Faber, 1973).

    5. Reuben Gold Thwaites, ed., *The Jesuit Relations and Allied Documents*, 73 vols. (New York: Pageant Book, 1959), 5: 85; 6: 101. Hereafter cited as JR.

    6. JR, 5: 115; 6: 27.
    7. Ibid., 6: 101.
    8. Lucien Campeau, S.J., ed. *Établissement à Québec (1616–1634)*, Monumenta Novae Franciae 2 (Québec: Les Presses de l'Université Laval, 1979), 135*–141*.
    9. JR, 6: 209, 213, 219, 223.
    10. Ibid., 5: 191.
    11. Ibid., 5: 35.
    12. Ibid., 5: 87, 109–111. See Thomas Grassman, "Pierre Antoine Pastedechouan," in *Dictionary of Canadian Biography*, ed. G. W. Brown (Toronto: University of Toronto Press, 1966), 1: 533–534.
    13. JR, 5: 107–113, 173–179, 215.
    14. Ibid., 4: 219; 5: 115.
    15. Ibid., 5: 117.
    16. Ibid., 5: 171.
    17. Ibid., 5: 159–161.
    18. Ibid., 5: 151.
    19. Ibid., 6: 27.
    20. Ibid., 7: 69–71.
    21. Ibid., 7: 71.
    22. Ibid.
    23. Ibid., 7: 55.
    24. Ibid., 7: 71.
    25. Ibid., 7: 107.
    26. Ibid., 7: 115.
    27. Ibid., 7: 139–143.
    28. Ibid., 7: 117.
    29. Ibid., 6: 165-167.
    30. Ibid., 7: 117.
    31. Ibid., 7: 63.
    32. Ibid., 7: 57.
    33. Ibid., 6: 179.
    34. Ibid., 6: 231.
    35. Ibid.
    36. Ibid., 7: 57.

37. Ibid., 6: 147.
38. Ibid., 7: 137.
39. Ibid., 7: 147-159.
40. Ibid., 7: 161; Frank G. Speck, *Naskapi: The Savage Hunters of the Labrador Peninsula*, 2nd ed. (Norman: University of Oklahoma Press, 1977 [1935]), 206–211.
41. JR, 7: 163.
42. Ibid., 7: 165.
43. Ibid., 7: 191.
44. Ibid., 7: 189.
45. Ibid., 7: 21–33.
46. Although scholars of religion have not reached a consensus on the problems of methodological orientation, I draw upon the following studies: Jonathan Z. Smith, *Map is Not Territory: Essays in the History of Religions* (Leiden: E. J. Brill, 1978); Joseph P. Cahill, *Mended Speech: The Crisis of Religious Studies and Theology* (New York: Crossroads, 1982); Clifford Geertz, "Religion as a Cultural System," in his *The Interpretation of Cultures* (New York: Basic, 1973), 87–125; Michael Banton, ed., *Anthropological Approaches to the Study of Religion* (London: Tavistock, 1966); Walter Holden Capps, ed., *Seeing with a Native Eye: Essays on Native American Religion* (New York: Harper & Row, 1976); Åke Hultkrantz, *The Religions of the American Indian*, trans. Monica Setterwall (Berkeley and Los Angeles: University of California Press, 1979); idem, *Belief and Worship in Native North America*, ed. Christopher Vecsey (Syracuse: Syracuse University Press, 1981); idem, "North American Indian Religion in the History of Research: A General Survey," *History of Religions* 6–7 (1966–1967) 6: 91–107, 208–235; 7: 13–34, 112–148; Sam D. Gill, "Native American Religions: A Review Essay," *Religious Studies Review* 5 (1979): 251–258; idem, *Native American Religions: An Introduction* (Belmont, CA: Wadsworth, 1982); idem, *Native American Traditions* (Belmont, CA: Wadsworth, 1983).
47. Wilfred Cantwell Smith, "Comparative Religion: Whither—and Why?" in *The History of Religions: Essays in Methodology*, ed. Mircea Eliade and Joseph M. Kitagawa (Chicago: University of Chicago Press, 1959), 31–50.

CHAPTER SIX. MONTAGNAIS MISSIONIZATION IN EARLY NEW FRANCE

1. The *Jesuit Relations* on which this study is based are largely the work of one man, Paul Le Jeune, superior of the Canadian Society of Jesus in the 1630s. For an evaluation of the accuracy of his writings, and of the uses to which they can be put, see Lucien Campeau, S.J., *Établissement à Québec (1619–1634)*, Monumenta Novae Franciae, 2 (Quebec: Les Presses de

l'Université Laval, 1979), 131–141; Eleanor Leacock, "Montagnais Women and the Jesuit Program for Colonization," in *Women and Colonization: Anthropological Perspectives*, ed. Mona Etienne and Eleanor Leacock (New York: Praeger, 1980), 26; and see Chapter Five.

2. Suzanna K. Langer, *Philosophy in a New Key*, 2nd ed. (Cambridge, MA: Harvard University Press, 1951).

3. Actually, to say that history may have alternative, culturally based causal explanations oversimplifies the situation. Native American senses of historical process may just as well be complementary as opposed to current historical assumptions. At present, the imperative is to push the possibility of taking seriously Native American reality assumptions. For some background on the challenge of cross-cultural interpretation, see Clifford Geertz, "Religion as a Cultural System," in *Anthropological Approaches to the Study of Religion*, ed. Michael Banton (London: Tavistock, 1966), 1–46; Keith H. Basso and Henry A. Selby, eds., *Meaning in Anthropology* (Albuquerque: University of New Mexico Press, 1976); Peter L. Berger, *The Sacred Canopy: Elements of a Sociological Theory of Religion* (New York: Doubleday, 1967); Joseph P. Cahill, *Mended Speech: The Crisis of Religious Studies and Theology* (New York: Crossroads, 1982); Mary Douglas, *Implicit Meanings: Essays in Anthropology* (London: Routledge and Kegan Paul, 1975); Victor Turner, *The Ritual Process: Structure and Anti-Structure* (Ithaca, NY: Cornell University Press, 1977).

4. For the historical literature that focuses specifically on the seventeenth-century Montagnais, see Alfred Goldsworthy Bailey, *The Conflict of European and Eastern Algonkian Cultures, 1504–1700*, 2nd ed. (Toronto: University of Toronto Press, 1969 [1937]); Lucien Campeau, S.J., *La Première Mission des Jésuites en Nouvelle France (1611-1613) et Les Commencements du College des Jésuites, 1626–1670* (Montreal: Éditions Bellarmin, 1672); Howard L. Harrod, "Missionary Life-World and Native Response: Jesuits in New France," *Studies in Religion* 13 (Spring 1984): 179–192; Cornelius Jaenen, "Amerindian Views of French Culture in the Seventeenth Century," *Canadian Historical Review* 55 (1974): 261–291; idem, *Friend and Foe: Aspects of French-Amerindian Cultural Contact in the Sixteenth and Seventeenth Centuries* (New York: Columbia University Press, 1976); Kenneth S. Lane, "The Montagnais Indians, 1600–1640," *Publications of the Kroeber Anthropogical Society* 7 (1952): 1–62; James P. Ronda, "The European Indian: Jesuit Civilization Planning in New France," *Church History* 31 (1972): 385–395; idem, "'We Are Well As We Are': An Indian Critique of Seventeenth Century Missions," *William and Mary Quarterly* 34 (1977): 66–82; idem, "The Sillery Experiment: A Jesuit-Indian Village in New France, 1637–1663," *American Indian Culture and Research Journal* 3 (1979): 1–18; Bruce G. Trigger, "Champlain Judged by His Indian Policy: A Different View of Early Canadian History," *Anthropologica* 13 (1971): 85–114.

5. For the Jesuit writings supporting the above generalizations, see Reuben Gold Thwaites, ed., *The Jesuit Relations and Allied Documents*, 73 vols. (New York: Pageant, 1959), 6: 157–317; 7: 7ff.; 8: 15. Hereafter cited as JR.

6. For the intellectual background of the Jesuits, and the role religion played in the colonization of New France, see James Axtell, *The Invasion Within: The Contest of Cultures in Colonial North America* (New York: Oxford University Press, 1985); Lucien Campeau, S.J., *La Première Mission des Jésuites en Nouvelle-France (1611–1613)* and his *Établissement à Québec (1616–1634)*; Olive Patricia Dickason, *The Myth of the Savage and the Beginnings of French Colonialism in the Americas* (Edmonton: University of Alberta Press, 1984); George W. Healy, "The French Jesuits and the Idea of the Noble Savage," *William and Mary Quarterly* 15 (1958): 143–167; John Hopkins Kennedy, *Jesuit and Savage in New France* (New Haven: Yale University Press, 1950).

7. See James A. Boon, *Other Tribes, Other Scribes: Symbolic Anthropology in the Comparative Study of Cultures, Histories, Religions, and Texts* (Cambridge: Cambridge University Press, 1982) and Richard E. Wentz, *The Contemplation of Otherness: The Critical Vision of Religion* (Mercer, GA: Mercer University Press, 1984).

8. Berger, *The Sacred Canopy*.

9. Geertz, "Religion as a Cultural System," 4.

10. Sam D. Gill, *Native American Religions: An Introduction* (Belmont, CA: Wadsworth, 1984), 11.

11. A. Irving Hallowell, "Ojibwa Ontology, Behavior and World View," in *Culture in History: Essays in Honor of Paul Radin*, ed. Stanley Diamond (New York: Columbia University Press, 1960), 19–52. Hallowell's work on the Ojibwa has been thoroughly discussed in a series of essays in *Ethos*. The most relevant of these is Mary B. Black, "Ojibwa Taxonomy and Percept Ambiguity," *Ethos* 5 (1977): 90–117. See also her "Ojibwa Power Belief System," in *The Anthropology of Power*, ed. Raymond D. Fogelson and Richard N. Adams (New York: Academic, 1977), 141–152. For a critical, although inadequate, critique of Hallowell's concept of person, see Åke Hultkrantz, "The Concept of the Supernatural in Primal Religion," *History of Religions* 22 (1983): 231–253.

12. JR, 11: 253.

13. Ibid., 7: 101.

14. Ibid., 11: 155–157.

15. Ibid., 11: 157.

16. Ibid., 11: 205.

17. Ibid., 6: 183.

18. Ibid., 7: 101.

19. Ibid., 6: 173.

20. This discussion is somewhat in advance of scholarly understanding of these categories in the sense that I assume that the three ideas are essentially linked. For the concept of person, I rely on A. Irving Hallowell, "Ojibwa Ontology"; for power, see Raymond D. Fogelson and Richard N. Adams, eds., *The Anthropology of Power*; and for gift see Marcel Mauss, *The Gift: Forms and Functions of Exchange in Archaic Societies* (New York: Norton, 1967 [1925]).

21. JR, 7: 23.

22. Ibid., 5: 57; 6: 159, 161, 171, 215, 233; 12: 7, 25-27. See also Frank G. Speck, *Naskapi: The Savage Hunters of the Labrador Peninsula*, 2nd ed. (Norman: University of Oklahoma Press, 1977 [1935]).

23. JR, 7: 23.

24. Ibid., 6: 199; 7: 181; 9: 113, 119; 11: 195, 259, 263, 265; 12: 7.

25. Hallowell, "Ojibwa Ontology," 29.

26. Speck, *Naskapi*, 79.

27. For references to the Jesuits' perceptions of these vices and virtues, see JR, 5: 123; 6: 45, 83-85, 231-235, 243-247, 255-261, 281; 7: 113-115, 177, 191; 8: 41.

28. This study is closely related to an earlier essay in which I explore this mythological connection in greater detail for the Wabanaki, who were the Montagnais' southern neighbors. See Chapter Four.

29. Speck, *Naskapi*, 103-127, 232-245.

30. JR, 5: 171, 179.

31. Ibid., 6: 249.

32. Ibid., 259. For related literature on the role of reciprocal exchange in Indian-European relations, see Wilbur Jacobs, *Wilderness, Politics and Indian Gifts* (Lincoln: University of Nebraska Press, 1966), and Cornelius J. Jaenen, "The Role of Presents in French-Amerindian Trade," in *Explorations in Canadian Economic History: Essays in Honour of Irene M. Spry*, ed. Duncan Cameron (Ottawa: University of Ottawa Press, 1985), 231-250.

33. See Black, "Ojibwa Taxonomy," 90-117 and her "Ojibwa Power Belief System," 141-152.

34. For related articles by Hallowell, see "Fear and Anxiety as Cultural and Individual Variables in a Primitive Society," *Journal of Social Psychology* 9 (1938): 25-47; "The Social Function of Anxiety in a Primitive Society," *American Sociological Review* 6 (1941): 869-881; "Some Psychological Characteristics of the Northeastern Indians," in *Man in Northeastern North America*, ed. Frederick Johnson (Andover, MA: Phillips Academy, 1946), 195-225.

35. JR, 8: 247.

36. Ibid., 6: 233.

37. Ibid., 11: 193.

38. Ibid., 5: 103; 7: 115–117; 8: 29-33; 9: 113–117, 213–215; 11: 117; 12: 21. See Speck, *Naskapi*, 67–70; Morton I. Teicher, *Windigo Psychosis: A Study of a Relationship between Belief and Behavior among the Indians of Northeastern Canada* (Seattle: University of Washington Press, 1960); and see Chapter Three.

39. JR: 9: 115.
40. Ibid., 5: 35; 9: 111; 11: 87, 215.
41. Ibid., 6: 173; 12: 15–17, 143–145.
42. Ibid., 12: 153–157.
43. See Chapter Five.
44. JR, 4: 203; 9: 17; 11: 181, 255.
45. Ibid., 6: 193–195; 8: 273; 9: 115.
46. Ibid., 12: 9–11.
47. Ibid., 12: 7.
48. Ibid., 5: 151.
49. Ibid., 11: 193–195.
50. Ibid., 9: 195–197, 207.
51. Ibid., 7: 301; 9: 69.
52. Ibid., 7: 277–279, 283; 9: 79ff., 95; 12: 153–157.
53. Ibid., 7: 85–87.
54. Ibid., 11: 253.
55. Ibid., 5: 151, 177; 6: 165–167; 7: 85–87.
56. Ibid., 11: 203, 261; 12: 155, 169.
57. Ibid., 7: 131; 11: 181, 259.
58. Ibid., 12: 151.
59. Ibid., 8: 179.
60. Ibid., 6: 257–259; 9: 193.
61. Ibid., 7: 285.
62. Ibid., 5: 5; 8: 21–23; 9: 79.
63. Ibid., 8: 255, 269, 271; 9: 39–41.
64. Ibid., 5: 109–111, 121–123; 6: 109; 8: 247; 9: 11–13, 25, 41–43, 59, 73–77, 193; 11: 83, 91–93, 111–113, 127, 137–139, 165, 235.
65. Ibid., 7: 295; 8: 247; 11: 87–89, 161–163; 12: 155.
66. Ibid., 11: 119.
67. Speck, *Naskapi*, 73.
68. JR, 6: 173, 203, 283; 7: 9.
69. Ibid., 7: 9.
70. Ibid., 8: 37.
71. Ibid., 7: 171, 175; 8: 29ff., 57; 9: 145–147.
72. Ibid., 7: 149–151.
73. Ibid., 8: 27–37; 9: 213.
74. Ibid., 8: 213.
75. Ibid., 6: 101.

76. Eleanor Leacock, "Status among the Montagnais-Naskapi of Labrador," *Ethnohistory* 5 (1958): 200–209; idem, "Montagnais Women and the Jesuit Program for Colonization," 25–42; Julius E. Lips, "Public Opinion and Mutual Assistance among the Montagnais-Naskapi," *American Anthropologist* 39 (1937): 222–228; Toby Morantz, "Northern Algonquian Concepts of Status and Leadership," *Canadian Review of Sociology and Anthropology* 19 (1982): 482–501.

77. See Chapter Five.
78. JR, 7: 123, 159ff., 295; 6: 37; 9: 19.
79. Ibid., 11: 89.
80. Ibid., 4: 201.
81. Ibid., 5: 223.
82. Ibid., 11: 259.
83. Ibid., 6: 157.
84. Ibid., 6: 157–159. For the relationship of Christianity and traditional religion in the twentieth century, see Jacques Rousseau and Madeleine Rousseau, "Le Dualisme Religieux des Peuplades de la Forêt Boréale," in *Acculturation in the Americas*, ed. Sol Tax (Chicago: University of Chicago Press, 1952), 118–126; idem, "Persistances Païennes chez les Amérindians de la Forêt Boréale," *Cahiers des Dix* 17 (1952): 129–155; and Jacques Rousseau, "Dualisme Religieux ou Syncretisme chez les Algiques de la Forêt Boréale," *Actes du VIe Congres International des Sciences Anthropologiques et Ethnologiques*, 2 (Paris: Musée de l'homme, 1962), 469–473.

85. JR, 11: 205.

CHAPTER SEVEN. BAPTISM AND ALLIANCE

1. Victor W. Turner, *The Drums of Affliction: A Study of Religious Processes among the Ndembu of Zambia* (Oxford: Oxford University Press, 1968); idem, *The Ritual Process: Structure and Anti-Structure* (Chicago: Aldine, 1969); idem, *Dramas, Fields, and Metaphors: Symbolic Action in Human Society* (Ithaca, NY: Cornell University Press, 1974).

2. I use the technical term "anomy" in the sense proposed by Peter Berger, *The Sacred Canopy: Elements of a Sociological Theory of Religion* (New York: Doubleday, 1969). For Berger, religion consists essentially of those acts of naming through which people give sensible order to their world. In this sense, anomy occurs when real-life experience does not fit the socially constituted, named, cultural order. In terms of oral tradition, the term refers to those situations in which people experience uncertainty because the named cultural order no longer applies.

3. For the background of the Sillery mission, see James Axtell, *The Invasion Within: The Contest of Cultures in Colonial North America* (New

York: Oxford University Press, 1985); Alfred Goldsworthy Bailey, *The Conflict of European and Eastern Algonkian Cultures, 1504–1700: A Study in Canadian Civilization*, 2nd ed. (Toronto: University of Toronto Press, 1969 [1937]); Lucien Campeau, S.J., *La Première Mission des Jésuites en Nouvelle-France (1611–1613) et les Commencements du Colleges des Jésuites (1626–1670)* (Montreal: Éditions Bellarmin, 1972); idem, *Établissement à Québec (1616–1634)*, Monumenta Novae Franciae 2, (Quebec: Les Presses de l'Université Laval, 1979); Denys Delage, *Bitter Feast: Amerindians and Europeans in Northeastern North America, 1600–64* (Vancouver: University of British Columbia Press, 1993); Olive Patricia Dickason, *The Myth of the Savage and the Beginnings of French Colonialism in the Americas* (Edmonton: University of Alberta Press, 1984); Gerard Gagne, "L'impact des Maladies Européenes sur la Mortalité Amérindienne à Sillery, aux Dix-septième Siècle," *Recherches Amérindiennes au Québec* 18 (1988): 17–18; John Webster Grant, *Moon of Wintertime: Missionaries and the Indians of Canada in Encounter since 1534* (Toronto: University of Toronto Press, 1984); Howard L. Harrod, "Missionary Life-World and Native Response: Jesuits in New France," *Studies in Religion* 13 (1984): 179–192; George R. Healy, "The French Jesuits and the Idea of the Noble Savage," *William and Mary Quarterly* 15 (1958): 143–167; Cornelius J. Jaenen, "The Frenchification and Evangelization of the Amerindians in the Seventeenth Century New France," Canadian Catholic Historical Association, *Study Sessions* 15 (1968): 57–71; idem, "Amerindian Views of French Culture in the Seventeenth Century," *Canadian Historical Review* 55 (1974): 261–291; idem, *Friend and Foe: Aspects of French-Amerindian Cultural Contact in the Sixteenth and Seventeenth Centuries* (New York: Columbia University Press, 1976); idem, "Conceptual Frameworks for French Views of America and Amerindians," *French Colonial Studies* 2 (1978): 1–22; idem, "French Attitudes towards Native Society," in *Old Trails and New Directions: Papers of the Third North American Fur Trade Conference*, ed. C. M. Judd and A. J. Ray (Toronto: University of Toronto Press, 1980), 59–72; idem, "Canada during the French Regime," in *A Reader's Guide to Canada History: Beginnings to Confederation*, ed. D. A. Muise (Toronto: University of Toronto Press, 1982), 1: 3–44; idem, "'Les Sauvages Amériquains': Persistence into the Eighteenth Century of Traditional French Concepts and Constructs for Comprehending Amerindians," *Ethnohistory* 29 (1982): 43–56; Kenneth S. Lane, "The Montagnais Indians, 1600–1640," Publications of the Kroeber Anthropological Society 7 (1952): 1–62; Eleanor Leacock, "Montagnais Women and the Jesuit Program for Colonization," in *Women and Colonization: Anthropological Perspectives*, ed. Mona Etienne and Eleanor Leacock (New York: Praeger, 1980), 25–42; Michael Pomedli, "The Concept of 'Soul' in the *Jesuit Relations*: Were There Any Philosophers among the North American Indians?" *Laval théologique et philosophique* 41 (1985): 57–64; idem, "Mythical and Logical Thinking: Friends or Foes?" *Laval théologique et philosophique* 42 (1986):

377–387; idem, "Beyond Unbelief: Early Jesuit Interpretation of Native Religions," *Studies in Religion* 16 (1987): 275–287; James P. Ronda, "'We Are Well As We Are': An Indian Critique of Seventeenth-Century Christian Missions," *William and Mary Quarterly* 34 (1977): 66–82; idem, "The Sillery Experiment: A Jesuit-Indian Village in New France, 1637–1663," *American Indian Culture and Research Journal* 3 (1979): 1–18; Bruce G. Trigger, *Natives and Newcomers: Canada's 'Heroic Age' Reconsidered* (Kingston and Montreal: McGill-Queen's University Press, 1985). See also Chapters Five and Six.

4. For my methodological orientation, see Berger, *The Sacred Canopy*; Raymond D. Fogelson and Richard N. Adams, eds., *The Anthropology of Power: Ethnographic Studies from Asia, Oceania, and the New World* (New York: Academic, 1977); Clifford Geertz, "Religion as a Cultural System," in *Anthropological Approaches to the Study of Religion*, ed. Michael Banton (London: Tavistock, 1966), 1–46; A. Irving Hallowell, "Fear and Anxiety as Cultural and Individual Variables in a Primitive Society," *Journal of Social Psychology* 9 (1938): 25–47; idem, "The Social Function of Anxiety in a Primitive Society," *American Sociological Review* 6 (1941): 869–881; idem, "Some Psychological Characteristics of the Northeastern Indians," in *Man in Northeastern North America*, ed. Frederick Johnson (Andover, MA: Phillips Academy, 1946), 195–225; idem, "Ojibwa Ontology, Behavior, and World View," in *Teachings from the American Earth: Indian Religion and Philosophy*, ed. Dennis Tedlock and Barbara Tedlock (New York: Liveright, 1975), 141–178; Marcel Mauss, *The Gift: Forms and Functions of Exchange in Archaic Societies* (New York: Norton, 1967 [1925]); Kenneth M. Morrison, *The Embattled Northeast: The Elusive Ideal of Alliance in Abenaki-Euramerican Relations* (Berkeley and Los Angeles: University of California Press, 1984), 1–11. See also Chapter Four.

5. I ground my understanding of Algonkian religious syncretism on the following ethnographic studies: Mary B. Black, "Ojibwa Taxonomy and Percept Ambiguity," *Ethos* 5 (1977): 90–117; idem, "Ojibwa Power Belief System," in *The Anthropology of Power*, ed. Fogleson and Adams, 141–152; J. Allen Burgesse, "Property Concepts of the Lac St.-Jean Montagnais," *Primitive Man* 18 (1945): 1–25; Fogelson and Adams, eds., *The Anthropology of Power*; Sam D. Gill, *Native American Religions: An Introduction* (Belmont, CA: Wadsworth, 1983); Åke Hultkrantz, "The Concept of the Supernatural in Primal Religion," *History of Religions* 22 (1983): 231–253; Eleanor Leacock, "Status among the Montagnais-Naskapi of Labrador," *Ethnohistory* 5 (1958): 200–209; Julius E. Lips, "Public Opinion and Mutual Assistance among the Montagnais-Naskapi," *American Anthropologist* 39 (1937): 222–228; Toby Morantz, "Northern Algonkian Concepts of Status and Leadership," *Canadian Review of Sociology and Anthropology* 19 (1982): 482–501; Jacques Rousseau and Madeleine Rousseau, "Le Dualisme Religieux des Peuplades de la Forêt Boréale," in *Acculturation in the Americas*, ed. Sol Tax (Chicago: University of Chicago

Press, 1952), 118–126; idem, "Persistances Païennes chez les Amérindiens de la Forêt Boréale," *Cahiers des dix* 17 (1952): 129–155; Jacques Rousseau, "Dualisme Religieux ou Syncretisme chez les Algiques de la Forêt Boréale," *Actes du VIe Congres International des Sciences Anthropologiques et Ethnologiques*, 2 (Paris: Musee de l'homme, 1962), 469–473; Frank G. Speck, *Naskapi: The Savage Hunters of the Labrador Peninsula*, 2nd ed. (Norman: University of Oklahoma Press, 1977 [1935]); Morton I. Teicher, *Windigo Psychosis: A Study of a Relationship between Belief and Behavior among the Indians of Northeastern Canada* (Seattle: University of Washington Press, 1960). For a critical introduction to the documentary character of the *Jesuit Relations*, see Campeau, *Établissement à Québec (1616–1634)*.

6. See also Chapter Six.

7. See citations to Hallowell, Leacock, Mauss, Morantz, and Speck in notes 4 and 5.

8. See citations to Black in note 5.

9. Reuben Gold Thwaites, ed., *The Jesuit Relations and Allied Documents*, 73 vols. (New York: Pageant, 1959), 8: 245–247. Hereafter cited as JR.

10. Ibid., 8: 247.
11. Ibid., 8: 273.
12. Ibid., 5: 233.
13. Ibid., 11: 89.
14. Ibid.
15. Ibid., 5: 161, 227; 6: 133; 11: 121–123, 133.
16. Ibid., 7: 297; 8: 219–221.
17. Ibid., 6: 117, 125; 8: 249, 253–255, 259, 265; 11: 107, 121, 137.
18. Ibid., 6: 129–131; 8: 267.
19. Ibid., 6: 129–131; 8: 267; 11: 121, 125.
20. Ibid., 8: 269.

21. Sometimes the Montagnais refused baptism in order to maintain solidarity with dead relatives who had gone to the traditional land of the dead. See ibid., 8: 271.

22. Ibid., 6: 117; 8: 255.
23. Ibid., 8: 259.
24. Ibid., 9: 9.
25. Ibid., 9: 11.
26. Ibid.
27. Ibid., 9: 13–15.
28. Ibid., 9: 97.
29. Ibid., 9: 95.
30. Ibid., 9: 69–79, 97.

31. Thomas Grassman, "Makheabichtichiou," in *Dictionary of Canadian Biography*, ed., G. W. Brown (Toronto: University of Toronto Press, 1966), 1: 481–482.

32. JR, 11: 149.
33. Ibid., 11: 157.
34. Ibid., 11: 161–163.
35. Ibid.
36. Ibid., 11: 165.
37. Ibid., 11: 215.
38. Ibid., 11: 177.
39. Ibid., 12: 179; 14: 131–133, 179; 20: 209–211.
40. Ibid., 11: 239–247.
41. Elsie McLeod Jury, "Pigarouich, Etienne," in *Dictionary of Canadian Biography*, 1: 548–549.
42. JR, 11: 251.
43. Ibid., 11: 253.
44. Ibid., 12: 149.
45. Ibid., 11: 255–259; 12: 9, 143.
46. Ibid., 11: 261.
47. Ibid., 11: 263–265.
48. Ibid., 11: 267.
49. Ibid., 12: 9.
50. Ibid., 12: 11.
51. Ibid., 14: 133.
52. Ibid., 16: 149–165; 18: 189–193.
53. Ibid., 12: 163–165.
54. Ibid., 12: 159–163.
55. Ibid., 12: 173.
56. Ibid., 12: 171–173, 177–179, 199, 203.
57. Ibid., 14: 215–217.
58. Ibid., 14: 133.
59. Ibid., 14: 135–137.
60. Ibid., 14: 137.
61. Ibid., 14: 139.
62. Ibid., 14: 139–141.
63 Ibid.
64. It is a compelling detail in this man's story that the people he accosted thought him mentally ill, contending that he was a fearsome windigo, a threatening cannibal. According to Le Jeune, "The Savages, wishing to get rid of him, spread a report that he had become a man wolf, and that he would eat all those who came near him. When we had learned of all this fine news, we had him brought to us, and succored him so effectually that this carcass again became a body, this corpse was resuscitated." Ibid., 14: 153.
65. Ibid., 14: 221.
66. Ibid., 14: 221–223.
67. Ibid., 14: 227.

68. Ibid., 14: 265.
69. Ibid., 16: 53–55.
70. Ibid., 16: 65.
71. Ibid., 16: 85.
72. Ibid., 16: 87–89.
73. Ibid., 16: 99.
74. Ibid., 16: 147.
75. Ibid., 18: 95.
76. Ibid., 18: 95–99.
77. Ibid., 18: 101.
78. Ibid., 18: 105–107.
79. Ibid., 18: 107.
80. Ibid., 18: 121, 155, 163–165, 175.
81. Ibid., 18: 173.
82. Ibid., 20: 143–147.
83. Ibid., 149–155.
84. Ibid., 18: 131.
85. Ibid., 18: 145.
86. Ibid., 149–151, 157, 217.
87. Ibid., 18: 191, 219.
88. Ibid., 20: 159.

CHAPTER EIGHT. THE SOLIDARITY OF KIN

1. They also left ample records of their relations with Iroquoian-speaking peoples—among them the Huron Confederacy, the Five Nations, and the central Algonkians. These peoples have not been the focus of these essays.

2. Francis Jennings, *The Invasion of America: Indians, Colonialism and the Cant of Conquest* (Chapel Hill: University of North Carolina Press, 1975).

3. Robert W. Hefner, "World Building and the Rationality of Conversion," in *Conversion to Christianity: Historical and Anthropological Perspectives on a Great Transformation*, ed. Robert W. Hefner (Berkeley: University of California Press, 1993), 3–44.

4. Ibid., 34; his italics.

5. Peter Wood, "Afterword: Boundaries and Horizons," ibid., 305.

6. Ibid.; his italics.

7. Ibid., 306.

8. But see Ann Fienup-Riordan, *The Real People and the Children of Thunder: The Yupik Eskimo Encounter with Moravian Missionaries John and Edith Kilbuck* (Norman: University of Oklahoma Press, 1991).

9. One should note here the interpretation of Lucien Campeau, who champions the missionaries and their moral success in converting Native Americans to Catholicism. As we shall see, Axtell strives for a more balanced interpretation, but in the end argues for conclusions that are not significantly different from those of Campeau. See Lucien Campeau, S.J. in Selected Bibliography.

10. James Axtell, "The European Failure to Convert the Indians: An Autopsy," in *Papers of the Sixth Algonquian Conference, 1974*, National Museum of Man, Mercury Series, No. 23, ed. Wiliam Cowan (Ottawa: National Museums of Canada, 1975), 274–290.

11. James Axtell, "Some Thoughts on the Ethnohistory of Missions," in his *After Columbus: Essays in the Ethnohistory of Colonial America* (New York: Oxford University Press, 1988), 47–57.

12. James Axtell, "Were Indian Conversions *Bona Fide*?" in *After Columbus*, 100–121.

13. In the discussion that follows, I limit my analysis to Axtell's treatment of French missions to the Algonkian peoples. Axtell's interpretation is much more ambitious because he essays a comparative treatment of French and English missions.

14. Axtell, "An Autopsy," 277.

15. Ibid., 277–278. Here Axtell quotes Peter Duigan, "Early Jesuit Missionaries: A Suggestion for Further Study," *American Anthrogologist* 60 (1958): 726.

16. Axtell, "An Autopsy," 278.

17. Ibid., 279.

18. Ibid. The Jesuits' linguistic ability has received considerable attention. See Remi Ferland, *Les "Relations" des Jésuites: Un Art de la persuasion: Procédés de rhetorique et fonction connative dans les "relations" du Pére Paul Lejeune* (Quebec, Éditions de la Huit, 1992); Victor Egon Hanzeli, *Missionary Linguistics in New France: A Study of Seventeenth and Eighteenth-Century Descriptions of American Indian Languages* (The Hague: Mouton, 1969); Margaret J. Leahey, "'Comment peut un muet prescher l'évangile?' Jesuit Missionaries and the Native Languages of New France," *French Historical Studies* 19 (1995): 105–131; John Steckley, "Brebeuf's Presentation of Catholicism in the Huron Language: A Descriptive Overview," *Revue de l'Université d'Ottawa/University of Ottawa Quarterly* 50 (1978): 93–115; idem, "The Warrior and the Lineage: Jesuit Use of Iroquoian Images to Communicate Christianity," *Ethnohistory* 39 (1992): 478–509; Peter A. Dorsey, "Going to School with Savages: Authorship and Authority among the Jesuits of New France," *William and Mary Quarterly* 55 (1998): 399–420.

19. Axtell, "An Autopsy," 280.

20. Ibid., 281.

21. Ibid., 281–282.
22. Ibid., 283.
23. Ibid., 284.
24. Ibid., 285.
25. Peter Wogan concludes, to the contrary, that there is "little evidence to support the view that Native North Americans in the seventeenth century perceived French missionary writing as especially powerful, suggesting that such early modern reports should be viewed with skepticism." "Perceptions of European Literacy in Early Contact Situations," *Ethnohistory* 41 (1994): 407. Wogan's essay presents a major critique of what might be called Axtell's "awe theory" about Native American responses to Europeans.
26. Axtell, "An Autopsy," 285.
27. Ibid., 286.
28. Ibid., 287.
29. Ibid., 288.
30. Axtell, "Some Thoughts," 48.
31. Axtell defines missiological as "a Jesuit historian or missionary." Ibid.
32. Ibid.
33. Ibid., 48–49; his italics.
34. Ibid., 49.
35. Axtell, "Some Thoughts," 50; his italics.
36. Ibid., 51. I do not follow Axtell's argument about the praying towns of New England because I focus on an assessment of Eastern Algonkian views of Christianity. In this essay, Axtell includes Maine in his argument, but only in a very general way.
37. Ibid., 56; his italics.
38. Ibid., 56–57.
39. Ibid., 57.
40. Axtell, "Indian Conversions," 100.
41. Ibid., 101.
42. Ibid., 100; my italics. This essay, like his earlier ones, treats English as well as French missionization. As before, I limit myself to the French sphere, here following Axtell beyond the French-Eastern Algonkian sphere of influence to include also the interaction of the French with Iroquoians.
43. David Blanchard, "To the Other Side of the Sky: Catholicism at Kahnawake, 1667–1700," *Anthropologica* 24 (1982): 77–102.
44. Cornelius J. Jaenen, *Friend and Foe: Aspects of French-Amerindian Cultural Contact in the Sixteenth and Seventeenth Centuries* (Toronto: McClelland and Stewart, 1976).
45. Bruce G. Trigger, *Natives and Newcomers: Canada's 'Heroic Age' Reconsidered* (Kingston and Montreal: Queen's University Press, 1985).
46. Axtell, "Indian Conversions," 102–103.

47. Ibid., 103. In Blanchard's view, "conversion" needs careful examination "in light of: 1. traditional Iroquois world view, 2. Iroquois religion, and 3. the historical context of early Iroquois contact with the French." Blanchard, "Catholicism at Kahnawake," 79. Axtell does not evaluate Blanchard's discussion of these variables.

48. Axtell, "Indian Conversions,"103–104.
49. Ibid., 104. For Axtell' s detailed critique of Trigger, see 119.
50. Ibid., 104.
51. Ibid., 108.
52. Ibid., 105.
53. Ibid., 105–106.
54. Ibid., 106.
55. Ibid., 107.
56. Ibid., 111.
57. Axtell, "Indian Conversions," 112; his italics.
58. Ibid., 113–114. On this element of Axtell's awe theory, see note 25.
59. Ibid., 116.
60. Ibid., 116–117.

61. He claims further that neither Blanchard nor Jaenen provides proof of either conscious or unconscious syncretism. Ibid., 117.

62. Ibid.; his italics.
63. Ibid., 118.
64. Ibid.
65. Ibid., 118–119; his italics.
66. Ibid., 120.

67. George E. Tinker, *Missionary Conquest: The Gospel and Native American Cultural Genocide* (Minneapolis: Fortress, 1993).

68. See Selected Bibliography: Classen; Classen, Howes and Synott; Eilberg-Schwartz; Gill; Johnson; Porteous; Rodaway; and Stoller.

69. Axtell, "Indian Conversions," 118.
70. Ibid., 13–17; quotation at 16.
71. Ibid., 278.
72. Ibid., 13, 16.

73. William G. Doty, *Mythography: The Study of Myths and Rituals* (University: University of Alabama Press, 1986), 33–34.

74. Ibid., 12, 14.

75. Anthony F. C. Wallace, *Religion: An Anthropological View* (New York: Random House, 1966), vi.

76. On Hallowell, see Chapter Two. See also Rodney Needham, *Belief, Language and Experience* (Oxford: Blackwell, 1972).

77. See Hallowell, "Ojibwa Ontology," 145–149.

78. On the category "person" as the northeastern Algonkians extend it to entities other-than-human, see Chapter Two. See also David M. Guss, ed., *The Language of the Birds: Tales, Texts, & Poems of Interspecies Communication* (San Francisco: North Point, 1985).

79. See Chapter Two.

80. Ramsey MacMullen, "Conversion: A Historian's View," *The Second Century* 5 (1985/1986): 67–89.

81. See Howard L. Harrod's useful argument that French and Native American realities ought to be conceptualized as life-worlds: "Missionary Life-World and Native Response: Jesuits in New France," *Studies in Religion* 13 (1984): 179–192.

82. Philip J. Deloria, *Playing Indian* (New Haven, CT: Yale University Press, 1998). See Introduction, note 14.

83. I have explored how this intellectual conundrum derived from an effectively illogical European way of reasoning about the relationship of "religion" as divine intentionality—the Sacred—to "culture" as a secular phenomenon without a religious rationale—the Profane. See the chapter entitled "The Sacred and the Profane: The Social Ideologies of Contact," in my book *The Embattled Northeast: The Elusive Ideal of Alliance in Abenaki-Euramerican Relations* (Berkeley: University of California Press, 1984), 42–71. In a complementary argument, Peter A. Dorsey traces the course of that logical impasse in the intellectual tradition the French missionaries established about the traditional lives of Native American peoples. See his "Going to School with Savages," 399–420.

84. See Axtell, *After Columbus; The Invasion Within*; his *Beyond 1492: Encounters in Colonial America* (New York: Oxford University Press, 1992); and his *The European and the Indian: Essays in the Ethnohistory of Colonial North America* (New York: Oxford University Press, 1981).

85. For a comprehensive discussion, see William F. Ganong, "Introduction: Father Chrestien Le Clercq, and His Gaspesian Work," in Father Chrestien Le Clercq, *New Relation of Gaspesia with the Customs and Religion of the Gaspesian Indians*, ed. William F. Ganong (Toronto: The Champlain Society, 1910), 1–41. Alfred Goldsworthy Bailey, *The Conflict of European and Eastern Algonkian Culture, 1504–1700: A Study in Canadian Civilization*, 2nd ed. (Toronto: University of Toronto Press, 1969 [1937]), 152–153, summarizes Le Clercq's account but does not offer an explanation. Olive Patricia Dickason, *The Myth of the Savage and the Beginnings of French Colonialism in the Americas* (Edmonton: University of Alberta Press, 1984), 103, publishes a picture of an "Acadian Amerindian or Micmac marked with the cross symbols that so intrigued and puzzled early missionaries." Calvin Martin, *Keepers of the Game: Indian-Animal Relationships and the Fur Trade* (Berkeley: University of California Press, 1978), 60–61, does not discuss the case of the Mi'kmaq cross. His treatment of Mi'kmaq Christianity describes Mi'kmaq tradition as obsolescent and decaying: "Under pressure from disease, European trade, and

Christianity, he [the Mi'kmaq] had apostatized—he had repudiated his role within the ecosystem. Former attitudes were replaced by a kind of mongrel outlook which combined some native traditions and beliefs with a European rationale and motivation." See also Bruce G. Trigger, "Early Native North American Responses to European Contact: Romantic versus Rationalistic Interpretations," *Journal of American History* 77 (1991): 1195-1215, and discussion of Trigger in Chapter One. Finally, G.-M. Dumas' comments should be noted: "As for the worship offered to the cross by the Indians of the Miramichi region, modern historians, without denying the fact, have tended to recognize in this cross the stylized figure of the tribal totem, which was originally a bird with outspread wings." "Le Clercq, Chrestien," in *Dictionary of Canadian Biography*, ed. George W. Brown (Toronto: University of Toronto Press, 1966), 1: 440. Ganong made the inference that the cross was a tribal totem. *New Relation*, 39.

86. Axtell, *Invasion*, 4; Brian Slattery, "French Claims to North America, 1500–59," *Canadian Historical Review* 59 (1978): 139–69, especially 145–153.

87. See Bruce G. Trigger, *Natives and Newcomers*, 50–163, for the early contact period.

88. David B. Quinn, ed., *New American World: A Documentary History of North America to 1612*, 5 vols. (New York: Arno, 1979), 1: 316, 2: 38–40, 130, documents Native American requests that Europeans heal the sick.

89. Le Clercq, "On the Origin of the Worship of the Cross among those Gaspesians called Cross-bearers," in *New Relation*, 146–158.

90. Ganong suggests that this account may have been also derived from Le Clercq, but its author, Bishop Saint-Vallier, explicitly associates it with another Frenchman, Richard Denys, who received it from an old Mi'kmaq man. Le Clercq, *New Relation*, 190, note 2.

91. Ibid. The text is in a note that quotes Saint-Vallier, *Estat present de l'Eglise* (1688).

92. Le Clercq, *New Relation*, 22, 32–33, 109, 144, 147–149, 151–152, 157, 176, 179, 189–190, 234, 251, 253–258.

93. Joseph François Lafitau, *Customs of the American Indian Compared with the Customs of Primitive Times*, ed. and trans. William N. Fenton and Elizabeth L. Moore, 2 vols. (Toronto: The Champlain Society, 1974), 1: 271–280.

94. Le Clercq, *New Relation*, 84, 173.

95. On Sillery, see James Ronda, "The European Indian: Jesuit Civilization Planning in New France," *Church History* 41 (1972): 385–395; idem, "The Sillery Experiment: A Jesuit-Indian Village in New France, 1637–1663," *American Indian Culture and Research Journal* 3 (1979): 1–18; idem, "'We Are Well As We Are': An Indian Critique of Seventeenth-Century Christian Missions," *William and Mary Quarterly* 34 (1977): 66–82.

96. See Karen Anderson, *Chain Her by One Foot: The Subjugation of Women in Seventeenth-Century New France* (London: Routledge, 1991).

97. Bailey, *Conflict*, 34–45; . Morrison, *The Embattled Northeast*, 77–79.

98. Robert Conkling, "Legitimacy and Conversion in Social Change: The Case of French Missionaries and the Northeastern Algonkian," *Ethnohistory* 21 (1974): 20.

99. Ibid., 20–21.

100. See Selected Bibliography: Jeanne Guillemin, Daniel N. Paul, Harald E. L. Prins, Jennifer Reid, Wilson D. Wallis and Ruth Sawtell Wallis, and Ruth Holmes Whitehead.

Selected Bibliography

Anderson, Karen. *Chain Her by One Foot: The Subjugation of Women in Seventeenth-Century New France.* London: Routledge, 1990.

Axtell, James. *After Columbus: Essays in the Ethnohistory of Colonial America.* New York: Oxford University Press, 1988.

———. *The European and the Indian: Essays in the Ethnohistory of Colonial America.* New York: Oxford University Press, 1981.

———. *The Invasion Within: The Contest of Cultures in Colonial North America.* New York: Oxford University Press, 1985.

———. *Natives and Newcomers: The Cultural Origins of North America.* New York: Oxford University Press, 2001.

Bailey, Alfred Goldsworthy. *The Conflict of European and Eastern Algonkian Culture 1504–1700: A Study in Canadian Civilization.* 2nd ed. Toronto: University of Toronto Press, 1969 [1937].

Beck, Peggy V., and Anna L. Walters. *The Sacred: Ways of Knowledge, Sources of Life.* Tsaile, AZ: Navajo Community College, 1977.

Berkhofer, Robert. *A Behavioral Approach to Historical Analysis.* New York: The Free Press, 1969.

Biolsi, Thomas, and Larry J. Zimmerman, eds. *Indians and Anthropologists: Vine Deloria, Jr., and the Critique of Anthropology.* Tucson: University of Arizona Press, 1997.

Blackburn, Carole. *Harvest of Souls: The Jesuit Missions and Colonialism in North America, 1632–1650.* Montreal & Kingston, McGill-Queen's University Press, 2000.

Bowden, Henry W. *American Indian and Christian Missions: Studies in Cultural Conflict.* Chicago: University of Chicago Press, 1981.

Brown, Jennifer S. H., and Robert Brightman, eds. *The Orders of the Dreamed: George Nelson on Cree and Northern Ojibwa Religion and Myth, 1823.* Winnipeg: University of Manitoba Press, 1988.

Brown, Jennifer S. H., and Elizabeth Vibert, eds. *Reading Beyond Words: Contexts for Native History.* Peterborough, Ontario: Broadview, 1996.

Brown, Joseph Epes. *The Spiritual Legacy of the American Indian.* New York: Crossroad, 1982.

Calloway, Colin G. *New Worlds for All: Indians, Europeans, and the Remaking of Early America*. Baltimore: Johns Hopkins University Press, 1997.

Campeau, Lucien, S.J. *Les Cent-Associés et le Peuplement de la Nouvelle-France (1633–1663)*. Montreal: Bellarmin, 1974.

———. *La Première Mission D'Acadie (1602–1616)*. Monumenta Novae Franciae, 1. Quebec: Les Presses de l'Université Laval, 1967.

———. *Établissement à Quebec (1616–1634)*. Monumenta Novae Franciae, 2. Quebec: Les Presses de l'Université Laval, 1979.

———. *Fondation de la Mission Huronne (1635–1637)*. Monumenta Novae Franciae, 3. Quebec: Les Presses de l'Université Laval, 1987.

———. *Les Grandes Épreuves (1638–1640)*. Monumenta Novae Franciae, 4. Montreal: Les Éditions Bellarmin, 1989.

———. *La Bonne Nouvelle Reçue (1641–1643)*. Monumenta Novae Franciae, 5. Montreal: Les Éditions Bellarmin, 1990.

———. *Recherche de la Paix (1644–1646)*. Monumenta Novae Franciae, 6. Montreal: Les Éditions Bellarmin, 1992.

———. *La Première Mission des Jésuites en Nouvelle-France (1611–613) et Les Commencements du Colleges de Jésuites (1626–1670)*. Montreal: Les Éditions Bellarmin, 1972.

Capps, Walter Holden. *Seeing with a Native Eye: Essays on Native American Religion*. New York: Harper & Row, 1976.

Carmody, Denise Lardner, and John Tully Carmody. *Native American Religions: An Introduction*. New York: Paulist, 1993.

Classen, Constance. *The Color of Angels: Cosmology, Gender and the Aesthetic Imagination*. London: Routledge, 1998.

———. *Inca Cosmology and the Human Body*. Salt Lake City: University of Utah Press, 1993.

———. *Worlds of Sense: Exploring the Senses in History and Across Cultures*. London: Routledge, 1993.

———. Classen, Constance, David Howes, and Anthony Synnott. *Aroma: The Cultural History of Smell*. London: Routledge, 1994.

Clifton, James A., ed. *The Invented Indian: Cultural Fictions & Government Policies*. New Brunswick, NJ: Transaction, 1996.

Comaroff, Jean, and John L. Comaroff. *Ethnography and the Historical Imagination*. Boulder, CO: Westview, 1992.

Crumrine, N. Ross, and Marjorie Halpin, eds. *The Power of Symbols: Masks and Masquerade in the Americas*. Vancouver: University of British Columbia Press, 1983.

Delage, Denys. *Bitter Feast: Amerindians and Europeans in Northeastern North America, 1600–64*. Vancouver: University of British Columbia Press, 1993.

Delanglez, Jean. *Frontenac and the Jesuits*. Chicago: Institute of Jesuit History, 1939.

Deloria, Vine, Jr. *For This Land: Writings on Religion in America.* New York: Routledge, 1999.

———. *God is Red: A Native View of Religion.* Golden, CO: Fulcrum, 1994 [1973].

———. *Red Earth, White Lies: Native Americans and the Myth of Scientific Fact.* New York: Scribner, 1995.

Devens, Carol. *Countering Colonization: Native American Women and Great Lakes Missions, 1630–1900.* Berkeley: University of California Press, 1992.

Dickason, Olive Patricia. *The Myth of the Savage and the Beginnings of French Colonialism in the Americas.* Edmonton: University of Alberta Press, 1984.

Dooling, D. M., and Paul Jordan-Smith. *I Become Part of It: Sacred Dimensions in Native American Life.* New York: Parabola, 1989.

Dowd, Gregory Evans. *A Spirited Resistance: The North American Indian Struggle for Unity, 1745–1815.* Baltimore, MD: Johns Hopkins University Press, 1992.

Eccles, William J. *France in America.* Vancouver: Fitzhenry and Whiteside, 1973.

Eilberg-Schwartz, Howard. *People of the Book: Jews and Judaism from an Embodied Perspective.* Albany: State University of New York Press, 1992.

Etienne, Mona, and Eleanor Leacock, eds. *Women and Colonization: Anthropological Perspectives.* New York: Praeger, 1980.

Fabian, Johannes. *Time and the Other: How Anthropology Makes Its Object.* New York: Columbia University Press, 1983.

———. *Time and the Work of Anthropology: Critical Essays, 1971–1991.* Philadelphia: Harwood, 1991.

Fixico, Donald L., ed. *Rethinking American Indian History.* Albuquerque: University of New Mexico Press, 1997.

Fogelson, Raymond D., and Richard N. Adams, eds. *The Anthropology of Power: Ethnographic Studies from Asia, Oceania, and the New World.* New York: Academic, 1977.

Geertz, Armin W. *The Invention of Prophecy: Continuity and Meaning in Hopi Indian Religion.* Berkeley: University of California Press, 1994.

Gill, Sam D. *Mother Earth: An American Story.* Chicago: University of Chicago Press, 1987.

———. *Native American Religions: An Introduction.* Belmont, CA: Wadsworth, 1982.

———. *Native American Religious Action: A Performative Approach to Religion.* Columbia: University of South Carolina Press, 1987.

———. *Native American Traditions: Sources and Interpretations.* Belmont, CA: Wadsworth, 1983.

Grant, J. W. *Moon of Wintertime: Missionaries and the Indians of Canada in Encounter since 1534*. Toronto: University of Toronto Press, 1981.
Grim, John. *The Shaman: Patterns of Siberian and Ojibway Healing*. Norman: University of Oklahoma Press, 1983.
Guillemin, Jeanne. *Urban Renegades: The Cultural Strategy of American Indians*. New York: Columbia University Press, 1975.
Hall, Robert L. *An Archaeology of the Soul: North American Indian Belief and Ritual*. Urbana: University of Illinois Press, 1997.
Harrod, Howard L. *The Animals Came Dancing: Native American Sacred Ecology and Animal Kinship*. Tucson: University of Arizona Press, 2000.
———. *Becoming and Remaining a People: Native American Religions on the Northern Plains*. Tucson: University of Arizona Press, 1995.
———. *The Human Center: Moral Agency in the Social World*. Philadelphia: Fortress, 1981.
———. *Renewing the World: Plains Indian Religion and Morality*. Tucson: University of Arizona Press, 1987.
Henry, Jeanette. *Textbooks and the American Indian*. San Francisco: Indian Historian Press, 1970.
Hoxie, Frederick E. *The Indian versus the Textbooks: Is There Any Way Out?* Chicago: Newberry Library, 1984.
Hultkrantz, Åke. *Belief and Worship in Native North America*. Edited by Christopher Vecsey. Syracuse, NY: Syracuse University Press, 1981.
———. *The Religions of the American Indians*. Berkeley: University of California Press, 1979.
Irwin, Lee. *The Dream Seekers: Native American Visionary Traditions of the Great Plains*. Norman: University of Oklahoma Press, 1994.
Jaenen, Cornelius J. *Friend and Foe: Aspects of French-Amerindian Cultural Contact in the Sixteenth and Seventeenth Centuries*. New York: Columbia University Press, 1976.
Jenness, Diamond. *The Ojibwa Indians of Parry Island: Their Social and Religious Life*. National Museum of Canada, Bulletin 78. Ottawa, 1935.
Jennings, Francis. *The Invasion of America: Indians, Colonialism and the Cant of Conquest*. Chapel Hill: University of North Carolina Press, 1975.
Johnson, Mark. *The Body in the Mind: The Bodily Basis of Meaning, Imagination, and Reason*. Chicago: University of Chicago Press, 1987.
Kennedy, J. H. *Jesuit and Savage in New France*. New Haven: Yale University Press, 1950.
Krech, Shepard, III, ed. *Indians, Animals, and the Fur Trade: A Critique of Keepers of the Game*. Athens: University of Georgia Press, 1981.
Kugel, Rebecca. *To Be the Main Leaders of Our People: A History of Minnesota Ojibwe Politics, 1820–1898*. Ann Arbor: Michigan State University Press, 1998.

Lafitau, Joseph François. *Customs of the American Indian Compared with the Customs of Primitive Times*. Edited and translated by William N. Fenton and Elizabeth L. Moore. 2 vols. Toronto: The Champlain Society, 1974.

Landes, Ruth. *Ojibwa Religion and the Midewiwin*. Madison: University of Wisconsin Press, 1968.

Le Clercq, Chrestien. *New Relation of Gaspesia with the Customs and Religion of the Gaspesian Indians*. Edited by William F. Ganong. Toronto: The Champlain Society, 1910.

Loftin, John D. *Religion and Hopi Life in the Twentieth Century*. Bloomington: Indiana University Press, 1991.

Martin, Calvin, ed. *The American Indian and the Problem of History*. New York: Oxford University Press, 1987.

———. *Keepers of the Game: Indian-Animal Relationships and the Fur Trade*. Berkeley: University of California Press, 1978.

Martin, Joel. *Sacred Revolt: The Muskogees' Struggle for a New World*. Boston: Beacon, 1991.

Merkur, Daniel. *Becoming Half Hidden: Shamanism and Initiation among the Inuit*. Stockholm: Almqvist & Wiksell International, 1985.

Meyer, Melissa. *The White Earth Tragedy: Ethnicity and Dispossession at a Minnesota Anishinaabe Reservation, 1889–1920*. Lincoln: University of Nebraska Press, 1994.

Mihesuah, Devon A. *Natives and Academics: Researching and Writing about American Indians*. Lincoln: University of Nebraska Press, 1998.

Miquelon, Dale. *New France, 1701–1744: A Supplement to Europe*. Toronto: McClelland and Stewart, 1987.

Moore, J. T. *Indian and Jesuit: A Seventeenth-Century Encounter*. Chicago: Loyola University Press, 1982.

Morrison, Kenneth M. *The Embattled Northeast: The Elusive Ideal of Alliance in Abenaki-Euramerican Relations*. Berkeley: University of California Press, 1984.

Nicolar, Joseph. *The Life and Traditions of the Red Man*. Fredericton: Saint Annes Point Press, 1979 [1893].

O'Brian, Jay, and William Roseberry, eds. *Golden Ages, Dark Ages: Imagining the Past in Anthropology and History*. Berkeley: University of California Press, 1991.

Paper, Jordan. *Offering Smoke: The Sacred Pipe and Native American Religion*. Moscow: University of Idaho Press, 1988.

Parkhill, Thomas C. *Weaving Ourselves into the Land: Charles Godfrey Leland, 'Indians,' and the Study of Native American Religions*. Albany: State University of New York Press, 1997.

Paul, Daniel N. *We Were Not the Savages: A Micmac Perspective on the Collision of European and Aboriginal Civilizations*. Halifax, NS: Nimbus, 1993.

Pflug, Melissa A. *Ritual and Myth in Odawa Revitalization: Reclaiming a Sovereign Place*. Norman: University of Oklahoma Press, 1998.

Porteous, J. Douglas. *Landscapes of the Mind: Worlds of Sense and Metaphor*. Toronto: University of Toronto Press, 1990.

Prins, Harald E. L. *The Mi'kmaq: Resistance, Accommodation, and Cultural Survival*. Fort Worth: Harcourt Brace College Publishing, 1996.

Reid, Jennifer. *Myth, Symbol and Colonial Encounter: British and Mikmaq in Acadia, 1700–1867*. Ottawa: University of Ottawa Press, 1995.

Richter, Daniel K. *The Ordeal of the Long-house: The Peoples of the Iroquois League in the Era of European Colonization*. Chapel Hill: University of North Carolina Press, 1992.

Rodaway, Paul. *Sensuous Geographies: Body, Sense, and Place*. London: Routledge, 1994.

Ronda, James P., and James Axtell. *Indian Missions: A Critical Bibliography*. Bloomington: Indiana University Press, 1978.

Smith, Donald B. *Le Sauvage: The Native People in Quebec Historical Writing on the Heroic Period (1534–1663) of New France*. History Division, Mercury Series, Paper 6. Ottawa: National Museum of Man, 1974.

Smith, Theresa S. *The Island of the Anishnaabeg: Thunderers and Water Monsters in the Traditional Ojibwe Life-World*. Moscow: University of Idaho Press, 1995.

Speck, Frank G. *Naskapi: The Savage Hunters of the Labrador Peninsula*. 2nd ed. Norman: University of Oklahoma Press, 1977 [1935].

———. *Penobscot Man: The Life History of a Forest Tribe in Maine*. Philadelphia: University of Pennsylvania Press, 1940.

Stoller, Paul. *Sensuous Scholarship*. Philadelphia: University of Pennsylvania Press, 1997.

———. *The Taste of Ethnographic Things: The Senses in Anthropology*. Philadelphia: University of Pennsylvania Press, 1989.

Swagerty, William R. *Scholars and the Indian Experience: Critical Reviews of Recent Writing in the Social Sciences*. Bloomington: Indiana University Press, 1984.

Tanner, Adrian. *Bringing Home Animals: Religious Ideology and Mode of Production of the Mistassini Cree Hunters*. New York: St. Martin's, 1979.

Tedlock, Dennis, and Barbara Tedlock, eds. *Teachings from the American Earth: Indian Religion and Philosophy*. New York: Liveright, 1975.

Thornton, Russell, ed. *Studying Native America: Problems and Prospects*. Madison: University of Wisconsin Press, 1998.

Thwaites, Reuben Gold, ed. *The Jesuit Relations and Allied Documents*. 73 vols. New York: Pageant, 1959.

Treat, James, ed. *Native and Christian: Indigenous Voices on Religious Identity in the United States and Canada*. New York: Routledge, 1996.

Trigger, Bruce G. *The Children of Aataentsic: A History of the Huron People to 1660*. 2 vols. Kingston and Montreal: McGill-Queen's University Press, 1976.

———. *Natives and Newcomers: Canada's 'Heroic Age' Reconsidered*. Kingston and Montreal: McGill-Queen's University Press, 1985.

Trudel, Marcel. *Histoire de la Nouvelle-France*. 2 vols. Montreal: Fides, 1963, 1966.

Underhill, Ruth M. *Red Man's Religion: Beliefs and Practices of the Indians North of Mexico*. Chicago: University of Chicago Press, 1965.

Upton, L. F. S. *Micmacs and Colonists: Indian-White Relations in the Maritimes, 1713–1867*. Vancouver: University of British Columbia Press, 1979.

Vecsey, Christopher. *Imagine Ourselves Richly: Mythic Narratives of North American Indians*. San Francisco: HarperSanFrancisco, 1991.

———. *On the Padres' Trail*. Notre Dame, IN: University of Notre Dame Press, 1996.

———. *The Paths of Kateri's Kin*. Notre Dame, IN: University of Notre Dame Press, 1997.

———. *Religion in Native North America*. Moscow: University of Idaho Press, 1990.

———. *Where The Two Roads Meet*. Notre Dame, IN: University of Notre Dame Press, 1999.

Vincent, Sylvie, and Bernard Arcand. *L'Image de l'Amérindien dans les manuels scolaires du Québec*. Montreal: Hurtubise, 1979.

Wallis, Wilson D., and Ruth Sawtell Wallis. *The Micmac Indians of Eastern Canada*. Minneapolis: University of Minnesota Press, 1955.

Weaver, Jace, ed. *Native American Religious Identity: Unforgotten Gods*. Maryknoll, NY: Orbis, 1998.

Weaver, Jace. *That the People Might Live: Native American Literatures and Native American Community*. New York: Oxford University Press, 1997.

White, Richard. *The Middle Ground: Indians, Empires, and Republics in the Great Lakes Region, 1650–1815*. Cambridge: Cambridge University Press, 1991.

Whitehead, Ruth Holmes. *The Old Man Told Us: Excerpts from Micmac History, 1500–1950*. Halifax, NS: Nimbus, 1991.

Williamson, Ray A. *Living the Sky: The Cosmos of the American Indian*. Boston: Houghton Mifflin, 1984.

Index

Abenaki. *See* Wabanaki
acculturation. *See* culture change
Adam, 83, 98–99, 138
alcohol
   abstinence from, 90–91, 94
   Catholic critique of, 96
   devastating impact, 4, 74–75, 87, 151, 165
   prayer and, 92
   punishment for, 144
Algonkian. *See also* Catholicism, cosmogony, cosmology, culture change, dialogue, ethics, disease, ethnocentrism, God(s), history, individualism, interpretation, Jesuits, Mi'kmaq, Montagnais, Ojibwa, mythology, religion, Wabanaki, war, worldview
   alienation of, 61–62
   contact liminality, 4–5
   critique of literature on, 11, 17–38, 60, 147–172
   missions to, 2, 5, 11–12, 69–77, 86–98, 103–114, 122–129, 135–146
   religious conservatism of, 108, 115, 119, 124, 126–127, 144–145, 148, 151, 155, 162–163, 165, 168, 172
   tradition, 6, 10–11, 39–41, 48–49, 51–58, 59–78, 81–86, 98–101, 115
Anderson, Karen, 169
Anishnaabe. *See* Ojibwa
   usage, 180n 25
Anthropology. *See* interpretation
Apache, 15
Arbman, Ernst, 45–46
Attikamegou, 137
Axtell, James, 14, 147, 149–160

Bailey, Alfred Goldsworthy, 18–21, 23
baptism. *See also* conversion, culture change, Mi'kmaq, Montagnais, syncretism, Wabanaki
   and alliance with French, 116–117, 123–124, 132, 135–136, 138, 141, 145, 158
   and burial, 136
   and death, 88–89, 92, 134–135, 214n 21
   economic motivation for, 154
   French godparents, 75, 132, 135–136, 142
   and heaven, 92, 126
   as medicine, 96, 122–124, 126, 134–135, 137–138, 142–143, 158
   missionary hesitancy, 88, 94, 135, 139, 155
   numbers of, 123, 134
   preparation for, 95
   and punishment, 137–138
Baptiste, Jean, 143–144
Beck, Peggy V. and Anna L. Walters, 6–9
belief
   assessed, 22–24, 31–34, 40, 114–115, 119, 134, 139–140, 160, 162, 164, 180n 27
   continuity of, 77, 93
   as faith, 10, 14, 22–23, 48, 56, 59, 64, 66–69, 70, 73, 76–77, 79, 81, 86–87, 89–90, 92–93, 106, 111, 114, 123, 128, 135, 143, 151–152, 154–156
   in Gluskap, 99

belief *(cont.)*
  religion as, 1, 5, 8–10, 38, 45, 52, 59, 75, 79–83, 88, 91–92, 98–99, 117, 138–139, 150–151, 154, 159–160
Berger, Peter, 104, 118, 211n 2
Berkhofer, Robert, 3, 103
Bigot, Jacques, S.J., 95–96
Bishop, Charles A., 21
Black, Mary Rogers, 40, 122
Blackburn, Thomas, 15, 173n 5
Blackfoot, 15
Blanchard, David, 153–154

Campeau, Lucien, S.J., 105–106, 217n 9
Cannibal Giant. *See* Windigo
Carigonan, 109–114, 137
Cartier, Jacques, 23
Catholicism. *See also* alcohol, Baptiste, belief, Carigonan, conversion, councils, culture change, Gluskap, God(s), hunting, Jesuits, LaNasse, missions, Mi'kmaq, Montagnais, Nenaskoumat, Pastedechouan, Pigarouich, power, Sillery, syncretism, Wabanaki, windigo
  apostasy from, 106–107
  claims of superiority, 109, 112, 151, 161
  charity, 72–73, 125
  criticism of, 73, 151
  and emotions, 150
  and grace, 38, 69, 72–73, 83, 94, 98, 134, 142–143, 146, 154–155, 159–160
  impact of, 22, 30, 95, 138, 143
  Mohawk, 154
  myth of Christian civilization, 6, 8, 148, 150–151, 159, 166
  resistance to, 107, 149, 151–152, 158, 171
  theology, 43, 47–48, 61, 72–73, 88–89, 97, 154, 160
  as universal, 148–150, 153, 156–158, 161
  view of history, 4–6
causality. *See also* intentionality, interpretation, intersubjectivity, manitou, objectivism, power, spiritual, subjectivism, supernatural
  ethnohistorical, 116, 207n 3
  extra-physical, 19
  forces, 7–8, 14, 59
  materialism, 101
  mechanical and impersonal, 10, 20–21, 24–26, 53, 57, 121
  mystical, 19–20
  relational, 31, 46, 83, 101, 103, 120, 132, 168
  variables, 116
Chenoo. *See* Windigo
Chumash, 15
colonialism. *See also* Catholicism, ethnocentrism, Jesuits, missions, Wabanaki
  contemporary, 12–13
  genocide, 5, 159
  intellectual, 17
  interpretive context, 3, 103, 129, 148, 153–154, 157–159, 168
  missions as, 129, 138, 148, 157
Conkling, Robert, 170–171
conservatism. *See* Algonkian, culture change, missions
conversion. *See also* culture change, missions, syncretism
  as apostasy, 196n 73, 154
  critiqued, 91, 93, 115–116, 128–129, 131, 147–149, 153–155, 158–162, 170–172, 219n 47
  as *bona fide*, 150, 155
  as giving assent and rediscovery, 128–129
  Greco-Roman, 162
  Jesuit advantages in, 150–151
  Jesuit expectation of, 58, 72, 91, 128, 134, 141, 150, 158, 169
  and kinship, 73, 95, 97, 158
  obstacle to, 18–19, 151–152
  process versus results, 148–149
  as protective coloration, 154, 157
  redefined, 11–12
  religious change as, 12, 14–15, 73–74, 80–81, 95, 97, 116, 147–149, 157, 161–163
  as repudiation of tradition, 128, 153

test of, 155
tradition and, 69, 104
Wabanaki, 74, 88, 91, 170–171
of windigo, 66
cosmogony. *See also* Gluskap, mythology
Christian, 162
Cree and Ojibway, 26–27, 57
as primitive, 19
Wabanaki, 83, 163
cosmology. *See also* cosmogony, councils, culture, dreams, magic, nature, person, power, solidarity, spiritual, supernatural, worldview
Christian, 41, 61, 131, 162
comparative, 11, 13–14, 16, 19–20, 25, 47, 61, 114, 160–161, 163, 171, 189n 81
Europe, 145
heaven, 42, 92, 96,135, 126, 134–136, 142,145, 159
hell, 91, 95, 98, 123, 126, 135, 138, 145, 159
as hierarchy and authority, 24, 27–28, 38–39, 40, 43, 160
interpretive context, 9, 12–14, 34–35, 38, 43–44
land of the dead, 126, 136
Montagnais, 121, 128–129, 134, 145–146, 158
as nature, 62, 134
Ojibwa, 26–29, 41–43, 49, 57
principles of, repudiated, 22
purgatory, 145
as society, 3, 9, 15, 20, 24–26, 28–29, 34–35, 39–40, 50–51, 53, 55–56, 59, 76, 79, 86, 98, 120–121, 128–129, 163
as spiritual, 22–24, 59
underworld, 98
as universe, 7, 46–47
Winter, 62
Wintu, 49–51
world-ejection, 43–44
Yoeme (Yaqui), 184n 7
councils
Christian, 139, 141, 143–144

in cosmogonic traditions, 6, 28
Mi'kmaq, 167–168
culture. *See also* causality, cosmology, culture change, ethics, gift, hunting, worldview
Bailey's view of, 19
causality and, 19, 24
comparative, 13, 28, 34, 41, 45, 47
existential and normative principles of, 1–2, 4–6, 15, 37, 40, 53, 56–57, 61, 80, 120–121, 127, 133
material, 18, 24
and personality, 36
popular, 3
study of, 1, 16, 28, 31–36
culture change. *See also* baptism, colonialism, conversion, dialogue, ethics, Jesuits, missions, pragmatism, ritual, syncretism
apocalypticism, 3, 7
Axtell on, 149–160
as cognitive and value reorientation, 4, 31, 69
conservatism in, 60, 72, 80, 88, 92, 96–98, 117, 128–129, 132, 146, 161
as cultural intersection, 12, 69, 72, 76, 116, 104, 127, 129, 131, 133, 138, 145, 161–172
dialogue and, 15, 43, 60, 73, 77–78, 93, 100, 103–105, 109, 113–114, 119, 127–128, 131–132, 147, 150, 160–161, 164
ecological change, 3–4, 69, 71, 140
education in, 74
ethics in, 3–5, 72–73, 77, 165
ethnocentric parameters in, 60
ideology in, 21, 31, 118, 120, 129
Jesuit goals, 74, 97, 129, 160–161
as liminal, 132
need to understand, 1–2, 115, 133, 147–149
revitalization, 81, 86–99, 164–168, 170
social change, 71–72, 170–171
tradition in, 72, 78, 80, 95–96, 100–101
culture hero. *See also* Gluskap
Messou, 120, 128Wisekejak, 27

culture hero (*cont.*)
  Wisekejak, 27

dialogue. *See also* intersubjective
  in Algonkian history, 6, 11, 26, 164
  religious life and, 40, 43, 56–58
  scholarly, 101
discourse. *See* dialogue
disease. *See also* windigo
  in Algonkian history, 3–4, 22, 30, 72–74, 87–89, 90–92, 95–97, 110, 116, 122, 124, 132, 134, 136–137, 140–142, 151, 165, 167–169, 171
  Catholic cures of, 89, 91–92, 126, 137 143
  and religious anxiety, 96–97, 109, 132, 134–135, 139, 143, 145
  theory of, 19, 57, 63–65, 68, 72, 86–87, 95, 97, 108, 113, 123, 165, 167
Doty, William, 159
dreams
  condemned, 108, 118, 123, 125, 139, 142
  as cultural evidence, 26, 53–54, 56–57
  post-Christian, 127, 135, 138, 144, 156, 162, 171, 201n 67
  as revelation, 54, 66, 85–86, 92, 108, 125, 139, 140, 165–168
Druillettes, Gabriel, 74, 88–93, 171, 200n 52, 200–201n 59

Eastern Algonkian. *See* Algonkian. *See also* Mi'kmaq, Montagnais, mythology, Wabanaki
ethics. *See also* cosmology, culture, culture change, gift, Gluskap, intersubjectivity, person, power, pragmatism, religion, religious, religious specialist, responsibility, solidarity, worldview
  as anti-social, 14, 161, 163
  communal values, 61–62, 77, 82, 103
  comparative, 33, 72, 118
  evil and, 83, 114
  French, 122
  human-animal reciprocity, 27, 121, 129

  moral principles, 4, 11, 13, 46, 59, 79, 103, 117–122, 133–134
  mythology and, 11, 27
  and Native American life, 3–4, 13, 57, 160–161
  pimadaziwin, 55
  post-contact crisis, 86–87
  reciprocity, 27, 55–56, 121, 126, 129, 137, 145–146, 160–161, 209n 32
  respect, 40–41, 86, 112, 120
  sharing, 111–112, 133
  theory of otherness, 39–40, 42–43, 53, 55, 59, 68–69, 121, 131, 160
  values, 14–15, 121
ethnocentrism. *See also* colonialism, Jesuits, religion
  Algonkian, 60, 100, 106–108, 119
  attempts to circumvent, 18, 36, 60, 100
  claims about 2, 5–6, 8–11, 23, 35, 37–39, 41
  intellectual, 12, 14–16, 17–18, 22, 26, 32–33, 56, 115, 118, 131, 161, 163–164, 171
  Jesuit, 74, 90, 108, 113, 196–197n 3
  of rationalists and romantics alike, 34–35
  religious, 9, 22, 29, 37
  as superiority, 163
  terminology, 24, 25–26, 32, 34, 59, 115, 159
ethnography. *See* Anderson, Axtell, Bailey, Bishop, Black, Blackburn, Blanchard, Conkling, Goldschmidt, Hallowell, Hultkrantz, Irwin, Jaenen, Jenness, Jones, Landes, Lee, MacLeod, Martin, Morrison, Paul, Redfield, Ronda, Saler, Smith, Snow, Speck, Tanner, Trigger, Turner, Wallace, Wax, Witthoff
ethnohistory. *See* interpretation
Etinechkaenat, 141
evil. *See* alcohol, disease, individualism, windigo

Five Nations, 70
Fléché, Jesse, 155
folklore. *See* mythology

fur trade
  Mi'kmaq motives in, 22–24, 165, 166–167
  overtrapping, 71–72
  religious motivation of, 30, 31–32, 169, 180–181n 31
  rationalism as interpretation of, 32, 150

Geertz, Clifford, 104, 118
gift. *See also* ethics, Gluskap
  baohi''gan (helper), 86
  culture as, 189n 81
  of power, 42, 54, 166–167
  religious economy, 15, 35, 133, 145
Gill, Sam D., 6, 8–10, 115, 118–119
Gluskap. *See also* ethics, power
  and Catholicism, 98–99, 164, 172, 203n 105
  ethical character of, 11, 64, 79, 83–84, 103
  teaches relational ethics, 84
  and Winter, 62
  and Woodchuck, 83–84
God(s). *See also* cosmology, culture hero, Gluskap, person, sacred, supernatural
  Christ, 99, 107, 138
  divinity, 8–9, 24, 43, 71, 91, 107–108, 112, 117–119, 125, 134–135, 138, 140, 142–143, 145, 156–159, 162, 166, 171
  Europeans as, 23–34
  Great Being, 98–99
  great Captain, 129, 142
  Great Spirit, 27–28, 41–42, 98–99, 186n 26, 200–201n 59
  He-Who-Made-All, 41, 72–73, 90, 98, 124, 127–129, 134, 136–137, 141, 145–146, 158, 162, 171, 186n 26, 200–201n 59
  Jesus, 91, 96, 99, 109, 119, 124, 127–128
  kitchi manitou, 27–28, 41–42, 185–186n 19
  master of demons, 92
  monotheism, 15, 41, 62, 134
  as the Sun, 28, 128, 168

superhuman, 25, 29
theism, 7–8, 28–29, 38, 41–42, 120, 125
Thunder, 128
  as transcendent, 43, 45–46, 119
Goldschmidt, Walter, 50–51, 185n 12

Hallowell, A. Irving, 10, 13–15, 24, 27, 29, 32, 35–36, 38–39, 40–41, 47–48, 51–58, 59, 84, 115, 119–120, 122, 131, 160
Hearne, Samuel, 26–27
Hefner, Robert, 148
history. *See also* causality, colonialism, conversion, culture change, ethnocentrism, intentionality, interpretation, missions, syncretism
  Algonkian, 10–12, 98–99, 121
  Indian-White Relations, 2–4
  mission, 147–172
  religious, 11, 14, 39
  representation, 3, 4, 60
  social, 34, 174n 7
  western views of, 4, 5, 121
Hultkrantz, Åke, 10, 37–51, 56, 184n 7, 188n 58, 188n 59
hunting. *See also* ritual
  Catholicism ensures, 95, 98, 112, 126–127, 132, 138, 144–145, 162
  Catholicism undermines, 138, 201n 65
  Master of the Game, 121, 127
  overtrapping, 116, 122, 127, 141, 145
  ritual, 109–110, 114, 120, 126, 140
Huron, 70, 75

idealism. *See* romanticism
Indian-Indian relations, 4, 6, 34. *See also* councils, war
individualism. *See also* subjectivity
  Algonkian revulsion toward, 11, 61–64, 68, 79
  Algonkian religion as, 81
  and French culture, 108, 111, 122, 124, 164–165
  as historical motivation, 23, 32–35
  as subjectivity, 8, 16, 50
intentionality. *See also* ethics, gift, pragmatism, religious, responsibility, ritual

intentionality *(cont.)*
  being, 26
  defined, 10
  motivation, 16, 38, 40, 55, 57, 165, 166
  as power, influence, 28
  ritual and, 132
  supernatural beings and, 37
interpersonal. *See* intersubjective
interpretation. *See also* ethics, ethnography, causality, colonialism, cosmology, culture change, ethnocentrism, gift, history, individualism, intentionality, intersubjective, language, magic, meaning, Native American Studies, nature, objectivism, person, power, pragmatism, rationalism, reification, religion, religious, Religious Studies, romanticism, solidarity, spiritual, subjectivity, supernatural, symbol, worldview
  Algonkian-Jesuit relations, 77, 80–81, 114, 152
  anthropology, 1–2, 14, 47, 131, 148
  baseline, 18–20
  behavior, 10, 11, 15, 26, 28–29, 34, 40, 48, 52, 103
  cultural relativism, 30–34
  ethnohistory, 1, 2, 9–10, 14, 18, 21, 22, 35, 47–48, 116, 147, 152–157, 166, 207n 3
  ethnometaphysics, 48
  and the human sciences, 36, 38
  life as, 1, 15–16, 19, 24, 36, 51, 53, 55, 57, 64
  materialism, 150
  local perspective, 149
  person, power, and gift, 15, 120, 127–128, 133–134
  primitive, 19–20, 24, 51, 62, 163
  qualitative, 34
  Rationalist versus Romantic, 17–36, 163–164
  problems, 10, 178n 51
  sociolinguistic, 204–205n 4
  sociology of knowledge, 103–104, 116
  and theism, 8, 162
  thick description, 104
  typified, 17
  victimization 3, 18, 24, 32, 100, 103, 152–153, 158, 161
intersubjective. *See also* ethics, dialogue, politics, responsibility, ritual, solidarity
  as cultural principle, 22, 24–26, 28–29, 48, 51–58, 65, 79, 82–86
  interpersonal adaptations, 60, 77
  missions as, 104, 114, 127
  relational logic, 10–11, 15–16, 19, 26, 31, 34–36, 39–40, 51, 103, 163–165
Irwin, Lee, 46

Jaenen, Cornelius, 153–154
Jenness, Diamond, 20, 28, 46–47, 52
Jennings, Francis, 147
Jesuits. *See also* colonialism, ethnocentrism, missions, religious specialist, windigo
  accommodation to Algonkians, 73–76, 92, 97, 125
  Algonkian views of, 11, 74–78, 87–88, 90–93, 124, 134, 143, 151, 218n 25
  bias of, 106–107, 117
  education and, 151
  criticism of French culture, 73
  and "frenchification," 150
  goal of conversion, 60, 72, 128, 150, 168
  linguistic ability, 150, 217n 18
  relativism, 73–75, 92, 97, 107, 117–118, 136, 150
  and ridicule, 110–111, 113, 124–126, 151
  selfishness, 124
  selflessness, 89, 125, 136
  threats of damnation, 95
  view of Algonkian culture, 81, 100, 158–159
  world view of, 20, 155–156
Jesuit Relations, 60, 69, 80, 100, 104–109, 112–114, 115–118, 132–133, 142, 194n 50, 196–197n 3, 206–207n 1
Jones, William, 49

Kennebec. *See* Wabanaki
kinship. *See also* baptism, conversion, ethics, Gluskap, intersubjective, responsibility, solidarity
  French as, 73, 135–136
  solidarity, 6, 32, 39, 64–67, 73, 78, 82, 121, 144, 163–165, 169–171
  in mission life, 97, 112
  ntu'tem relationships, 84–85
  with other-than-human persons, 49, 52, 72
Kiwakwe. See windigo
Kwakiutl, 188n 58

Lalement, Charles, S.J., 107
LaNasse, 73
Landes, Ruth, 28, 41–42
Langer, Susanne K., 116
language. *See also* ethnocentrism, Montagnais, reification
  the animate, 41, 52–53, 113–114, 187n 53, 120, 122, 160
  English, 9–10, 26, 29, 43, 50, 160, 164
  Jesuit study of, 103–109, 111, 120, 150–151, 162
  orality, 9, 106, 108–109
  personification, 20, 29
  socio-linguistics, 9, 12, 15, 24, 38, 40, 48, 56–58, 103, 116, 121, 148, 204–205n 4
  verbal and non-verbal, 104, 108–109, 115
  Wintu, 49–50
  Wabanaki, 75–76, 80, 88–90, 97, 172
Lee, Dorothy, 49–51
Le Clercq, Chrestien, Fr., 70–71, 165–168
Le Jeune, Paul, S.J., 70–71, 73, 105–114, 117, 119, 122, 123, 134,–143, 150

MacLeod, William Christie, 18
MacMullen, Ramsey, 162
magic. *See also* causality, manitou, power, ritual
  as incantation and exorcism, 19
  Calvin Martin's use of, 24–27, 29, 31
  magical world, 24
  magician, 84, 86, 110, 140
  as power, 29, 76, 99
  religion as, 56, 151, 171, 173n 5
  skepticism about, 179n 19
  supernatural as, 51
Makheabichtichiou, 119, 125, 138–141
Maliseet. *See* Wabanaki
Malsum, the Wolf, 83
manitou. *See also* God(s), power
  assessed, 48–49, 120–121
  as being, 42, 127–128, 165
  as charms, 90
  as religious specialist, 73, 120
  as spirit, 28
Manitouchatche. *See* LaNasse
Martin, Calvin
  despiritualization, 31, 180n 23, 196n 73
  religious ethnography, assessed, 21–30, 35
  and methodological impasse, 17
  and supernatural, 14
meaning. *See also* baptism, conversion, cosmology, ethics, gift, kinship, intentionality, interpretation, language, religious, responsibility, solidarity, syncretism, worldview
  contested, 2, 6
  contextualized, 10, 35
  as interspecies sociality, 29
  interpretation of, 59, 115–116, 133
  meaning making activity, 9–10, 118–119
  religious, 1, 3, 6, 15–16, 35, 103, 114
Mestigoït, 113, 137
Micmac. *See* Mi'kmaq
Mi'kmaq. *See also* fur trade
  and Calvin Martin, 22, 25–26
  baptism of, 155
  economic motivation of, 23–24
  famine cannibalism, 70–71
  religious sociality of, 165–169, 220–221n 85
  stories of, 59, 62, 65–68, 76–77, 99
missionaries. *See also* baptism, conversion, culture change, Jesuits, syncretism

missionaries *(cont.)*
  ethnocentricism of, 12, 59, 104, 117, 131
  motivation, 150
  Recollets, 150
missions. *See also* Algonkian, baptism, Catholicism, colonialism, conversion, culture change, intersubjective, Jesuits, Mi'kmaq, Montagnais, Wabanaki, Sillery, syncretism
  ambivalence about, 94
  cognitive dissonance, 129
  as conversation, 2, 103
  as contested encounter, 2, 4–5, 11–12, 114, 127–128
  interpretation of, 17, 103–104, 115, 152–157
  as refuge, 93
  St. Francis, 75
Montagnais. *See also* Algonkian, baptism, Catholicism, conversion, cosmology, culture change, missions, syncretism, war
  alliance with Wabanaki, 74, 170
  anxiety of, 122–128, 132, 134–136, 138, 141–143, 145–146
  belief attributed to, 105, 108, 119, 120, 125, 135, 137–141, 143–144, 150
  and cannibalism, 70
  Christian power and, 76–77
  contact history, 116
  discernment of Catholicism, 116–117, 122, 129, 133–134, 137–138, 143, 169
  Jesuit descriptions of, 105–107, 109, 116–117, 127, 133
  language, 109, 113–114
  missions, 11, 60, 73–75, 81, 88, 97, 168–170
  insiders' view of, 116
  motives for French alliance, 108, 123, 133, 141
  religious conservatism, 111, 113, 116–117, 119, 122, 126–127, 158
  religious knowledge of, 127, 158
  view of the French, 122, 127
  women, 112, 127, 139, 143–145

Montagnais-Naskapi. *See* Montagnais
Morrison, Kenneth M., self-assessment, 10–16, 59, 79, 103, 115, 131, 164
Muller, Werner, 81
mythology. *See also* cosmogony, cosmology, ethics, gift, worldview
  assessment of Europeans, 93, 99, 164
  deevaluation of, 69
  as documentary resource, 2, 11–13, 39, 59–61, 63, 77–80, 98–101, 147, 164, 177n 36
  Passamaquoddy, 83–84
  Penobscot, 83–84, 87, 99
  tradition as consensus, 6
  Ojibwa, 26–28, 41–43, 53, 56, 59, 64–67
  and value formation, 61, 99
  Wabanaki, 11, 82–86, 98–99

Native American Studies, 1, 14, 16, 51, 57, 79, 131
nature. *See also* cosmology, interpretation, reification, worldview
  as causal, 19–20, 46, 55, 134
  as cultural representation, 9, 13–14, 20, 53, 59
  humans as, 38
  natural laws, 7–8, 24, 47–48
  reified, 24–29
Navajo, 188n 57
Negabamat, Noel, 143
Nenaskoumat (François Xavier), 141–142
Nicholas, Andrea Bear, 12
No-chi-gar-neh, 85, 87, 200–201n 59
Nomlaki, 50–51, 185n 12

objectivism. *See also* interpretation, rationalism, reification
  as method, 34–36, 52
  as rationality 8, 10–11, 19, 23, 55–56, 62, 160
  terms, 26
Odawa, 15
Ojibwa. *See also* Black, cosmogony, cosmology, Hallowell, Hulkrantz, Jenness, Landes, Martin, mythology, Smith

ontology. *See* person
oral tradition. *See* mythology

Pastedechouan, Pierre Antoine, 106–107, 109–113, 137
Passamaquoddy. *See* Wabanaki
Paul, Dr. Peter, 80, 85, 90, 99, 197n 4, 199n 34
Penobscot. *See also* Wabanaki
  King Philip's War, 93
  Speck on, 81, 87
  windigo and, 64–65
person. *See also* ethics, God(s), ethics, Hallowell, hunting, intersubjective, kinship, language, ritual, solidiarity, subjectivity
  animals as, 26–28, 41, 62, 83, 95, 124
  animism, 41, 62, 160
  anthropomorphism, 24, 53–54
  assessed, 15, 40, 120–121
  attributes of, 54–55, 57, 120
  and anthropomorphism, 20, 24, 54
  Catholic persons, 124, 128, 134, 145, 162, 171
  communication with, 84–86, 98, 113–114, 120, 122–123, 132, 163, 165–167
  demons, 92, 95, 108, 125, 135, 137, 139, 142–144
  history and, 3, 6, 11, 35, 121
  misunderstood, 160
  ontological similarity, 36, 42, 46–48, 54–56, 62, 83, 159–161
  ontology, 13–15, 19, 24, 36, 40, 48, 131, 133
  as personification, 20, 28–29
  as rationality, 128, 131, 133, 165
  as a spirit, 20, 23, 25–29, 45–48, 52, 64, 67, 76, 85–86, 90, 96, 98, 119, 140, 165, 171
  stories as, 53
  superhuman forces and beings, 19, 26, 45
Pigarouich, 124, 125, 139–141, 143
Pirouakki, 94
politics
  authoritarian, 79, 108
  consensual, 43, 62

  intratribal, 86–87, 90, 139, 143–144
power. *See also* causality, culture hero, ethics, gift, Gluskap, Jesuits, intentionality, magic, manitou, Montagnais, person, pragmatism, religious specialist, ritual, spiritual
  abused, 85, 87, 92, 93
  achieved, 84
  as authority, 7, 43, 117
  as being, 20, 29, 49, 63, 128, 139, 160
  Catholicism and, 72–74, 91–92, 97–100, 123–125, 127, 129, 134, 136, 140, 145, 155–156, 160, 170
  as causal relations, 24–26, 32, 121, 133
  comparative, 49, 117, 145
  concepts, 49
  of drum, 89
  ethical purpose of, 26, 43, 64, 67–68, 72, 82–87, 92, 121–122, 126, 133–134, 140, 146, 160, 163
  as impersonal force, 6, 8, 14, 19, 25, 49, 53, 55, 59, 62, 77, 90, 96, 120, 127, 133, 151
  as interpretive category, 15, 37, 54, 117, 120–121, 127–128
  ktaha'ndo, 85
  as knowledge, 35, 40, 42, 47, 79
  manitou, 23, 25–26, 28, 90, 120, 160
  as metamorphosis, 26–27, 47, 54, 56, 83, 85, 122
  of objects, 98, 140
  percept ambiguity and danger, 40, 54, 86, 121–122, 124, 134, 136, 138–141, 188n 57
  personalized, 73
  as ritual principle, 26
  and shamanism, 193n 29, 82
  shared by human and other-than human persons, 54, 63
  as spiritual potency, 19, 20, 24–26, 28–29, 45, 64, 76, 85, 159
pragmatism
  comparative, 122
  as motive, 73, 113, 117, 121, 134
  religious, 7, 16, 31–34, 51, 59, 79, 88, 92–93, 107, 120, 126–127, 135, 139–140, 146, 159, 162, 169

Quebec (Canada), 11, 116

Racle, Sebastien, S.J., 75
Ragueneau, Paul, S.J., 70
Rale, Sebastien, S.J. *See* Racle
rationalism. *See also* fur trade, interpretation, objectivism, pragmatism, subjectivity
    critiqued, 10, 14, 17, 33, 77, 147–148
    and European superiority, 151
    Martin as, 24–26
    as materialism, 21, 23, 30, 31, 55
    Trigger on, 30–35
    as self-interest, 32
reciprocity. *See* ethics
Redfield, Robert, 36
reification. *See also* nature
    as abstract representation, 2, 6–7, 9–10, 15–16, 35–36, 52–53, 57, 161–162, 164
    and cultural policy, 4
reincarnation, human and animal, 57
religion. *See also* Catholicism, baptism, belief, causality, cosmogony, cosmology, culture change, disease, God(s), hunting, individualism, magic, mythology, nature, power, religious, ritual, sacred, spiritual, supernatural, symbol, syncretism, war, worldview
    Axtell's view of, 160
    compared to Algonkian, 18–20, 41, 72, 159–160, 162
    as culture, 1, 9, 14, 20, 32, 33, 35, 39–40
    deistic, 128, 134, 146
    as dogma, 117, 128–129, 135, 146, 157, 160
    ethnocentric assumptions about, 6, 15, 17, 38, 103, 117, 163–164
    European reasoning about, 220n 83
    as holism, 19, 32, 39, 50, 57, 118, 160, 166–168, 203n 114
    as immanence, 119–120
    as knowledge, 8, 39–40
    as performance, 9, 40, 115
    as temporal-spatial orientation, 114–115
    Trigger's view of, 31–34
    sin and salvation, 79, 83, 117, 137, 145–146, 166
    study of, 206n 46
religious. *See also* ethics, intersubjectivity, meaning, pragmatism, religion, responsibility, ritual, solidarity, symbol
    defined, 6–7, 8–9, 39–40
    as economic, 35
    heterogeneity, 127–128
    non-utilitarian and non-rationalistic, 32
    relational, 31, 103, 164–165, 168
    sociality and 11, 13, 14, 45, 56, 165
    study of, 19
religious specialist. *See also* Carigonan, Jesuits, manitou, Pigarouich, power
    ambivalence towards, 82, 92, 124, 132, 137–138, 140
    ethics of, 35, 62–64, 81–82, 85–87, 89, 119, 140, 193n 29, 199n 34
    cure of, 89–90
    failure of, 72, 74, 76, 92, 127, 137, 200n 43
    Hole-in-the-Sky, 42
    Jesuit as shaman, 76, 90, 124–126, 136, 140, 143, 196n 73
    medicinal power of, 86, 120
    and metamorphosis, 122
    missionary as, 76–77, 88–91, 124–126, 136, 156, 170–171, 200n 52
    missionary opposition to, 108, 118, 125, 127, 139, 151
    opposition to missionaries, 73, 88–89, 98, 108, 139, 151
    rivalry among, 87
    and tradition, 82, 85–86, 92, 127–128
Religious Studies
    and conversion, 148
    criticism of social sciences, 38
    and misrepresentation, 13–16, 37, 47
    and otherness, 118, 160
    goal of, 1–3, 9–10, 14–16, 36, 115–116, 131, 166
responsibility
    as historical cause, 3, 87, 90, 126, 131, 137, 167

in religious life, 8, 40, 42, 79, 85, 121, 143, 160
scholarly, 2, 15
ritual. *See also* baptism, disease, hunting, Martin, responsibility, power, pragmatism, religion, symbol, war
  cannibalism, 69–70
  as communal, 81–82
  as communication, 62, 86, 89–90, 114, 120–121, 132–134, 136, 160
  bear ceremonialism, 29
  Catholic symbols in, 95, 98, 104, 117, 129, 146, 154, 159, 162
  and cosmos, 40, 51, 56–57, 133
  curing, 108, 120
  as diagnostic and redressive, 3–4, 6, 131–132, 167
  "Eat-all" feast, 112, 138–139
  and food cycle, 86, 91, 109, 112, 114, 120, 126–127
  liminality and, 4–5, 132, 143
  mass, 91, 97–98, 150, 154
  midewiwin, 42
  myth rationalized as, 8, 159
  as performance, 9
  rejection of, 143
  shaking tent, 110, 140
  study of, 116
  as superstitious, 159, 169
  sweat lodge, 138, 144
romanticism. *See also* interpretation, objectivity, rationalism, subjectivity
  dismissed, 10, 21–23
  critiqued as relativist ideology, 14, 17, 30, 35–36
  as irrational, 31
Ronda, James, 168–169

sacred. *See also* supernatural
  holy, 29
  as religious category, 7–9, 24, 29, 38, 45, 110, 119
  as substance, 29
  texts, 103
Saler, Benson, 44
shamanism. *See* religious specialist

Sillery, mission at, 60, 75, 94–97, 104, 115–116, 128–129, 139, 141–144, 146, 168–170
Smith, Theresa S., 41–43, 48–49
Smith, Wilfred Cantwell, 114
solidarity. *See* baptism, ethics, gift, kinship, responsibility
  erosion of, 87, 134, 144, 146, 164
  religious meaning of, 11, 13, 59, 82, 164
  as social and religious goal, 3–4, 6, 34, 78, 79, 82, 85, 103, 123, 133, 143–144, 161, 172
  threatened, 87
Snow, Dean, 30
Speck, Frank G., 29, 81–82, 83, 89, 126
spiritual
  assessed, 22–24, 29, 159, 164
  despiritualization, 31
  as explanation, 14, 55–56, 59, 69, 72, 79
  potency, 25–26, 29, 63, 76, 85, 96
  religion as, 92, 107, 156, 158
  as religious subjectivity, 8, 63, 68, 77, 156, 176n 29
subjectivity. *See* belief, dream, ethnocentrism, individualism, intersubjective, objectivism, reification, spiritual
  as emotion 8, 14, 22, 150
  as ideology, 18, 21, 30, 35
  mystery/mysticism 8, 19, 20, 26, 29, 48, 154–155
  as paradigm 10, 31, 36, 52, 55–56, 61, 164
  projected 3, 20
  as rationality, 11, 14, 19, 52, 55
supernatural. *See also* cosmology
  assessed, 10, 14, 27–29, 33–34, 37–58, 119, 159–160
  beings, spirits, 19–21, 23
  causal significance, 55
  as exalted, 48–50, 55
  rejected term, 14, 19–20, 23, 27–28, 39, 159
  scholarly usage, 43–45, 49–51, 173n 5
  and vertical superiority, 38, 40, 42–43, 51

supernatural *(cont.)*
  as worldview, 27, 53
symbol. *See also* ritual
  cross, as, 165–168
  defined, 133
  integration of, failed, 146
  and religious life, 7, 9–10, 37, 46, 62, 67, 70, 73, 76–77, 92, 95, 97–98, 114, 116, 118–119, 123, 129, 131–136, 138–140, 144–146, 151, 156
syncretism. *See also* conversion, culture change, Gluskap, God(s), windigo
  emotional reasons for, 156–157
  as incorporation and overlay, 154
  as making sense, 5, 14, 81, 91–92, 98–99, 115–129, 131, 140, 154, 161–172
  missionary induced, 91–92, 156
  missionary domination of, 156–157
  scholarship on, 213–214n 5

Tanner, Adrian, 29
Thompson, David, 27
Tinker, George, 5, 159
Trigger, Bruce
  Axtell's view of, 153–154
  critique of Calvin Martin, 21
  romanticism v. rationalism, 30–35
Turner, Victor, 4–5, 132, 175n 15

Vaultier, Jacques, S.J., 94

Wabanaki. *See also* Catholicism, conversion, cosmogony, cosmology, culture change, disease, ethics, language, Mi'kmaq, Montagnais, Morrison, mythology, Passamaquoddy, Penobscot, war, windigo, worldview
  Catholicism, 2, 11–13, 60, 79–101, 162, 171–172
  colonialism and, 12–13
  and French alliance, 92, 93–94
  Kennebec, 14, 74–76, 80, 87, 93, 100, 171–172
  Maliseet, 62, 64–65, 80, 84

  relations with New England, 93
  religious adaptation, 86–98
  traditional moral history, 62, 65–69, 82–86
Wallace, A. F. C., 160
Walters, Anna L. and Peggy V. Beck, 6–9
war
  Algonkian, 86, 199n 38
  Five Nations-Huron, 70
  Indian-animal, 22, 29–30
  King Philip's, 75, 93–94, 96
  Montagnais-Five Nations, 71–73, 86, 107, 116, 120, 123, 139, 141, 145, 169–170
  religion and, 4, 11, 57, 120, 123, 141, 143, 151
Wax, Murray and Rosalie, 24
Williams, John, 98
windigo
  cannibalism, 69–70
  case studies, 65–69, 123
  Catholicism and, 76–77, 123
  characterized, 63–64, 103, 111, 164, 183n 72
  cure of, 66–68, 215n 64
  and disease, 64–65, 71
  essay on, 11, 13, 59–78
  and Jesuits, 68, 70, 77
  psychosis, 59, 63, 69–70
Wintu, 49–51
Witthoff, John, 29
Woodchuck, 83–84
worldview. *See also* Algonkian, cosmogony, cosmology, culture, ethics, interpretation, nature, meaning, mythology, person, pragmatism, religion, religious, supernatural, responsibility, Wabanaki
  Algonkian, characterized, 20, 24, 26–29, 43, 51–59, 74, 81–82, 160–161
  coherence of, 15, 19, 28, 120, 131
  comparative, 104, 115, 155, 160–161
  European, characterized, 11–12, 17–18, 23, 28, 57, 131
  as hierarchy, 28, 160

as historical motivation, 31–35
as interpretation, 6, 22–23, 43
intersection of, 161–172

traditional rationality, 11, 12, 13, 15, 16, 31–32, 131, 158

www.ingramcontent.com/pod-product-compliance
Lightning Source LLC
Chambersburg PA
CBHW020648230426
43665CB00008B/347